By the Editors of WORKING WOMAN with Gay Bryant

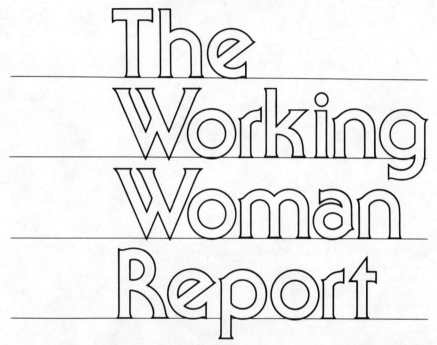

The Working Woman Report

Succeeding in Business in the 80s

Simon and Schuster

Copyright © 1984 by Working Woman Ventures, Inc.
All rights reserved
including the right of reproduction
in whole or in part in any form
Published by Simon and Schuster
A Division of Simon & Schuster, Inc.
Simon & Schuster Building
Rockefeller Center
1230 Avenue of the Americas
New York, New York 10020
SIMON AND SCHUSTER and colophon are registered trademarks of Simon & Schuster, Inc.
Designed by Jacqueline Schuman
Manufactured in the United States of America

10   9   8   7   6   5   4   3   2   1

Library of Congress Cataloging in Publication Data

Main entry under title:

The Working woman report.

   Bibliography: p.
   Includes index.
   1. Women—Employment—United States. 2. Vocational
guidance for women—United States. I. Bryant, Gay.
II. Working woman.
HD6095.W74   1984   650.1'4'024042   84-14003

ISBN: 0-671-47454-5

Acknowledgments

This book was written in my capacity as editor of *Working Woman* magazine. From the initial stage—when what I had in mind was just another how-to book for working women—to the much more ambitious report that it became, the preparation of *The Working Woman Report* was a classic case of a superlative group of professional women working together. The book reflects the expertise of everyone involved. Three editors, Jacqueline Giambanco, Basia Hellwig, and Julia Kagan wrote parts of this book. Jacqueline Giambanco wrote the chapters called "Getting Started" and "Getting Ahead." Basia Hellwig wrote "Managing in the 80s," "The Efficacious Office," and "Being Your Own Boss." Julia Kagan wrote "Benefits and Rights of Work" and Appendix A, "The Legal Safety Net."

Vicki Robinson researched, compiled, and prepared all the material for this book. Her thoughts and opinions were as invaluable as her endurance.

Wendy Menzies constantly revised and typed the manuscript, and her unflagging support was of immense help.

Maria Caliandro put her copy-editing skills to work on the chapters as they formed.

Tom Mellors helped organize some of the more unwieldy material.

John Wilcock also lent his considerable talents to the project.

Bruce Campbell's design expertise enriched the chapter on office environment. Also of great help and support were Paula Gribetz Gottlieb, Jacqueline Paris-Chitanvis, Lauraine Merlini, Heather Twidale, Marcia Ruff, Nancy Gagliardi, and Heidi Lang. Not forgetting Stacey Lucas for her early work on the project and for her sense of humor throughout.

Angela Harris wrote "Motherhood and Career"; "Where Most Women Work: The 80 Percent" was reported by Elizabeth Welbourne; "What

Women Earn" was reported by Debra Rubin. Much of "Working Smart" was written by Julie Gray. Parts of "Psychological Issues" were written by Donna Brown, the rest by Sharon Luebbers.

I am grateful to Donna Lenhoff of the Women's Legal Defense Fund for looking over the legal appendix and to Bob Classon for checking the rights and benefits material.

Special thanks for their editorial assistance go to Catherine Shaw and to Simon & Schuster's Donald Hutter and Barbara Berson.

The Working Woman Report is informed throughout by the thinking of Editor-at-Large Kate Rand Lloyd, without whom much of this would not have been possible.

G.B.

Contents

Introduction

For more than seven years *Working Woman* magazine has been documenting and discussing a new phenomenon: women's sweep into the workforce. In these few years we have seen the status of women who work rise substantially. Once "just a fad," they are now the norm. Women are employed at all levels of the workforce and in all industries. They are valued wage earners and decision makers, not just peripheral components of the business scene. These women and their need for knowledge about the business world, and for the advice and skills to get ahead in that world, have made *Working Woman* one of the fastest-growing magazines in America today. Its circulation has quadrupled in four years.

The world of business is still strange, complex territory for women, and a place where things change very fast. The magazine's editors have their hands full, researching and reporting these changes and the business problems that accompany them, responding to readers' needs for information and advice, and illuminating new aspects of their lives. Women are changing the business world as it changes them.

In its brief history, *Working Woman* has been in a constant and rapid state of evolution—one that mirrors its readers' development and the changing face of the work world of women. Both their development and the magazine's can be seen in terms of four stages:

Phase 1. In the late 1960s it was still a strange and, for many people, disturbing thing to be told that the average woman could, or should, work. By late 1976, when the premiere issue of *Working Woman* was published, women had made some inroads into the workforce, but the market for the magazine was uncertain. The magazine's readership was made up largely of women who were entering the workforce for the first time and for different reasons: financial need, self-fulfillment, self-assertion, a desire to contribute to the family income. All constituted some measure of social change. The goal was to get women and men used to the idea that women belong in the workplace, and in those early days of publication, *Working Woman* supplied reassurance, reinforcement, and a lot of very specific instructions. For example, women who had never anticipated the need for a résumé learned how to write one that made the best of their usually limited experience. Most important, the magazine told women that it was all right to work—that it wasn't immoral, unnatural, or unfeminine.

Phase 2. By the end of the decade it was clear that women were entering the workforce in large numbers. They had their foot in the door; now they needed a guide to this new territory. *Working Woman* was called upon to provide the sort of information that men impart to each other in locker rooms and bars and on the train in the morning—how to score in office politics, how to hire and fire, how to negotiate for perks, and other concrete information. The how-to-write-a-résumé refrain was taken up by other magazines. *Working Woman* readers were prompted to scout out the executive suites and the boardrooms of the corporate world.

Phase 3. A couple of years on, a new attitude informed the magazine. It was taken for granted that women work—now most of them did—and increasingly women were becoming a familiar sight on executive row. Still, there were many battles to be fought, and plenty of sexual politics. *Working Woman* showed women how to contend, but also how to relax, reward themselves, enjoy the fruits of their labor. This was the time for the guiltless materialism of the newly arrived.

Phase 4. Now *Working Woman*'s outlook reaches beyond so-called women's issues. The readers are still ambitious, still materialistic, but in the mid-eighties their concerns transcend sex-related, parochial matters and focus on larger issues relating to the success of business itself—ethics, productivity, management skills. America's business is now women's business.

Social and political issues change, but for working women certain realities abide. The corporate landscape is still mined with stereotypes and false perceptions on both sides. There is still much to resolve about child care. The salary gap is as large as ever. Pay equity is years away. Working women still need all the help they can get.

By 1983, as editor of *Working Woman* I began to see that we had accumulated a vast body of information at the magazine that was not available to people other than its two-million-plus monthly readers. Women in or entering the workforce need information and help. There are books aimed at working women, books on how to write a résumé, how to dress for success. But such books concentrate on getting in, getting ahead, surviving, and looking out for Number 1. Nothing in them goes beyond and pulls the whole world of work together for women in one handbook.

This is the first book to address women as an integral part of the workforce—contributors influencing everything in the work world, from office décor to strategic planning. Women are now intimately involved with the structures and methods of the business world. This book assumes that unless you know how the business world is run, you cannot begin to succeed in it.

Freud was right when he said that we need love and work to keep ourselves sane. Work is what we do in our offices, but it also informs and shapes everything about our lives, down to our very identities. Work affects our

Inner strength and sense of self
Access to and choice of partners
Personal and sexual relationships
Current and future life styles
Childbearing and child raising
Happiness and sense of fulfillment

... and for all these reasons there can be no more important subject in the fast-moving 80s than women and work.

Gay Bryant

1

Where We Are

The sweeping influx of women into the workforce over the past twenty years has been described by Eli Ginzberg, chairman of the President's Commission for Manpower, as "the single most outstanding social phenomenon of this century . . . an unprecedented revolution." About 17 million women were employed in 1950; by 1983 that number had mushroomed to 45 million. And for 1985 the Census Bureau projects that 57 million women will hold jobs. How much further can it go? Ginzberg suggests that eventually 80 percent of women over the age of sixteen will be working.

Increasingly women are regarded not just as other people to hire, but as employees of preference. This was borne out even during the recession of 1979–82, when the ranks of working women grew by more than 3 million; the comparable figure for men was only 200,000. Looking ahead, it is estimated that women will fill two-thirds of all the jobs created between now and the end of the century.

Some of the figures on women's financial power are equally impressive. In the late 1970s the gross national product generated by working women in the United States was bigger than the total GNP of any other country; in fact, it constituted nearly 44 percent of the entire U.S. GNP for 1981. This earning power contributes, in turn, to women's enormous buying power. According to the U.S. Department of Commerce, women control the spending of 80 percent of all consumer dollars—nearly $1 trillion a year.

Looking at the picture another way, if a substantial part of America's 49 million working women were to quit work, go home, and expect someone else to support them, the country would plunge into an economic state worse

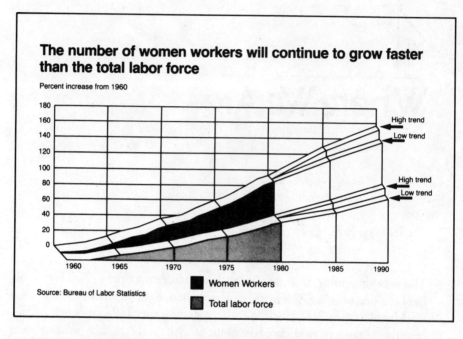

The number of women workers will continue to grow faster than the total labor force

Percent increase from 1960

Source: Bureau of Labor Statistics

Women Workers

Total labor force

than the Great Depression. The money women make keeps a roof over many families. The goods and services women buy with their pay checks keep the economy rolling. Women don't just make a substantial contribution to the economy—they are a central part of it. Without women's productivity, the economic pie would be much smaller.

Women have always worked, of course. In addition to keeping house and raising children, they have worked as field hands, as servants, as factory workers, as shop assistants, as secretaries, as nurses and teachers. And by and large they have worked out of necessity, not for pin money, even though traditionally many women, particularly those of the middle class, have held jobs only in the years between father's and husband's support. After marriage they ceased being wage earners and assumed responsibility for home and family as their "rightful place."

There have been times of special economic opportunity for women. In the colonial period, for example, more than 9 percent of the merchants in Boston and about 2 percent of those in New York were female—and this at a time when merchants comprised the summit of the colonial economy. In today's vastly larger and more complex economy, positions of comparable power and prestige would be those of president or chairman of the board of major business corporations.

After the Revolution, women—at least middle- and upper-class women, those who had a choice—rarely ventured into the workplace. The ideology of "true womanhood" held that women should keep away from commerce and politics. Lower-class women, who had to earn a living, continued to work in agriculture, domestic service, and factories. There were some women in businesses in the nineteenth century, but most of these were immigrants who managed to parlay a pushcart into a storefront, as opposed to the merchant princesses of the colonial period.

The desire of women not to just hold a job but to pursue a career never died out entirely. One-third of a group of teenage women surveyed in the mid-1920s, for example, said they wanted careers even if that meant not having a husband and children. But such aspirations had little impact on the economic realities of the times; the percentage of women in the workforce increased only by 4 percent from 1900 to just before World War II.

It was this war that set in motion the wheels of the "unprecedented revolution." With so many men in the armed forces, and so many defense-industry and related jobs available, it became women's "patriotic duty" to work. Rosie the Riveter was a war heroine, along with the many other women who conquered tough new jobs with surprising ease. The number of employed women swelled 10 percent to 6 million—36 percent—during the war years.

With peace, women were expected to withdraw from the workplace. In that era the pressure was intense to go home and make it all nice for the men returned from war. "Togetherness" and the nuclear family were the order of the day. But women hardly stopped work en masse. In fact, the number drawing pay checks grew at a remarkable rate.

On the surface, the 1950s were "Happy Days," the era of the Organization Man. Underneath, however, major changes in attitude were brewing that would shake just about every assumption of this smug decade.

Changing male attitudes and behavior toward the two traditional pillars of manhood—job and family—would soon compel women to seek economic independence. One of these attitudinal changes—worked out in Hugh Hefner's "Playboy Philosophy" from the early 50s on—told men it was all right to stay single and have a good time rather than marry and support families. Barbara Ehrenreich, in her recent book *The Hearts of Men*, combines the effects of this attitude with those of another social phenomenon of the time: the Beat Movement. The Beatniks of the 50s and 60s asserted that it was not only unnecessary for men to have families, it was also unnecessary for them to work, at least at high-pressure careers. Ehrenreich also traces another change, one created by the wide publicity given to new medical information about the dangers of overwork. It became popular perception that those high-pressure jobs—which men endured primarily to support wives and children they didn't have to have in the first place—caused an alarming number of heart attacks. Men were working themselves to death for reasons that were no longer compelling. Under these circumstances, some men began to find it more acceptable for their wives to work, while easing themselves into more "natural," lower-paying vocations; some even concluded that it was unnecessary to assume family responsibilities at all, or to keep the ones they had.

At the same time men were altering their attitudes, life was turning sour for their helpmates. Reading Betty Friedan's *The Feminine Mystique* (published in 1963), housewives began to realize that things were terribly wrong. A vague, deep sense of depression was identified as a frustrated need for women to break out of their subservient or secondary roles and fulfill their own capacities and desires for achievement.

The self-actualization movements of the 60s and 70s, and the growing women's movement, extended the changes that had been brewing in people's minds during the 50s. When the dust cleared two decades later, society was standing on its head. Many men couldn't or wouldn't support a wife and kids; many women couldn't accept, or didn't want, the housewife-and-mother role as their exclusive lot.

Some women who had expected to leave their jobs to marry and have children came to appreciate their rewarding careers and found themselves reluctant to leave. Many of these chose to postpone marriage and children, or not to marry at all. More recently, women have been finding that they may not really have the option, with too few single men to go around. The situation has reached the point where there are around 30 million single women for just 21.5 million single men. The female/male disparity is particularly great in the thirty-five-to-thirty-nine age group, where there are 128 single women for every 100 single men. As Rochelle Distelheim wrote in *Working Woman:*

> For women past 35—just when the biological clock is ticking the loudest—it is the toughest of all. Since most American women tend to marry men who are three or four years older than they are, women born at the beginning of the baby boom lose out because relatively few men were born during World War II.

Not only has the marriage rate declined since World War II, the divorce rate is up to 50 percent. More women who have to take care of themselves. More women for the workforce.

But most of all, there are more women who *want* to work. The social changes of the 60s and 70s transformed working women from objects of pity (they didn't have men, or their families didn't have enough money) into objects of respect. Women with jobs had choices their housebound sisters lacked. By the early 70s, an increasing number of women regarded working as a desirable option, a matter of choice. Reliable, easily available birth control measures and the markets for a college education had emancipated them sexually and intellectually. At the same time, feminism was teaching them to assert themselves as human beings with equal rights and limitless potential. The message was clear—women could, should, and would go out to work.

Ginzberg's "unprecedented revolution" has also been fueled, in the past decade and a half, by the coming of age of the post–World War II baby boom, as Distelheim implies. There are simply more women around, and many of them have heightened aspirations: better jobs, better homes, longer vacations, and a better quality of life than their parents had. Few single incomes can give two people the good life they have come to expect. Single or married, most of these women feel that they have to work.

Ambition, necessity, choice, changing mores, and sheer numbers of women all help explain why there are now close to 50 million working women. What about the rewards attached to the work these women do? Here there is reason to applaud, but also to ponder. The worst news first: for 80 percent of working women, the employment revolution might just as well not have occurred. These women fill the low-status, low-paying jobs that women have always held. They type letters and wait tables. They sell dresses and operate switchboards. They clean house and work on assembly lines. In terms of pay, responsibility, recognition, and opportunity for advancement, the vast majority of these pink- and blue-collar women are stuck.

For women in professional, technical, and managerial positions, the picture is much brighter. There are women executives, surgeons, lawyers, pilots, bankers, and brokers. There are "firsts" galore at the highest levels—first woman on the Supreme Court, first woman on the nightly news, first woman on the New York Stock Exchange, first woman in space, first woman bank president. The list goes on and on.

It is no longer surprising to hear that women are getting high corporate jobs or are stocking middle management. At entry level and a few steps beyond, the battle for women's acceptance in business seems all but won. The new generation of educated women entering corporations no longer start in the typing pool. A growing number are receiving the same kind of preparation for management as men. In fact, about a third of college and university graduates in professions are women.

Faced with this growing corps of ambitious, well-trained women, corporations are recruiting female students in record numbers. Like their male classmates, these graduates begin their careers in training programs. And in nontechnical areas, the women trainees often equal or outnumber the men. Many of these women aspire to top-level management and eventually, perhaps, a place on the board of directors.

In 1950 there were just under 700,000 women managers, officials, and proprietors. In 1982 there were more than 2.5 million. It is safe to say that managerial women are in the business world to stay.

But for all this progress, even among managers and professionals, there are severe limits to the advances women have made. Women in business often find themselves in a female ghetto in the new corporate landscape. They tend to hold staff jobs—public relations, personnel, advertising, administration—that are low in power and not on career paths to the top. These jobs are the first to go when budgets are slashed, because it is not staff jobs but line jobs—in production, sales, and marketing—that directly contribute to the bottom line.

But what of the future? Women *are* moving up, yes, but slowly. For all the successes women have had, there is today only one female chief executive officer among the nation's 1,000 largest industrial companies: Katharine Graham, who heads the Washington Post Company, a firm she inherited. A few women have reached the top in service and retail businesses, and more are expected, but even here there is more talk than action. For all the hoopla over the selection of women to corporate boards of directors, no more than 300 to 400 have served, or are serving, in this capacity—hardly a fair top-management representation considering the number and economic clout of working women today.

One might expect women to reach their rightful place by sheer weight of numbers. The more women who work in a given organization, the greater will be the opportunities for success. Since management consultant and Yale professor Rosabeth Moss Kanter's now classic *Men and Women of the Corporation* was published in 1977, the popular perception has been that things are most difficult for women in situations where they are "tokens." Then, Kanter writes, women become "symbols of how-women-can-do," and thus "stand-ins for all women." Men respond to the infiltrators by exaggerating their differences, disparaging their work style, and focusing attention on weaknesses. Once the numbers begin to balance out and women are freed from the spotlight, Kanter predicts, corporate life will become easier.

But it may not be simple, according to a 1980 study by Anne Harlan and Carol Weiss, both of the Wellesley College Center for Research on Women.

When Harlan and Weiss compared two large retail companies owned by the same corporation—one with 6 percent women managers and one with 19 percent—they found that the women at the 6-percent company could change jobs more easily. With fewer women in the organization there was less labeling of what constituted a "man's job" and a "woman's job." But with greater numbers of women managers, enclaves of women formed (personnel, fashion buying), and the men stayed clear of these areas. This meant that women in the 19-percent company had fewer direct dealings with senior management and therefore less chance of getting onto the right career paths for the top jobs.

Does this mean Kanter is wrong? Not necessarily. It becomes a progressive thing. At first, as women become more visible, men begin to recognize them as a real threat. As women's numbers grow, so does the threat, and things can get tough. But, then, somewhere around the 35-percent mark (and middle-management women are still a long way from that point), the female "critical mass" becomes so large that men have to realize they can no longer fight the invaders, and they accept women managers fully.

Throughout the corporate world—faster in some industries, slower in others—the door to real power for women has opened. But it is just ajar. Women may already be in middle management, but the steps from there up to the senior hierarchy are likely to be slow and painstakingly small. Partly because corporations are structured as pyramids, with many middle managers trying to move up into the few available spots, and partly because of continuing, though more subtle, discrimination, a lot of women are hitting a "glass ceiling" and finding they can rise no further.

But then, so are a lot of men. This is a structural reality of the pyramid that ambitious and capable women have to accept no less than their male counterparts. What working women do *not* have to accept is the inequities to which they are subjected because they are women—inequities of pay, responsibility, and opportunity.

There is no simple way to correct the imbalances, though the new wave of qualified young women working as entry-level managers will help. And certainly part of the solution lies in women's preparation for the world of work, preparation that begins in school.

Women have made remarkable progress in education. More than 50 percent of college graduates are women. But the progress this statistic represents is not always of the right kind. The college education many women get is often the one that helps them least in business. This may not be deliberate on society's part, but it is a fact of the new emphasis on coeducation. Carl

Schafer, financial vice president and treasurer of Princeton University, unwittingly put his finger on the problem in a recent speech:

> Actually the smartest thing Princeton has done from a budgeting standpoint since I've been here ... was coeducation [instituted in 1973]. You talk economies of scale—pardon the industrial terminology, but that's what it is. Where we had excess capacity was in the humanities and the social sciences, which are the areas that women are still disproportionately going to take. Coeducation was a superbly timed financial bargain.

But what may be a superb "financial bargain" for institutions of higher learning is not such a wonderful deal for women. Generally speaking, degrees in the humanities and social sciences do not put women on career tracks that lead to the top. One reason colleges have so much "excess capacity" in the liberal arts is that male students are concentrating on other subjects—such as business and engineering—that are more direct preparation for the work world.

Yet it should be acknowledged that while women are not as likely as men to think this way, they are at least beginning to catch on. Several years ago the *Chronicle of Higher Education* surveyed freshmen women to ascertain their career goals. The journal found that only 10 percent of these women hoped to be elementary or secondary school teachers, as opposed to 38 percent in 1969. Those hoping to be business owners or executives were up from almost none to about 10 percent. Because of this shift in aspirations, women now constitute nearly 25 percent of those enrolled in undergraduate schools of business, compared to 13 percent in 1972. There is also an impressive increase in the numbers of women candidates for a master's degree in business administration (MBA). Late in 1983, *Working Woman* surveyed ten of the top graduate schools of business to determine the increase in female degree candidates. Here is what we found:

WOMEN IN ENTERING CLASS (%)

	1972–73	1977–78	1982–83
1. UCLA	13	33	39
2. Columbia	13	35	37
3. Northwestern	7.2	25.7	34.7
4. Sloan (MIT)	4.9	23.8	27.3
5. Chicago	14	20	27
6. Tuck (Dartmouth)	4	18.8	26.8
7. Wharton (U. of Pennsylvania)	16.9	27.5	26
8. Michigan	6.2	20.1	24.3
9. Harvard	7.2	19.1	24.2
10. Stanford	11	22	24

All the preparation in the world does not solve another problem that women seem to encounter: being in the wrong place at the wrong time. Indeed, their very presence in a line of work may *make* it "the wrong place." There are indications that when a field "turns" female-intensive, it drops in commercial prestige and compensation. According to the Urban Institute's Policy Research Report, occupational segregation is a primary link in the vicious circle that prevents women's earnings from achieving parity with men's. The circle begins with women's failure to realize that, today, the average married woman with children can expect to spend twenty-five years in the labor force. Poor career or job preparation results, insuring women's relegation to low-paying jobs to which they feel little commitment. Thus women are viewed as secondary wage earners within their own families, and as less stable workers than men by their employers. These employers in turn become even less interested in training women or advancing them to higher-paying positions. The circle closes with women being locked into low-paying, dead-end, "women-only" occupations.

Part of the reason for unequal pay practices has to be the mind-set common to both men and women that there is women's work and there is men's work—and that men's is better. Child-care workers (mostly female) earn less than parking-lot attendants (mostly male). Librarians (mostly female) often earn less than liquor-store clerks (mostly male).

Do women flock to female-intensive fields because of cultural conditioning, poor career planning, lack of the right college preparation? Or is it because they have different expectations of what a job should be? One of the most astonishing revelations in a series of articles in *Working Woman* in 1983, analyzing the Public Agenda Foundation's survey of work, concerned women and job satisfaction. Despite more than a decade of protest against the low salaries and limited opportunities that women encounter in the job market, the study shows women to be no more dissatisfied with their jobs than men. This equality of dissatisfaction is especially disturbing because fewer women than men report themselves earning good pay, or are ambitious to get ahead, or even feel they have a say in important decisions. Women do report higher levels than men of other factors that seem to be related to job satisfaction. They are much more likely to believe that their jobs fill certain human-relations needs, to feel like part of a team at work, and to say that the people for whom they work treat them with respect and care about them. More women than men are proud of their companies. And women managers and professionals with higher incomes are more likely to describe their jobs as challenging and as opportunities to learn new things.

Psychic income at the expense of real income? The balance is still not right, but there may be progress. Leviticus 27:3–4 asserts that women of working age are worth 30 silver shekels while men are worth 50. The salary gap has hovered around the same 60 percent ever since those biblical times. But a mid–1983 survey by the U.S. Bureau of Labor Statistics showed that it may finally be starting to close. The survey indicates that women are now earning 66 percent of men's weekly salaries across the board, with women professionals earning 71 percent of men's salaries. These are preliminary figures, to be sure, and they may not hold up, but they are promising.

Next, a look at what women earn, and where.

2
What Women Earn

If the salary gap were closed, the gender gap might no longer exist. The disparity between what women earn and what men earn is a sharp thorn in the side of any female who works. Though many factors contribute to the size of the salary gap, the full explanation can only be discrimination against women. Why else would the female child-care workers mentioned in the previous chapter earn less than male parking-lot attendants?

Discrimination isn't the whole story, of course. Women, through education or conditioning, may be working in low-paying fields, or they may have less seniority than their male coworkers and hence be less able to compete for promotions. In addition, they may put other things ahead of money, settling for jobs that are less than equal in opportunity and pay, and for psychic income in lieu of financial rewards.

While the human relations aspects of a job can provide bona fide satisfactions, so should the pay check. In too many cases this is not so. Sixty percent of employed women earned less than $10,000 a year in 1982, according to the Bureau of the Census—and $10,000 is just about the poverty level for a family of four in America. At the other end of the salary scale things look just as bleak. Out of 45 million women working in 1982, only about two million received over $25,000 a year for their work. And in truly high-salaried jobs, women are rare. In the entire country only 42,000 women were in the $75,000-plus range—less than one-tenth of one percent of the women who work compared to the 14 percent of men who work. Discouraging as this figure seems, it contains an element of hope: it represents a nearly 100 percent increase from the year before.

A comparison of salary statistics for 1981 and 1982 demonstrates other, less dramatic salary increases for women. In 1982, a higher percentage of women made more than $10,000, a higher percentage made more than $20,000, and so on up the line. On the other hand, men also show increases in each salary level: though the rates of increase are not as great, there is a much higher percentage of men at each salary level. Expressed more simply: men make more money. Still.

The following table illustrates the pervasiveness of salary inequities:

MEN AND WOMEN: SAME JOB, DIFFERENT PAY*

Job Title	Average Weekly Earnings Men	Average Weekly Earnings Women	Average Earnings Ratio(%): Women to Men
Lawyers	$653	$492	75.3
Engineers	592	479	80.9
Health administrators	587	394	67.1
Social scientists	580	420	72.4
Bank financial officers and managers	574	336	58.5
Computer systems analysts	568	428	75.3
Elementary and secondary school administrators	566	338	59.7
Physicians	564	412	73.0
Life and physical scientists	553	378	68.3
Public relations specialists	550	341	62.0
Operations and systems analysts	547	417	76.2
Personnel and labor-relations workers	530	354	66.7
College and university teachers	528	415	78.5
Designers	526	302	57.4
Public administrators	501	392	78.2
Computer programmers	478	382	79.9
Accountants	468	325	69.4
Vocational and educational counselors	459	348	75.8
Editors and reporters	451	325	72.0
Advertising agents, sales workers	449	286	63.6
Real estate agents	435	292	66.8
Insurance agents, underwriters	419	284	67.7
Wholesale, retail buyers	412	271	65.7
Elementary school teachers	411	339	82.4
Secondary school teachers	411	357	86.8

* Job titles are those with approximately 50,000 or more each of men and women. Survey includes only earnings from salaries, not self-employment.
Source: Bureau of Labor Statistics, Current Population Survey, 1982.

Yet women are making some progress on the salary front, and the law is helping. A recent federal study compared action among companies that are federal contractors, which are required to have affirmative action plans, with companies lacking such plans. In the seven years preceding the Reagan Administration, about seven times as many women got jobs at companies that had affirmative action plans; women's participation in the contractors' workforces grew by 15.2 percent, as opposed to 2.2 percent in noncontractors' workforces. Upward mobility was also greater for women, and for minorities, where there were affirmative action requirements.

Thus federal law has joined the array of tools women can use to adjust the imbalance, but they are not neglecting the need for job-specific education. These days more women are going for the degrees that will bring them income—whether it is an M.D., an M.B.A. or a certificate in word processing. As the following graph shows, more and more women are studying engineering, dentistry, law, architecture, and accounting—occupations that pay better than those traditionally pursued by women. In addition, training is going beyond the classroom and the laboratory. Women are more savvy about the world of business today and are committing the extra time and effort needed to make progress both at entry level and throughout their careers.

It takes planning to get ahead, and women are only now beginning to plot their careers the way men have done traditionally. But even that is not

Growth in Number of Degrees Earned by Women in Selected Fields

Percent Change 1965–1980

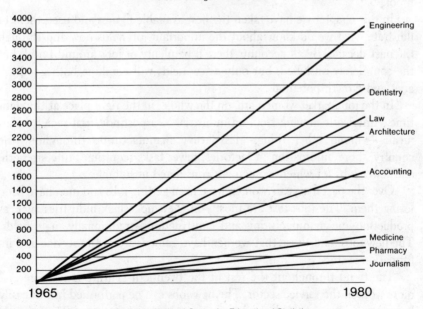

Source: Digest of Educational Statistics, National Center for Educational Statistics.

enough. It's one thing to plan a career but quite another to plan it in a field that offers adequate challenge and financial compensation for a lifetime of effort. More than one woman has prepared diligently for a career only to discover that it does not provide her with sufficient scope or money. Teaching is the most obvious example, and social work is another.

One way to avoid taking a dead-end route is to study employment forecasts. The government, industry trade associations, and other groups compile data on the number of people in various job categories and the salaries they earn. These sources also project the number of openings in these jobs in the years to come. The problem with such projections is that they may not be entirely accurate. Different employment forecasters, looking in different crystal balls, sometimes make different predictions. For example, some assert that the ranks of middle management will swell in the future; others say they will shrink as fat corporations try to become "lean and mean." The Department of Labor expects the number of bank tellers to soar, but the proliferation of automatic teller machines suggests that soon there may be no tellers' jobs at all. And while many employment prophets foresee strong growth in job openings for video display terminal operators, the computer industry is in a state of extraordinary technological flux. It could be that newly developing means of computer access will make the VDT operator of tomorrow as obsolete as the key-punch operator of today. No career field is absolutely risk-proof.

In this chapter we have taken the best available figures and used them to illustrate what we *do* know about the important job fields now and through the next decade. By all accounts there'll be plenty of jobs around for all but the completely unskilled, but only a few fields will combine both good salaries and growth potential.

In the job market women are, on the whole, in the right place at the right time. America is moving from an industrial to a postindustrial society. This means—among other things—less heavy manufacturing throughout the country, more automation in factories, fewer tasks requiring brute strength, and fewer jobs for which women are considered unsuitable.

Over the past five years women have been getting jobs and men have been losing them. The jobs lost are mostly in the smokestack industries such as production-line manufacturing and construction—traditionally male fields. The new jobs, and those that women have gained, are in the service and information sectors.

The trend throughout the rest of the twentieth century is to more and more work in the service sector. The new jobs can be performed just as easily by women as by men, and women may even have an advantage. They already have a substantial presence in many service areas, from information processing through banking to social services, teaching, food service, and, of course, clerical and domestic work.

This, then, is why there'll be plenty of jobs—though not all good ones—for women. For the good jobs, look to forecaster John Naisbitt's Information Society. Subtract information or knowledge workers from the service sector, says Naisbitt, and you have only 11 percent of the workforce left. By his interpretation, a full 60 percent of the workforce is involved with information, to the point where he renames the postindustrial society the information society. Naisbitt argues that while in preindustrial societies people have to struggle against nature, and while in industrial societies people must struggle against the world they have made and are making, the central focus of an information society isn't a struggle at all. It is people interacting with people, and it requires the kind of human relations skills at which women have traditionally excelled. Indeed, an emphasis on brains over brawn and on interpersonal relations over hardnosed competitiveness is becoming increasingly evident in a number of today's jobs, even at the top levels.

The service sector or the information society, whichever it is called, needs everything from the kind of analytical skills that apply to computer work, to the management skills that go into motivating people, to the technical and organizational skills that are involved in processing information. The following table shows jobs with growth projections that are substantially above average. Here we see that jobs in the service and information sectors—and the technical jobs that support them—are the wave of the future. The second table projects entirely new job categories for the future, and the number of openings predicted in them.

JOBS WITH GOOD GROWTH POTENTIAL

Occupation	Job Growth, 1990s (%)
Paralegal	109–139
Computer systems analyst	68–80
Occupational therapist	63–71
Physical therapist	51–59
Computer programmer	49–60
Speech pathologist/audiologist	47–50
Health services administrator	43–53
Aerospace engineer	43–52
Registered nurse	40–47
Licensed practical nurse	42
Dietician	38–46
Electrical/electronic engineer	35–47

Source: Bureau of Labor Statistics.

JOBS OF THE FUTURE

Occupation	Job Openings, 1990s
Geriatric social worker	610,000
Housing rehabilitation specialist	500,000
Industrial robot production specialist	400,000
Industrial laser process specialist	360,000
Energy conservation specialist	310,000
Computer modeling and simulation specialist	300,000
Hazardous waste management specialist	300,000
Computer software writer—financial management	250,000
Computer software writer—marketing	200,000
Genetic engineering specialist	200,000
Holographic inspection specialist	160,000
Computer assisted graphic artist	150,000

Source: Occupational Forecasting, Inc.

The surveys on the following pages describe and classify according to comparative salaries the twenty-two main fields of professional employment today, and offer projections for the next decade. Some fields are covered in greater depth elsewhere in the book—for example, management in Chapter 7, clerical jobs and federal government jobs in Chapter 18, and entrepreneurial fields in Chapter 17.

ACADEMIA

Salaries for those who teach at the college level vary according to the institution and the discipline. Large universities and Ivy League schools usually pay more than small private colleges, and professors of business and engineering generally earn more than their counterparts in fine arts or literature.

Academia offers its teachers a very flexible work life. Hours are not long, contact with students can be stimulating, and there is a chance to work on individual projects. Indeed, the latter is a necessity as far as tenure is concerned. However, with fewer students attending these days, many academic institutions are starting to "think small." The total number of professors is expected to decline over the next ten years.

Women have enjoyed some success in reaching the highest levels of college administration. According to a survey done by the American Council on Education, the number of women college and university presidents has nearly doubled since 1975, but they earn less than their male counterparts. Women occupy a substantial number of lower-level administrative positions as well. Pay varies according to the size and wealth of the institution. Again the story

COLLEGE AND UNIVERSITY PROFESSORS

Employed	Women (%)	Job Growth, 1990s (%)
601,000	35.4	−9

Position	Salary*	
	Men	Women
Professor	$39,507	$35,390
Associate professor	28,713	26,961
Assistant professor	23,918	22,016
Instructor	18,669	17,198
Lecturer	21,717	18,643

* All salaries are for nine-month teachers.
Source: National Center for Education Statistics, U.S. Education Department.

COLLEGE AND UNIVERSITY ADMINISTRATORS

Employed	Women (%)	Job Growth, 1990s (%)
130,000	36.2	N/A*

Position	Salary	
	Men	Women
Chief executive officer	$56,120	$46,261
Chief academic officer	45,000	39,200
Chief budget officer	36,032	28,288
Administrator, grants and contracts	36,000	24,782
Director, human resources	34,920	24,600
Director, admissions	30,145	24,600
Director, student financial aid	27,500	20,800
Bursar	27,125	19,026
Director, news bureau	24,752	19,884

* N/A, here and throughout, means "not available."
Source: College and University Personnel Association.

is the same—with academic enrollment declining in many institutions, the number of openings for administrators seems unlikely to grow.

ACCOUNTING

Jobs for accountants range from government positions at the low end of the pay scale to partnerships in the Big Eight firms, where the financial compensation runs well into six figures but where women are currently outnumbered 100 to 1. The partnership ranks of the Big Eight all include women, but just barely. Peat Marwick Mitchell & Co., for example, is the nation's largest accounting firm, but counts only 10 women partners out of 1200. The inequities do not end there. Women are reportedly more likely to handle administrative functions that deal with clients and may earn only a third as much as their male colleagues.

Below the top tier, accounting looks good for women. Forty percent of all accountants in the United States are women, a figure that has more than doubled in five years. And the Bureau of Labor Statistics predicts a 25–34 percent growth for the accounting field through the 1990s.

In the past, when women entered a profession in significant numbers it sometimes lost its status and salary levels dropped. This doesn't seem to be happening in accounting. "Accountants are no longer pencil pushers; they are managers, executives, and advisers to executives. Business cannot function without accounting," says Lyzatte Hale, a full professor and head of the School of Accountancy at Utah State University. Accountancy is also preparation for other careers in business because accounting is the language of business.

ACCOUNTANTS

Employed	Women (%)	Job Growth, 1990s (%)
1.2 million	38.6	25–34

Position	Salary*
Public accountant (manager/large firm)	$35,000–55,000
Public accountant (manager/medium firm)	32,000–45,000
Public accountant (entry/large firm)	18,000–19,500
Public accountant (entry/medium firm)	16,500–18,500
Corporate accountant (manager/large firm)	33,000–50,000
Corporate accountant (manager/medium firm)	28,500–33,000
Corporate accountant (entry/large firm)	14,000–16,000
Corporate accountant (entry/medium firm)	14,500–16,500

* Figures vary depending on whether you have a C.P.A. or just an M.S.
Source: Robert Half of New York, Inc.

ADVERTISING

Though it is widely thought of as a lucrative industry, salaries for lower-level jobs in advertising are no higher than for comparable positions in other industries. In some cases they are even lower, because there is so much competition to get into this glamorous field. In 1983 salaries for top advertising executives went up, but there was no appreciable rise at lower-level positions.

Male ad executives outearn females by an average of almost $14,000. The fact that men generally hold their jobs longer than women explains part of this disparity, but not all. In advertising as in so many other industries, women are still regarded as less than equal to men.

Women have for years enjoyed considerable success in the creative side of advertising (copywriting, art direction), and now are making a big impact on the marketing side too. There is still some resistance at major ad agencies to making women account executives: the thinking seems to be that "the client prefers to have a man and the client must be pleased." Otherwise there are women at every level of advertising, though just a few at the very top. New York, the nation's advertising capital, pays the highest salaries.

ADVERTISING

Employed	Women (%)		Job Growth, 1990s (%)	
130,000	46.9		N/A	
Position		Salary		
	Combined	Men	Women
Corporate sales promotion manager	$30,800	$36,000	$27,000
Corporate advertising manager	45,000	49,000	36,500
Agency copywriter	25,200	28,700	22,000
Agency art director	24,200	26,000	21,000
Agency account executive	28,000	30,000	26,000
Agency media department head	34,500	46,500	27,800

Source: *Adweek*, 1983 survey.

ARCHITECTURE

Today there are as many students in architecture schools as there are practicing architects. In other words, the market for architects is glutted. Consequently salaries are lower in architecture than for any other profession of comparable prestige.

Women represent half of the architecture students but a much smaller percentage of those employed in the field. Women who do work for architectural firms often don't get the good assignments and a great many of them find themselves performing routine tasks (like drafting or model building) with no real chance to learn or advance. Women are low on this totem pole and earn only two-thirds as much as men.

Because of these problems in established firms, many women architects are seeking opportunities elsewhere. One way they are doing this is by starting their own firms. This requires several years of experience—to pass licensing examinations—but many women report that working as an independent architect is worth it.

ARCHITECTS

Employed	Women (%)	Job Growth, 1990s (%)
94,000	8.5	33–41

Position	Salary	
	Base (Average)	Bonus (Average)
Principal (head of the firm)	$31,430	9,170
Supervisory (supervises people, projects, hires contractors)	24,000	3,000
Technician (designing, site planning, etc.)	18,500	1,800

Source: American Institute of Architects, 1981 salary data.

BANKING AND OTHER FINANCIAL SERVICES

One reason why banks have so much money is that they don't give much to their employees. Tellers and other clerical workers have a long tradition of earning less than their sister clericals (90 percent of bank clerical workers are women) in other industries.

Officers, who make up about one-fourth of the bank workforce, are not highly paid either. The median annual salary of the membership of the National Association of Bank Women is $21,200. Bank officers do, however, have relatively good job security and the opportunity to advance through in-house training programs. Higher pay usually comes with seniority and depends on the size of the bank. As a general rule, the greater the assets of the bank, the bigger the pay check.

The titles "vice president" and "assistant vice president" in banking cover a wide range of job descriptions, and it is not possible to give meaningful salary ranges for them. MBAs can usually expect to start at higher salaries than trainees without the degree, and increasingly, as banking goes through widespread changes, the industry is looking for people with knowledge of computers.

Like banking, the insurance industry employs an enormous number of people at the clerical level. Also like banking, insurance generally has lower pay levels than most other industries. The main exception is the insurance agent who earns a commission on the policies she sells and who consequently may, with time and experience, find herself making a five-figure income. Women insurance managers earn an average of $67,000.

Some financial jobs are more or less unique to the insurance industry: actuaries design insurance policies; underwriters decide which risks their companies will take; and claims representatives settle claims.

Women considering a career on Wall Street can forge ahead knowing that there are probably more women earning six figures in the securities

BANKING/FINANCIAL OFFICERS & MANAGERS

Employed	Women (%)	Job Growth, 1990s (%)
731,000	37.1	26–33

Position	Salary	
	Medium Firm	Large Firm
Corporate controller	$37,000–50,000	$61,000–95,000
Corporate credit manager	25,000–32,000	33,000–49,000

Position	Small Bank	Medium Bank	Large Bank
Senior loan manager	$33–37,500	$31–35,000	$32–49,000
Bank branch manager, commercial loans	22–28,000	22–28,500	26–34,000
Bank operations officer	16–20,000	20–27,000	23–29,000
Cashier	21–28,500	24–31,000	28–37,000

Source: Robert Half of New York, Inc.

INSURANCE
(Agents, Underwriters)

Employed	Women (%)	Job Growth, 1990s (%)
646,000	26.2	18–29

Position	Starting Salary
Agent (5 years experience)	$23,000–25,000
Actuary	16,000–20,000
Underwriter	18,500
Claim representative	17,000

Source: Insurance Information Institute.

SECURITIES SALES
(Stocks and Bonds)

Employed	Women (%)	Job Growth, 1990s (%)
197,000	19.8	26–44

Position	Salary	
	Base	Bonus
Broker (institutional)	$150,438	
Broker (retail)	62,788	
Senior municipal bond trader	52,449	$64,016
Senior over-the-counter trader	49,458	$35,801
Junior municipal bond trader	20,005	6,936
Junior over-the-counter trader	19,416	4,859

Source: Securities Industries Association.

industry than in any other. Recent securities industry statistics show earnings for senior municipal bond traders averaging over $116,000 (more than half of that made up of commissions). Both brokers, who earn commissions, and traders, who earn salaries but get bonuses on the profitability of their transactions, must produce to earn well.

Experts predict the generation of a million and a half finance-related jobs by 1990—jobs requiring computer, marketing, communications, and administrative skills, as well as jobs more immediately concerned with the provision of financial services.

CLERICAL WORK

Clerical work is the fastest-growing employment in the United States today. A quarter of all the new jobs in the 80s will be clerical, and clericals are already one-fifth of the workforce. Eighty percent of all clerical workers and 99 percent of all secretaries are women. In fact, of every three women in the labor force, one is a clerical worker. In 1983 clerical employees averaged $262 per week. Salaries range from a high of $339 for executive secretaries/administrative assistants to a low of $195 for file clerks, the only position that averages less than $200 a week. The introduction of office automation is transforming the field, and it is not yet clear how it will all turn out for women. For more on this subject see Chapter 18, Where Most Women Work.

COMPUTERS

A woman, Lady Augusta Lovelace, was the first computer user. In 1842 she began working with Charles Babbage on applications for the computer he had invented, and found her place in history. Women today make up the fastest-growing group of personal computer users, because women are recognizing that a knowledge of computers can provide a competitive edge in obtaining and remaining in professional jobs.

Just about every industry in the United States has been affected by the computer revolution, and computers will be a growth field for years to come. Predictions for job growth in the computer industry range from the wild to the astronomical, but all need to be kept in perspective. Though high-tech jobs as a whole probably will grow at a rate three times as fast as employment growth overall, the total *number* of new high-tech jobs will add up to only 7 percent of all new jobs during the rest of the decade. For example, employment for computer systems analysts will have grown by over 100 percent between 1978 and 1990, netting 200,000 new jobs, while for the same period some 1.3 million new jobs are projected for janitors, nurses' aides, and orderlies. Even if the number of high-tech jobs doubles or triples in the next dec-ade, it will hardly make a ripple in the overall job market. However, it is predicted that a disproportionate number of the jobs that *do* get created will go to women.

Computer programming is not just a technical skill anyone can pick up with a little training. It requires creativity and a good business sense, and, be-cause the field is changing so rapidly, long experience is not a significant fac-tor in one's advancement. While the computer boom still has its share of busts, salaries and staff sizes have been rising steadily since the 1960s. Even secretaries with word-processing skills are doing well, earning a 9.7 percent av-erage pay raise in 1982.

Computers are quickly becoming an essential part of modern life. Anyone who does not acquire at least a passing familiarity with the computer world is going to be at a disadvantage in almost any field, particularly in busi-ness/management.

There are three basic job categories in the computer field: data processors, who operate the equipment, put the data in and receive the printout, and run checks on the system; programmers, who write instructions for the computers to follow; and systems analysts, who analyze the particular computer needs of a company and the personnel needed to run different systems.

COMPUTER SPECIALISTS
(Systems Analyst, Programmer)

Employed	Women (%)	Job Growth, 1990s (%)
751,000	28.5	68–80 (Systems Analyst)
		49–60 (Programmer)

Position	Salary
Vice president, data processing	$50,469
Director, data processing	39,185
Manager, systems analyst	35,247
Lead systems analyst	29,837
Senior systems analyst/Programmer	28,726
Senior applications programmer	26,427
Systems analyst/Programmer	24,302
Applications/Programmer	21,288
Junior systems analyst/Programmer	18,719

Source: *Datamation* magazine.

DENTISTRY

Women have been slower to enter the field of dentistry than any of the other prestige professions. Only in the past ten years have women made inroads into dentistry, and the number of female dentists is extremely small. Nevertheless, the percentage of female dental students has accelerated steadily and now stands at about 17 percent. Female practicing dentists have achieved virtual parity with their male colleagues in the fees they receive. If women earn less than men in this field, it is only because they work fewer hours.

Yet the view is not all rosy. The number of dentists has been increasing faster than the population as a whole, which has led to speculation that dentistry may one day be an overcrowded field. Competition among dentists has clearly been on the rise (witness the advent of the cut-rate clinic). Yet dentistry is still a promising and profitable profession. As with other professions, specialists often earn more than those in general practice. The average income of a specialist is $80,373, and specialists make up about 13 percent of dentists. The two fastest-growing specialties are oral surgery and orthodontics.

	DENTISTS	
Employed	*Women (%)*	*Job Growth, 1990s (%)*
121,000	3.3	23
Salaries		
Net income (average)		$65,912

Source: *Dental Management* magazine.

ECONOMICS

The vast majority of economists—about 75 percent—are in private industry (working with management, analyzing trends in business and finance markets for short- and long-term investments, assisting in strategy development preparing economic forecasts). Another 10 percent teach in colleges and universities, and an equal number work for federal and state governments (again analyzing markets, preparing forecasts, and presenting economic material that bears on decision making). There are relatively few economists in private practice; those who do private consulting are mostly professors.

Economists enjoy good job prospects, no matter what the economic picture happens to be. Almost everyone who earns a Ph.D. in the field gets a job. The Bureau of Labor Statistics expects the number of economists to increase to 183,000 by 1990, a faster growth rate than is predicted in most job areas.

One curious note: half of all women earning Ph.D.s in economics take college teaching positions, where the pay is relatively lower.

ECONOMISTS

Employed	Women (%)	Job Growth, 1990s (%)
200,000	28	26–32

Position	Salary		
By Industry		By Sex	
Securities/Investments	$47,900	Men	$43,000
Banking	47,000	Women	35,000
Consulting	45,000		
Manufacturing	44,000		
Government	40,000		
Academia	33,000		

Source: National Association of Business Economists.

ENGINEERING

Less than 3 percent of working engineers are women, but educators and employers are vigorously recruiting women to meet the increasing demands of the field. Female enrollment in engineering programs has risen from 1 percent in 1970 to a current high of 25 percent in some entering classes. The demand for engineers has climbed 30 percent in just the past two years, and is expected to rise.

Engineers are needed in many different areas: chemical engineers, who design the processes required for chemistry; metallurgical engineers, who work with mining procedures; petroleum engineers, who design methods for

ENGINEERS

Employed	Women (%)	Job Growth, 1990s (%)
1.57 million	5.7	27–37

Position	Salary		
	All Levels	5–9 Years Since B.S.	Starting Offers
Petroleum	$52,500	$42,320	$30,816
Chemical	46,800	37,800	26,736
Mechanical	43,000	34,440	25,152
Electrical/Electronic	42,290	34,880	25,536
Aerospace	42,125	31,564	24,048
Civil	38,845	31,500	22,428

Sources: College Placement Council, National Society of Professional Engineers.

extracting oil; environmental engineers, who deal with water and waste problems. There are also, of course, engineers in industry, mechanics, electronics, and research and testing areas. The largest number of engineering jobs will be in public utilities, petroleum-allied firms, and the areas of chemicals and drugs. The fastest-growing branches of engineering are mechanical and electrical.

Because of the great demand for engineers, the salary gap in the field has been closing. Men and women now start with equal salaries, and in 1983 female engineering graduates *outdistanced* men in salaries offers in almost all engineering fields.

HEALTH CARE

General prospects for continued growth in the number and variety of health care occupations are good to excellent. Employment opportunities are greatest in hospitals, nursing homes, and extended-care facilities. Women make up some 80 percent of the health care labor force but hold only 10 percent of the higher-level jobs. The high-paying category of health administrator is still predominantly male. (Information about the professional categories of medicine and dentistry is given separately in this chapter.)

HEALTH ADMINISTRATION

Employed	Women (%)	Job Growth, 1990s (%)
228,000	50.9	43–53

Position	Salary		
	Large	Medium	Small
Hospital Administrators	Over $80M	$20–40M	Up to $7M
Chief executive officer	$70,000	$55,000	$35,000
Associate administrator	53,700	45,400	28,300
Director, nursing services	49,800	38,500	25,500
Director, medical records	29,300	24,600	16,700

Source: *Modern Healthcare* magazine, 1981–82 figures.

In health care the fastest job growth is expected to be in the category of health technologists and technicians. Most of these jobs are new occupations requiring a one- or two-year program of course work or an equivalent amount of hospital training. On the average, technologists have longer formal training, higher pay, and greater levels of responsibility than technicians. Most of the occupations center on operation or monitoring of new hospital equipment.

Note too that nurses' aides are one of the five categories expected to produce the most new jobs in the 80s. (The others are janitors, sales

OCCUPATIONAL THERAPIST

Employed	Women (%)	Job Growth, 1990s (%)
28,000 (1983)	95	63–71

Years of Experience	Director/ Manager	Staff
15+	$26,272	$20,707
10–14	25,501	20,577
5–9	22,784	19,540
0–4	19,595	17,378

Source: American Occupational Therapy Association.

clerks, cashiers, and waiters and waitresses.) Other important health care areas include:

OCCUPATIONAL THERAPY

There are currently a relatively small number of occupational therapists, almost all of whom are women. As is to be expected in a female-dominated profession, salaries are modest, pay increments small. Yet rapid growth in this field is expected, in line with the aging of the population and the continuing growth of the health care industry.

PHYSICAL THERAPY

The typical physical therapist is female, young (around thirty), and in great demand. This demand is expected to continue through the coming decade. The vast majority of physical therapists work in hospitals, where they may rise to administrative positions. Self-employed therapists generally make substantially higher incomes than those on staff.

PHYSICAL THERAPIST

Employed	Women (%)	Job Growth, 1990s (%)
42,000 (1983)	70 (industry estimate)	51–59

Position	Salary	
	Men	Women
Self-employed	$35–50,000	$25–35,000
Salaried	25,35,000	18–21,000

Source: American Physical Therapy Association.

SPEECH PATHOLOGY/AUDIOLOGY

A fairly well-paying, female-dominated profession with good employment prospects for the coming years.

NURSING

Women and nursing are so nearly synonymous that a male in the profession usually requires a qualifying term before his title. (A man who is a registered nurse usually is listed as "male nurse.") The effect of such complete female dominance is predictable: nurses are not paid as much as they should be. To quote *The American Almanac of Jobs and Salaries*, "Such low salaries for such highly responsible work have had an adverse affect on the profession. By 1980, for example, more than 25 percent of all nurses had left the field completely, and only 60 percent of all nurses were working at any given time; moreover, 90,000 to 100,000 nursing vacancies existed nationwide, leaving 88 percent of all hospitals with nursing jobs unfilled. The acute shortage of nurses has become such a serious matter that some hospitals are recruiting personnel from overseas." Given the enormous demand, one might expect a dramatic increase in salaries. It doesn't seem to be happening.

SPEECH PATHOLOGISTS/AUDIOLOGISTS

Employed	Women (%)	Job Growth, 1990s (%)
50,000	85 (industry estimate)	51–59

Position	Salary	
	Ph.D.	M.S.
Private Practice	$29,722*	$22,642*
Hospital	31,185	19,065
Academia	26,571	17,643

* All figures from 1981.
Source: American Speech-Language-Hearing Association.

REGISTERED NURSES

Employed	Women (%)	Job Growth, 1990s (%)
1.41 million	95.6	40–47

Position	Salary
Nurse anesthetist	$27,574
Nursing administrator (hospital)	24,486
Nurse practitioner	20,448
Nurse clinician	19,739
Assistant nursing instructor	19,806
Clinical nurse specialist	19,419

Source: American Nurses Association.

HOTEL AND MOTEL MANAGEMENT

The hotel and motel industry is the seventh-largest service industry in the country, and we may remind ourselves that the service sector is expected to grow faster than any other occupational group through the 1980s and 1990s. Hotel/motel employees are usually categorized as professionals (general managers, personnel directors, administrative chefs); middle management (auditors, executive housekeepers, front-office management); and service (housekeepers, food-service workers, and uniformed staff). Once relegated primarily to the clerical, housekeeping, and food-service areas, women have made major advances into middle and upper management in the past ten years. How fast and how high a woman can go in this business depends on her education and training, the size of the hotel/motel she works in, its location, and whether it is independent or part of a chain. Many women get hotel-administration degrees at college and then join management-training programs run by hotel corporations. Others take a somewhat slower and less certain route and work their way up without formal training. Whichever path a woman takes, opportunities for advancement are best in large metropolitan hotels or chains such as Sheraton, Hilton, Ramada Inn, and Holiday Inn.

HOTEL/MOTEL MANAGEMENT

Employed	Women (%)	Job Growth, 1990s (%)
1,119,000	N/A	34–47
	Position	Salary*

Position	Salary*
General Manager (includes living allowance)	$26,000–68,000
Food and Beverage manager	15,600–27,745
Hotel controller	14,400–30,000
Executive chef	12,000–45,000
Executive housekeeper	12,500–21,600
Manager trainees	12,000–14,000

* Salaries vary according to location and size of hotel or motel.
Sources: American Hotel & Motel Association and Statistical Abstract of the United States.

LAW

Between 1950 and 1970 the number of attorneys nationwide increased at a steady rate of about 4,000 a year. Then the dam broke. Over the next twelve years the total number of lawyers in the country more than doubled and the number of women lawyers increased more than seven times. The female proportion of the legal profession rose from approximately 5 percent to an estimated 15.5 percent.

Are there more lawyers in this country than there is legal work? The American Bar Association *Journal* reports that there are three and one-half lawyers for every thousand adults and the number is rapidly approaching four—a far higher ratio than is necessary. Competition for jobs is stiff among graduating law students, and the lawyer glut will affect women more than

ATTORNEYS		
Employed	Women (%)	Job Growth, 1990s (%)
606,000	15.5	25–39
Position		Salary*
Law firms		
Associate		$38,660
Partner		96,443
Corporations		
Chief legal officer		$117,000
Nonsupervising attorney		45,554
Recent law school graduates		30,000
Federal Government		
Lower level (GS 9)		$21,811 (average figures)
Middle level (GS 12)		32,065
Higher level (GS 14)		45,713

* Includes benefits.
Source for private companies: Altman & Weil, Inc.
Source for federal government: Bureau of Labor Statistics.

men because there are more of them in the less prestigious law schools—and those schools have the most trouble placing graduates. In a recent article, the lawyer and sociologist Donna Fossum warns: "Women in the legal profession are beginning to fear that just as they reach the cupboard, it may be bare."

According to the Bureau of Labor Statistics there are 606,000 practicing attorneys in the United States and 94,000 of them are women. Three-fourths of the total number of attorneys are in the private sector (either working for law firms or self-employed); 15 percent work for the government (the judicial system included); and about 10 percent work in private industry. A random sample taken by the ABA *Journal* shows a median personal income of $33,000 for female lawyers and $53,000 for male lawyers.

Surprisingly, women attorneys report that they are warmly accepted as colleagues by male attorneys and are satisfied with their jobs even though they work in a male-dominated field, according to a study conducted by the public opinion research firm Kane, Parsons & Associates. But newcomers in the field must also take into account the fact that many male lawyers do not think women can bring in as much business as their male colleagues. These perceptions may help explain why 70 percent of all women lawyers are salaried employees of law firms, government agencies, and businesses, while 60 percent of men are in the higher paying private sector.

MASS COMMUNICATIONS

The field of mass communications encompasses many jobs in the radio, television, print, and motion picture industries. These jobs are often perceived as glamorous. Some of them are, of course, but for the rank and file, glamor comes in about as low a quotient as pay. This is especially true in radio and television. There *are* high earners in local television news (for example, anchorwomen) and among television general executives. But entry-level TV jobs and behind-the-scenes technical jobs are not well paying. Still, there is a fairly fast turnover in television and radio, and so there is room for upward movement.

Since the communications field has traditionally favored entrants with a good liberal arts education, competition for jobs is strong in all areas of mass

MASS COMMUNICATIONS

BROADCASTING *Number Employed*	*Women (%)*	*Job Growth, 1990s (%)*
191,982	34.5	N/A
Position		*Average Salary*
Television		
Television Entry level		$10,140
General managers		$74,700
General sales managers		59,400
Program directors		35,500
Radio		
Radio Entry level		$ 8,840–13,000*
General manager		$82,836
General sales manager		$26,000
Program director		$16,120
PRINTING AND PUBLISHING		
1,287,800	40.8	N/A
Average yearly income: $19,240		
Newspapers		
424,500	39.6	N/A
Average yearly income: $19,260		
Periodicals		
100,100	59.3	N/A
Average yearly income: $20,134		
Books		
92,000	53.6	N/A
Average yearly income: $18,283		

* Salary depends on area of entry.
Sources for broadcasting: National Association of Broadcasters, *Editor and Publisher, Television, Radio Age.*
Sources for printing and publishing: Bureau of Labor Statistics.

communications. But at the same time, new opportunities are opening up, especially in cable television and such areas as videotext and electronic publishing. The videotext industry estimates that it will provide up to 5,000 new jobs by the end of the century, and the cable industry has created a need for communications-related skills such as engineering, marketing, sales, and business administration, as well as production and programming skills. And even within cable new areas, such as interactive cable, are opening up.

The print industry never reaches the heady heights of pay that television and motion pictures do, but there is a similar story as far as competition and lower-level pay are concerned. Still, the outlook is not bleak. The latest figures, from 1982, show an increase in job openings in newspapers and magazines.

MEDICINE

A 1983 article in the *New York Times* features a number of young physicians lamenting that costs and competition will keep them from setting up lucrative Manhattan practices. The Congressional Office of Technology Assessment forecasts a surplus of 185,000 physicians by 1990. Yet the medical profession is the best-paying one in the country. The American Medical Association regulates the number of students admitted to medical school each year, and there still is a great need for physicians in small towns and rural areas.

There should, then, be ample opportunities for women, who form an ever increasing part of the medical profession—15 percent of all doctors today. They will, if current medical school admission trends continue, make up around 30 percent of the doctor population by the year 2000.

Women doctors tend to cluster in the lower-paying areas of their profession: psychiatry, for example, public health, and teaching (although

PHYSICIANS		
Employed	*Women (%)*	*Job Growth, 1990s (%)*
486,000	14.8	32
Position		*Salary**
Neurosurgeon		$142,500
Plastic surgeon		127,920
OB/GYN specialist		108,330
Family practitioner		74,580
Pediatrician		72,110
All physicians		93,270

* All figures are net earnings.
Source: *Medical Economics* magazine.

women do not occupy many senior teaching posts). There are signs that women are shifting to more lucrative specialties. The specialty currently most popular with women is internal medicine, and more women are also taking up obstetrics/gynecology.

Earnings in private practice can easily reach as high as $200,000.

PERSONNEL LABOR RELATIONS

Managerial positions in personnel were among the first to open up to women, who today are firmly established in this part of the corporate world. It is, in fact, the original velvet ghetto. The responsibilities are many; they include staffing the organization, employing and supervising the training of employees at all levels, maintaining equitable compensation for employees, developing personnel policies and procedures, and planning human resource needs for the future. Corporate personnel managers often specialize in one of these.

Personnel is a field in which women do well and it is a business function every corporation needs. However, though women may rise to the top of a personnel department, few advance from there to the top of the corporation.

PERSONNEL/LABOR RELATIONS

Employed	Women (%)	Job Growth, 1990s (%)
423,000	49.6	15–22

Position	Salary	
	Large Company	Small Company
Top personnel/Industrial relations head	$97,300*	$50,300*
Personnel/Corporate development manager	59,900	34,600
Benefits administrator	22,900	21,400
Personnel assistant	16,100	15,100

* All figures are averages and include bonuses.
Sources: American Society for Personnel Administration and A. S. Hansen Company.

PHARMACY

Pharmacy is another profession that women are entering at an increasing rate. Enrollment in college pharmacy programs is up, and the percentage of women pharmacists has risen from around 17 in 1978 to nearly 24 today. This drive may be too much too late. The number of openings for pharmacists is expected to rise modestly in the coming years, and there may not be enough jobs for today's students.

Pharmacy is not a particularly lucrative profession. Average salary for drug-chain pharmacists in 1982 was $27,651. Generally speaking, the best-paying positions are at the administrative level in the larger hospitals. Pharmacy is a good career for those seeking some independence; about 25 percent of all pharmacists are self-employed.

PHARMACISTS

Employed	Women (%)	Job Growth, 1990s (%)
168,000	23.8	10–20

Position	Salary
Chain store	$27,651
Independent	25,275

Source: *Drug Topics* magazine.

PUBLIC RELATIONS

The job of a public relations person is basically one of promotion—promoting a corporation, a research foundation, a college, or a political action group by maintaining good media contacts and writing news releases and press copy. In addition to offering vital information (new products, new research, new ventures, new campaigns) a PR person is in the "image making" business. In this sense, the job is not unlike that of advertising.

PR is another field in which women are highly visible but where there is the usual salary gap. Women earn only two-thirds of what men get in the PR business. Women at the top may earn over $100,000 a year, but lower-level positions are very lowly paid. PR is another glamor field with plenty of competition to get into it. The prominence of women in the industry will probably continue, since half the students taking PR courses in college are female.

PUBLIC RELATIONS

Employed	Women (%)	Job Growth, 1990s (%)
134,000	50	18–26

Position	Salary
Public relations firms	$48,800
Industry	45,600
Consumer product firms	44,000
Trade associations	40,000
Government	37,500
Banking	35,000

Source: *PR Reporter*.

RETAIL AND SALES

In the traditional women's field of retailing, women today are clustered in behind-the-counter jobs at the bottom of the salary scale. Women are also in the majority up to the level of middle management, where buyers, for example—those who purchase for resale—earn in the low twenties (though, with bonuses, some take home over $60,000 a year). The few who are senior executives do very well. A 1983 Korn/Ferry study found that senior women executives in the retail field are the highest paid among top female managers in the country, averaging $107,000 annually. While there is a conspicuous dearth of women at the vice presidential level and beyond in retailing, given women's longevity in the industry, they should soon move to the top. The Carter Hawley Hale retail chain has three female store presidents, and in November 1983 Dawn Mello was named president of its flagship store, Bergdorf Goodman in New York. Geraldine Stutz, president of the famous Henri Bendel specialty store in New York, now owns the store.

Retail sales will produce new jobs at all levels through the next decade because of anticipated expansion, and because high turnover means plenty of replacement openings.

In all industries sales traditionally has been a path to upper management for men, and now it has become a career field with great potential for women. Sales success is based entirely on results—not necessarily on education or on previous experience—and so it offers an excellent chance for women of any age to get ahead. It can be pursued at any level, and working hours are often flexible.

Statistics seem to back up the selling ability of women. In March 1981, 45.5 percent of the business and industrial sales force was female. Today women make up 10 to 15 percent of all corporate sales people, and their numbers are expected to grow rapidly. Selling is what is called a "fast-track career."

Sales positions are divided into three categories: *inside* (retail sales, tele-

	BUYER	
Employed	*Women (%)*	*Job Growth, 1990s (%)*
195,000	43.1	20–27
Position		*Salary*
Entry		$19,120
Mid-level		23,633
Top-level		35,570

Source: Bureau of Labor Statistics.

phone marketing, sales support and services), *outside* or *field* sales (wholesale, industrial), and *direct* (to consumers in homes).

Average salaries in sales range from $25,000 to $75,000 a year and beyond, including or plus bonuses and commissions. Of all people who earn more than $50,000 a year in this country, 65 percent are in sales, according to Barbara Pletcher, founder of the National Association for Professional Saleswomen.

SCIENCE

Scientists are in demand to develop new products, combat disease, protect the environment, and develop new sources of energy. Job outlook is related to an expanding economy and increased spending on research and development. Both government and industry expect such increases through the next decade. The majority of scientists work for private industry or government, where salaries are higher than in teaching.

Women scientists make up only 10 percent of the field, a figure that has not changed since the 1920s. Nevertheless, attitudes are changing and career possibilities are better now.

Chemistry is a particularly good area for women, especially analytical chemistry and biochemistry, and a background in chemical engineering can get you into the industrial or high-tech companies. Dr. Sheila Pfafflin, former president of the Association of Women in Science, says that career-oriented women should move away from the overcrowded biological sciences and study applied physics and physical chemistry. (Physical chemistry, which deals with energy transformation, is considered the real growth area of this discipline.)

CHEMIST

Employed	Women (%)	Job Growth, 1990s (%)
133,000	20.3	18–24

Years Since B.S. — *Salary—By Degree*

Years Since B.S.	B.S.		M.S.		Ph.D.	
	Men	Women	Men	Women	Men	Women
30–34	$40,000	$31,050	$41,104	$27,500	$48,000	$35,346
15–19	36,800	26,050	35,000	28,300	40,000	33,000
5–9	26,400	23,000	27,000	24,619	33,840	33,450
0–1	19,600	19,000	N/A	N/A	N/A	N/A

Source: American Chemical Society.

SOCIAL SERVICES

Social work has never been a particularly lucrative field, but it has a wealth of humanitarian value. Social work offers a genuine opportunity to *help people*.

It is also, reportedly, a very frustrating profession. Social workers often choose social work because they want to work closely with people, but many find that they also have to do a lot of administrative paper work and become familiar with the workings (and nonworkings) of bureaucracy. They end up spending only 25 percent of their time in client contact.

The profession reports frequent cases of "burnout," and the turnover in social agencies is high because of it. Ambitious social workers are going into private practice or becoming consultants to industry.

Social workers are in great demand—there are more than twice as many jobs in the field as there are trained people to fill them. Until social priorities change and wages rise, however, social work is a profession that will remain one of life's true vocations.

SOCIAL SERVICES

Employed	Women (%)	Job Growth, 1990s (%)
407,000	73	20–24

Position	Salary
Beginning social worker	$15,220
Graduate social worker (M.S.W.)	18,990
Certified social worker (M.S.W. and 2 years experience)	21,980
Advanced social worker (doctorate)	26,660

Source: National Association of Social Work.

TEACHING (ELEMENTARY AND HIGH SCHOOL)

Teaching, like social work, offers a chance to work with people. In this case it is a chance to shape young minds, a prospect that is very attractive to many people. But, again like social work, teaching has its stress and burnout problems. Only 22 percent of teachers say they would definitely choose teaching if

*TEACHING PUBLIC AND PRIVATE SCHOOLS**

Employed	Women (%)	Job Growth, 1990s (%)
2,375,000	66.6	11.7

Position	Salary
Elementary (public school)	$20,000
Secondary (public school)	21,100

* Private school salaries vary according to the size and wealth of the school but generally are lower.

they had it to do over. Furthermore, it is a field crowded with women and not well paying.

THE NEXT STEP: PAY EQUITY

As we've seen throughout this chapter, the salary gap between men and women is still very wide nearly everywhere. Our job listings show fields—often those only recently desegregated, such as engineering—that offer high salaries and good advancement opportunities for women, but most women still work in the low-paying, traditionally female jobs. And though they may not be pleased with the pay, many can't or don't want to switch fields. What's more, it's unlikely that enough women could ever become business executives or union electricians or telephone installers to even out the salary differences between the sexes. It's unfair to women—and bad for society—to insist that the only way a woman can earn a fair wage is to leave nursing or secretarial work for a better-paying job.

To deal with the salary gap we have to address the underlying problem: a salary structure which values the jobs women do less than it values those of men. To solve the problem women are now turning to the fight for pay equity, equal pay for work of comparable value. It's becoming clear that just demanding equal pay is not the solution.

Take the Equal Pay Act, passed by Congress in 1963 to fight sex discrimination in salaries. It covers only men and women who have virtually identical jobs—jobs that require equal skill, effort, and responsibility under equal working conditions in the same company. This type of legislation does nothing to solve most unfair practices, such as the discrepancy in pay between the child-care worker and the parking-lot attendant.

The inequities may be reachable via another antidiscrimination statute, Title VII of the 1964 Civil Rights Law. Title VII is broader than the Equal Pay Act. It forbids, among other things, job discrimination in salaries on the basis of sex, without requiring that a salary comparison be made within the same company.

In a historic 1981 case, *County of Washington [Oregon] vs. Gunther,* the U.S. Supreme Court found that Title VII applies when an employer evaluates the worth of jobs held by men and by women even when those jobs are different. The case was brought by female prison matrons. The county had done a study evaluating the jobs of male prison guards and female prison matrons and found that the women's jobs were worth 95 percent of what the men's jobs were worth. Yet the county continued to pay the women only 70 percent of the men's salary. The court said that this was a form of wage discrimination on the basis of sex.

Job evaluation studies such as the one Washington County did are the basis of the pay equity push. It's important to understand how these studies work. Researchers look at all the different components of a job—the skills and training required, its difficulty, what the actual work involves (heavy lifting, supervising people, making certain decisions)—and, according to a point system, rate the job on a scale. This sort of study provides a method of comparing the way different jobs are valued by an employer, and seeing whether the way such jobs are valued has any relationship to which sex predominates in the category.

In 1983 such a study bore fruit again when a U.S. District Judge Jack E. Tanner used it to find that the state of Washington had practiced "direct, overt and intentional sex discrimination" by paying women in female-dominated jobs less than men in male-dominated jobs that were determined to be of comparable value to the state. In *American Federation of State, County and Municipal Employees* vs. *The State of Washington*, the judge ordered the state to pay $800 million to $1 billion in back pay and increased wages for women workers. He also ordered that new pay formulas be calculated; they are expected to raise the pay of Washington State's women employees by about 31 percent.

Pay equity is the first tool that may offer relief for the large number of women working in traditional jobs without requiring them to switch to male jobs to earn what they are worth. Finding out whether your salary and those of other women in your firm is lower than that of men in comparable jobs may be difficult if you work in private industry, where salary information is not a matter of public record. If you file a lawsuit, though, the company will have to reveal this information in the course of what is called the discovery phase of the proceedings (before the actual trial is held).

However, pay equity is not a panacea. One limitation is that it applies only to those who work for a single employer. For example, pay equity would insure that secretaries and teachers employed by a city government are paid fairly compared to city maintenance workers; but pay equity would not require a driving school in one town, whose employees are predominantly female, to pay wages that match those of the predominantly male driving school in the next town if those two schools have different owners. What's more, to win a pay equity case sex discrimination must be proved, and courts are still developing ways of establishing this proof.

But pay equity does offer one of the strongest hopes for helping correct at least some of the historic inequities in the job market. Some eighteen states and a number of cities have undertaken studies like the one conducted in Washington State. Twenty-two legislatures have considered pay-equity laws or resolutions, and California, Iowa, Minnesota, and Washington have amended their civil service laws to require pay equity. Minnesota avoided a case similar to the one in Washington by correcting voluntarily the inequities its pay-equity study found. The cost of phasing in the wage increases over a four-year period: 4 percent of the state payroll. The first two years of increases cost the state $21.7 million.

Whatever kind of job or profession you choose, or think of switching to, the decision will require many considerations beyond pay or salary level. In fact, getting started in a field, though in most cases easier for women than it has ever been, calls for a broad understanding of business realities and a lot of know-how. We'll take up these considerations next.

3
Getting Started

The life of a college student has its rewards and agonies. So does the first job in a chosen career field. But they are quite different. Moreover, the passage from studying to working, an exciting one that can result in great payoffs— money, prestige, power—requires a new kind of maturity and readiness to deal with others. These are the prerequisites for grasping the opportunities the world of work offers: the chance to discover one's talents and strengths, to grow and master skills, to meet and learn from a variety of people, to be part of a team, and to make important decisions.

Of course more and more women are preparing themselves for careers by getting a college education. In June 1983, 480,000 women received bachelor of arts degrees from colleges and universities across the country—76,000 more than in 1973. Of the 1983 figure, some 73,806 women earned degrees in business and management (including accounting), and 14,513 women earned the coveted MBA.

Today's women want to work and must work, and they are beginning to face these realities by learning marketable skills, such as computer program- ming and accounting. But for the individual woman, competition for a job is greater than ever. In addition to preparing herself for a career, a woman has to prepare herself for the *job* of finding a job. Though students in a few disci- plines are pursued by the recruiters who flock to colleges each year, most women must find jobs the old-fashioned way: by pounding the pavement.

There are three major concerns for any first job: preparing for it and get- ting it; keeping it and learning skills; and getting out of it—that is, getting promoted.

53

THE JOB OF FINDING A JOB

The basic entrée to any job is the résumé. This list of educational credits and work experience is intended to introduce you to an employer. As Richard Nelson Bolles says in his classic manual for job hunters, *What Color Is Your Parachute?*, "The key to an effective and useful résumé is very simple: You must know why you are writing it (to open doors for you), to whom you are writing it (the people who have the power to hire), what you want them to know about you, how you can help them and their organization, and how you can support this claim so as to convince them to reach a favorable decision about you."

For a first job, the résumé doesn't have to be a work of art; for example, it needn't be printed on high-quality paper. But its appearance is important: it must be a neatly typed, well-organized document.

Although job experts have different opinions on what a résumé should include, most agree that it should state, usually in this order:

1. Who you are: the identification section
2. What you want to do: the job-objective section
3. What you can contribute: sections on education and experience

In a résumé, how you say something matters as much as what you say. When you are listing previous areas of responsibility, pay special attention to language. Use "action" verbs. A résumé manual prepared by Catalyst (see Appendix C, Other Resources) suggests using words such as:

administered	handled
analyzed	implemented
conducted	improved
contacted	invented
contracted	maintained
created	managed
cut	negotiated
designed	operated
developed	organized
directed	oversaw
edited	planned
evaluated	prepared
exhibited	presented
expanded	produced

reduced costs	taught
researched	trained
sold	was promoted
supervised	wrote
supported	

Use such verbs to construct brief, clear phrases: "Managed staff of 12 student editors"; "Reduced overhead by 25 percent."

First-job seekers may feel that they have nothing to say about themselves or their "careers." If you haven't worked for pay before, list other kinds of activities. Don't overlook volunteer work: "Ran volunteer nurses' aide program at local hospital." Put down part-time employment: "Supervised hosiery department part time at local store." Emphasize student activities: "Organized student/faculty orientation meetings." Your objective is to be able to translate these types of experience to the job you are seeking.

Do not list the names of your references. Instead, say that they are available on request. Do not give salary figures, either present salary or expected salary. This is a subject to discuss at interviews. Omit personal information such as marital status, children, health, height, nationality, race, weight, and age. None should be relevant to the job, and some are illegal to ask about. A résumé should be limited to one page, one side only, of 8½-x-11-inch paper. Although most résumés cover the same general points, there are different formats for different needs. A recent graduate may want a straightforward format, such as the Harvard Business School résumé. Someone upgrading her career or reentering the job market may find the chronological or the functional résumé more appropriate.

The *Harvard Business School Résumé*, devised by the school for its graduates, is clear, simple, and popular. It lists educational background followed by a chronology of jobs (latest job is listed first).

The *chronological résumé* has a number of pluses: It is the kind most interviewers know best and it has a simple structure. It highlights long-term, steady employment, but it also exposes breaks in employment. It puts equal emphasis on every job experience and does not focus on skills.

The *functional résumé* spotlights marketable skills and emphasizes growth and development; it is great for burying a spotty employment record and playing down jobs that are not relevant to career growth. This format lacks specific job titles and descriptions, though, and the interviewer may request these as well as more chronological information.

The *combination résumé* plays down earlier and less significant experience, emphasizes relevant and important experience, and smooths out employment breaks. If the writer is not careful, this format can become too lengthy.

Harvard Business School Résumé
Résumé of Mary Smith

Columbia National Bank
2220 Nebraska Place
Denver, Colorado   80222
Phone: (409) 555-2000

Home Address:
1119 Lafayette Street
Denver, Colorado   80218
Phone: (409) 555-2748

Job Objective

To work in banking industry in the areas of institutional investment, loans, and portfolio development.

Education
1981–1983

WHARTON SCHOOL, UNIVERSITY OF PENNSYLVANIA
Master in Business Administration, June 1983. Second-year electives in administration of nonprofit institutions, banking law, institutional investment, tax accounting, government policy and management relations. Major project on investment policies of the Ford Foundation.

1977–1981

WILLIAMS COLLEGE, WILLIAMS-TOWN, MASS.
Bachelor of Arts Degree in Economics, June 1981. Research papers in economics included: "Polaroid and the Marketing of Technology," "Women as New Resource in the Labor Market," "The Impact of Inflation on the Nonprofit Institution," "Comparisons of Growth Potentials in the United States, West Germany and Japan." Other research papers included: trends in the commodities market, government restrictions on product manufacture, and the future of financing of small colleges.

Business Experience
1983–Present

COLUMBIA NATIONAL BANK
Officer in the trust department of the largest bank in Colorado. Involved in in-

vesting for portfolios totaling $250 million. Handled customer relations for central branch. Wrote forecasts and semiannual reports for department.

1982   CITIBANK, NEW YORK
Summer management intern. Conducted investment research for institutional department.

1981   ROCKEFELLER BROTHERS FUND, NEW YORK
Intern in financial office.

Personal background   First woman page on the floor of the San Francisco Stock Exchange; father was military attaché to Lebanon and Greece. Interests include running and Charlotte Bronte.

References   Available on request.

Chronological Résumé

Susan Jones
123 Black Road
Anytown, State 02159
(617) 555-5334

Job Objective   Administrative Assistant

Work Experience
1980–Present   Administrative Assistant to President
Western Technology, Inc.
Lincoln, Massachusetts
* Responsible for day-to-day operations of ten-person office.
* Prepare annual stockholders' report.
* Handle calendar, appointments, and travel for president.
* Authorize expenditures of $250,000 operating budget.
* Review audits, projections, and financial statements.

1978–1979   Assistant to Chief Financial Officer
Western Massachusetts Labs
Andover, Massachusetts
* Managed office.

	* Processed payroll, kept attendance records, ordered office supplies.
	* Set up appointments and meetings.
1977–1978	Secretary/Assistant to President Techtronics Development Corp. Lincoln, Massachusetts
	* Directed president's office.
	* Served as liaison with stockholders.
	* Organized president's calendar and travel.
Education	B.S., Rice Institute, 1977. Electrical engineering major.

Functional Résumé

Ann Johnson
456 Blue Avenue
Anytown, State 94610
(415) 555-3165 (Office)
(415) 555-6609

Qualifications and Experience:

Project Development

Conducted research into reading and learning problems of minority students in urban junior and senior high schools. Secured funding for major study in the field. Coordinated and administered the project. Was accountable for the $465,000 funding of the project. Project is being used as model for similar projects across the country. Developed reading-testing program for disadvantaged junior and senior high-school students.

Writing

Published reports on evolution of projects. Specialist in grant projects.

Research

Gathered and processed wide variety of educational information. Working knowledge of statistical data processing.

Administration and Management

Organized research teams of up to 25 members.

Public Relations

Wide experience with speaking before community groups.

Education:

Austin College, B.A., American History, 1973.
Columbia Teachers College, M.A., Learning Disorders, 1974.

Combination Résumé

Elizabeth Osgood
789 East White Street
Anytown, State 10019
(212) 555-1369

Project Management:	Responsible for product supervision and quality control. Made all major advertising and policy decisions. Brought sales up 60 percent over the previous year.
Research and Marketing:	Developed marketing strategy for total product line. Introduced new line of bath products and room perfumes.
Merchandising:	Worked closely with cosmetics executives in major chains, developed on-counter videotapes to show use of products. Coordinated merchandising and advertising with retail outlets.
Sales:	Developed close contact with buyers; worked personally behind counters.
1962–Present:	Fragrance Catalysts Started out in sales and worked up to current position as Product Manager.
1958–1962:	Senses, Inc. Covered Northeast territory as sales person. Ran $20,000 to $30,000 above other reps annually.
Education:	B.A., Finch College, 1958.

A covering letter should accompany your résumé. You can, of course, send the letter and résumé to a company's personnel department, but it is better to write to the person who heads the department you're interested in. Call the company and ask whoever answers the phone (usually the receptionist) for the name, its correct spelling, and the title of the person in question.

Keep your letter short and type it (single spaced) on good paper. In the first paragraph introduce yourself—explain who you are and what you are doing. Mention any contacts you have. For example: "I am graduating from

ABC College in June with a degree in accounting. Professor Mary Smith has told me that you are looking for accountants in your department."

In the next paragraph, expand on information the résumé gives: "As my résumé shows, the senior project for my class was to form a corporation. As accountant for this corporation, I served as internal auditor, performed tax services for the company, and devised a pension plan."

Your final paragraph should be a call for action: "I am very much interested in investigating career possibilities with the XYZ Company, and would welcome the opportunity to talk with you. I will telephone you early next week in the hope that we can arrange an appointment."

Even if you have never held a job before, you have a network of people you can approach for possible job leads. It's important to take advantage of your contacts because, according to experts, 80 percent of job vacancies are never advertised.

To find one job, you may have to network with scores of people. Start with the people closest at hand. Ask your friends, former schoolmates, and neighbors how they got their jobs. Tell them you're job hunting and ask for suggestions and contacts. Don't overlook anyone; your neighbor's aunt may know someone in broadcasting or social services or offshore drilling. *How to Get a Job in Boston (or Anywhere Else)*, by Renee Levine (fourth edition), suggests the following people for your network:

professional colleagues	relatives and neighbors
employers	building inspectors
coworkers	small store owners
sports friends	salespeople in your grocery store
your doctor	barber or hairdresser
your dentist	people at parties
your clergy	real estate agents
the druggist	family
your banker	secretaries in your office
insurance agents	alumni of your school
faculty	classmates (gym, adult ed, high-school reunion)

In addition to people to consult, the same book suggests places and organizations, such as consultants in your field, appropriate local, state, or federal government departments, trade shows, volunteer groups, temporary employment agencies, chambers of commerce, professional associations, local newspapers, trade journals, Sunday and Wednesday editions of major newspapers, and college placement offices. Get names and addresses from the classified telephone directory as well as friends and acquaintances.

Pay special attention to the many local women's newspapers that are published in cities around the country. For more on the realities of networking, see Chapter 6, Who You Know.

Polishing your résumé and making contacts are only part of the job-hunting picture. The candidate who is well informed about a prospective company (its goals, products, history, and so on) has a better chance of making a good impression, asking the right questions, and matching her skills with the employer's needs. If time permits, write to the companies you are interested in and request an annual report. In your library, research the companies in such books and directories as: *How to Find Information about Companies*, Washington Research Staff, editors (Washington Researchers); Standard & Poor's two directories, *Corporation Records* and *Register of Corporations, Directors and Executives*; Dun & Bradstreet's reference works, *Middle Market Directory, Million Dollar Directory, Principal International Businesses*. Finally, Moody's puts out an *Industrial Manual* and a *Bank and Finance Manual* which contain financial information about publicly held companies. Read the business press for current information about companies. Ask people you know who work at companies you're interested in or in the same industry about the business.

Once you've written your résumé and covering letter and sent it off to the right people, follow up with telephone calls. Introduce yourself, remind the person of your résumé, and ask for an appointment. Talk to the person who does the hiring. If you have trouble getting past the secretary, call early or late in the day because there's a better chance that before the secretary arrives or after she leaves, the person in charge will answer his or her own phone. Even if there are no job openings, request an interview. You'll be able to explore the industry this way, find out more about what the job you're seeking entails, get a salary range and leads. Most important, you become a face to that particular interviewer, not just a piece of paper.

After applying for a specific job, you may be invited to interviews with a series of people in one company. This is an auspicious sign—it means you're getting closer to a job offer.

At some point in the process everyone succumbs to "interview nerves." This is normal, but try to keep all interviews in perspective. They are not meant to be a test of your self-worth. Be prepared and do the best you can. That's all anyone can ask of you, and that's all you should ask of yourself.

Sometimes it's impossible to explain why one person gets the job instead of another. A lot depends on chemistry; if the interviewer likes a particular job candidate, that person has an advantage. This doesn't mean that the interviewer wants to be best buddies with you; it means that the person feels comfortable with you and gets a good feeling from you. And since many people form a lasting impression of someone within seconds, it's obviously best to create a likable, professional impression.

Keep these pointers in mind:

How you look counts. Your clothing, makeup, hairdo make a statement about you. There's no need to invest in the whole dress-for-success uniform (see Chapter 12) for interviewing for a first job, but a suit is a good choice; a skirt and jacket are fine, too. Keep it simple and neat. The guideline here is not to look like what you are (a recent college graduate or a job-hunting homemaker) but to look like what you want to be (a bank trainee, a sales person). It is true that different fields have different dress codes; what's correct for a law firm, for instance, may seem too formal in a graphic-arts studio. If in doubt, opt to make a more conservative impression.

Be confident. The interview is two-sided. While the company is checking you out, you are checking *it* out. The decision is as much yours as theirs. So be assertive. Talk with confidence about your skills and talents and be prepared to answer questions about your work habits, your experience, and your goals. Such questions include: How do you respond to pressure? What are your strengths and weaknesses? How do you handle stressful situations? How do you feel about working for a workaholic? How do you feel about working overtime?

Ask questions. You need to get information about the company and the job in order to form an impression and arrive at a decision if you are offered employment. You might want to ask:

Is there a job opening?
What department is the job in?
Who is the supervisor?
What are the duties?
What happened to the people who held this job before? You want to know if they quit (perhaps the supervisor is impossible to please) or were promoted or went on to a better position at another company.
What are the future plans for the department?
What kind of training will you get?
What are the pressures of the position? Are there daily deadlines? Is regular overtime expected?

If I do well at this job, what are the promotion possibilities?

What is the salary? Is that a negotiable figure? What are promotions and pay raises based on? (A word about salaries: If this is your first job, you may not have much negotiating power. Nevertheless, be wary of accepting a salary that is too low. If you do, you may start to feel exploited and not do your best work; that can have career consequences.) Investigate salaries in the field at the library (the *Occupational Outlook Handbook* and the *Dictionary of Occupational Titles* are two primary sources for this type of information) and through professional associations, so that you'll know what is reasonable. It's best, though, to get the interviewer to name a salary range.

If offered this job, when would I start?

Also ask about hours, overtime requirements, benefits such as medical insurance and vacation policy.

During an interview a prospective employer will ask you many questions about your background and experience and other subjects that relate to the job. But it is against the law for a prospective employer to ask the following questions: Are you married? What is your husband's name? Where does your husband work? Are you single? Divorced? Engaged? Living with anyone? Do you have children at home? How old are they? Who cares for them? Do you plan to have more children? How old are you? How tall are you? How much do you weigh? Have you ever been arrested, convicted, or spent time in jail? Do you have a disability? What is your nationality? The nationality of your husband and parents? Of what country are you a citizen? What is your native language? What is your religion? Do you own your own home? Do you rent? Any comments or references to sex are also unlawful.

You can answer such questions, ignoring their illegality. Or you can simply say, "I don't think that my age/marital status is relevant to the requirements of the position." Tactfully steer the conversation back to what is relevant, such as your experience and background.

In *What Color Is Your Parachute*, Bolles points out that writing a thank-you letter is one of "the most essential steps in the whole job-seeking process—and the one most overlooked by job-seekers." *Hardball Job Hunting Tactics*, by Dick Wright, states simply: "You have to write a thank-you letter for the interview. It is the ultimate 'weapon' in destroying your competition." This kind of correspondence gives you the chance to extend a professional courtesy and once again state your qualifications for and interest in the job. Wright gives the following outline for a thank-you letter:

1. I want to take this opportunity to thank you for the time you spent with me on _____, regarding your position for _____.

2. After talking with you, I am convinced that my skills in _____ [list them, starting with the most important to the job opening] can be transferred quickly to your systems and methods so that I can make an immediate contribution.

3. I look forward to hearing from you soon.

KEEPING YOUR JOB AND LEARNING SKILLS

You've beat out competition and have been offered the job. The first days are crucial. You must become acquainted with your surroundings, your boss and coworkers, and the basic routine and office systems. You want to become productive immediately and get on with learning and working so that you will establish yourself as a productive employee.

Your immediate supervisor or a delegate should take you around the office to introduce you to your new associates and explain where supplies are kept, where different departments are, how to work the telephone system. Make sure all such questions *are* addressed. After the introductions, get your work space set up and organize your work tools: Is the phone installed? Do you have a typewriter? Word processor? Computer? Pens, pencils, stationery? If not, ask a coworker or your boss how to get the necessary items; then get them. Don't rush to decorate your work space. See what other employees have done; check on company policy (there may be rules against putting pictures on the walls, for example).

Your job at this point is to learn your job. Ask questions. *Working Woman* contributing editor Shirley Sloan Fader, an expert on the workplace, has this advice: "There is no such thing as a 'stupid question.' Your boss wants you to become productive as soon as possible. When you don't know something, ask. For example, 'How does our company handle this kind of memo?' Your boss will be more pleased if you ask and then do it correctly than if you guess and later have to waste time doing it over."

If your boss doesn't know how something is handled, ask her to suggest the proper person for you to go to.

Discuss the basic office routine with your supervisor. Does she want you to answer her phone? How? Should you answer: "Ms. Johnson's office"? "Sarah Johnson's office"? "Marketing"? Maybe she would rather have you answer with your name (which is the way you should answer your own phone). Work out specifics about office hours and lunch hours: Should you and your boss have lunch at different times so that the office is covered?

What about reporting methods? Would she like to meet with you at a specific time each day to go over daily priorities? How is the filing system organized? Is she happy with the system, or should you revamp it? Your goal here is to adapt to your boss's style and to make her job easier.

After you're settled in and know the basic general systems and priorities, start honing your skills. If your company has a formal training program, you'll report there. For many positions, though, there is no official program, so you will learn by actually performing the job.

What do you need to know to do your job well? Do you have to learn how to write department reports? Interpret financial figures? Organize a department? Read the files of your predecessors to find out how things are done. Read material that crosses your desk to see what's important to the company and to your boss.

Make appointments with your boss for training sessions (don't wait for her to come to you), or have her appoint someone else to teach you. Attend seminars, workshops, and courses that relate to your work. (Your company may pay for these.) If you don't make the effort to acquire the necessary skills, your boss will feel you are not performing well and decide you are not able to contribute to the company's goals.

Also, it's important to keep in mind the psychological aspect of one's first, entry-level job. After being a star student in college it can be very hard to admit you don't know certain things; you'll often feel "green" and very young. You should accept the fact that you'll be making mistakes and own up to them without falling apart, even if your supervisor reprimands you.

After three months on the job, set up a meeting with your boss to go over your performance so far. This way you and she can assess your progress and define the skills you need to learn or improve. Tell your boss if you are having a problem mastering a particular part of your job. Be prepared for criticism and accept it with a professional attitude. Your boss, who hired you, wants you to succeed, so examine her remarks carefully. Perhaps you do forget to follow up on important matters. (What's important to your boss is an important matter.)

There are also some general work pointers that are important to keep in mind on your first job:

Keep busy. If you have a free moment, don't read the newspaper, read the files. They can teach you about the organization and how it operates.
Don't let your work area get too messy; messiness often implies disorganization.

Show that you're enthusiastic about working. Get to the office early and stay late.

Absorb all the information you can and save your suggestions until you're confident that you know what your company needs.

Never promise anything you can't or won't deliver; your reputation for responsibility is career gold.

Assume nothing; the times your assumptions are wrong can be crucial. For example, never assume your boss will be flexible about a deadline or work hours.

Enjoy yourself. Work needn't be a painful experience.

Keep on learning in a positive and rewarding way.

ON THE JOB ETIQUETTE

Getting along with coworkers and supervisors is a key element to success. This is why etiquette is a valuable tool. "The base point of etiquette for office interaction is to abstain most of the time. Do not let your hair down and tell all to your coworkers. Do not bare your soul, do not display all parts of your personality, do not tell them your hopes and dreams, plans and schemes." This excellent advice comes from George Mazzei's *The New Office Etiquette: A Guide to Getting Along in the Corporate Age*. The point is that work relationships are different from personal relationships. Don't give in to the urge to "tell all." People you work with may be friendly, but they shouldn't be considered or treated like personal friends.

No matter where you work, you have to find a way to work with people you may not like or who are "difficult." In either case, you should stick strictly to work topics, maintain your silence during any temper tantrums, learn to respect the person (at least in business dealings), and, above all, avoid confrontations that will make the office atmosphere even more strained. Consideration for others makes life easier for everyone involved and makes the work more efficient. People deserve to work in a pleasant, cooperative atmosphere that is reasonably free of conflict. Good manners also include always spelling people's names correctly and being exact about people's titles. (There's a world of difference between a senior vice president and a vice president.)

OFFICE POLITICS

"Office politics" is a phrase you may recoil from instinctively. The words have an ominous sound because they convey backbiting and manipulation. But there's no escaping the politics around you, and mastering the art of politics works to your benefit as well as giving you a psychological boost. Office politics covers such territory as:

Knowing what's going on; being plugged into the office grapevine
Identifying your allies and enemies
Deciphering who has power
Wielding clout and getting things done

Doing your job conscientiously and efficiently isn't enough. Women sometimes insist that they be judged and rewarded only for the quality of their work. But work life isn't so clear-cut. The successful person combines job competence and an understanding that job relationships matter.

You don't have to become a phony or a cutthroat to learn the game of politics. You just need to be conscious of what's going on around you—basically, who has power for what over whom.

The official power structure in a company is usually easy to identify. An organizational chart or even a walk around the offices (who has the corner office? who occupies a tiny interior space?) will give you the formal hierarchy. But there's also an "invisible" hierarchy. For example, on paper all vice presidents are equal, but in reality one may have more influence than others and greater access to the seats of power. Out of three department managers, one may be on the fast track while the others are in dead-end jobs. The personnel director may have a formal method for applying for promotions but not have the power to grant them. Notice too that people with modest positions may wield great influence. The president's secretary, for example, has the power to control access to him or her. There are other considerations that cloud the formal power chart. The company may employ relatives of the chief executive officer, or office romances may be going on, or perhaps the elder statesman who seems to be out of the picture has great clout because of seniority.

Fader warns you to choose your office friends carefully: "As long as you and your own career goals do not come between co-workers and their objectives, there's no reason why you can't form genuine friendships." But once you and a coworker compete for a promotion or lobby for a new system or try for a sale, you would be wise to watch what you say so that you can guard your ideas.

Though many people find it an unsavory topic, it is important to understand that "inherited" enemies come with any position. If you were hired over people already in the company, you have enemies. If people are jealous of your position, your access to the boss, or your talent, you have enemies. It takes some diplomacy to defuse these feelings. Try to turn envious coworkers into allies. Show them how your success can help their success—that a mutual friendship can be beneficial to everyone. In situations with coworkers it's important not to take sides on issues that immediately concern you or your department. Listening to both sides but remaining neutral is the best policy.

GETTING PROMOTED

Once you have established your place in the company, and have mastered the basics of your job and made allies, you're ready to press for something more. There's no universal timetable for promotions, but when your present position is no longer challenging, and when you realize you've learned all that's possible there, it's time. During your stay in the entry-level position, you should keep a list of duties you've performed, new responsibilities you've taken on, skills you've mastered, and any other information that shows your progress and will support your claim that you're capable of handling the next step.

Take this list with you to your performance appraisal. If the company does not have formal reviews, request one with your immediate supervisor. Performance appraisals should take place at least twice a year. If you're new on the job, you may want formal feedback more often, perhaps every three months or so.

For all you need to know about The Next Big Step, see Chapter 5, Getting Ahead.

REENTERING THE JOB MARKET

Perhaps you have been absent from the work world while raising a family or for other reasons and are now ready to crack the job market. Unfortunately, reentering this market is a struggle for most older women. Many do not, or believe they do not, have the necessary job skills, and they may give up the search in despair or settle for a dead-end position.

Nevertheless, there *is* encouraging news for older workers who are seeking employment. Several studies conducted by the Bureau of Labor Statistics comparing middle-aged workers with their younger counterparts have shown that older workers exhibit more stability. They have steadier work habits, waste less time, are more reliable, have a lower rate of absenteeism, show more loyalty and responsibility, have a more serious attitude toward the job, require less supervision, and are less distracted by outside interests.

Other studies also attest to the stability of older workers. In fact, turnover among older women is 88 percent lower than for younger women, according to one study.

Despite these studies, finding a job is still a great challenge for older women. In our youth-oriented society it seems that women are expected to stay young forever. For women aging is not equated with experience, growth, and maturity—especially not in the business world. Until recently corporate America hardly perceived older women except as secretaries, and the chances for reentry women to advance in a career are still not good.

The career picture in corporate America is quite different for men over forty. At this age men are thought of as being mature, experienced, and in the prime of their careers. They are wooed for top-level corporate positions; they conduct mergers, close million-dollar deals, and run conglomerates. Such men, of course, have almost always been working and gaining experience for two decades.

Older women who are looking for work these days fall into several categories. They are widows, divorced women, "empty nest" mothers, former professionals, women switching careers in midlife, and women who are forced by economic conditions to look for a job to supplement the family income.

All these women share one characteristic: they are not totally prepared for the struggle ahead. Self-evaluation, the primary step in the process of reentering the job market, is often the most difficult one for these women. They lack self-confidence because they feel they have no skills to offer an employer. The reality is that some women do have marketable skills but don't see them, and others don't have any at all. Their low self-image is reinforced by the negative view the business world has of homemaking as a career. But homemaking is *work*. Many women overlook the fact that running a home, being a wife and mother, and taking part in community affairs have helped them develop valuable skills in budgeting, dealing with people, problem solving, and other areas of responsibility, says Eleanor Berman in *Re-entering: Successful Back-to-Work Strategies for Women Seeking a Fresh Start*.

Any woman preparing to reenter the job market or change careers should evaluate her potential by asking these questions:

First, why do I want a job? For money, security, or a challenge? Perhaps it's for all three reasons. List your motivations in order of preference and determine which are the least important and can be eliminated if necessary.

How much time do I want to give a job? Do I want to work part time or full time? Some jobs require overtime work and traveling. Research your prospective career field and consider such factors.

What have I done, what do I like to do, what don't I enjoy? List your strengths (interpreted as skills) and weaknesses.

What would I like to be doing five and even ten years from now?

You may have gained marketable skills through volunteer work. Now you need to translate these skills into the business language an employer will understand. For example, Betty Brown *organized* a political campaign, *worked* as an administrator for a foundation, *sold* ad space for her particular group's newsletter, *balanced* the budget for her area's nursing home. Skills should be highlighted in this way on your résumé and at job interviews, in addition to any other work experience. Include any retail or day-care experience.

Almost the same advice holds for career changers. You must learn to take the skills you've acquired in one position and make them applicable to the position you want. In *Salary Strategies: Everything You Need to Know to Get the Salary You Want,* Marilyn Moats Kennedy suggests that you begin with a skills analysis. The best way is to define on paper what you really do on your present job. This information will be the basis of your résumé. Kennedy recommends using a worksheet like the one below (this one was done for teachers who want to change careers):

Task	Procedure	Skills Used
Lesson planning	Deciding on content, order of presentation, organization of material	Research, writing skills, logic, planning, organization of material, developing examples, presentation techniques, selling the ideas
Grading papers	Deciding whether the paper meets the assignment and how well	Developing criteria for judgment, evaluating results, prioritizing results, modifying judgments

You may find that personnel agencies and departments are sticklers when it comes to qualifications. They want evidence of the right educational background, the right skills, and a proven track record. In this case you will have to sell harder. Your skills—those that can be transferred to the company's needs—and your enthusiasms are key selling points. You may also find it worthwhile to take advantage of the numerous career-planning courses and workshops across the country that are conducted by colleges and universities, community groups, women's resource centers, YWCAs, and state and local commissions on the status of women. These outlets provide group support, encouragement, and discipline.

In addition, career counseling is available on an individual basis from professional counselors. Individual counseling can be valuable, but before making a commitment you should check the counselor's credentials, make sure the materials in the office are up to date, get the names of former clients for their appraisal of the experience, and determine whether the counselor has set ideas about a woman's "proper" place. (See page 108 for more about career counselors.)

The worst thing you can do is keep your job hunting a secret: remember that 80 percent of jobs not are advertised. Use your network (see Chapter 6, Who You Know). Being an older person may be an advantage. You have more contacts, know more people.

Older women do encounter age discrimination, and even though it is illegal (see Appendix A), it is difficult to prove. Avoid discussing your age. You are not required to give an exact age on any job application, and you can write "over 40" in the space provided. Remember that it is against the law for the interviewer to ask your exact age. If she or he does, simply repeat aloud what you put down on your application. (After you are hired, you may have to give your exact age on company records.)

Think carefully before enrolling for further education in pursuit of a career. Many people say a degree is the key to better paying jobs, but it is not always a substitute for experience. A degree can also make you be considered overqualified for many openings. For an older woman, undertaking one or two years of technical training without any assurance that it will lead to a job wastes too much time.

One way of combining education with on-the-job experience is through the internship programs offered at many colleges and universities, usually for credit. Internships, in which a person "works" for a business or organization without pay or for a nominal fee in exchange for on-the-job training in a particular career field, are a valuable experience for adults even without college credit. You can set up an internship on your own or through an advocate—someone who will present the concept to the organization in a way that shows the advantages for it as well as for the intern. An advocate can be a friend within the organization, a professional career counselor, or a representative of your former college's career planning and placement center. Internships provide an introduction or reintroduction to the world of work. Even more important, they offer experience, contacts, and a relevant résumé listing. If you are interested in participating in an internship, you should be prepared to accept supervision (often from people much younger than yourself); to get involved in as many aspects of the work as possible; and to complete each task (no matter how simple) competently.

An added benefit to doing your best is that interns are often hired outright; being *there* can be the best way to get a job.

Volunteering is another way for reentry women to gain experience. It's important to choose the field and the position carefully, with future job interests, goals, and priorities in mind. Enter the volunteer arena with the attitude of a professional; later you will take the fund-raising, leadership, organizational, and interpersonal skills you have developed and use them to get a job. There even may be a career for you in your volunteer organization.

Another option is to become a paid temporary worker. Demand in the temp field is directly affected by the economy, but in good times or bad, temps are necessary to businesses. In a recession there is less demand, but companies often hire temporary workers instead of full-timers. In a prosperous economy there is a big increase in the demand for temps. In 1981 there were approximately 3.5 million temporary workers, and they earned $3.7 billion from temporary agencies. It is estimated that 10 to 20 percent of the people who start in temp work move on to permanent positions in the job area they originally chose.

Though you may associate temp services with clerical work, temps are in demand in fields besides traditional office work. The fastest-growing of these fields are health care, marketing, data processing, technical, and light industrial. In fact, the demand for operators of data- and word-processing machines is so great that some temporary agencies, such as Olsten, Manpower, and Kelly Services, have set up free word-processor training programs. There are also temp opportunities in professional fields such as accounting, library science, engineering, paralegal, and publishing. Temping is a good way to introduce yourself to different fields and companies.

Fader recommends that to get the most out of being a temp you should:

Register with a number of agencies. They expect you to do this to keep yourself employed.

Take as many different kinds of skill tests as you can. The more types of jobs you register for, the greater your chances of being kept busy.

Indicate whether you can work only certain hours and days.

When you upgrade a skill, inform the agency, since charges to employers vary depending on the level of your skills. The service then will send you on different kinds of jobs and pay you at a higher rate.

Register with both large, well-known temp agencies and smaller local organizations. Although large national services have the advantages of size and backing, a good small service can also have high-quality openings. Look in the telephone Yellow Pages and Sunday newspaper ads to locate agencies that specialize in certain fields such as accounting and publishing.

Check whether the different agencies offer such benefits as paid vacation and sick leave, and find out how long you have to be with a particular service to qualify for these benefits.
Check what fees and percentages they take.

Learning the proper way to conquer the ins and outs of getting started will prepare you for the career climb ahead. Be patient and, above all else, persevere, and the rewards will come.

4
Working Smart

Having landed a job, a woman cannot afford to stay grounded for long. She must concentrate on her flight up the corporate ladder. Some women have contracted a serious disease, though, which seems to block their path upward. It's called the "good little girl syndrome." How'd they get it? For years their parents, teachers, husbands, and bosses told them that if they did everything right, made everyone happy, and worked *very* hard, they would get their just deserts. This isn't necessarily so in the grown-up world. Knocking yourself out to please the crowds won't earn you a great deal of respect and it will probably cause you to burn out prematurely. Put bluntly: While you are working late writing the perfect memo, your male rival is probably out playing tennis with the boss.

What does he know that you don't? That the much-sought-after secret of success isn't really hard work, it's smart work. Instead of compulsively trying to do *everything* perfectly, your rival targets his efforts so that he does the right things well, and that can leave him the time to cultivate contacts on the courts. But what are the "right" things? How did he decide that playing tennis was more important than dotting the i's on a memo? He set goals for himself.

GOAL SETTING

Setting goals sounds tedious and dry. It's amazing, though, how liberating it feels to know what you want to do at work and how you're going to do it. Plenty of experts will tell you how to set goals; one threesome, for example,

74

believes that you should plan every day for the next *year* in a single session. But a few common-sense rules are all you really need.

Setting goals is the process of deciding what you have to do, what you have done, and how to close the gap between the two. For example, think about what you have to do this month. Aside from routine tasks like making courtesy calls to clients, perhaps all you really have to do is produce your department's quarterly report. Producing that report, then, will become your goal. What have you done so far? You and your staff have collected background material. So your first subgoal will be to organize that material. Your second subgoal might be to make a tentative outline of the report. Your third subgoal might be to go through the outline, deciding who on your staff will produce what and by what dates. The result of all this is going to be a list or series of lists. To make sure that everything on these lists gets done, you either check them daily (perhaps several times daily) or transfer the list into your daily calendar. The latter is better; you don't want lots of lists floating around your office.

You should always work with a daily "to-do" list. It's the only way to stay on top of things. Include on your list every task you hope to accomplish, from the most trivial to the most serious and assign priorities to each task. Be realistic and don't draw up an impossibly long list. You'll get discouraged if you never come to the end and you'll just wind up transferring the same unfinished tasks from daily list to daily list.

Goal setting also works well for the long term. Perhaps you'll decide that by the end of the year you want to increase your plant's production capacity by 5 percent. Achieving this single goal may involve a number of steps, such as the purchase or reconditioning of equipment or the addition of new staff. During the year ahead you will have to pick and act on these alternatives, and as you do so you'll create short-term goals. You may even have to revise your original long-term goal. But going through the long-term process will help you get a sense of the big picture.

The only catch to setting goals is that having decided *what* to do, you have no choice but to *do* it. And in order to do it, you have to know how to manage time.

AGAINST THE CLOCK

Not without reason do women feel that their lives are becoming more and more complex. Between work and home, family and friends, bosses and lovers, women have a lot more to juggle than ever before. And that "good little girl syndrome," that wish to do it all—perfectly—persists, resulting in pressure, stress, and guilt. Time-management newsletters, books, and seminars that promise to help women gain control of their lives *and* still have time left over for themselves are proliferating. Their advice ranges from the pragmatic to the pedantic. Some books tell you to calculate the price of all your actions: Two experts say that uninvited office guests cost an average of $5 a visit and the cost of picking up a piece of paper and putting it down again unattended to is 50 cents. Another school spurns these formulas and stresses attitude, concentrating on women's tendency to obsess about details instead of going after the big projects.

What the theorizing boils down to is a stock of tried and tested ideas to cope with two of life's inescapable truths: most of us produce 80 percent of our work in only 20 percent of our time; and work expands to fill whatever time we have available.

Here, then, are the basics:

Draw up a life plan. Before you start on your time-saving scheme, give yourself some additional incentive by writing down everything you want to accomplish in life. Doing so will show you just how *much* you want to do and in how little time, and will reinforce, once and for all, the necessity for learning to use time well.

Plan. Make a "to-do" list for days, weeks, months, even years if you want to. Write tomorrow's list today, before you leave work.

Set priorities. Alan Lakein, one of the gurus of time management, uses a simple ABC system: The A tasks are top priority, B tasks are less important, and C tasks can often be postponed indefinitely. Use Lakein's ABC system with this twist: Keep a list of your A and B tasks on top of your C pile, so that every time you are tempted to knock off an easy C task, you must confront your list of more urgent and important As and Bs. Lakein even suggests filing the C tasks away so that they're literally out of sight and mind.

And speaking of priorities, remember that there are two kinds: the ones you set and the ones others set for you. The most effective time managers know how to say no to some of the priorities that their bosses try to dictate. Weigh your priorities against your boss's and determine the postponability of both. This may mean that you must challenge your boss (not easy but indispensable). You cannot allow yourself to accept passively a deadline or assignment that you know, in your heart of hearts, you can't handle. If you don't speak up, you'll let your boss down and damage your reputation.

Know your schedule. Take time to figure out your biological highs and lows, and attack your tasks accordingly. Are you a morning or an afternoon person? Schedule a B task for a low-energy morning slot and an A task for after lunch when your energy has picked up.

Delegate. This is a biggie on the list of time management techniques, so big in fact, that it has a section all to itself later in this chapter. If you are one of those managers who's still saying, "It is quicker to do it myself," then it's your own fault if you are overwhelmed. You owe it to yourself, to your restless subordinates dying for a challenge, and to your company, to learn how to delegate.

Schedule "Quiet" and "I'm Available" hours. The average executive is interrupted once every eight minutes, so set up times when you will be sociable and others when you will be reclusive. Send out a memo to your staff telling them when you're generally available. Get an "Only if It's Urgent" sign to post on your office door during certain hours. Avoid phone interruptions by having your secretary screen your calls and by making all your outgoing calls at one time of day.

Use technology. Personal computers, dictation systems, even the primitive calculator save time.

Never handle a piece of paper more than twice. Or once, if you listen to some experts. Look at it, make a decision about it (to give it to your secretary to handle, to file it, to dump it), and go on.

Don't smoke or drink while you work. Many people rely on cigarettes, coffee, and soda to perk them up. A better way to increase your energy is to get at least fifteen minutes of exercise a day. A brisk walk at lunch time, for example, will get your pulse rate going, increase your circulation, and help you shake off lethargy.

Cut down on business reading. You may decide to take a speed-reading course, but it makes more sense to read fewer things well than lots of things quickly.

Do business during coffee breaks and lunch. But beware the buildup of stress. Sometimes you need to take a break and forget it all.

Don't attend meetings unless you absolutely must. And when you do go to meetings, leave if they become irrelevant.

Special tips for procrastinators:

Delegate the tasks you hate. Don't just put them off month after month.
Set time limits. Estimate how long a task will take and then stick to the estimate.
Create artificial deadlines. Plan another event right on the heels of a deadline, so that you have to meet the deadline.
Weigh the alternative. Write down the pros and cons of doing something versus putting it off. You will probably persuade yourself to do it right away.

Break a big job down into small jobs. Do a big job in nibbles rather than one huge bite.
Reward yourself for finishing. Buy yourself a new suit, catch a movie.
Surrender. Do absolutely no work at all for fifteen minutes. The enforced slowdown will make you long for action.

OK, so you've got all this down. Kudos. You now can claim to be what Peter Drucker calls an effective executive. You're not only getting more things done, you're getting the right things done. However, even the effective executive can easily fall prey to the lions of disorganization at home. Time-management techniques, though, can prove just as practical in personal life. Organize each cupboard and room at home as you would your desk at work. Enlist the cooperation and help of your kids and husband as you would your staff. Forget Supermom—children *can* make beds, men *can* make breakfast. Asking them to take on these reponsibilities is another form of delegation, not abnegation. Hire people to help you—housecleaners, accountants, personal shoppers, and the like. But keep your delegating urges in check. Don't give tasks to your office staff that should be handled at home. Working women have long understood the frustrating ignominy of being sent out to buy a birthday present for the boss's wife.

Schedule those personal errands you must do yourself around your business appointments. If your shoe repair shop is next door to your best client's office, drop off your shoes the next time you meet the client. Make doctor's appointments for the beginning of the day, so that you can stop in on your way to the office. Don't waste time on television (except for "Wall Street Week" and "Hill Street Blues"). The list goes on and on. You may have to break some habits and form new ones. Don't worry—that's the name of the game.

DELEGATING, NOT DUMPING

One of the smartest moves an executive can make is to delegate. But delegating should not be a euphemism for dumping. No good comes of bursting into Jane Doe's office in a frenzy because you've suddenly realized that you'll never be able to write a report *and* plan next year's budget on time, throwing your notes and half an outline for the report on Doe's desk, and then fleeing to your own office and the unfinished budget. Instead decide exactly what it is that needs to be done. Conserve your time and effort for those parts of the job that only you have the authority or skills to handle and resolve to give the rest to others. Then decide who on your staff has the skills and experience to take on the project. If Doe doesn't, who does? (If you decide that no one does, then you have one of two problems: you're operating under the delusion of indispensability or you're not spending enough time training your staff.) Next, review the work load and vacation schedule of your potential lieutenant to make sure she or he has the time to take on this new task.

That done, sit down with Doe. Outline the task, establish goals, give clear instructions, and set deadlines. Get her feedback to make sure she understands exactly what must be accomplished. Ask Doe for her input—people work better if they feel that they are involved and not merely carrying out orders. Agree on dates for progress reports, so that if Doe makes a mistake you'll have time to help her fix it.

Remember that when you pick somebody for a task, the finished product is not going to end up exactly as it would if you had done it yourself. But if you have decided that others are smart enough to do the job in the first place, then you must admit that they are smart enough to have their own ideas about how to do it. You can't expect people to be clones of you, so give them the freedom to be themselves. Besides, you're interested in *results*, not methods. And although their way may not be your way, it could be better.

A final caution: Try not to let your staff delegate back to you. If your office door is too far ajar, if you constantly, even gratefully, agree to answer their every question about a project or to take back problematic assignments—you're in trouble. Encourage your staff to take the initiative and responsibility to resolve problems themselves, using the guidelines and instructions you've given them. Remind them that you have given them the authority to make decisions. You can always doublecheck on what they've done during progress reviews.

READ IT, WRITE IT, SAY IT

An executive may be perfectly well organized and tremendously productive, but if no one else in the company knows about her, she's sunk. Like the male rival on the tennis court with the boss, an executive has to conduct her own public relations campaign, letting others know what she has done. How? The most obvious way is through memos, letters, and reports. How do you make sure that people read them? Here are the basics:

Be succinct. Everyone in business is short of time; no one wants to wade through pages of material to find the point of your memo or report buried in the next-to-last paragraph. State clearly in the first sentence the reason you're writing your report or memo. ("Our department could save $200 a month if we purchased our copier rather than leasing it.") If you're going to suggest a solution to a problem, for example, present it immediately. Save discussion of the pros and cons of other options for later in the memo, *after* you've made your case for your own solution. Most memos probably can be confined to one page; if your boss needs more information, she'll ask for it. And writing short, pointed memos makes good political sense—your boss will be more likely to read them.

Don't mince words. No one is fooled by jargon or long, windy sentences. Write as you talk. You would never say, "A decision was made that the proposal submitted by you does not conform to our productivity-enhancement standards and thus will not be implemented," would you? You'd probably say, "I have decided to reject your proposal because it won't help us increase production." The second sentence sounds more natural and it conveys information. It tells who made the decision and why; the first sentence does neither. That sentence, in fact, contains examples of the three most common writing faults:

> *The passive voice.* Saying "a decision was made" prompts the sensible reader to ask, "Who made it?" By leaving that question unanswered you arouse the reader's distrust. The reader assumes that you're ignorant and simply don't know who made the decision, or that you're evasive—you do know who made the decision but you aren't telling. In some cases, of course, political expediency may require that you be evasive in order to hang on to your job. ("A mistake in the budget was made.") Except for these rare cases, stay away from the passive voice.
> *Wordiness.* Why did the writer say "the proposal submitted by you" when she could simply have said "your proposal"? Once you think critically about every sentence you write, you will discover hundreds of ways of pruning. As Kenneth Roman and Joel Raphaelson point out in their excellent guide, *Writing that Works,* instead of writing "despite the fact that," write "though" or "although." Instead of "at the present time," write "now." In other words, *simplify.*
> *Jargon.* Sometimes, when no other word can express exactly what you mean, there is a reason to use technical, specialized language. More often, writers use jargon to sound knowledgeable—and end up sounding pompous and silly to most intelligent readers. Steer clear of meaningless words like "implement" (try "carry out" instead), "finalize" (try "finish") or "initiate" (try "start"). As with avoiding wordiness, the key to eliminating jargon is simplicity and straightforwardness.

Edit. Too often we put something down on paper and stop there, exhausted by the effort. But all good writers know the real work begins after you've come up with a first draft. Reread your memo or report and ask yourself the following questions:

Are my thoughts well organized? See if you can outline them; if you can't, there's something wrong with your reasoning.

Are all words used and spelled correctly? Double-check the spelling and meaning of any words you have even the slightest doubt about. Be particularly careful of such misused and confused pairs of words as disinterested/uninterested, effect/affect, farther/further.

Is my grammar correct? It may seem troublesome to check, but it's not nearly as difficult as you think. You probably already know all the grammar you need—you just need to be careful about applying it. For example, many writers are careless about the agreement between subject and verb, especially in confusing sentences like "One of the reasons is/are." "One," not "reasons," is the subject here: use "is."

READING

Even if you write only one-page memos, everyone else probably writes ten-pagers. You and most American managers are drowning under a data deluge. How do you sift through the "must read" books, magazines, newspapers, reports and memos?

Say no. Refuse to read memos from your subordinates that are longer than one page, or ask subordinates who turn in long reports to mark the most important sections for you.

Delegate. Ask your assistant to read and prepare written summaries of material. Or get a clipping service to identify important articles for you.

Do something else while you read. Read while you commute or while you're stuck on the phone with a long-winded caller.

Skim. Look at the table of contents or the major headings of a report before you begin reading and decide what is important. Read only the essentials; for example, check the news digest in your daily paper to see which stories are important to you. Read the introduction and conclusions of long reports, skipping the sections outlining the methodology.

Concentrate. Once you decide that something is worth reading, read it carefully. Take notes or ask assistants to make copies of important sections. Keep an eye out for statistics, anecdotes, or background material you could use in a speech or report.

SAYING IT

OK, so you can write it and you can read it. But can you say it? In front of a tableful of people? A roomful? An auditorium-full?

Women seem to be afraid of public speaking. Although many know their stuff, they still lack confidence and so they revert to the "shy little me" routine in public. They trail off at the end of sentences, they speak too softly and breathily, and they practice that Valley girl trick of softening statements by making them sound like questions—hardly the kind of power talk that will make a woman a convention speaker along the lines of Lee Iacocca. And as the women's movement has taught us, if we can't be heard we are powerless.

Poor speaking is comprised of little vocal inadequacies which, isolated, are hardly worth mentioning, but which, together, create an impression of weakness. Bad habits like giggling and squeaking can be overcome with practice. But practice is more than a lot of "Peter-Piper-picked-a-peck-of-pickled-peppers" exercises. Learning to speak well is closer to Acting 101: the aim is to present yourself convincingly to an audience. Think about:

Breathing. This is basic. Women who take quick, nervous breaths sound like shaky schoolgirls. To breathe properly you must use your diaphragm and abdomen. If your shoulders are moving up and down as you breathe, then you are breathing shallowly through your chest.

Pitch. A high, squeaky tone also undermines authority. Worse, it makes you sound like a whiner, and *nobody* likes a whiner. To lower your voice, pause, breathe deeply and evenly, open your mouth, relax your jaw, and use more of your breath to project or throw your voice forward and out to your audience rather than keeping it back in your head.

Articulation. Open your mouth and try to enunciate each word clearly. The result may sound theatrical and exaggerated to you, but it won't to your audience. Opening your mouth when you speak will not only give you an energetic, crisp, authoritative sound but help your jaw and throat relax, so that your voice sounds deeper and less shrill.

Body language. Use descriptive gestures; pause for emphasis or to build suspense; make eye contact. Don't stand there like a post.

Speed. Pace your delivery and watch your audience for clues. Have several members thrown down their Mont Blanc pens in disgust because they can't keep up with you? Or has your ponderous delivery lulled some to sleep?

Starting and ending. While memorable anecdotes, statistics, and quotations can be most helpful to a speech's success, consider lighter, perhaps humorous openings or closings. But be careful. You don't want to sound like a Las Vegas comedian working the casino crowd. Above all, avoid clichés.

Relax. Before you speak in public, sit down, close your eyes, and take several deep, slow breaths. Don't forget to exhale! Relax your muscles by rotating your head in a complete circle. Think about removing all tension from your body. And try to keep things in perspective. What's the worst that can happen? So you lose your place for a minute—take a deep breath and go on.

Above all, rehearse. Try listening to yourself on a tape recorder or practice in front of coworkers. If you're lucky, you may be able to watch a videotape of yourself, a painful but revealing exercise.

Sometime in your career you will be asked not only to speak but to give a presentation complete with visual aids in front of a large, or at least important, audience. The actual content of your presentation depends on your purposes and your audience. Think about why you're speaking. Are you trying to persuade clients to buy a product or are you reporting to the home office on the results of your research? Think also about the members of your audience—what are their backgrounds and how will these affect their reactions to your presentation? A group of hardbitten bottomliners won't be moved by tales of your childhood. Just as the members of the International Federation of Business and Professional Women's Clubs were not amused in 1983 by President Reagan's joke about women as a civilizing force without whom men would still be carrying clubs and wearing "skin suits." Ask yourself what the audience expects from your presentation—inspiration, information, entertainment? Then make sure that every sentence of the presentation helps you further your purposes and satisfy your audience's needs.

As you plan your presentation, think about what kind of audiovisual aids would strengthen your message: charts, diagrams on a blackboard, handouts, slides, overhead transparencies, videotape presentations. If you decide to use any of these, get professionals to help you prepare them so that the results look slick. If you are not going to have any assistance, be sure you know how to operate the equipment.

Think too about your audience's comfort. They won't listen to you if they're hot or cold, so make sure the temperature is comfortable and the room well ventilated. Also, if possible, make sure there won't be any distracting interruptions, like a pair of workers on scaffolding outside the window behind you or a large crane moving tons of concrete in the empty lot next door.

Consider your audience's attention span—it's much shorter than you think. Some experts think that twenty or thirty minutes is the maximum, although others give audiences more credit, saying they'll stay with you for an hour. Whether you take half an hour or twice that, you must change pace every ten or fifteen minutes if you want to hang on to your audience. You can do this by shifting from lecturing to presenting slides or charts, or by having someone on your staff presenting one aspect of your topic.

Above all, start and end on time. Nothing will make your audience lose sympathy for you faster than disrespectfully rushing in late or droning on when everyone else longs to get back to work.

Whether you make your speech from notes, recite it from memory, or read it from a script depends on your self-confidence, experience, and the formality of the occasion. If you're announcing a controversial new policy, every nuance of every word is important, so read from a script. If you have a complicated audiovisual show with slides and charts, follow a script so that you can coordinate the text with whatever visual image is being flashed on the screen. On the other hand, your speech at a retirement dinner won't seem heartfelt if it's read, so try to memorize your remarks. And for a presentation at a department meeting, a prepared text will look too formal, so use notes to carry you through. If you are one of several speakers at a large meeting or convention, be sure to provide other speakers with the text of your remarks so that they can adjust their speeches accordingly and ask them to extend you the same courtesy. If someone is going to introduce you, provide her with a copy of your résumé and speech.

Most presentations and speeches are followed by question-and-answer sessions. It's important to carry these off well if you want to maintain the credibility you've worked for in your speech. Do your homework, try to anticipate questions and rehearse answers. When asked a question, repeat it for the audience's sake and to give you time to order your thoughts. Rephrase it slightly to suit your answer if necessary, but try to answer the question; everyone in the post-Watergate world can spot evasive responses. However, don't hesitate to say, "I don't really think that is relevant to our discussion because . . ." or to turn the tables by answering a question with a question: "You may have a point, but don't you think that . . ." Finally, don't be afraid to admit that you don't know the answer to a question. Usually you can offer to get back to the questioner later with the relevant information.

MANAGING YOUR BOSS

To work smart, then, you have to be self-centered. You must think about how to organize and present yourself and your accomplishments most effectively. To develop a second, equally important set of "smarts," though, you must think about others and how you work with them. The first "other" who probably comes to mind is your boss.

Bosses may sit on the throne, but their subordinates are truly the power behind the throne, and they can topple it with a few well-timed pushes. They can withhold information; they can drag their feet on important projects or execute them sloppily. In short, power flows both ways, and for both the throne and the power behind it to succeed, the two must work together as partners. Keep the following principles in mind as you work with your boss:

Know your boss. Does she like to read long background reports or does she prefer short oral summaries? Does she prefer action to rumination? Does she want to work with you as an equal or does she prefer a more authoritarian arrangement? Does she like to keep on top of details or does she prefer that you carry things out as you see best? Does she like to plan or to play by ear? Is she, for example, under unusual pressure to prove herself by cutting costs or raising output?

Once you know the answers to these questions, act on your knowledge. Don't submit ten-page reports you know she hates reading. If she wants to keep things moving, don't interrupt her directions by suggesting that she convene a meeting of department heads to discuss a plan of action. If she's under pressure to come up with ways to cut costs fast, don't draw up a six-page, $3-million proposal for a new word-processing system. In other words, use what you learn about your boss's needs and interests to help you work *with* her, not against her.

Compensate for your boss's weaknesses. If she's rude to others, you may have to smooth hurt feelings. If she writes terribly, you may tactfully suggest minor improvements (or perhaps go ahead and make them). If she tends to rush forward with plans without considering important angles, you may have to try to exert a gentle, moderating counterforce. Generally, all but the most insecure or most self-confident bosses will be grateful for your quiet intervention, even if they think you're wrong. Your concern at least shows that you care and are thinking. But if your boss never accepts your suggestions or seems annoyed by them, shut up. Either you don't yet know what you're talking about (in which case you should keep quiet and learn), or your boss does not like team playing, which she regards as interference (in which case you should keep quiet and look around for a more compatible player).

Always be honest. If you don't understand what your boss wants, ask. If you know you can't possibly complete an assignment by the deadline she's given you, say so. If you're certain that she's making a mistake, gently question her. Of course, if you go too far you'll be looked upon as a presumptuous upstart, but, couched the right way, your cautious objections and questions will be considered conscientious and thoughtful. By the same token, don't try to hide bad news from your boss. Let her know that you made a mistake calculating the monthly sales totals before she goes to the chairman of the board to brag about a nonexistent increase.

Don't be a naysayer. If your boss asks you to do something, don't waste her time and yours by trying to think up reasons why the task is impossible. Try, and if it really is impossible, come back later with suggestions for a more reasonable goal or a different means to the same end.

Always keep the lines of communication open. Don't let resentment or undone work build up. Keep your boss up to date on the broad outline of your work but don't burden her with all the details.

PICKING AND COACHING A TEAM

Let's turn the tables now and look at the smart ways to work with your subordinates. The smartest move you can make is to hire good people. The knowledge we all have about how to float through interviews is indispensable in this regard. There are all sorts of scientific ways (and consultants) to "screen candidates," as they say in the personnel business, but for lower-level jobs you don't usually have the luxury of this specialized and pricy advice and in large part you must stick to your instincts.

Some of the best advice on hiring staff comes from Bradford Smart, a Chicago management psychologist who has interviewed hundreds of candidates. Many of the following tips come from him.

Write a job description before you do any recruitment at all. Don't merely list title and responsibilities. Try to define important personal qualities such as emotional maturity or pragmatism.

Ask candidates to fill out an application. As a skilled job hunter you should be well aware of tricks you can play with résumés. Getting everyone to fill out applications will give you a standardized means of comparison, and the very appearance of the applications will help you judge whether the candidate is neat or sloppy, wordy or succinct.

Weed out candidates. You can do this either by short telephone interviews or by very short personal interviews. If you don't have the time, delegate the job to your assistant or to the personnel department. Invite the top candidates to longer interviews with you, say forty-five minutes. The two or three who most impress you can then come back for in-depth interviews with you and your staff. If this process sounds too time-consuming, you can skip the forty-five-minute interviews and pick the top two or three candidates whom you'll interview in depth through phone interviews.

Keep the candidate talking. Prepare a list of the questions you want answered and be sure you cover them. Don't let the candidate sidetrack you into talking about your last vacation. Bradford Smart suggests that you ask several questions at once, so that while the candidate is answering them you have time to take notes and think of other questions. This device also frees you from the stiff formality of the question/answer format.

Ask coworkers to interview candidates. Getting a second and third perspective is helpful, and candidates may sometimes reveal more to others than they revealed to you.

Check references but don't be overwhelmed by them. Before you check references, make sure you have the candidate's permission. If you don't have the time to do the checking yourself, ask the personnel department. Be careful about uncritically accepting everything you hear—perhaps the reference really is an ogre whose unflattering description of the candidate isn't fair. Try to make the reference your ally—apologize for taking her time, tell her how important it is that you choose the best person, and promise to keep everything she tells you in confidence. Ask the reference to list strengths first, so she will feel less guilty about telling you the candidate's weaknesses later. Be sure to ask why the candidate left.

Recruiting a good team doesn't necessarily mean you'll be able to field a good one—unless you are a good coach. A good coach:

Delegates. No one will be able to develop her talents unless you let her practice. You must give your staff the chance to take on new and challenging responsibilities. Part of delegating involves encouraging your staff to take on assignments even when they're not sure they're ready for them. Remind them that you're the best judge of their capabilities.

Builds on strengths. Encouraging people to test their limits is good, but forcing people to take on responsibilities for which they're clearly unsuited is not wise. You'll wind up with a demoralized and unhappy subordinate and a badly done project. Work with all your employees to assess and build on strengths, and to overcome or compensate for weaknesses. But don't force a highly skilled engineer to become a sales person.

Insists on good work. Don't reward bad work by holding your tongue because you're afraid you'll hurt employees' feelings if you criticize them. Nor should you let employees off the hook by relieving them of assignments when they have trouble with them. Your employees will be far more hurt when you have to fire them later because their work wasn't up to par. Tell people what they're doing wrong, then discuss solutions with them and help them work these out.

Rewards achievements. Many of us are uncomfortable giving praise and we often assume there's no need for it in any case because our employees know they're doing a good job. Everyone needs constant encouragement; no one objects to a compliment, however unnecessary it may seem to you.

MEETING ADJOURNED

One of the best ways to build a team is through meetings, but too many executives convene too many of them. If seven attorneys who bill their time to clients at $100 an hour hold a three-hour luncheon meeting, the cost in billable time alone is $2,100. The true cost of the meeting, including overhead and the lunch itself, is much higher. It's unlikely that the seven lawyers actually produced even $2,100 worth of work. We all know that most meetings are aimless affairs in which most of the time is frittered away on side issues that could have been decided elsewhere by just one or two people. And for many women meetings are more than a waste of time. All too often they are just another breeding ground for male chauvinism, with decades of conditioning prompting familiar female deference to male opinions. Most executives, men and women, long to learn how to hold brief, purposeful meetings. Below, a few guidelines:

Cut back. Before you call a meeting ask yourself whether you could accomplish your purposes through a memo, a few phone calls, or a conference call rather than interrupting your department.

Schedule carefully. Decide who needs to attend and make sure that key people are free before you set a meeting time. Give plenty of notice, so that you disrupt other people's schedules as little as possible.

Provide an agenda. A day or so before the meeting, send participants an agenda that lists how much time will be spent on each topic. Such an agenda reminds participants about the meeting, allows them to prepare for it, and clues them to how much of the meeting they should stay for. If someone's specialty will not be discussed until midway through the meeting, she may arrange to skip the first half.

Start and finish on time. Don't waste the time of prompt arrivals to accommodate latecomers. So the meeting doesn't drag on interminably, schedule it for half an hour before lunch or late in the afternoon, so that there's an incentive to finish quickly.

Summarize. Leave a few minutes at the end of the meeting to summarize the ground covered, then send all interested parties a memo describing what was accomplished and who is going to follow up on what in what ways.

Leave time for questions and answers. Although you should structure the meeting tightly, you can't be inflexible. Not permitting discussion causes misunderstandings.

Stick to schedule. If you have distributed an agenda before the meeting, staying on schedule will be easy. You can tactfully remind long-winded participants that the ten minutes you've allotted to that topic have passed and you'll have to move on. (Of course, if the group really is accomplishing something, don't cut discussion short simply to conform to the schedule.) If you've asked some people to make presentations, let them know ahead of time that you will hold them to a five- or ten-minute time limit.

Be a leader. Get meandering discussions back on track, even if it means stealing the show from overbearing participants by thanking them for their observations, citing the need to keep on schedule, and moving on. Cut short antagonistic encounters in the same way. Make sure to invite silent staff members to chip in.

Participants in meetings have responsibilities as well. Remember that you are being paid to attend meetings; they are not supposed to be the equivalent of a group coffee break. Pay attention, speak up, take notes. If you are asked to attend a meeting that is clearly irrelevant for you, tactfully ask whether it might not be more sensible for you to send a representative, attend only part of the meeting, or get a copy of the minutes after the meeting.

Finally, as a woman you must be careful to hold your own ground at meetings. Prepare for them so that you feel confident about making contributions. Sit as close as you can to the meeting chair or to other powerful members, so that the aura of their authority envelops you as well. You can develop contacts this way too. If you're asked to run out for coffee, it may be wiser to assent for the moment and talk privately with the people involved later. If you are asked to get coffee more than once, try to establish a rule that whoever calls the meeting is in charge of such details as providing coffee. Often, though, you can politely decline by saying you'd prefer not to miss any of the meeting. People will get your message.

LETTING GO

Despite your best efforts at recruiting and coaching staff members, you will occasionally have to fire someone. Don't be too hasty in writing off troublesome or inefficient employees, though. Before you fire people, you must try to help them reform. Meet with them. Tell them what they're doing wrong and what they need to do to improve. Set dates to review their progress. Keep records of the criticism and warnings you've delivered and the unsatisfactory work or incidents that prompted you to do so. This record will be useful if an employee sues you after she's been fired; but the most important reason for keeping it is to demonstrate to the employee that your decision hasn't been hasty or personally motivated. Your record documents the reasons that made your decision inevitable and irrevocable and shows the employee that you thought carefully before you acted. You do not have to show this record to the employee, of course, but it will refresh your memory and help you plan your talks with her.

If all your coaching and warnings don't work, you may be able to transfer the employee to another job or division where her skills could be put to better use. Perhaps early retirement is an option. If none of these solutions work, then you must discuss the firing with the personnel department and your superiors before you do anything. Your company may have formal grievance procedures that give employees a chance to present their side.

If you must fire someone, pay attention to where and when. Always fire people in your office with the door shut. It's cruel to drop by someone's office casually, as if you were going to have a friendly chat instead of being the bearer of such bad news. Before you fire someone, always check to see if the day you've picked is her birthday or a holiday. Also consider the employee's personal situation—if someone in her family has just died, firing her would be unpardonable.

There are two schools of thought about the best time of day and week to fire someone, and both sides mount convincing cases. You'll have to be the judge. Some people think the best time to deliver the news is late on a Friday afternoon, so the person doesn't have to face coworkers and can clean out her desk in peace. Others think that firings should be done early in the morning and early in the week, so that a person who is too stunned and hurt during the actual firing to argue her side can come back and talk things over once she's collected her thoughts. By firing people on a Friday, this school argues, you force them to stew for the whole weekend without a second chance at discussing the reasons for your decision with you. If your company offers outplacement counseling, then you probably will have to do the firing early in the day, since many counselors like to meet with people immediately after they have been fired.

The actual course of the conversation is difficult to predict, but to spare hurt feelings and confusion you should avoid making these common mistakes:

Beating around the bush. This will keep the employee in painful and needless suspense. The person you're firing may not have done a good job, but she's no fool and has probably guessed the real reason for your talk. Get straight to the point with a brief, straightforward explanation of why you are firing her. Employees deserve to know this, and the explanation may prevent them from making the same mistakes at their next job.

Dwelling on your affection for the employee. Under the circumstances, protestations of deep friendship sound insincere and confuse the employee. You don't want to sound callous, of course, but it's better to touch quickly on your feelings for her and get on with the unpleasant task at hand.

Stressing your guilt and discomfort. Your employee may resent your preoccupation with your own feelings. *Her* feelings, not yours, should be paramount.

Acting brisk and businesslike. Although you want to avoid making this into an emotional catharsis for both of you, you can't be icy. Be sure to point out the employee's strengths and express your regrets. Conclude the session on an upward note, if possible, thanking the employee for past service to the company.

Holding out false hope. Don't hint that there may be a position elsewhere in the company unless there is one. And don't try to imply that the decision wasn't really yours. Doing so encourages the employee to waste time trying to reverse the decision instead of looking for a new job.

Allowing the employee to stay on indefinitely. Make the discharge effective immediately. If the employee hangs around she may lower office morale or waste her time trying to do a super job so that you'll change your mind. In some fields it is customary to allow employees to stay until they find a new position; for example, associates at large law firms who are not asked to become partners, often stay with the firm for a few months.

Forgetting to describe the company's termination policy. Make sure you learn what kind of outplacement counseling, severance pay, and insurance coverage your company provides to employees who have been fired. After briefly describing these, give the employee a written policy statement, since she may be too upset to understand or remember everything you've said.

Once you've done this difficult task, don't discuss your reasons with others ("Glad I got rid of that lazy lout"). Nor do you have to explain to clients or professional associates why an employee has left. Simply say that the employee is no longer with the firm and let them draw their own conclusions. Coordinate with the employee as to what you will say to potential future employers. You may agree to say that the employee resigned. If you feel honor bound to say that you fired her, you may agree that you will emphasize the areas at which you felt she excelled.

TECHNOLOGY

An important key to working smart is to make good use of the technology that daily infiltrates the workplace.

Telephones. Sitting on your desk is a piece of equipment that no longer simply connects two people. Your phone may tie you into a central transcribing and word-processing unit so that you can dictate reports and memos from your office, home, or hotel. You can set up conference calls with it and avoid expensive travel; (Hoffmann-LaRoche, the pharmaceutical company, recently saved $200,000 by holding a national sales conference involving a thousand people at forty locations by phone). If you have an answering machine, you can avoid all calls or screen calls, taking only the most urgent. If you are on the road, you can use a remote control unit or the mere sound of your voice to trigger your answering machine to play back messages it recorded while you were out. Some answering machines can carry on "conversations" with callers. Activated by the sound of the caller's voice, these machines can ask questions to record customers' orders, for example. Check with your secretary or office manager to see what more mundane but useful capabilities your phone has. These probably include call waiting (a beep indicates that another caller wants to speak to you; with a push of a button you can put your first caller on hold while you speak to the second) or call forwarding, which permits you to transfer your calls to a different number.

Dictation equipment. Many offices have dictating equipment, but even its manufacturers admit that few executives use it, despite studies and personal testimonies showing that dictating letters, memos, and reports saves time and money. Equipment varies from pocket-size lightweight portable dictating units that can accompany executives wherever they go, to the transcribing units that sit on a secretary's desk, to the central systems that link an entire company and its executives (whether at the office, on the road, or at home), to a pool of transcribers. The newer equipment has such features as two-speed settings (at the slower speed, the machine can record twice as much material, so that a thirty-minute tape runs for sixty minutes) and electronic cuing (by pushing a button you insert "beeps" on the tape to mark the location of special instructions and the beginnings and ends of jobs, so the transcriber can play quickly through the tape and gauge the work load).

Calculators. The most advanced calculators can now be programmed, and some computers themselves are about the size of calculators, but the simpler calculator models retain their own identity and usefulness. Since they're extremely small and easy to use, they meet the needs of the executive who doesn't often work with numbers, or who does but spends a lot of time on the road so that portability is important. Don't get tricked into buying more machine than you need. Some calculators have all sorts of scientific, financing, or engineering functions that are useful only to specialists; others have fancy extras, like alarm clocks. Two other observations: the tiny keys on the very small calculators are hard to punch, and the portable calculators that print out numbers are useful for double-checking long calculations.

Typewriters. You may have breathed a sigh of relief when you reached a position where there wasn't a typewriter on your desk, or you may work in an office where to be seen within ten feet of one signals "secretary," but you should try to overcome these inhibitions and learn something about the capabilities of the new generation of typewriters. This will give you a better idea of what kinds of things your secretary can do with them. The old IBM Selectric is no longer the pinnacle of typewriter technology, because IBM and other manufacturers have developed sophisticated electronic and memory typewriters that verge on being word processors. Your secretary may be able to do the following on her typewriter (and she may need your encouragement to try): automatically center and hyphenate words; move letters, words, and paragraphs around without having to retype a thing; direct the typewriter to search documents for words, abbreviations, or numbers; store form letters and then run out reams of them simply by typing up a list of names and addresses to fit in with them.

That's working smart.

5
Getting Ahead

Now that the door to real power is ajar, it is more important than ever for women to research, study, and plan their careers. "Luck" may account for some successes, but most women give luck more credit than it deserves. The people in power have made their own luck by managing their careers well—by placing themselves in the right place at the right time, by being bold about their career goals and taking risks to achieve their long-term objectives.

The first risk you take is accepting an entry-level job and the second is leaving it. Once you have learned the basics of the work world and excelled in a specific job category, it's time to move up.

Before you ask your boss for a promotion, you need to ask yourself many questions about your short- and long-term goals, your ideal job, your present job, and your present company. And you need to assess your achievements and formulate your objectives so that you will be able to present a strong, persuasive case for your promotion. One way to do this is to co-opt top managements' method and give yourself a performance evaluation. Corporations use this kind of evaluation as a means of measuring an employee's progress and planning her future with the company. Some evaluations are very formal one-on-one meetings with many forms to fill out; others are more casual. Either way the same points are covered by the staff person and her manager.

EVALUATING YOURSELF AND YOUR COMPANY

To get an objective picture of your on-the-job performance, play manager and rate yourself on the following:

Quality of work. What are the standards of performance for the job I hold? How well do I meet them?

Special skills. What skills and talents does my job require? Do I possess them? How have I developed them? What areas need improvement?

Initiative. Do I sense what needs to be done and do it? Do I require direction too often? Have I learned to take charge?

Follow-through. Does my work get done on time? Do I attend to all the necessary details? Have others had to prod me into getting my job done, or have I worked in a self-directed way?

Innovation and flexibility. Have I found new and better ways to do my job, or mimicked what was done before? Am I receptive to change and to the ideas of others?

Motivation. Do I work with dedication? Have I demonstrated a genuine interest in my work and in the goals of my company? Do I seek more responsibility and work?

Quantity of work. Do I devote enough hours, effort, and energy to my job and turn out the volume of work expected? Is there a problem with attendance and punctuality?

Attitude. Do I have a positive or a negative attitude about my job? Which attitude do I communicate to the people I deal with?

Personality. How well do I work with others? Which of my personality traits add to my effectiveness on the job and which diminish it?

Development. Am I in a job that uses my talents? Have I honed and developed them over the course of my employment?

Future. Am I ready to assume more responsibility? How much? How do I expect to grow in my job over the next twelve months, and how does that correspond with what would be expected of me?

Training. Do I need more training to improve my performance, and, if so, what do I imagine my boss would suggest?

If you manage a staff you should also address the following matters as you perform your self-evaluation:

Departmental performance. How well has the department and its staff performed under my leadership?

Decision making and delegation. Do I make the necessary decisions and communicate them effectively? Do I delegate responsibility or try to do everything single-handedly?

Planning. How well do I plan and set priorities for my department and its staff?

Staff selection. Have I demonstrated good judgment in hiring new staff?

Staff development and leadership. How about the development and training of the staff? Have I worked to develop people of superior talent? Do I lead and motivate my staff well? Do I deal effectively with performance problems?

Affirmative action. What is my record on hiring, developing, and evaluating minority-group, women, and handicapped staff members?

Communications. Do I communicate effectively with my staff? With management? Am I willing to hear and accept the thoughts of staff members?

Be as concrete as possible as you prepare your self-evaluation. Include examples of your good work. Did you show initiative by setting up a new, more efficient filing system? Did you volunteer to head a research and development project? How many new clients have you brought in? Did your innovation result in a computerized bookkeeping system? What have your staff members accomplished?

After you have evaluated your performance and are aware of your strengths and weaknesses, do an evaluation of your *job.* Clarify to yourself what you want from a job, decide whether your present job is suitable, and assess whether it can grow as you do.

Shirley Sloan Fader has prepared a list of job characteristics that can help you define what you need in a job and what you're better off avoiding:

Lots of people contact
Concentration on job tasks, done privately and independently
Predictable daily routine
Varied routine
Undemanding work
Constant challenge
Strictly prescribed work hours, Monday to Friday, nine to five
A "career" position that requires putting in extra hours
Security (a job you can depend on for years)
Promotion possibilities (a job you can leave behind)
High income
"Worthwhile" work with intrinsic social value
Interesting work
Power
Status (title, work surroundings)
Uncertain income (such as when pay checks depend on your output, as in sales)
Convenience (commuting ease)

Potential (you'll relocate or adjust your personal life)

Your response to the list will help you crystallize the job area you're best suited for. For example, you may think that sales would offer you a lot of opportunities, but if you dislike lots of people contact, sales is not for you. Matching the right person (you) to the right job is an important factor in achieving success.

After evaluating your own performance and taking a hard look at your aspirations, the logical next step is to grade management. You need to know whether you are working for a company that will help you develop your talents and reward you for excellent work. Even if you are a dynamo and your boss recognizes it, your career can stagnate because of poor departmental management or corporate sexual politics.

Start by assessing the situation of women in your company. Many companies are bottom-heavy with women, and to a new recruit this may indicate that management has a real interest in hiring women. But don't stop there. The initial assessment may be correct, but does management have a real interest in training and promoting women? To determine this, find the answers to these questions:

How many women are in middle management and above?
How did these women get their jobs? Were they promoted from within or recruited from outside?
How large are their staffs? Budgets?
Are their salaries equal to those of their male counterparts?
Do they have any real authority? Do their recommendations become policy? Are they included in important meetings? Are they part of management's decision-making method?
What is the "unofficial" word about women? Are they tolerated but not respected? Are their staffs loyal or eager to transfer? How are they treated by equals and superiors? Are they gossiped about and put down?
Do they have the ear of top management?

Of course, you can't parade around the halls of Big Business, Inc., querying everyone you meet about the "women situation." But you can raise many of these questions during the hiring interview or with the personnel department. Later, approach women managers in the company and ask if they will help you find the answers.

Beyond the assessment of management and women, try to ascertain the future of your immediate boss, your department, and the company as a whole:

> Is there room for advancement in the company? Or is there virtually no turnover in areas in which you would like to be promoted?
> Is the firm growing, getting into new areas?
> Is your department or division well regarded and well managed, or is it considered a dumping ground for dead-ended personnel?
> Is your immediate boss someone on the way up, with access to top management? Or is she or he running scared, underqualified, overqualified, in a rut?
> How will technology affect your job? Will technology upgrade your work or disintegrate it?
> Do people advance in an orderly way, getting promoted for merit? Or do people move up as a consequence of shrewd politicking, resulting in the advancement of some who don't deserve or can't handle promotion?

Answering these questions will give you a feel for your future with your present company. You need to know if advancement is a real possibility for you or if you should plan a strategy for moving to another company.

SETTING GOALS AND DEFINING OPTIONS

You have evaluated your performance on the job, defined your area of interest, and graded your present company. Now you are ready to set concrete career goals. Each day you accomplish small goals, and to do so quickly and smartly you probably draw up daily to-do lists and assign priorities to each task (see Chapter 4). The same principle holds true for long-range goals.

A goal should include a well-defined objective *and* a time frame. Everyone has a head full of vague professional and personal goals: to get a raise, to have a nice office, to increase staff, to buy a house in the country. Norma Carr-Ruffino reminds us in *The Promotable Woman* that in order to be attainable, goals must be specific. She gives these examples:

Vague Goals	Specific Goals
To make more money	To earn $30,000 next year
To move up in the company	To be General Manager of a regional branch by 19__
To get ahead in life	To have a net worth of $500,000 by 19__
To go back to school	To have an MBA degree by 19__

To have more free time	To have at least one month free time per year by 19__
To travel more	To travel to the Far East for three weeks in 19__
To start a family	To own a house and have two children, one in 19__, and one in 19__

Project your objectives for the next six months, the next year, the next five years, the next ten years. Analyze the situation of the people on the next levels above yours. How long have they been working? How long have they been in their current positions? What's their seniority? What kind of education do they have? What salary range are they in? What's their family situation?

Defining your goals and placing them in context will help you focus on the strategies you need to adapt for career success.

There are a number of ways to go about advancing your career, and each has its pros and cons. Getting a promotion within your current company means advancing on familiar territory where you know the system, the people, and the politics. But even if your title and responsibilities change, colleagues may continue to see you in your old role. If, for example, you are an administrative assistant turned sales person, coworkers may still insist on taking complaints about the photocopying machine to you. To change your image as well as your position, it's often better to switch to another company. Being brought in from the outside commands a certain respect. Of course, changing jobs also means starting from scratch to prove yourself all over again. And you are bound to suffer from culture shock for a while; perhaps it will take several months to get settled and knowledgeable about the company and its operations. There are lots of unknowns that can make life complicated for the job switcher. You may discover, for example, that the kind person who interviewed you is actually a tyrant or that coworkers resent outsiders and try to sabotage your efforts.

As you plan your career you may also want to consider making a lateral move either within your present company or to a new firm. A lateral move may seem less glamorous than a step upward—indeed, people often refuse to consider a job that deviates from the vertical route—but it is an effective way to develop top-management skills and broaden experience. Men who are being groomed for high-level positions often move from staff to line and back again, to cover manufacturing, sales, technical support systems, marketing, and so on. Progress needn't always be in a straight line upward. A lateral move may not be accompanied by a fancy executive title or a jump in salary, but it can prepare you for the long haul.

MAKING MONEY: HOW TO GET WHAT YOU'RE WORTH

Thinking about your short- and long-term career goals and tackling the questions presented in this chapter are good preparation for real action. But knowing what you want is only a prerequisite. Now you have to get what you deserve. And the best way to measure where you stand is by the bottom line: your salary.

Women have shied away from negotiating aggressively for money because they believe it is unfeminine to do so, or they think that someone else (in this case the boss, the management, the system) will take care of them. But management is also being measured by a bottom-line figure: how much money it doesn't spend. By paying you as little as possible, they come out winners. And obviously you lose. You don't get your fair share unless you ask for it and prove that you deserve it.

Pay is based on tangible and intangible factors: what you think your work is worth, what your employer thinks it is worth, what it is really worth in the marketplace, and what your boss thinks has to be paid to get or keep you. To find out all these aspects of the figure, you have to do some research. Get the facts and figures of the salaries in your field. Start with the want ads of major newspapers to see what's being offered for comparable positions. Make diplomatic inquiries within your company; talk to people on your level and above you. They may not give exact figures, but by opening up salary discussions you can piece together a picture of salary ranges. Request information from professional associations and societies; many publish annual salary surveys. Find an executive search firm and consult them when looking for a job; they know who is paying what for whom. The local Chamber of Commerce may also be a source of information. Confront your boss directly: "What salary can I expect in the job I'm aiming for?"

After you find out where you stand in relation to the industry as a whole, you need to learn what your work is worth to your own company. Get to know your company's salary system. Many companies have a definite salary structure, which consists of a number of levels or grades and a salary range for each. There's a minimum, a mid-level, and a maximum figure for these jobs. Other companies operate less formally, but management always has figures in mind for every job—from entry-level compensation to the salary ceiling.

Your immediate supervisor can probably give you salary ranges; if not, try the personnel department. Here too discussions with coworkers can help you determine company policy and salary ranges. By knowing what the company is paying for people at your level you know how it values you. Are you on the low end despite the fact that you have equal responsibility with others on your level? Are you progressing up the pay scale as quickly as others?

Pay attention also to the benefits your company offers. These noncash extras can add up. Be familiar with your existing medical and insurance coverage. Try to get a breakdown of benefits in dollars and cents. Check into pension plans and the timetable for vesting (when you become eligible for the plan). Some companies offer profit-sharing plans and savings assistance. Such programs have a dollar value to you.

Since tax laws and inflation affect your take-home money, you should research taxable versus nontaxable income. Salary is a taxed form of income; medical insurance is not taxed. Use of the company car and company-paid membership dues for professional organizations may or may not be taxed. You should take these matters into account when you negotiate a raise or start looking for another job.

Every company has a policy about salary increases. In some companies there's a set time each year (perhaps January or July) when every worker comes up for salary review. Other companies use the employee's hiring anniversary as the review date. Some companies or managers are more flexible. It's important for you to find out how your company and your boss operate in this realm. Determine the size of the average increase—this is often expressed as a percentage—and find out if increases vary with performance and/or present salary level.

The best way to get more money out of your present employer is to get a promotion. Keep in mind that promotional increases can add up to a sizable percentage of your current salary, but remember too that the best kind of promotion is a real job change that offers more responsibility and authority. Don't get duped by a title: find out what the job behind the title is. In good companies the raises handed out with promotions are larger—they should be much larger—than normal merit raises. That's one reason why it's essential to know what the usual company increase is; with a promotion you deserve a far greater sum.

If your company has no salary review, initiate one. Prepare your boss by explaining what you want to discuss—your future with the company and your compensation. Then prepare yourself for the sell.

No one gets a big pay hike for merely fulfilling the basics of her job. The average worker gets an average salary increase. Many people don't get extra monetary rewards; some are lucky even to hold onto the job. This is the sort of worker you want to differentiate yourself from. You want to show that you've been doing something above and beyond the call of duty, that you've expanded your job description. This holds true for all job levels; even entry-level personnel should follow these guidelines. You are asking for a raise and are setting yourself up as a candidate for a promotion. The information you gathered in your self-evaluation is your arsenal.

Now you're ready to set up a review meeting. Don't forget that a crucial element here is the ability to negotiate. A successful negotiation leaves both sides feeling as though they have won: a "win-win" situation. No one likes to be a loser, and if you force management into what it sees as a "no win" position, it may decide it doesn't need you around at all.

One way to approach negotiations is to devise a strategy that meets the other person's needs. Why should management give you a promotion just because you want one? By convincing your boss that a promotion for you both helps his or her advancement and is good for the company, you're more likely to make an ally. To do this, focus on the company's needs and on the areas in which you've had to branch out in order to keep your department running smoothly.

Give careful thought to the time and place of the meeting. Many career counselors warn against asking for a raise on a Monday or a Friday. Aim for a midweek morning. And plan for enough time; don't give the impression that your request is so inconsequential that it can be handled during a coffee break.

Begin and end the session on a positive note. You're there to help the company solve problems, not to make trouble. Appear as confident as possible—after all, you're only seeking what is right and equitable.

Many women give up or make concessions prematurely. Don't. Hold your ground, but know on what points you will be flexible. If the other side gives a totally unacceptable answer, do nothing—respond with total silence. Keep calm. A poker face may help. Remain positive, but keep your tone matter-of-fact.

Be persuasive. Cite evidence of your growth in very specific terms: you increased sales by 10 percent, you decreased production losses by 20 percent. Stress that your raise will be an incentive for you to continue to work extra hard in solving company problems and leading it into the future.

Take notes. As each point is agreed on, jot it down. This information will help you write a new job description and make sure promises are fulfilled.

Ask for more than you expect. Decide on the minimum you will accept and add X dollars to that. If you start by asking for a $5,000 raise, management may offer $2,500. Counter with $4,000. You may decide to agree on

$3,500. Even if the boss sounds as if she or he won't budge from the original offer, try to bargain. You have nothing to lose by asking for more. People don't get fired for asking for a raise. Even if you don't get the full amount you went in asking for, you will probably get more than people who ask for nothing. The worst management can do is say no; and then you know where you stand and can plan accordingly.

No matter how unyielding management is, never issue an ultimatum unless you are ready to act upon it and bear the consequences. "If I don't get this promotion, I'm resigning" is an assertion that can put you on the unemployment line. On the other hand, having a job offer from another company can give you a power base. Tell your boss about the offer—why the new job interests you, and what the financial package is. Say that you have a few days to make up your mind. And tell him or her that you have valued the time at the present company and would be happy to continue working there if it could be made more rewarding for you. This gives the employer a chance to get into the bidding. But beware: This method may backfire if your present employer interprets your new opportunity as disloyalty.

You may, of course, receive an offer that you intend to take. In such a case you should inform your employer of your decision without implying that you are open to negotiation. It's not fair to seduce your boss into a bidding war if you have no intention of negotiating honestly.

If you have presented your case well, but management won't agree to a raise or promotion, ask to have a review again soon, in three months, say, instead of the usual six. Negotiate for a bonus or perks instead of a salary increase: additional insurance, extra travel and entertainment allotments, a company car, deferred income (see Chapter 8, Benefits and Rights of Work).

SKILLS AND VISIBILITY

Skills and visibility are key ingredients in getting ahead. You must gain expertise *and* make yourself known to the right people.

The main method of acquiring skills is on-the-job training, learning as you do. But sometimes learning on the job is not sufficient; then you have to go outside to find the best skills.

Seminars often fill the bill. Management associations and professional groups offer workshops on everything from how to get organized to basic management to finance for the nonfinancial manager. Ask your supervisor which seminars would help you in your present job and give you insights into the next level up. Many companies have tuition reimbursement programs that cover the cost of job-related outside training; check with your boss about which courses are covered and, if you want a course that is not on the company's approved list, get your expenses cleared in advance.

You may meet with some resistance if you want to attend a women-only management seminar. Men and women have to learn the same management techniques, it is reasoned, so why the need for a special course for women only? *Working Woman* columnist Betty Harragan points out that though this attitude seems logical, it repeatedly assumes that the "general" courses being offered are bias free. In fact, these courses are geared for men and their experiences. "There is a monumental void in 'general' training programs that totally exclude women's business experience," Harragan says. "Women do not share the life conditioning, social culture, and real-life experiences of men—in or out of the work force." In addition, women managers evoke different responses from their coworkers and subordinates, and they must learn to deal effectively with that fact of life.

Someday—let us hope in the near future—men and women will be able to benefit from the same courses, because they will have more of the same reference points. Until then, courses for women have a legitimate reason for being.

Seminars give you the opportunity to meet speakers, network with other women managers, and become more visible—and visibility is an essential tool in getting ahead. You can hardly expect to be singled out for advancement if no one notices you. Although gaining visibility takes time, there are now some key ways to move the process along.

Skills themselves increase visibility. First of all, concentrate on doing the best job possible and always strive to sharpen your skills. Word will get around that you're the resident computer whiz or a number-one sales person. Becoming an expert in a hot, in-demand field, such as the high-technology industries, will help get you noticed, too. So will getting into print. Consider writing articles for professional associations or in-house newsletters, or send letters to the Op Ed page of local and major newspapers. Route copies of your by-lined piece to your superiors. Find out about trade events and investigate the possibility of speaking at such functions. Join and become active in a professional association. Volunteer to moderate panels, seminars, and workshops; become an officer (see the networking discussion in Chapter 6). Take on "impossible" assignments—you'll get a reputation as a problem solver.

Paying attention to your image and grabbing the spotlight may seem calculated to some people, but you are the only one responsible for making sure your work gets recognized.

HELPING YOURSELF THROUGH OTHERS:
MENTORS AND SPONSORS

Contacts outside your company can help you with job mobility and make you a better professional; in many industries, cultivating outside contacts is an essential part of one's job. Nevertheless, it is sometimes important to ally yourself with someone within your company who can help you look after your career progress. No one gets ahead entirely on her own. You need people to give you trustworthy advice, to listen to your ideas, to guide you through the political maze, to bolster your confidence and open up opportunities. Two kinds of people are of particular help here, mentors and sponsors, and they differ according to function.

In her book *Paths to Power*, Natasha Josefowitz defines a mentor (an inside contact) as someone who helps with your immediate needs and teaches you what you need to know to do your job. The relationship is that of teacher and apprentice. A sponsor, on the other hand, is a more influential person and is interested in promoting your long-range interests. This is more of a collegial relationship. As Josefowitz puts it: "A mentor will help by telling you what issues to focus on at the next regional meeting, a sponsor will help by introducing you to the regional vice president."

Ideally, mentors and sponsors are transitional figures who change as your own areas of responsibility change. Allying yourself with a series of people also helps you avoid some of the pitfalls of working with a mentor or sponsor. It broadens your own sphere of influence and protects you in the event that a mentor or sponsor dies, gets transferred, or leaves the company.

A woman must also be mindful of the advantages and disadvantages of having male mentors and sponsors. Because top corporate hierarchies are still predominantly male, having a male sponsor to promote your interests and provide an entrée to otherwise inaccessible informal networks can make a big difference. The political savvy to negotiate the unspoken rules of a male team is another lesson you can learn from a male mentor or sponsor.

On the other hand, male-female sponsoring relationships have special dangers. Paternalism is one. Deep down your sponsor may not regard you as a peer, and therefore his advice may not be directed toward developing your full potential but toward creating an executive handmaiden. On your side, the fatherliness in the relationship may encourage your passivity and create a dependence on the man's perceived power to make your career.

Sex, either real or apparent, is another problem. First there's the boor who thinks mentoring is the new casting couch. He's easy to identify and avoid. It is more difficult when you are genuinely attracted to a mentor or a sponsor. A study by Nancy Collins reports that 20 percent of her respondents said they had slept with their mentors and, without exception, had regretted it. Such behavior does nothing to convince other people of your abilities, and when the affair is over you'll suffer professionally more than he will. In the case of a mutual attraction the best thing to do is acknowledge it to yourself and discuss it with him. That way you can both decide not to let it interfere with your working relationship.

Even if you are not sleeping together, office gossip may say you are. After Mary Cunningham and William Agee's no-we-weren't, yes-we-are melodrama at Bendix, an employment manager in a Fortune 200 company put it succinctly: "A pair is a pair is a pair. 'We're just good friends' will be replaced by the similarly dubious 'We have a mentor relationship.' Raised eyebrows help no woman's career." Unimpeachable professionalism is the key here to preventing gossip. And if your being married doesn't stop the "more-than-protégée" speculation, it's a good idea for the three of you to be seen having lunch or a drink together occasionally. (This is also a good idea if your husband is uneasy about the relationship.)

There's another caution to keep in mind about mentor relationships. When you need to change mentors, it should be handled diplomatically. Don't break off the relationship abruptly; continue to seek out a previous mentor for advice from time to time and always be polite and friendly. You don't want a mentor to feel he or she has been used and discarded—you may still have to work with that person or meet him or her again in another company, and mentors are powerful people. Besides, you don't want to give anyone the impression that your loyalties are fleeting.

Mentors are easier to find than sponsors because it's relatively easy to ask for help with specific tasks. Usually a mentor is a coworker or your boss. Finding someone influential enough to be a sponsor requires you to be assertive and to put yourself in a position to be noticed.

Make it known that you're interested in getting ahead and increase your visibility by taking on challenging projects. Watch the informal social structure of the office—who has lunch with whom, who is sought out for advice, who hands out the interesting work. Look for someone who can help you improve your skills.

After you've identified a possible sponsor, introduce yourself by asking for some help in a problem-solving situation or a career decision. If you get good advice, acknowledge it and ask if you may come back with similar requests. If he or she follows up on your work and seems interested, continue the dialogue.

Upon reaching middle management, you'll not only have new sponsors and mentors, you'll also start acting as a mentor yourself. Many benefits accrue to mentors and sponsors. You gain political power within the organization by being associated with the up-and-comers as well as getting the fresh input of your protégée's ideas. It's a way to promote the company's interests by bringing up talented new people. It's a gratifying way to pass on the experience you've accumulated. It's a way to pay back the help you received from your own advisers. And it's a way to advance your own career. By acting as a mentor or sponsor to the new generation in your company, you build a power base of loyal, dedicated people, and you gain a reputation as someone who has the skill for developing talent in others.

Here are some tips on being a good sponsor:

Cultivate your protégée's sense of confidence.

Encourage her to push at limitations, to look at the big picture.

Develop a collegial relationship; convey a sense that you will be peers someday.

Listen well to your protégée's aspirations, so that you advise according to her needs, not yours.

Act to promote her interests: mention her name to others; invite her to attend important meetings as an observer or a participant; give credit—don't circulate her work under your name only.

Recognize when the relationship is changing—accept her new status as she is promoted; deal with jealousy or competition if it arises.

PROFESSIONAL JOB FINDERS

There are many professionals whose job is to help people find jobs. They fall into three major categories: employment agents; career counselors; and executive recruiters or search consultants. The three operate very differently, and it is important to understand their functions before you invest time and money in the wrong place.

Employment agencies are looking for people to fill positions that generally pay less than $30,000; they are often a means of finding entry-level or lower-level positions. They are paid in a variety of ways—sometimes by the client company, sometimes by the job seeker. Occasionally the two share the fee, which is up to 10 percent of the job's annual salary.

Employment agencies vary widely in quality, so it is important to find one with a good reputation. (Check with friends, colleagues and professional associations.) Since many of them specialize in certain industries, look for those in your field.

Career counselors, on the other hand, are paid by the job seeker, and though they sometimes offer placement assistance, actual job finding is not their primary goal. You, the individual, are their client, rather than a company, and for your money you will get decision-making guidance and help in developing strategies to move ahead in your own field or to transfer to another one. Counselors offer self-evaluation exercises to help pinpoint your skills, interests, and values; they research and clarify career options; and they help you prepare an effective résumé and develop good interview skills.

A career counselor's fee can be enormous—sometimes up to $3,000—and is paid up front and regardless of whether you come out with a job. There have been recent investigations into some career counselors who are one thin step away from being frauds—misleading applicants by claiming access to otherwise unavailable companies and by guaranteeing job placement. Counselors may help you with a job search, but they are not placement agencies.

That said, however, career counselors can be helpful if you want advice about finding the career that's right for you. This kind of counselor shouldn't be very expensive and is best found through local colleges, YWCAs, and women's centers.

Executive recruiters are the glamorous members of their community, the ones to know if you're looking for management or executive-level positions. Because these "headhunters" are paid by a company to find the right person for its opening, they are busy seeking out candidates rather than waiting for them to walk in. They generally deal in jobs that pay over $30,000 and often much higher. Estimates of how many positions headhunters fill annually go as high as 100,000 throughout the world, with probably a fifth of these paying $100,000 and more. It makes sense for recruiters to start a search with people they already know about, so it's worth the effort to bring yourself to their attention.

When is the time to do that? The best time is when you are already working, particularly in a management position. Though you may not be looking to move now, you are at your most desirable when you are already employed, and that is when you should get enrolled in the headhunters' talent banks.

Who are they looking for? Headhunters want someone with a demonstrated track record whose earnings are equal to or above industry averages. They want people with a history of concrete achievements that have made visible contributions to their company's profits. They want someone who is known in the industry so they can call up other executives for references.

If you have these characteristics, here are some ways to get a headhunter's attention.

Send a straightforward résumé to each local and regional search firm in the geographical area you're interested in, and to each national firm within a thousand miles of the area. Emphasize your concrete achievements but keep the résumé plain and professional. One headhunter pointed out that a résumé with too hard a sell makes one assume that the person is losing her job. Definitely include the salary you want, and most headhunters want applicants to include age, marital status, and hobbies. In many cases this is not a good idea, but headhunters claim that companies looking for executives want to know about a candidate's background and interests. The covering letter with your résumé need not say that you want a job now, just that you would like to be considered in the future.

Be aware that some firms specialize in certain industries or management disciplines. *Consultant News* publishes an annual *Directory of Executive Recruiters*, with names and addresses cross-indexed geographically and by specialty.

The standard advice for getting ahead applies here too. You must become visible in your field. Join professional societies and try to become an officer; publish articles in the best journals you can; get to know business and community leaders and speak to groups. These are all resources for headhunters seeking new talent.

Get frequent mentions in the places headhunters look regularly: get yourself listed in industry directories by name, title, and company; make sure your promotions are announced in the financial press or trade magazines along with a photograph; get on select mailing lists by subscribing to obscure, elite journals (recruiters often buy these lists).

Get to know recruiters. If one calls you to get a recommendation for someone else, be cordial and let him know that you might be interested in a new position at some point. If you are not prominent enough to be a resource for headhunters, you can set up a courtesy interview. The emphasis here is courtesy—it's not the recruiter's job to find you a job. If one agrees to see you, be direct, brief, and get what advice you can about good people to see.

Being approached by a headhunter for a challenging and well-paying job somewhere else may seem like the ultimate free lunch, but remember that headhunters are basically sales people, selling you on this "wonderful" new job and selling the company on the "wonderfulness" of you, their candidate. You will be hampered by the confidentiality of the process (they may not tell you who the company is until late in the process), but don't take a passive role. There are many recruiters who want only to make the best match, but don't forget that the company is their client, not you, and you have to watch out for your own interests. The best headhunters are paid on a retainer and will get their fee whether they find someone or not, but even then they may be under pressure to keep up a good placement rate. Other headhunters are paid on a contingency basis and their fee depends on getting a candidate hired. Find out which way your recruiter is paid. Get other details of the hunt spelled out ahead of time. For example, if you have to travel to an interview, your expenses (air fare, hotel and meal bills) should be reimbursed by the interviewing company. And before you allow a recruiter to use your name, you may need to discuss confidentiality: you don't want to jeopardize your present job.

When a headhunter is wooing you, guard your interests. Get frequent updates on how the process is going and pin him or her down. If he or she seems incompetent, withdraw. If the job seems attractive and the headhunter is not going fast enough, ask if you can approach the company yourself.

You should get the job specifications and qualifications early, so that you can decide whether you are really qualified. Some headhunters want to offer a long list of candidates to a client and will include marginally qualified people as filler. You don't have the time to waste on that.

On the other hand, make sure that there are other good people on the list for a job you do want. Recruiters may submit two "dummies" plus you to make you look good in comparison. That's not fair to the company or to you.

A caution about unethical recruiters: Arrant headhunters can turn a confidential job search into a nightmare. Such recruiters may call you about a job that you seem perfect for, and then you hear nothing for weeks. Meanwhile, though, you start to get calls at home from personnel directors of companies you've never heard of or applied to. You may even get calls from other headhunters. Pretty soon word gets around to your associates and your boss that you're interested in changing jobs.

If you want to protect yourself from such practices, send a covering letter with your résumé stating that the agency is liable for suit if your current job is jeopardized. The idea of a lawsuit may have an effect on the firm. After all, a reputation for discretion is important in this industry. (Filing a lawsuit against an agency is a complicated matter. You'll need good legal advice, and keep in mind that a suit may take years to win.)

One special warning for women using headhunters is to make sure the position they have been recruited for is fairly compensated. Some headhunters, especially if they are on a contingency fee and do not have the search exclusively, may try to offer a woman candidate at a bargain rate to get an edge over male candidates other recruiters are offering. Check what men in that position are being paid and make sure you get it.

FOND FAREWELLS

Updating and honing skills, networking with people in the know, finding the best professional help to keep your career progressing will eventually pay off in a shiny new job. But before moving on, you have to make a gracious exit from your present job. How you handle your leaving is as important to your professional reputation as any other aspect of your business life. Daydreams of telling off the boss or squealing on coworkers have no place in exiting etiquette. No matter how bad things were for you, don't voice your complaints or badmouth management. There's nothing to be gained and plenty to be lost if you wind up working again with people you've ventilated about.

When you do decide to leave, inform your immediate supervisor first. People who report to you will be directly affected by your leaving and should be notified as soon as possible after you tell your boss. After that, inform staff members and management above your boss. Then let peers, associates, and clients know of your departure.

The two weeks or so before you leave are an important measure of your professionalism. Keep functioning as though you were going to work there forever; don't give in to the temptation to cruise along and renege on responsibilities. Your behavior during this time will be watched very closely, so be sensitive to coworkers' feelings. By gloating about your new-found job, you'll make them feel uncomfortable and perhaps jealous. It's probably best to display some ambivalence about leaving: you are both happy and sad about it; it's a new opportunity, but it's been such a rewarding experience to work for the present company.

Because of an exaggerated sense of loyalty, women often feel that they have to give as much notice as possible when they decide to leave a job. But there is an acceptable cut-off date, and the standard practice of giving two weeks' notice makes sense for most managers. The hard fact for women to accept is that they are not indispensable; most employees can be replaced without too much trouble.

Many jobs include access to confidential, sensitive information. Some tricky situations can arise when people in such jobs move on to other companies. If you are privy to trade secrets, you may want to consult a lawyer about what information you can take with you (including clients) and what belongs to your former employer. Getting legal advice is especially important if you have been working under contract.

Because of the sensitive nature of some industries, there are employers who prefer that employees leave the premises the day they resign. Don't be surprised if you are thanked for your services, told you'll be missed, and then asked to clear out your desk and return your ID and keys that same day. A superior or a member of the personnel department may escort you back to your office and watch as you pack your personal belongings and then see you to the front door.

Job hopping has become a trend among fast trackers. The thinking is that each new job can bring greater challenges, a better title, more experience, and more compensation. And in many cases the mobile executive has her stay-in-one-place counterpart beat. Job hoppers, though, should be prepared to explain their jumping around. The reason for change is as important as the move itself. Interviewers may assume that the changes weren't the employee's choice.

When making any job change, especially if you've been hopping around, determine whether the mobility is helping you and your long-range career plans. Have you stayed in one place long enough to prove yourself and learn new skills? Is the move one that gives you greater opportunities, or are you going just for the sake of movement? Does the salary make the move worthwhile?

Frequent mobility may best serve the executive at the beginning of her career, when she needs to learn many skills, increase responsibility, and get into a high salary range. But job hopping to get fancier titles and higher salaries may not be the best way to climb to the top. A survey by Russell Reynolds Associates, an executive recruiting firm, found that 76 percent of chairmen or chief executive officers had been with their company for more than ten years. Fifty percent of them had remained with one company for more than two decades.

BOARD MEMBERSHIP

You know you've made it when you receive an invitation to sit on a corporate board of directors. This is one of the business world's highest accolades, offering tremendous prestige and the chance to work with—and learn from—the best business minds. But with this "reward" comes great responsibility.

Board members represent the stockholders of a company and are responsible for overseeing the wisdom of a company's major policy decisions. They spend much of their time listening to reports from the chief executive officer, committee chairpeople, and heads of subsidiaries. Their overriding concern is financial planning, managerial succession, and, increasingly, corporate ethics and government relations.

On the average, directors spend about 123 hours a year on board-related work and generally are compensated on both an annual and a per-meeting basis, averaging $17,000 total. Perks often include travel expenses, deferral of these board fees until retirement, and extra insurance coverage.

Currently most board members are men—of the 16,000 directorships in Fortune 1300 companies, only 3.3 percent are held by women. The main reason for this lopsidedness is that board members are chosen from the very top ranks of business, where women have just begun to penetrate. However, as the business climate becomes more competitive, companies need more than rubber-stamp boards made up of insiders; many now look for outside directors with pertinent expertise. The number of attorneys and commercial bankers on boards has declined, while the percentages of specialists, academics, and former government officials are on the rise.

Directors are selected through an elite and discreet network, either by recommendation or through recruiters. Sending in an application or résumé is considered a faux pas and a reflection of the naïveté of the applicant. Such ingenuousness is not the material boards look for.

If you're interested in future board membership, the best way to prepare yourself for an invitation is to develop high visibility and advance through the ranks to the top. Other desirable qualities include being adept at evaluating corporate strategy, knowing how to conduct industry analyses, and understanding the legal issues concerning the functions and responsibilities of corporations and their boards. Reading the *Harvard Business Review*'s column "From the Boardroom," *The Corporate Director, Directorship*, and *Director's Monthly* will make you conversant with such important topics.

The heady heights of the corporate boardroom are not for everybody. Flying this high calls for time, energy and devotion to a career beyond almost all else. Nevertheless, getting ahead, at *any* stage in the game, is no small matter. And neither is the reward. The payoff for all the work comes when you make that next step up. And with the payoff comes immense satisfaction.

6

WhoYou Know

Women are often ambivalent about using contacts to progress in work. They may describe their reluctance in various ways: "It's not nice to call someone only when you want something"; "We haven't been introduced"; "It's a sign of weakness to ask for help"; "Asking for help makes you obligated to people." Such attitudes show a lack of understanding of how contacts are used in the business world or of how the give and take of the phenomenon known as "networking" generates action and forward movement. Without people reaching out, there is no movement and eventually everything grinds to a halt.

Making and using contacts is an essential part of business communication. It's what justifies expense-account eating and drinking. People meet after work and go on talking about work. They lunch and dine together, and nobody assumes that they are doing it just because they like one another. Women still think that the best way to operate is to be likable, not pushy—by doing things through the proper channels. But working hard and keeping your nose down, hoping your reward will come in heaven, does not serve you or your company well.

Professional contacts in and of themselves will not get you a new job, but they can get you invited to interviews and inform you about employment opportunities that never make it to official channels. And when you are on the hiring side, trusted contacts can help you find the best possible candidate for the job.

Contacts help in all fields, but the smaller the field, the more important they are. In a limited field such as advertising, everyone is very visible and known. Sally Koslow wrote about another "closed" field in *Working Woman*: "The textile and garment manufacturing industry, though it serves most of the country, essentially is a tiny, Manhattan-based profession crowded into an area literally only ten blocks long and wide. Occasionally, openings are advertised in *Women's Wear Daily*, the trade newspaper, but it is very hard for an outsider to come into the industry. Getting jobs depends on whom you know, and connections are the only way employers can decipher what a person's experience really has been." In this industry, when you capitalize on a connection, it shows a certain aggressiveness that is looked upon favorably.

As we've already stressed in this book, finding a good job is not easy. And it's the job seeker's responsibility to use every resource she can. Both getting and doing a job, you need a network. Beyond friends, family, former colleagues and neighbors, your network can expand to include mentors, sponsors, professional associations, and business clubs. Some "experts" have been quick to point out that women are at a disadvantage when it comes to this kind of networking; they don't have ties similar to the ones the old-boy networks rely on, don't know the lingo of teams, and since many are relatively new to the work world, they don't have many favors to call in. But by taking a look at how men handle networking, women have learned the basics and adapted the system to their own needs.

Beyond their official groups, for example the Business Roundtable, men also have more informal support systems. Men learn strategies and game plans from other men in locker rooms, on the golf course, in fraternities and bars. Moreover, they see early in life how to work on a team in order to win. This is a lesson that serves men well in the business world. Women often shy away from bonding with people they wouldn't otherwise choose as friends— very likely because they were channeled away from sports at a young age. It is also true, as Rosabeth Moss Kanter points out, that "Lots of women know perfectly well how to play on teams, but it is very hard to play on a team that doesn't want you on it."

Talent and ability sometimes have less influence on success than background, and old-boy clubs offer good examples of this. Not until January 1982, for example, was The Century Club in New York forced to admit women into its lounge (at certain times), against the "better judgment" and stalwart opposition of many of its prominent male members. Such clubs are exclusive, elitist, white, male organizations where people who have power hoard it. Only occasionally do members of an elite share power with others, and then only with those carefully selected and judged to be sufficiently like themselves. This is not the stuff of networking.

Women in professional positions long ago realized that affirmative action

could take them only so far in the business world. They also saw that exchanges of information vital to that world were taking place in their absence.
This pointed to the need for some sort of organized network in which women
could get together with other professionals for mutual advancement.

Mary Scott Welch, who wrote the definitive book on networking for
women, gets the credit for turning "network" from a noun to a verb. Here is
her definition: "Networking is the process of developing and using your contacts for information, advice, and moral support as you pursue your career.
It's linking the women you know to the women they know in an ever expanding communications network. It's building a community of working
women across professional and occupational lines, outside the old boys'
network. It's helping each other to become more effective in the work world
—with more clout, more money, more know-how, more self-confidence.
It's beating the system that isolates women as they move up in male-dominated environments. It's asking for help when you need it—knowing *when*
you need it, knowing whom and how to ask for it. It's giving help, too,
serving as a resource for other women. In sum, it's getting together to
get ahead."

Any woman, whether she is a vice president of a corporation or its newest
trainee, can use networking for mutual support and professional benefit.
What's more, in today's high-tech society, information is power, connections
are a means to that power, and networking is a megatrend.

It's important to note that networking takes on two meanings. The less
structured method of networking is what people have been doing all along to
find jobs: they call on the people they know in order to meet people in their
chosen field. In the 1970s a more formal definition took hold. Women began
forming groups—networks—with fairly stable memberships that met regularly at each other's homes or in company conference rooms. The purpose of
these groups was much like that of informal networking—to meet the right
people. But these networks went a step further, because they set up a mutual
support system. Each member was not only looking for advice and information, she was willing to assist other members up the ladder by offering advice
on everything from the best headhunter to the best babysitter.

FINDING YOUR GROUP

To join an existing network, find women who are members of networks and
ask to attend their meetings to get an idea of the goals and activities of the
groups, and decide on the one that best suits your needs. Here are some tips
on joining a network:

Have a clear idea of your own goals—the reason to network.

Go to functions where you will meet professional colleagues (seminars, conferences, trade meetings).

Follow up on the first lead you get; you may talk to someone who can get you into her network with little trouble. If that first lead doesn't pan out, follow up on subsequent ones.

Make going on lunch dates and to parties and conferences a priority.

Make sure people begin to recognize who you are and what you do.

Set yourself time goals. Mary Scott Welch suggests that if you are serious about networking, you try to make three new contacts a week. One way to accomplish this is to set aside three lunches for networking activities (if your work requires meeting people for lunch, try to find equivalent after-hours time).

Know how to present yourself and give a good description of what you do.

Organize yourself. If you are planning extensive networking, you may find it useful to write down each new contact on a file card (also collect business cards), then cross-reference name, company, and occupation.

Make your personal limits known: "Don't call me at home during the evenings/on a Sunday."

Don't go network crazy. Be cautious about joining groups. Welch advises attending a couple of meetings, finding out about plans for the future, and then deciding.

Call ahead before you refer someone; this is network courtesy.

Don't be discouraged if you can't find the right group. It may not exist. In that case you may want to consider forming your own.

A woman or a group of women can start such a network organization themselves. Like any other major project, it can be approached with a step-by-step plan. The payoffs: Role models, others' experience to learn from, advice on how to juggle professional and personal imperatives, contacts for future job referrals.

Here are some pointers for starting a network (from Mary Scott Welch in *Working Woman*):

List twenty women you'd like to include in your network.

Include women who can offer good specific advice (a lawyer, a public relations specialist, someone with media contacts, a computer expert, a banker).

The best way to find women who are interested in forming a network is to get the word out about what you are trying to do. To find the names of top women in different fields, plug into various professional associations. Approach people carefully. Emphasize that the time commitment will be minimal but that during the formative weeks of the network you will need input and advice. This, says Welch, may appeal to their sense of duty to the women's movement.

Try to have at least three women who are known to be "doers," women who have a reputation for throwing themselves into fledgling organizations.

Set the date, time, and place for the first three meetings. Promise a report for those who want to join but can't make the meetings.

At the first meeting write a tentative statement of the purpose of the group.

Have ready for everyone: a list of those attending, with names, addresses, and phone numbers; name tags; a copy of the agenda. It's also a good idea to take a tape recorder along (unless the session is going to include confidential information).

Soon after the first meeting, talk to people to get their reactions.

Arrange for someone else to chair the next meeting—rotating leadership is important.

Formalize a way for the group to evaluate themselves every now and then. Set up a suggestion box.

One caution about networking is worth mentioning. Since it has become a major trend among both men and women, its potential for abuse has greatly increased. Many people with power in their fields have become disenchanted with the networking process because impatient networkers can be rude, expecting immediate interviews or breakfast or lunch meetings based on some tenuous connection or with a vague purpose.

If you are going to call one of your new executive contacts, you can counteract these impressions by suggesting a meeting in the person's office and by coming to it well prepared and with a clear purpose. Be courteous and keep the meeting short—half an hour is the limit.

Despite these precautions, it is a little easier now, in the mid-80s, to start or join a network than it was in the 70s. Beginners can benefit from the experiences of a decade of networking. In 1977, Diane Winokur founded the Bay Area Executive Women's Forum by approaching women in the San Francisco area with the idea of bringing together women with "like minds and similar experiences." This impressive network grew tremendously and now boasts of a membership of about 125. Here Winokur talks about the recent history of working women's networks.

Like many ideas that seem simple on the surface, the concept of women's networks was fraught with latent complexities. The first sign of trouble usually came during the organizational phase of their development. Should the network be a formal organization with bylaws, articles of incorporation, election of officers, rules of operation—or should it be informal? The dilemma was disturbing because there were no easy answers to these questions. There were no answers because an organized and informal network had never existed before. Men had informal networks and formal clubs. Women had formal clubs and, to a lesser extent, informal social networks. A totally new organization concept was needed, but at the time, few recognized this and they continued to force the networks into one or the other of the historical organization molds.

Another part of the crisis was leadership conflict. Like groupings of amoebae who are undecided whether to follow the leadership group or not to, women's networks had their own reservations about leadership and exercised a great deal of care to prevent members from taking over too much of the authority of the group. The leaderless group unfortunately is also the powerless group, as many women soon learned. While stating in principle that networks had been formed to grow and groom leaders, women suffered from confused and conflicting ideas on the nature and desirability of authority. Feeling that they had been repressed by authority most of their lives, women wanted to avoid anything that hinted at further domination.

Definition of purpose became the second impasse. Historically, women's organizations were founded and supported on the basis of their devotion to some greater good. As it became apparent that the prime purpose of the network was to enhance individual members' personal goals, there was much soul searching and discomfort. Every member looked to the network for fulfillment of her own needs, and priority of self often took precedence over urgent issues and matters of a pragmatic, administrative nature. Women mingled, women talked, cards were exchanged—some complained about the price of dinner, the price of drinks, the price of membership, MBA's balked at managing organizational paperwork, superwomen couldn't find the time to attend committee meetings.

Programming became a great ideological debate. No program suited everyone. Perspectives were distorted. Programs were only the means to bring women together. They were not intended to be the end also. The objective was to develop a network.

The most wrenching self-appraisal occurred, however, in the matter of membership criteria. Women who had themselves been excluded from membership in men's groups were unwilling to discriminate against other women. Yet many recognized that their own purpose in joining the organization could best be served if most members were at comparable professional levels. The battle lines were drawn on the front of elitism vs. sisterhood. There was a clear dichotomy in philosophy on the issue of membership. On the one hand, there were the true progeny of the women's movement who believed women were all in the battle together. This group favored networks open to all comers with no distinction based on career objectives or achievements. The message was that those who had moved up had a sisterhood obligation to pull others along. They assumed that unless they were bonded together, achieving women would abandon the younger or less experienced women who needed their support. The second group of networks was selective. These established membership criteria usually based on the level of positions held. Most of these groups included women from middle management on up. A few took their slice off the very top and required that a prospective member be the highest-ranking woman in her company and have distinguished herself professionally and personally. This second group looked to each other for support and for access. Their assumption was that through their collective power, they could push one, then another of the group into higher-level corporate positions, boards of directors, or significant appointments. In this way, they would open new frontiers and broaden the opportunity for all women . . .

In spite of the problems, networks did not become extinct; they matured. Darwin's evolution theory prevailed. Successful strategies begot survival. The membership policies of both groups underwent subtle refinements. Attitudes on the business of running a network grew more sophisticated with the introduction of paid administrators. Programming, in many cases, moved beyond the original soft programming of assertiveness training and dressing for success to the harder-line mainstream business and economic issues with which the moving-up women were more and more concerned.

In addition, new kinds of groups were formed. In some cases, they were called roundtables, or lunch groups—very informal; lunches—usually once a month, a changing group of members with a small permanent core, someone taking responsibility for bringing a program when there is a program, but often no program at all.

TWO AT THE TOP

Two women's networks stand out as prime examples of the power they can attract in terms of high-level members and sheer numbers. The Women's Forum, founded in 1973, now boasts about 600 members from Atlanta, Chicago, Denver, Los Angeles, San Francisco, and New York. The membership includes women who are well known in business, the professions, and the arts (including such women as Jane Pauley and Helen Reddy). The goal of the Women's Forum, beyond networking, is to consolidate its members' power and, in doing so, to rival such male professional bastions as the Business Roundtable.

The Committee of 200, founded in 1982, grew out of a research project by the National Association of Women Business Owners to identify the country's leading women entrepreneurs. To become a member a woman must own a business with an annual volume of at least $5 million or run a corporation or a corporate division with more than $20 million in corporate sales. There is also a required minimum level of income for membership. Hence the membership of the Committee of 200 includes the likes of Christie Hefner (Playboy, Inc.), Katharine Graham (Washington Post Company), Sherry Lansing (former president of 20th Century-Fox) and other top women in banking, retailing, manufacturing, and publishing. A glance at the membership roster makes it easy to understand why the Committee of 200 describes itself as the "vanguard" of a "rapidly growing economic force." President Patricia M. Cloherty says, "We are women who are accustomed to taking control and shaping the world we operate in."

Although the Committee of 200 claims diversity in terms of age, region, and industry/profession, as the *New York Times* pointed out, "The women in the Committee of 200 have only one thing in common: power."

These two networks have come under criticism for being elite. The *New York Times* writer put it this way: "Their selectivity is both their greatest strength and potentially most serious weakness." The women who belong to these two networks see themselves as being among equals, and in that sense the elitism is understandable. Jane Evans, the founder of the Committee of 200, says, "We all worked pretty hard for ten or fifteen years to get where we are. Now we can sit back and figure out what it takes to get there, the common bonds of our success. We can learn from one another and pass on our knowledge and experience to women still building businesses and climbing the corporate ladder. We do represent the power base of women in business in this country."

Whether exclusive or nonexclusive, "outside" networks are only one way for businesswomen to meet and exchange information. Women in many companies have also set up internal networks. Management is sometimes wary of this kind of network, fearing that it is too close to an organized movement or a union, or that it will lead to a cliquishness that can undermine team spirit. Anyone who wants to start an internal network usually has to proceed cautiously. When Alina Novak founded the Equitable internal network in 1976, she discovered how a network can evolve and the benefits it offers employees, despite management's possible concern. Novak talked to many women at Equitable and found support for developing a network. She then told the head of the personnel department what the group had in mind. Novak was encouraged to go ahead because Coy Ecklund, CEO of Equitable at the time, was sympathetic to the concerns of women and their careers.

Novak says that the network alleviated much of the isolation women in the corporation had felt. As time went on, top management got used to the idea and saw it as "something viable and nonthreatening." Eventually, informality somewhat broke down the network's structure. Meetings are now monthly and people see one another mostly at lunches or parties. Novak says that most women admit they now value the Equitable network more for friendships than for job opportunities. In fact, one of an internal network's shortcomings, Novak feels, is not enough anonymity about jobs. "It was like getting your résumé on the street," she complains. "No precautions could really be taken when discussing, say, boss problems."

Even if an internal network evolves itself out of existence, it's a signal to top management that women are serious about tackling the obstacles that may stand in their way of success.

It should be clear by now that there is no standard "women's network," but rather a whole gamut of them. In addition to the types of networks we've discussed, there are broad occupational/professional networks such as Women in Communications alongside narrow-cast occupational networks such as Women in Cable and exclusive occupational networks such as Women in Media. (It is conceivable that one woman in a media profession will belong to these three groups and more.) There are internal networks within corporations—those that are women-only networks and those that end up networking almost entirely with men. (It was interesting that men tended to show up for network functions in the Equitable internal network when the topic included money.) The kind of network a woman chooses depends on her reasons for networking in the first place.

Often power still lies in male groups, and the dangers of "separate but equal" must be obvious to most people by now. Many women find that women's networks are fine for consciousness-raising and peer support, but for power brokerage they also need to belong to groups that include men. Either way, the wide-eyed assumption some women had that belonging to a network, any network, would automatically put their careers on the fast track has given way to an understanding that networking is just one of many professional activities. Novak points out that women may need to belong to three kinds of professional organizations to get all the benefits: one that has both women and men, one for women in the particular field, and a women's network.

Many women's networks have a similar philosophy to some of the women's business clubs that are springing up across the country. That is, even though women have fought long and hard to get into male clubs because decisions are made there, women need what men have had for years without even a murmur of the word "separatist"—a place in which to gather strength and come out fighting.

Women's clubs are nothing new; they have been around since the 1830s. What's new is that now women's clubs are geared to the needs of business and professional women, and not to the social life of upper-class women.

While the cream of women's networks still tend to have a restricted membership, as a rule the new clubs are "open." "Inclusion" is their theme. The belief is that *all* businesswomen want, and need, a place to work, to take a client, to attend seminars, to combat professional isolation, to belong to a powerful lobby, or simply to unwind and have a drink with peers.

Some clubs are dual-sex and some are women only. Some are having start-up problems due to mismanagement, undercapitalization, and delays in construction. Some have strong support and for some of them support is slowly growing. But at least half a dozen women's clubs now flourish. Here is a listing of some of the popular women's clubs in North America:

THE BLAISDELL PLACE, 2322 Blaisdell Ave., Minneapolis, Minn. 55404; 612-872-2325
Facilities: Restaurant, nonalcoholic bar, informational lunches, art gallery, gym, exercise room, sauna, whirlpool.
Membership costs: Dues $1,000 for a lifetime; $250 for a regular membership; $100 for a social membership that allows the use of the dining room (20 percent discount in restaurant for all membership categories).
Eligibility: Regular memberships open to women only, men permitted to join as social members.
Nonresident memberships: Dues: $50 per year. No overnight accommodations.

THE CENTRAL EXCHANGE, 1020 Central Ave., Kansas City, Mo. 64105; 816-471-7560
Facilities: Restaurant (lunch), bar/lounge, programs and seminars.
Membership costs: Initiation: $250. Dues: $20 per month; $10 monthly minimum in the club's restaurant.

Eligibility: Women or men.
Nonresident memberships: Initiation: $250.
Dues: $25 per year.
No overnight accommodations.

THE ELMWOOD CLUB, 18 Elm Street, Toronto, Ont. Canada M5G 1G7; 416-977-6751
Facilities: Restaurant (open to public), lounges, bar, library, private dining/meeting rooms, gym facilities, hot tubs, sunbathing areas, and a fully equipped spa.
Membership costs: Annual membership: $1,000 per year or $100 per month; life membership (individual): $4,000 initiation, $450 annual dues; life membership (corporate): $5,500 initiation, $450 annual dues.
Eligibility: Women only.
Nonresident memberships: Life membership: $2,000 initiation, $150 annual dues, $7 user fee for health facilities.

THE EXECUTIVE CLUB INC., 1110 Vermont Ave., N.W., Suite 1150, Washington, D.C. 20005; 202-296-4775
Facilities: Two dining rooms, conference facilities, health spa, computer room, library, cocktail lounge, concierge services.
Membership costs: For individual: Initiation: $2,000. Dues: $65 per month. Corporate and association memberships also available.
Eligibility: Women only, by invitation or with two club sponsors. Male guests permitted to use conference facilities and dining rooms.
Nonresident memberships: Initiation: $1,000. Dues: $35 per month. Overnight accommodations.

LIBERTY CLUB, Executive Offices, 345 East 56th St., New York, N.Y. 10022; 212-593-2036. Temporary club space: 3 West 51 Street
Facilities: Bar, dining room, meeting room, music room, athletic facilities, spa, lounge.
Membership costs: Initiation: $850–1350. Dues: $750–1250. Fees range according to member's age.
Eligibility: Women or men, by invitation or sponsorship.
Nonresident memberships: Fees not set yet.
No overnight accommodations.

THE MCGILL CLUB, club and offices, 21 McGill St., Toronto, Ont., Canada M5B 1H3; 416-977-4122
Facilities: Restaurant, meeting rooms, gym, pool, exercise classes, nursery, lounges, private working areas, seminars, spa, sunbathing area on roof, bedrooms for naps.

Membership costs: Initiation: $500. Dues: $1,035 per year; members must invest in a $1,500 debenture.
Eligibility: Women only.
Nonresident memberships: Initiation: $500; $1,500 debenture. Dues: 40 percent of existing resident member dues.

WOMEN'S ATHLETIC CLUB OF THE BOSTON YMCA, 140 Clarendon St., Boston, Mass. 02116; 617-536-0991
Facilities: Restaurant, meeting rooms, lectures and seminars on career issues, investment club, full gym and fitness classes, pool, sauna, steam room.
Membership costs: Initiation: $150 for a full member, $50 for a social member. Dues: variable.
Eligibility: Women only; men permitted to use dining rooms as guests.
Nonresident memberships: Same costs as regular members. Overnight accommodations available through the Berkeley residence.

WOMEN'S COMMERCE CLUB, 1112 Peachtree St. N.E., Atlanta, Ga. 30309; 404-872-1091
Facilities: Three dining rooms, four conference rooms, lounge.
Membership costs: Initiation: $500. Dues: $30 per month.
Eligibility: Women or men.
Nonresident memberships: Initiation: $250. Dues: $15 per month. No overnight accommodations available.

Successful clubs have a few things in common, such as a full-time staff or professional manager to run the club; a restaurant or access to food facilities; educational programs and seminars; and addressing women's needs with fitness facilities and other perks. By fulfilling these requirements, women's clubs are becoming an attractive supplement to the networking scene.

A darker side of the "who you know" phenomenon is what has been called "the horizontal approach"—sleeping one's way to the top. There's not much to say on the subject apart from a brief reminder that sleeping "up" is usually hazardous to a woman's career; however good her professional skills are, she won't stay at the top for long if she alienates colleagues by her "special" status. Suffice to say that this is advice most women don't need because the casting couch phenomenon is more a product of the male imagination than the female game plan. Besides, it is clearly not a very successful stratagem; as one observer put it, "If women can sleep their way to the top, how come there aren't more of us up there?"

7
Managing in the 80s

One hardly thinks of the 1970s as revolutionary times in the United States, but for many corporations profound changes were underway. For the first time women began to appear in significant numbers in the ranks of corporate managers. From 1970 to 1979, the number of women managers and administrators more than doubled, reaching 2.5 million. And after two decades of hovering around the 15 percent mark, the proportion of women in these positions jumped up in the 70s. By 1982 it had reached almost 28 percent.

This "unprecedented revolution" coincided with other shocks to the American corporate system. After decades of steady growth, the formula that had kept America No. 1 lost its magic. Stable corporations that were the backbone of the economy faltered; some even disappeared. Whole new industries sprang up in completely different regions of the country. Foreign competition ravaged American markets.

Business leaders caught in the turmoil began casting about for new ways of managing. Fresh theories seemed to crop up every few months: MBO (management by objectives), job enrichment, Japanese management, theories X and Y, theory Z. Although none has proved to be the quick fix for America's ailing industries that many people were hoping for, all have contributed to the general ferment in management thinking and practices.

One striking result of this ferment has been the transformation of many American companies from rigid hierarchies to more flexible, decentralized structures with participative management styles. These new approaches would seem to augur well for women. They extend the definition of what is "managerial" beyond the military stereotype to include characteristics that

126

are thought of as traditionally female: an understanding, cooperative attitude, sensitivity to others, good listening skills, the ability to communicate openly and to work with others.

If indeed, as some experts think, women do tend toward a more caring, collaborative management style, with less attention to defending turf and establishing hierarchies, then why aren't more women getting promoted to top management? For one thing, it may be too early to tell how deep the transformations have gone. Corporate attitudes tend to change with glacial slowness. Despite the influx of women, sex discrimination is still a problem, according to Margaret Hennig and Anne Jardim, coauthors of the pathbreaking *The Managerial Woman* and deans of the School of Management at Simmons College in Boston.

Many male managers, according to Hennig and Jardim, want to eat their cake and have it. They acknowledge the success of the new management techniques, but underneath they still feel the macho style is valid. If they promote men, they tell themselves, and the new style doesn't pan out, the man can revert to being macho. But for women, they reason, it's not a style but their real personality. Women, then, are grappling with what *Working Woman* calls the "wimp factor." Any manager who allies herself with the new style takes the risk of not appearing tough enough to do the job.

But sex discrimination isn't the only barrier to advancement. Change itself is causing men *and* women to feel that the ground is shifting under their feet. The thinning of middle management ranks in the recent recessions may signal more permanent changes in corporations. In a sense, today's executives are always managing *for* change. Figuring out what makes companies tick and what you need to know to be an effective (and promotable) manager isn't easy. That's why as a manager you must take a close look at your company's structure and management style. Ask yourself: How do *I* fit into this particular organization? What qualities does this company value in its managers? What skills do I need to be effective there?

To answer these questions, it helps to understand the dramatic changes that have taken place over the last two decades—changes in corporate structures and cultures, indeed, in America's very way of doing business.

OLD-STYLE MANAGING: MILITARY MODE

For years—and with successful results—companies were modeled on the military. Even today the military metaphor dominates many people's thinking about management. CEO generals commanded middle-management majors and captains in a hierarchy in which commands flowed in one direction—from the top down. How did women fit in? Not well. As management consultant Betty Harragan points out in *Games Mother Never Taught You,* "Not only do women have no useful military background, [but] those who are career-minded and ambitious find the thought anathema. Striving women are naturally inclined to be independent, rebellious and assertive . . . so the well-known army requirements of obedience, mass living and taking orders are repellent." Even those men who lack military experience are able to understand and accept it more easily than women do, Harragan argues, for most were exposed to it as they grew up (through cops-and-robbers games, uncles' war stories, playing with toy soldiers).

To be sure, these military-inspired operations called in human-relations specialists and industrial psychologists to make the well-oiled machine run more smoothly, but on the whole, businesses were standardized mass production machines, operated according to "scientific" principles. Impressive organization charts divided managers and workers into specialized functions, with clear lines of command. Professional managers took over the planning and monitoring that operating people didn't have the time or knowledge to attend to. Thus the separation of line and staff, of the doers from the thinkers. Business was run according to a predetermined set of rules, and efficiency was the key.

For half a century, until the late 1960s, the system ran pretty much like clockwork. That is, men ran things and women (and other men) took orders. America's productivity grew at an average rate of 2.3 percent a year, and U.S. companies became—and remained—world leaders in such industries as automobiles, steel, petrochemicals, electrical equipment. Stability reigned: many of the companies that dominated the economy in 1920—U.S. Steel, B.F. Goodrich, International Harvester, for example—still did so fifty years later.

Ironically, just at the time when French editor Jean-Jacques Servan-Schreiber was calling on Europeans to meet the "American challenge" of our management genius, things began to fall apart. Starting in the mid-1960s, the growth rate in productivity began to slow down. In the years from 1979 to 1981, productivity itself actually declined. Foreign competitors—especially the Japanese—made inroads into the very industries that had been the bedrock of American prosperity. By 1981, the United States was importing about a quarter of its cars and its steel. Newer industries weren't faring any better, either. Sixty percent of televisions, radios, and stereo equipment was imported. What was causing the great industrial machine to falter?

Business leaders pointed to a number of causes: high energy costs caused by OPEC oil-price hikes, the straitjacket of government regulation, double-digit inflation that eroded profits, record-breaking capital-investment costs resulting from soaring interest rates, uncertain monetary and fiscal policies. While all these events took their toll, of course, they didn't fully explain the sluggish American economy. As business professors Robert H. Hayes and William J. Abernathy observed in a 1980 *Harvard Business Review* article, other countries fared better under similar, or even worse, conditions. They pointed out, for instance, that Germany imports 95 percent of its oil, compared to our 50 percent. In addition, the German government takes an even greater share of its country's gross domestic product than the U.S. government does. "Yet Germany's rate of productivity growth has actually increased since 1970 and recently rose to more than four times ours."

Aside from the political and economic shocks of the decade, other forces challenged the complacency of American business. For the first time since World War II, the United States had to compete with world-class rivals in a world market. American corporations found their own techniques of competitive pricing and innovative technology being used against them. During the 1970s, according to Department of Commerce figures, the United States' share of world markets declined by 23 percent.

The acceleration of technological change was yet another force affecting the business environment. New production methods and products could make traditional manufacturing or marketing systems obsolete overnight. To get a competitive edge, companies had to be agile. And so did managers. They were no longer supervising a predictable economic machine.

Transformations in the workforce added another new dimension to the corporate world of the 1970s and 1980s. More and more women, many of them with children, were working, and a growing number of them were rising above secretarial and clerical positions. Indeed, the two-wage household became the norm rather than the exception. Workers were better educated, and a larger proportion were young. Their attitudes too were very different from those of the 1950s. The 60s counterculture hadn't killed the work ethic, but it certainly had changed it. No longer were workers willing to obey their employers' demands unquestioningly. They wanted jobs that not only paid well but offered a chance for self-fulfillment, for growth and responsibility. They expected more of a say in how and when they did their work, and they wanted more time for themselves and their families.

All these pressures did not lead to immediate and sweeping changes in the way companies were run. And the changes that did occur often seemed misdirected. One reaction of corporate management has been what many observers consider an obsessive attention to the bottom line, an emphasis on short-term financial returns over deeper changes that could lead to long-term corporate health. Top executives, who increasingly come from financial and legal rather than production backgrounds (as Hayes and Abernathy show), have responded with what they know best—numbers. If a product line isn't doing well, the instinct is to sell off the unprofitable division rather than focus on the quality or marketing of the product.

As the economist Robert Reich points out in *The Next American Frontier*, instead of responding with technological or institutional innovations, the "innovations [have been] on paper . . . based on accounting, tax avoidance, financial management, mergers, acquisitions, and litigation. Gradually over the past fifteen years, America's professional managers have become paper entrepreneurs." These maneuvers, he points out, do not create new wealth. "They simply rearrange industrial assets."

Executives have also turned to Japan in their search for answers, and Japanese management has become the pet subject of seminars, books, and business articles that seek to explain the secret of Japan's global business success. But adding a few quality circles to a company is not going to make up for the shortcomings of rigid corporate structures and autocratic or shortsighted management practices. American companies can learn from the Japanese experience, but it won't provide them with any quick solutions to their problems.

The picture of the last fifteen years hasn't been all doom and gloom, however. Some American companies have managed to combine strategies, structures, and what has been dubbed "corporate culture"—a sense of shared values and beliefs—and have thrived even during the hard years.

Let's look first at some of the structural innovations that companies have made. Many of these changes reflect attempts to become more flexible: companies had to be able to respond quickly to unpredictable and rapidly changing market conditions. Sometimes, too, the changes were designed to deal with ever more complex business decisions and with the character of the new workforce. These new approaches spelled good news for women. Because many such changes were evolving while the "unprecedented revolution" was underway, women could operate within them to broader and better advantage than in the old system.

THE MATRIX

A common modification to the traditional rigid functional hierarchy has been the matrix organization. This structure was developed by NASA to coordinate the work of the many contractors and subcontractors needed for the exceedingly complex moon-landing program. The apparent ability of the matrix organization to handle large, multifaceted problems by drawing on the input of various functions led to its adoption by many corporations.

Basically, the matrix cuts across the columns (functions) on the organization chart, linking people horizontally as well as vertically. An engineer, for instance, may report to several bosses—directly to the head of engineering, say, on the vertical chart, and then in a "dotted line" to the head of a particular product line or market segment. A number of cross-functional "teams" may exist in a company at a single time, each working on a different project. Individuals may work on several teams at once, while continuing to operate in their own functional groups. The network of horizontal teams superimposed on the functional lines thus forms a matrix.

In a multiple-reporting system, a senior manager in the functional line might find herself reporting to a lower-level manager whose specialty makes her the natural leader of a project team. Andrew Grove, president of Intel Corporation (the company that invented the computer memory chip and microprocessor), tells of such an experience in his book *High Output Management*. As a member of a strategic-planning group, he reports to the division controller who is its chairman, thus inverting the expected situation of controller reporting to president. The system, Grove says, "allows me to serve as a foot soldier rather than as a general when appropriate and useful. This gives the organization important flexibility."

An advantage of the matrix is that people with the knowledge and various technical skills to solve a particular problem can be brought together on a team, which has the authority to make decisions. In theory, this means more efficient and effective decision making.

Some experts argue that the matrix can be conducive to innovation as well. Rosabeth Moss Kanter studied fifty companies over five years to explore the conditions that lead to innovation. (She reports on her findings in *The Change Masters: Innovation for Productivity in the American Corporation*.) Kanter found that matrix-like conditions cutting across organizational boundaries encourage innovation because they give people "an incentive to move beyond the box of their own job." For innovation to occur, "complexity is essential: more sources of information, more angles on the problem, more freedom to walk around and across the organization."

The complexity of the matrix may cause trouble, though. The lack of clear reporting lines can be confusing to all participants. Which of four bosses holds real authority, people may wonder. And bosses may struggle with one another over whose priorities should come first on a subordinate's to-do list. Because of the potential for conflict in a matrix system, managers must understand the importance of communication and be able to deal with conflict openly. Typically "feminine" characteristics—mutual supportiveness, two-way communication, sensitivity to others—thus become prized managerial qualities, which is a promising sign for women.

Another pitfall of matrix systems is that the paperwork necessary to coordinate the many project teams can mean additional layers of staff and bureaucracy just to manage the matrix. As Thomas Peters and Robert Waterman, Jr., found in their study of excellent companies for McKinsey & Company, the project team or task force can become "just another part in the rigid system it was meant to fix." Their book *In Search of Excellence* reports that in some companies "paper pushing and coordination took the place of task-directed activity. Stodgy, formal, paperbound, rule-driven institutions layered the task force on a maze that lay beneath, rather than using it as a separable, action-inducing chunk. Task forces became nothing more than coordinating committees—with a different name." In one company they studied, not one of the 325 task forces in existence had completed its work in three years.

Texas Instruments is a good example of what can happen when the matrix gets out of control. That company's much-heralded matrix management, with its strategic and operating components, has been blamed recently for many of the firm's financial troubles. The planning system had become cumbersome and slow-moving—"a paperwork mill," according to one former employee. Managers of profit-and-loss centers lost control of their own strategic planning and no longer oversaw production of the products for which they were responsible. A recent reorganization restored some vertical integration, giving managers responsibility for all aspects of their product lines.

A *Business Week* cover story on Texas Instruments reported that the matrix may also have suffered from what some company insiders see as top management's autocratic management style. While the firm's founders allowed ideas and product innovation to percolate up from below, the inheritors of the firm imposed their will from above, a style more in keeping with strict hierarchical organizations.

ADHOCISM

To avoid such drawbacks of the matrix, some companies have tried variations in organizational design that go by such names as adhocracies and parallel organizations. The emphasis here is on temporary teams.

In an adhocracy (a term coined by management professor Warren Bennis), various self-managed work teams are brought together for a particular purpose or project and then disbanded. The corporate structure is a fluid, flexible one.

Successful task forces or work teams follow certain rules, according to Peters and Waterman:

They are small, typically ten or fewer people.
Task force members have the authority to "make stick whatever they recommend."
They are pulled together rapidly, when needed, and don't have formal written charters.
Follow-up is swift.
No permanent staff ("paper shufflers") is assigned to them.
Reports are informal and often scant, keeping paperwork to a minimum.
Communication is intense among the team members.

In Kanter's "parallel organization," a set of flexible, temporary teams is set up parallel to the line or operating organization. As in the matrix, team leaders are drawn from all levels of the company. The mandate of the teams, as Kanter sees it, is to innovate and solve problems: to continually "reexamine routines; explore new options; and develop new tools, procedures and approaches—that is, to institutionalize change."

A steering committee coordinates the teams and links their work to the operating organization. It makes sure, for instance, that any new procedures the teams devise are implemented. The steering committee also focuses the work of the various groups, avoiding a situation in which they report to no one and have no firm assignment. And as issues change and new problems come up, it can pull together a new configuration of teams. Such a system insures the cross-fertilization of ideas and the participation of all levels of the organization that are so necessary for innovative action.

One of the keys to any kind of multiple-reporting system, of course, is to make sure that coordination doesn't take the place of the task at hand. According to Grove: "We should mercilessly slash away at unnecessary bureaucratic hindrance, apply work simplification to all we do, and continually subject all established requirements for coordination and consultation to the test of common sense."

INTRAPRENEURSHIP

To foster innovation, some companies are going so far as to encourage their managers to set up entrepreneurial ventures within the company. Acknowledging that innovation requires different conditions in which to flourish, these companies are breaking off small ventures from the company bureaucracy, often giving them all the manufacturing, engineering, marketing, and other supports that any new business needs.

To provide incentives to "intrapreneurs," companies are experimenting with special compensation packages that give a percentage of the return to successful innovators. Management consultant Jay Galbraith, in an address to the Conference Board, a New York–based business advisory organization, gave some examples of these schemes: Some toy and game companies have offered a royalty to inventors, both inside as well as outside the company. A chemical company put aside 4 percent of the first five years' earnings from a new business venture, creating a pool of funds to be distributed to the initial venture team. Some companies have experimented with duplicating the free-market process—giving internal people the same venture-capital opportunities they would have on the outside.

Unfortunately, many of these corporate ventures have failed within five years. According to Gifford Pinchot III, the consultant who coined the term "intrapreneur," and who has helped major corporations start new businesses, the cause of failure is often management techniques that stifle entrepreneurship rather than encourage it. Still, the experiments reflect an ongoing concern with revitalizing corporate structures and strategies.

LEAN MANAGEMENT

The recession of the past few years compelled many companies to make even more dramatic changes in their company structures. In tight times, many simply could not support the large staffs they had built up in the fat times of the 60s and 70s. Companies began to shrink the size of their middle-management ranks, laying off as much as 40 percent of their staffs or even eliminating several layers in the hierarchy. There were other reasons for the move to "lean, mean" structures as well. Smaller, cheaper, and more "user-friendly" computers could take over the information-gathering and dissemination role of some staff positions. Executives also wanted to speed up the decision-making process, while making it more effective and responsive. By whittling down the size of their staffs and pushing decision making down the hierarchy, companies hoped to get closer to the customer.

For middle managers, this thinning of the ranks has meant more competition for fewer jobs. Women, too, have added to the number of competitors. And without enough opportunity to go around, women have often become a convenient target for the resentment of stymied male managers.

CULTURES

Imaginative corporate structures are not in themselves a guarantee of improved business performance. Researchers have found that truly well-run, successful companies have strong corporate cultures—a set of values or guiding beliefs shared by people at all levels of the organization. These values may be summed up in simple maxims such as "IBM means service," or they may be left unstated, existing merely as a sense of "the way we do things around here," as one McKinsey consultant put it. Whatever form the values take, they become a motivating force, spurring people to add "something extra" to their jobs and feel proud of the products or services they deliver.

How excellent firms develop cultures and transmit them to their employees is the subject of *Corporate Cultures: The Rites and Rituals of Corporate Life*, by Terrence Deal and Allan A. Kennedy. From the outside, a corporate culture can look odd, even incomprehensible, with its seemingly corny rituals and awards for performance. But it is through these rites and rewards that a company's beliefs are cemented and transmitted. These firms have heroes—individuals whose devotion to the corporate values often takes on mythic proportions. Heroes become role models. Deal and Kennedy tell the story of Mary Kay Ash, founder of the $300-million Mary Kay Cosmetics. Her message is that success is possible, and she uses herself as an example. Saleswomen are trained "not simply to represent her, but to believe that they *are* Mary Kay." To reinforce the identification, she awards diamond bumblebee pins to top saleswomen. The bumblebee, with its tiny wings and heavy body, shouldn't be able to fly. But bumblebees don't know this, and so they fly anyway. "The message is clear: Anyone can be a hero if they have the confidence and the persistence to try."

Cultures, according to Deal and Kennedy, have their storytellers (who transmit corporate values through legends) and their gossips (who do the same through the grapevine). The tales often travel far beyond the confines of the company, generating a mystique about the firm and its products. Those told about Delta Airlines and its employees' fanatic devotion to the company are an example.

The innovating firms that Rosabeth Moss Kanter studied all convey a sense of excellence to their employees. This "culture of pride" makes people feel important and special, and as a result, Kanter writes, they tend to be more confident about themselves and others. Innovating firms have, above all, "cultures of change," a commitment to new ideas and directions as a positive value, not an aberration. One computer firm Kanter studied, for example, characterizes itself as "a company with 10,000 entrepreneurs."

A company's culture naturally has a big influence on how well its structures work. In a culture that emphasizes action, task forces probably won't become bureaucratic tangles. In one that emphasizes "getting the job done," the confusion of a dual-reporting system will more likely be successfully resolved.

WHAT MANAGERS DO

There have been all sorts of changes in corporate structures and cultures. Still, the manager may ask, What exactly is my job? Given the uncertainty and complexity of today's business world, how do effective managers get their jobs done? Indeed, what does a manager do?

In answering these questions it's hard to make generalizations, because managers must, to some extent, suit their practices to their company and the people with whom they work. That's why, as we mentioned earlier, it's very important, even before joining a company, to assess how compatible your personal characteristics and style will be with a company's structure and culture.

One thing is clear, though. Managers—even good ones—are not the careful, methodical planners they were once thought to be. In fact, the stereotype of the manager as one who coolly controls, plans, and organizes doesn't seem to fit at all with recent findings on managerial behavior. What emerges from studies such as those by business professors Henry Mintzberg and John P. Kotter is a less structured, more haphazard picture.

Managers work long hours (we all knew that) and at an unrelenting pace (not surprising, either). But managers' days do not unfold according to a carefully devised plan, with large chunks of time set aside for distinct activities. In fact, much of a typical managerial day is unplanned, with managers reacting to others' initiatives to shape a large part of their day's activities.

Indeed, managers spend most of their time with others, according to the Kotter study. The most effective managers build up networks of hundreds of people in addition to their subordinates and bosses, often going outside the formal chain of command, or even the company, to make their contacts. The many conversations they engage in tend to be short and disjointed, switching from topic to topic and covering subjects well beyond typical "management" concerns. These exchanges often include a good deal of joking and nonwork topics that even the managers themselves seem to consider a waste of time. And they rarely seem to result in "big" decisions.

Managers tend to be strongly action-oriented and to dislike reflective activities, according to Mintzberg. They are unlikely to rely on formal sources of information, preferring a quick phone call or meeting to a report or the company's Management Information System. They typically ask a lot of questions. Intel's Grove, for instance, applies his Principle of Didactic Management: ask one more question. Face-to-face meetings allow managers to gather information and at the same time share it with others.

Let's take a closer look now at the skills today's effective managers must have. If managing is defined as getting something done through people, a strong corporate culture and good organizational structure will obviously make the manager's job a lot easier. Where employees share a common sense of values—a culture to guide their day-to-day behavior—and a system with the resources and structures to encourage creative and productive work, one might almost think there was no need for managers. But, of course, there is no ideal company in which the sheer elegance of its organizational design and a completely coherent culture motivate and guide people to make all the right decisions at the right time. As Kotter points out, managers must "figure out what to do despite uncertainty, great diversity, and an enormous quantity of potentially relevant material and [they] must get things done through a large and diverse set of people despite having little direct control over most of them."

Bogged down in paperwork, coping with seemingly intractable problems, and trying to reconcile contradictory demands, managers can easily lose a sense of purpose. Focusing on day-to-day efforts, managers can lose sight of the goal: to produce results for the company. They have always needed to use special skills and tools to meet the demands of their jobs and at the same time hold on to the longer view, but today many of the skills that were useful in the old-style hierarchies are no longer appropriate. The managerial role is changing.

Here are some of the skills all effective managers put to work:

A participative, cooperative management style. Kanter tells a story in *The Change Masters* that vividly illustrates the cost of not encouraging people's participation in an enterprise. A new textile-plant manager wanted to improve communications with the plant employees and get them more involved. During talks with people at the plant the manager met a worker who suggested a way to solve a longstanding yarn-breakage problem. The shocking thing was that the worker had thought of the solution thirty-two years earlier! "Why didn't you say something before?" the manager asked. The reply: "My supervisor wasn't interested, and I had no one else to tell it to."

Good managers know the value of the people who work for them. They solicit their ideas, involve them in making decisions, and encourage them to contribute. But what of the wimp factor? Will women appear weak if they espouse a participative management style? Jardim thinks that women can identify with the new style by their actions, without making an issue of it.

Participative management doesn't mean issuing edicts to contribute or dumping distasteful tasks on subordinates. It does mean giving them a piece of the action, delegating responsibility *and* the authority to get a job done. Friendly chats by the water cooler don't necessarily mean you're practicing participative management, either. Much more important is thoughtful concern about a subordinate's work. Participative managers set high standards, keep in close touch about work, ask lots of questions, and follow up on jobs they delegate.

A manager's role as boss is only one context in which she will find herself working with others. Teamwork is a fact of corporate life today, whether it's on a labor/management committee, a quality circle, an innovation task force, or as part of a matrix. If these teams are to be productive, back-room plotting, carving out a turf and defending it, and pulling rank are out. Cooperation is essential. Naturally, the corporate culture will have a great influence on how well teams operate in a particular company. But individual managers can set a tone too.

Although women tend not to pay excessive attention to territories, they may still be at a disadvantage when it comes to teamwork. Like the army, team sports are not part of most women's growing up experiences. As Harragan points out, women have a lot to learn about team playing: putting the good of the team and the success of the common effort first, taking defeats in stride, understanding that criticism of your performance by teammates is done to guide you and correct mistakes, not to insult you personally, knowing that you can't win (or lose) them all.

Working in groups requires a manager's patience. Decision making can be laboriously slow and involve many hours of meetings. And while browbeating or railroading may be the quickest route to a decision, this kind of behavior obviously short-circuits participative management. Managers must use other tools to lead groups and streamline decision making.

Ability to sell ideas, persuade others. Managers can no longer bark orders and expect to be obeyed. Workers are not willing to obey unquestioningly, and in any case, more and more companies are trying to push decision making down through the ranks. The most effective managers, then, rarely give commands. As Kotter's study found, "instead of telling people what to do, they ask, request, cajole, persuade and [even] intimidate" in order to influence others. Intel's Grove comments that for every clear directive managers give, "they probably 'nudge' things a dozen times."

Powers of persuasion—political skills—are a must for managers, who increasingly work with people over whom they have no direct authority or control. Intrapreneurs must sell management on their project if they want to get the venture funded. Matrix managers must vie with other managers for their subordinates' time. Managers who draw on diverse functions within a company to get their work done have to be able to build a team. This often means fighting for a share of one's peers' or even superiors' scarce time. Some of the skills needed here are the same ones required for playing office politics. Women, who may be conditioned to put others' office priorities ahead of their own, have to pay special attention.

The "Susan Robinson" case study published by *Working Woman* last year reveals some of the skills needed to build a team. Prepared by management consultants Rosabeth Moss Kanter, Allan R. Cohen, and Tana Pesso, the case study shows how Susan recruits people for a task force that her boss, Frank, has asked her to form. The task force's assignment is to design a performance-appraisal system for the sales force of a new group of products. Here's how Susan gets Jim O'Neill, an executive in her company, to join her team.

When Susan approaches Jim, his first reaction is that he's too busy. His questions to Susan are revealing, though: "Who knows about this already? Is anyone backing Frank?" When Jim finds out that he is the first person Susan has approached and that Home Office doesn't know about the project yet, he is worried. "I don't know, Susan," he says. "It sounds awfully risky to me."

The questions Jim asks give Susan some clues about what is important to him and what points she should play up. Jim is obviously very political, always tracking who is up and down in an organization. Susan's approach to Jim builds on this point.

"Let me tell you why this would be useful to you. There's a possible reorganization coming, and all of us could be in jeopardy. This task force guarantees us a chance to talk to a lot of people about something dear to everyone's heart: money. Furthermore, we're guaranteed an audience with Frank's boss at Home Office and probably with his staff as well. If we do a halfway decent job, we get some terrific exposure. Could that hurt when they start to shuffle jobs down here?"

Susan manages to get Jim on board by pointing out how membership on the task force could enhance his position in the department and by showing him that she has political smarts, too. To recruit people successfully to your team you need to listen carefully to each person and point out what stake she or he might have in joining.

Ability to communicate. If more ideas from more people mean better decisions, then promoting open communications is vital for managers. Indeed, the best companies, according to Peters and Waterman, have "rich ways of communicating informally." Hewlett-Packard values "Management by Wandering Around," Levi Strauss calls its open-door policy "the fifth freedom."

Good managers, it seems, spend a lot of time talking to other people and asking questions. They rely on informal sources—conversations, phone calls, meetings, even gossip—for both gathering and giving out information. Managers obviously need to know the facts and issues to make intelligent decisions, to put together a picture of how things are going and what needs to be done. As Kotter reports, the managers who develop the best agendas do so "by more aggressively seeking information from others (including 'bad news'), by more skillfully asking questions."

But these exchanges are equally important for imparting information. Subordinates need information to do a job: no delegation will be successful without it. Subordinates need not just facts but a sense of how the manager wants things done. By communicating your objectives, priorities, and preferred approaches, says Grove, you "nudge an individual or a meeting in the direction you would like." In other words, managers communicate both the corporate culture and their personal styles.

Making decisions. Businesses face increasingly complex issues today, and managers need to be able to make decisions in a climate of ambiguity, change, diversity. Often, too, decisions are not left in one person's hands. In teamwork, for instance, the individual abdicates her decision-making power to the group. This means she has to be willing to trust her colleagues and stand by the group decision.

What's more, she has to gain the trust of her colleagues. This may be tough because many men in corporations still haven't learned to trust women managers. The problem often is that women just don't fit the conventional idea of a manager (which is, of course, male). In other words, they're not managerial clones; they're different. At senior levels, according to Hennig, "it has less to do with whether you're a competent financial person—by now you've proven that—than with your ability to be seen . . . as the kind of person [male managers] can basically trust." And it's hard to combat this individually, she says. Only the continued and increasing presence of women in top corporate jobs will really help.

In group decision making, discussions may drag on in no obvious direction and with no end in sight. In a group of peers or in a situation where it's not always clear who's in charge (as in a matrix), people may be confused about who has the authority to make a decision. Or they may be afraid to stick their necks out or sound dumb. Even without these problems, decision making is complicated and time-consuming.

This handy list of questions (drawn up by Grove) may help you to focus the process before it begins: "What decision needs to be made? When does it have to be made? Who will decide? Who will need to be consulted before making a decision? Who needs to ratify or veto the decision? Who will need to be informed of the decision?" It helps to keep in mind a tip from management expert Peter Drucker as well: thinking about what will be acceptable, rather than right, only muddies the issues. You always have to compromise in the end, but if you don't know what is right, you may make the wrong compromise.

A good decision can't be rushed. All the issues must be raised—even the "bad news." As Grove points out, this means getting beyond the superficial comments that often dominate early stages of a discussion. But once disagreements have been thoroughly aired, it is equally important to push for a decision.

There can be pluses to group decision making. When American managers complain that the Japanese take so long to make group decisions, Japanese managers are apt to point out that once a decision has been reached, action follows quickly, whereas Americans make lots of quick decisions but it takes forever to implement them. When a group works together on the decision-making process, it's an easier step to turn a plan into action. Middle managers working in a matrix interviewed by Kanter confirmed this point.

Planning. Instead of the systematic, formal planning one might expect, for most managers planning is part of their everyday activities, something that often remains in their heads rather than on paper. Some kind of planning is important, though, to avoid the trap of responding equally to every issue that comes up. As Mintzberg writes in the *Harvard Business Review,* managers who respond abruptly as things come up "will never work the bits and pieces of information into a comprehensive picture of their world."

Management by objectives is one planning tool that managers can use to sort out and focus on the key results they want to achieve for their company. MBO gives managers a way to figure out where they want to go—their objective—and map out the concrete steps to get there. Managers draw up objectives jointly with their staff, establishing departmental and individual goals. By putting the goals in writing and adding a target date for achieving them, managers are less likely to be caught up in busywork. Goals should be achievable within months rather than years, and they should be specific. In the companies Peters and Waterman studied, they found that "activity-based" MBO systems ("Get the Rockville plant on line by July 17") were more common than financially based ones.

Another trap to avoid, of course, is setting too many goals. As the saying goes at Texas Instruments: "More than two objectives is no objectives." Too many goals means loss of focus.

Resolving conflicts. Conflict is practically built into the new corporate structures where authority is no longer automatically synonymous with the job title. All participants in a matrix, for instance, need to be able to resolve conflicts: the boss above two managers locked in a struggle over one subordinate, the managers themselves, and the subordinate. When people's jurisdictions are fuzzy, and there are fewer rules and regulations to govern how work gets done, managers need finely tuned negotiating skills to mediate conflicts. One thing to remember: Don't waste time placing blame or demonstrating how you're not guilty. It can be better spent working toward a solution to the problem.

Consistency. "A boss in whom people can believe," Eliza G. C. Collins writes in *Executive Success,* "is trustworthy, in the sense that people see her as consistent. Leaders don't make capricious decisions; [they] educate by example, through consistently embodying their own values in shaping their organizations over time."

Inconsistency in a manager can have disastrous effects on productivity and morale. People learn how to do a job successfully through feedback from their boss and by following her example. When managers give contradictory signals about what is important in a job, frequently change their minds about priorities and deadlines, or abruptly change standards by which work is judged, subordinates get confused and begin to doubt their own abilities. They hesitate to make decisions, fearful that they won't make the right ones, and they become anxious and insecure. Inconsistency is a terrible time waster, too. Jobs end up being done twice, or surbordinates check back with the manager at every step of the way, unable to predict what the best direction should be.

Where do all these changes in management styles, corporate structures, and cultures leave women? Some theorists argue that the best managers are neither stereotypically female nor stereotypically male but combine the best qualities of both in an androgynous style. Thus they are task-oriented, rational, tough-minded ("male") but also people-oriented, communicative, cooperative ("female").

But perhaps the emphasis on stereotypes simply perpetuates the idea that women and men always act in ways particular to their gender. One thing is certain: women managers must master the same management techniques as their male colleagues. The difference may lie, as Betty Harragan puts it, in the "road to learning these skills [which] must include recognition of the uniquely female barriers that women will encounter."

Women in middle management are on the front lines now. The challenge is to move up at a time when many of the rules are changing, and when relatively few women have done so before them. What's more, economic pressures are heating up the competition. The changes can be to women's advantage. In a way, they put women on the same footing as male managers, who must also learn the new rules. Nevertheless, the old guard still occupies many of the positions farther up the ladder. It is up to them to choose who shall be promoted to the top positions. If indeed they still have trouble seeing women as appropriate top executives, there may be a lot of frustrated ambitions in store for women managers. Still, the sheer force of numbers is certain to push more and more women into the upper echelons of corporate America. There is promise in that.

Benefits and Rights of Work

You think you're entitled to a vacation, a paid hour for lunch, and the Fourth of July off with pay? The grim truth is that you're entitled by law to none of these things. In fact, you're entitled to very little.

What your employer is required to provide for you is mandated by a combination of federal and state laws. Federal law requires a minimum wage for most employees plus paid overtime. Eligible employees are also entitled to Social Security benefits. State laws cover such areas as required breaks in the work day and workers' compensation or disability payments if you are injured or become ill. Unemployment insurance is also handled by the states. Almost everything else is up to your employer.

The things you're not entitled to include a paid vacation; paid holidays (even national ones, unless you are a government employee or work for a company that is required to shut down, such as a bank); sick leave with pay; a pension; health insurance; and disability benefits if you are injured or become ill for reasons that are not related to your job. (California, Hawaii, New Jersey, Rhode Island, New York, and Puerto Rico do have state programs that provide income for jobholders sidelined for non-job reasons.) You aren't even owed a paid hour off for lunch. Most states require only a thirty-minute break if you work more than six hours in one day.

However, this is a market economy with certain established practices. Employers can't get the good employees they need if they don't offer benefit packages that are competitive with other companies in the area. Many of

144

these benefits were won painfully over the years as some of the gains made by unions trickled into the job market as a whole. And once a job benefit is in a contract of any kind, the employer *is* required to provide it.

This chapter looks at both the rights you have as an employee (and must provide if you are an employer) and the job benefits that many companies offer.

YOUR RIGHTS

Though job benefits vary widely, three crucial legal rights apply to them.

First, although a company doesn't have to give the same benefits to everyone (unionized workers or high-level managers may have more benefits than other groups within a company), it may not discriminate in the benefits it provides solely on the basis of race, sex, national origin, religion, or age of the employee. An employer also cannot refuse benefits to pregnant employees that are provided to others (health insurance, for example) and, in most cases, cannot discriminate against the handicapped. (Some insurance plans refuse to cover people for conditions that existed *before* they came to work for their current employers, a provision that is legal but is problematic for handicapped people.)

Second, an employer is legally bound to give you what you were promised when you were hired. This includes statements made when you got the job as well as those in the employee handbook and in memos (the list of paid vacation days most companies circulate, for example). No employer can change these conditions of employment unless you are notified first. It's legal for your employer to notify you that, starting next year, you will no longer get the day after Thanksgiving as a paid holiday. It's not legal to tell you, after you took that day off, that your pay will be docked if that hasn't been the case up to now. That's why it's important to be aware of what promises are made and to keep copies of employee handbooks and memos.

The third important point is that once an employer does provide benefits, the kinds of benefits given may be controlled by laws. The most famous example of this is the Employee Retirement Income Security Act of 1974. This is the act that set standards for pension programs to insure that tiny rules in fine print and sloppy money management do not cheat workers out of pensions they are entitled to and counting on. ERISA does not require a company to offer pension plans to its employees, but it does apply to those companies that do.

A DAY'S PAY

The one thing an employer definitely does owe most employees is the minimum wage—currently set at $3.35 an hour—plus overtime pay at 1½ times their hourly rate if they work more than 40 hours a week. Can you get overtime pay if your regular work week is 35 hours? The answer is yes—but only if the employer has established a policy of paying time and a half after 35 hours or 37½ hours, as some routinely do. All employees covered by minimum wage laws are classified "nonexempt."

Several large and important categories of employees, though, *are* "exempt" from both overtime and the minimum wage. Surprisingly, at the head of that list are executives, administrators, professionals, and "outside" sales people with salary guarantees of over $250 a week.

To be considered exempt, according to the government, you need more than a title that says "administrator" or "professional." Each category is evaluated according to the duties required of someone in that slot. If they call you an administrator but you're not exercising "discretion and independent judgment," you may not truly be "exempt," should you decide for some reason that you wanted to fight that designation and claim overtime.

Certain employers are not covered by minimum wage laws. The list is long and complex, but among the most common groups are religious or non-profit organizations, certain small retailers (there's a dollar volume cutoff) and some agricultural employers. Casual and seasonal workers (babysitters, for example) also may not be covered.

If you have been denied the minimum wage, or denied overtime after 40 hours a week, and if you are in a job category that is protected by law, the place to complain is the nearest office of the Wage and Hours Division of the U.S. Labor Department. You'll find it listed in the phone book in many major cities.

WHEN YOU ARE DISABLED

The next group of job "rights" concerns what happens to you when you get sick. If you work, sickness and accidents divide themselves into two major groups: those that are work-related and those that aren't. Work-related injuries (your typewriter slipped off its table and broke your foot) and sicknesses (you developed breathing problems because of the chemicals in your workplace) are covered by workers' compensation laws, which every state provides. Non-work-related injuries and illnesses that leave you disabled beyond the time allowed by your sick leave (if you have sick leave) are covered by disability programs. Severely disabled workers may be eligible for Social Security disability payments, and also for additional money provided in some states. What does all this mean? Let's look at these programs in more detail.

Workers' compensation. To qualify for workers' compensation, you have to prove that your injury or illness arose "in and out of the course of work." In other words, if your job contributed to your problem in any way—even if, say, it simply made your bad back worse—you can make a claim.

What you will get varies from state to state. Generally, workers' compensation pays your medical bills and makes up at least part of your lost wages while you are disabled and cannot work. It may also pay for rehabilitation (occupational therapy or retraining) if you can no longer do your previous job, and provide a small allowance to support your spouse and children and a death benefit to your survivors if you die because of the accident or illness.

In general, you file for workers' compensation and are paid through your employer. To collect, you only have to prove that your problem is work-related—you don't have to show that the problem was the company's fault (and you can't be denied benefits because the company says the accident was your fault). The tradeoff for this no-fault policy is that the employer is shielded. No matter how negligent an injured person feels her employer was, she cannot sue the company for personal injury (even if she feels a court might award her much more money for her loss). Her only recourse beyond workers' compensation payments is to sue some third party—the company that manufactured the scaffolding system that fell on her as she walked into her building, for example.

The amount of money you will get depends on how much insurance your state requires employers to provide. In general, if you are totally disabled and unable to work, you will be paid two-thirds of your average weekly earnings up to a certain level. If you remain disabled, you will be paid for your lifetime. But if you recover and can work again, the payments will end. Some states allow for partial payment to people who don't recover completely and whose earning power is reduced as a result. Talk to your employer or to your state's workers' compensation agency.

If your employer disputes your claim to workers' compensation, consult an attorney and get in touch with the state's workers' compensation agency. (Federal workers have separate coverage and should get in touch with Employment Standards Administration, the federal agency in charge of these matters.) An employer may offer you a lump-sum payment in lieu of continued workers' compensation benefits. Before you accept it, check with an attorney. At the time of your injury or illness you may not be aware of its possible long-term effects.

Social Security disability. In addition to workers' compensation, disabled workers and their families may also be eligible for Social Security disability benefits. In 1981 alone Social Security paid over $17 billion to disabled

Americans and their families. This program is unlike workers' compensation in that your problem does not have to be job-related for you to collect benefits. You do have to meet very stringent qualifications.

Social Security is funded by taxes paid by both employers and employees. To be eligible for Social Security disability, you have to have paid into the fund for a specified period. Your payments are measured by "quarters" of work, three-month periods in which you have paid Social Security taxes on a certain amount of earnings (the rules for establishing these quarters are too complex to detail here). The Social Security Administration has delegated the running of this program to each state's disability determination office (usually part of the state vocational rehabilitation agency). It can tell you whether your earning history gives you "disability insured" status. It is important to note that self-employed workers also qualify for this program, and that there are special rules for workers who become disabled before they are thirty-one years old.

Having enough coverage to be considered for benefits is only half the problem—the much easier half. The real problem is convincing the Social Security Administration that you are disabled enough to receive payments. The burden of proof is on you, and what you must prove is that you have a physical, bodily, or mental illness or abnormality that doctors can confirm through clinical or laboratory diagnosis. Then you must demonstrate that this problem makes you unable "to engage in any substantial gainful activity" for at least twelve months.

"Any substantial gainful activity" is a tough test. Basically it means not only that you cannot do what you used to do but that—given your age, education, and past relevant work experience—you cannot perform any job that exists in the nation. The relevant words are age, education, and work experience.

If you can prove that you have a disability and that it makes it impossible for you to do the kind of work you did during the past fifteen years, the burden of proof switches to the Social Security Administration. To deny you benefits, it must show that a significant number of jobs exist in the nation that you *could* do despite your health problems. Whether such jobs exist in your area, whether there are available job openings, and whether it is likely that someone like you would be hired for them is completely irrelevant as far as the law is concerned.

Since 1979 the regulations have been liberalized to take certain vocational handicaps into account. The rules now recognize that older and illiterate workers have fewer jobs open to them, as do those who did skilled or unskilled work that was strenuous and that gave them no skills they could transfer to other occupations. But even these liberalized rules may not be of much help to many women. "A younger woman, particularly one with a college degree or even a high-school diploma, is going to have an extremely difficult time getting disability benefits unless she can show that she can literally do nothing at all," says attorney Marvin Schwartz, a former administrative law judge for the Social Security Administration and author of *The Trial of a Social Security Disability Case.*

There is, though, an official list of impairments that are considered automatic proof of disability. Among them: progressive, debilitating cancer; loss of both arms, both legs, or one arm and one leg; severe arthritis; serious kidney disease; and certain kinds of mental illness.

Applications for Social Security disability must be filed with your state's disability determination office, which will review your application and medical records and may require further tests (if more tests are needed, the government will pay for them). If you think you have a disability that would qualify, it's important to file your claim as soon as possible—the decision can take three to six months unless your illness is on the official impairment list. You also have to wait (regardless of when your application is approved) five full months from the onset of your disability to begin receiving checks (back benefits may be available if you filed late).

If you're turned down, you can appeal to your local office for reconsideration. If you still are denied benefits, you can appeal again and be heard before an administrative law judge. Two more stages of appeals—before the Appeals Council and to a federal court—can also be made. According to Schwartz, well over half of those who appeal eventually win benefits. A key factor in winning your case is choosing a lawyer familiar with the complex regulations that govern the process.

Once you are awarded benefits, they will continue as long as you are disabled. Your case will be reviewed once every three years. If your health is uncertain, you may be able to buy yourself a little time. You must notify the Social Security Administration if you recover and return to work. To enable people to try to resume working without risking a total loss of benefits, the administration allows a trial work period of up to twelve months. Check with an attorney and the administration before you start this process. There are strict standards of what is and is not permitted during the trial work period, and if you fall afoul of them, you could lose your benefits.

How much can you receive? As with regular Social Security, that depends on how much you contributed. The amount of money you receive monthly or as a lump sum from workers' compensation also affects your Social Security payments. A new law limits the amount you can receive from both sources to 80 percent of your "average covered earnings."

Cash sickness programs. As mentioned earlier, five states (California, Hawaii, New Jersey, Rhode Island, New York) and Puerto Rico offer benefits for non-job-related disabilities—if you broke both legs in a skiing accident and can't work for two months, for example. These programs last up to twenty-six weeks (thirty-nine in California) and provide weekly cash payments. If you live in one of these states, check with your company's personnel office or with the state government.

Workers' compensation, Social Security disability, and cash sickness programs are the only provisions the government makes for disabled jobholders. Disability insurance is also available from private insurance companies, and many enlightened employers offer it as part of their benefits packages. If yours does not, you would be well advised to look into a private insurance plan.

WHEN YOU RETIRE

When you're immersed in a job, retirement is probably the last thing on your mind. But even though the official retirement age—the age at which you *must* retire—is now seventy, most of us will have to face the issue eventually. Up to now the trend has been to earlier rather than later retirement—helped on by some firms' generous early-retirement benefits—but that trend may be about to reverse.

Working Woman's analysis of a major study of 846 American jobholders conducted in 1982 by the Public Agenda Foundation found that more than half of those fifty-five or older planned to keep working past the age of sixty-five. (Most hoped to cut back on their working hours, an option more companies may offer as the baby-boom generation ages and fewer younger jobholders are available to take over their responsibilities.) Certainly retirement will be delayed for millions when the new Social Security regulations go into effect, raising the age when we can retire with full benefits to sixty-six in 2009 and to sixty-seven in 2027. If you are thirty in 1984, you'll be only fifty-five in 2009—it's sooner than you think.

What will await you when they present you with your gold digital watch? That is, of course, impossible to predict, although it is safe to say that whatever happens to Social Security by 2009 or 2027, it is unlikely to be enough to live on, and that even if you are entitled to a pension, it may not meet your needs. What we can outline here is what you would be entitled to if you retired now.

Certainly by the time you hit forty, if not before, it makes sense to sit down and do some serious thinking about how you will support yourself in your later years. You probably already know about such tax-exempt retirement savings options as Individual Retirement Accounts, Keogh Plans, and annuity programs. But there are many other possibilities open to you, some with similar current tax benefits. A diversified financial plan is the safest choice, and the sooner you start one, the better off you will be. In your planning remember that a company pension is something to negotiate for, not a legal right. What is a legal right for those who have paid into the plan—at least until Congress changes the law—is Social Security.

Social Security. Recent headlines have been full of dire predictions about the fate of the Social Security system, many of them inspired by the well-publicized graying of America that will occur when the baby-boomers age in the first quarter of the twenty-first century. Experts estimate that by 2025 the current ratio of three workers to every retiree will fall to two to one. To save the system, Congress voted a number of changes in March 1983—including the rise in the age at which workers can receive benefits. Most people think that some form of Social Security will continue to be available by the time most of the people reading this book retire. Our guess is that, considering how many older Americans will be in the population by then, they'll have the votes to keep the program in business whatever happens.

And votes will be important. Unlike your life insurance or annuity plan, Social Security is a tax, not a contract. How and whether you can collect on the taxes you've paid in depends on the laws Congress passes. But right now retirees are entitled to receive full benefits at age sixty-five and reduced benefits at age sixty-two, if they are what is called "fully insured."

As with disability benefits, your status depends on how many quarters of coverage you have earned. Employees have been able to earn quarters through paying Social Security taxes on their earnings since 1936. Most self-employed people could not begin earning these quarters until 1950, when they were required to join the system, and some government and nonprofit organization employees are still exempt from Social Security.

Social Security taxes entitle you to payments for yourself, for your spouse, for your children who are under sixteen when you begin to collect benefits, and, when you die, for your surviving spouse (if he is sixty or older), children (under eighteen or nineteen), dependent parents (if they are sixty-two or older), and, in some cases, for divorced spouses and older, disabled children. As you can see from this list, the rules are complicated. If you want to check on your situation—and it pays to do so—the Social Security office will tell you how many quarters of coverage you have earned so far and what you are entitled to.

Because Social Security was set up for the traditional family with a single breadwinner and a dependent spouse, a married or divorced person may be entitled to a spouse's share of the husband's or wife's benefits as well as to any he or she has earned on their own. A retiree is entitled to his or her whole benefit plus an additional benefit for the spouse equal to half the worker's benefit (family total: 1½ times the breadwinner's benefit). When the bread-winner dies, the surviving spouse is entitled to 100 percent of his benefit, though if he or she is under sixty and not disabled, he or she will have to wait until at least age 62 to collect it. If you have been divorced after a marriage that lasted at least ten years, you are entitled to a wife's or widow's benefit.

Women who have spent many years at home may find that their wife's or widow's share entitles them to a larger check than their earnings do, because their years out of the job market and the low salaries most women earn do not entitle them to much Social Security income. In this case, alas, they cannot pick up both checks—just the larger one. They receive no more than a non-working wife who never paid any money into Social Security at all.

For more information on filing for benefits and how much money you can expect to receive, check with your local Social Security Office. To receive checks, you must apply there, and since it takes at least three months to receive your first check, you should start the ball rolling well before your retirement birthday.

Your pension. Roughly half of American jobholders are covered by private pension plans. If you belong to that lucky half, you are entitled to certain legal protections under the Employee Retirement Income Security Act. This includes the provision that you must be treated the same as other workers in your category (companies can't contribute a higher percentage of an executive's salary to the plan than they contribute for her secretary). It also means that you must be fully "vested" in—entitled to—your pension after ten years of work in your company (counting from 1975). Some pension plans, however, allow you to become partly or fully vested after fewer than ten years of work. There's one sneaky exception to the ten-year-maximum rule: if your company did not start the plan until after you went to work for it, your pre-plan years of service do not have to be counted toward vesting.

You can join the pension plan at age twenty-five, and your years of employment for vesting purposes will be counted from your twenty-second birthday. (These age limits are currently under fire in Congress because they disproportionately hurt women, who often go to work at eighteen, then leave the job market in their twenties for several years to raise a family, thus losing out on vesting rights.

ERISA requires that you get your pension at sixty-five unless you decide to work beyond that age, but companies may offer earlier retirement plans. Your company must give you a yearly report of how much money you have accumulated in your pension plan account and what you would receive at retirement.

What happens if you leave your job? If you're 100 percent vested in your pension, the benefits you have earned remain yours. Legally the company can hold the money until you reach sixty-five and then pay it in installments, but many employers prefer to give departing employees their accumulated pension funds in a lump sum. (The company has no legal right to keep your money after you leave if you *want* it in a lump sum—unless the specific terms of your pension program give them that right.) To avoid being taxed on that sum, you must invest it in an Individual Retirement Account (IRA) or other pension vehicle within sixty days.

What happens if your company goes bankrupt, is dissolved, or is merged into or acquired by another company? Basic vested pension rights in most company plans are protected by the Pension Benefit Guaranty Corporation, a government insurance program. When a company covered by this program goes bankrupt or dissolves, the government corporation will take over. It will not protect such special benefits as early retirement, though, and it does not cover every kind of pension plan. Professional-service corporations (groups of architects or physicians, for example), with pension plans including fewer than twenty-six people, are not covered. Even vested employees of such corporations may be entitled to no more than the funds they contributed to their pensions from their own salaries.

If your company becomes part of another company, you are still entitled to your vested rights in your original company plan and to be transferred to the new company's plan if it has one. Will your years of service with the first firm count toward vesting with the second? That depends—check with your new company's personnel office or with a pension lawyer. One good source of information on pensions is the Pension Rights Center (1346 Connecticut Avenue NW, Room 1019, Washington, DC 20036; 202-296-3778).

WHEN YOU LOSE YOUR JOB
Among the disasters employees fear most, getting laid off or fired has to rank near the top. You lose your job and the identity that comes with it, you lose what has probably been the central organizing structure of your life, and—

perhaps worst of all—you lose your pay check. Even if you hated your job and are glad to be rid of it, unemployment is a shock.

If you are called into your boss's office one morning, or find the dreaded pink slip in your pay envelope, the first thing to do is to try to get a letter from your employer summarizing the reasons you lost your job. Whether you can collect unemployment benefits depends on two factors: why you lost your job and whether you have worked long enough to be entitled to benefits. If you meet the requirements, unemployment benefits are a legal right.

You may be legally entitled to two weeks' notice, or to severance pay, or to a sum of money for sick days or vacation days you earned but did not take. A company that has a policy of giving such benefits—often based on length of employment—and that has detailed them in an employee handbook or promised them in some other official way, may be required to give them. Otherwise they are not required by law.

Unemployment insurance. Unemployment insurance is a federal and state program designed to provide an income to people who lose their jobs involuntarily. "Involuntarily" is the key word; if you resign instead of being laid off, you may not be entitled to benefits unless you can prove that you left for a good reason. State regulations about what constitutes a good reason vary. Work overload, unsafe working conditions, or sexual harassment usually qualifies a person for benefits if the condition can be documented. Some states will also pay benefits if you left your job voluntarily to accompany a spouse who was relocating.

You may also have difficulty collecting if you are fired. After filing for benefits you will be called into the unemployment office for a hearing. After talking to you and to your employer, the office will decide on your eligibility. If the firing is found to be justified because of misconduct on your part, you may receive a penalty of several weeks' loss of benefits before you can start collecting. If the office finds that you were guilty of "gross misconduct," you will be entitled to no benefits at all. You can appeal a finding of gross misconduct, however, if you do so within fifteen days after notification.

Because of these regulations it is sometimes better to try to get your employer to fire you instead of resigning voluntarily. They are also the reason for getting that letter documenting why you were fired. Some employers will give an employee one set of reasons and the unemployment office a different, more unflattering list that will make it difficult for her to collect. Why? Because the amount of money an employer has to pay for unemployment insurance depends on how many of the company's former employees have collected benefits. From the employer's point of view, this is why it is impor-

tant to document a staff member's unsatisfactory work through a perfor-
mance-evaluation system.

You receive benefits according to your quarterly earnings within a specified base period (at least a year). Usually you have to have earned money in at
least two quarters of the base period to qualify. About ten days after you file
for unemployment benefits, you will receive a statement of your quarterly
earnings. Compare it with your pay check receipts to make sure it is correct,
and keep this information even if you find you have not made enough money
to collect benefits at present. You may be able to combine these earnings with
others if you file for unemployment in the future.

Although unemployment insurance is run by each state, you can file an
interstate claim if you live in one state and work in another, or if you move to
a new state. You can also file an interstate claim if you have insufficient earnings in any one state to get insurance, but when you add up all your earnings
from jobs in several states you have earned enough to be eligible. There is
generally a one-week waiting period before you can begin to collect benefits,
so file as soon as possible. In most states you can collect regular benefits for
twenty-six weeks; a few offer longer periods. In times of high unemployment
the states and the federal government may extend the benefits period as long
as an additional thirteen weeks. When you go to the unemployment office to
collect your last check, ask about extended benefits.

Fighting an "unjust dismissal." Until recently employers assumed that
they had the right to fire any employee for any reason at any time, unless that
employee was protected by an employment contract, a union contract, or
some other agreement. This "right" is under attack in the courts and in some
state legislatures.

Legislation to set up state-run review boards to arbitrate disputes over firings is being considered in Michigan, New Jersey, New York, and Pennsylvania, and similar laws have been discussed in Colorado and Connecticut.

Under such an "unjust dismissal" bill, a discharged worker who had
completed a six-month probationary period would be eligible to file a request
for a review of her case by a state mediator. This official, after also considering
the employer's reply, might decide to uphold or disallow the firing and could
couple the decision with a financial payment—back pay or severance pay, for
example.

Such laws may not be in place for quite a while, but even without them
there is a growing awareness that employees deserve more protection, if only
in the procedures leading up to an actual firing. Many firms have demonstrated a new willingness to review and possibly amend these procedures.

This progressive state of affairs has been brought about, at least in part, by the astronomical rise of "unjust dismissal" suits, to which hardly any area of American business and industry has been immune in recent years.

Other businesses have responded to the threat of litigation with hard-nosed counteroffensives. Blue Cross/Blue Shield of Michigan's handbooks and job applications now warn that employees "can be terminated at any time without reason," and other companies have advised managers to build their cases against erring subordinates more carefully by using stronger discipline for each slipup. Some people think such moves will not only undermine management-employee relations but push white-collar workers into protecting themselves through unionization.

Politicians pressing for the new state-review-board bills don't expect them to be passed immediately—the theory is too new. But unjust dismissal is an issue to watch, and lawsuits are a possible avenue for employees who believe they have lost their jobs unfairly.

WHEN YOU ARE DISCRIMINATED AGAINST
American employees have the right not to be discriminated against because of their sex, race, religion, color, or national origin, or because they are pregnant, handicapped, or older. A number of national laws and executive orders (regulations signed by the president) protect us against discrimination at work. Because of their complexity, we have devoted a special section of this book (Appendix A, The Major Antidiscrimination Laws, which begins on page 309) to an in-depth description of these laws and regulations—how you can tell which apply to you, how to file complaints under them, how such complaints are processed, and what kinds of remedies you can receive if you win a case. If you are an employer, you too should study this section, so that you'll know which kinds of actions are illegal and what risks your organization runs by ignoring them.

Since women still earn an average of 60 cents for every dollar men earn, it's clear that these laws have not created equality in the job market. Nevertheless, they have enabled women to make inroads in previously all-male fields and to win several notable settlements from employers who have discriminated against them.

Are you a victim of discrimination? How can you tell if you're discriminated against? Consider some of these common situations:

You are the female manager of the First Street branch of the National Bank. You discover the salary of the newly appointed male manager of the Tenth Street branch is $5,000 a year more than yours. Is this unlawful discrimination? *Probably.*

After graduating from high school, you and a male classmate are hired by the local factory. He is hired for the heavy-work assembly line. You are hired to do light work at $1.50 an hour less than he earns. Your request for a job on the heavy-work line is denied. All your coworkers are women, all his men. Unlawful sex discrimination? *Yes.*

Your company has always been very cooperative about illnesses. When a fellow purchasing agent had open-heart surgery last year, the firm held his job open for him for three months, until he was able to resume it. But when you become pregnant and ask for assurances that your job will be held for you until you return from your maternity leave (the six to eight weeks your doctor says it will take for you to recover from childbirth), the personnel department says it cannot promise you your old job back. Unlawful sex discrimination? *Yes.*

You are an operating-room nurse at the municipal hospital and hold a B.S. in nursing. You discover that the town's tree trimmers, who are required only to have a high-school education, earn $4,500 a year more than you. Unlawful sex discrimination? *Maybe.*

These are, of course, only a few of many situations that you could encounter. If you think you have been discriminated against, you have to decide two things immediately. The first is whether your case comes under one of the federal antidiscrimination laws. After reading Appendix A, you should have a pretty good idea of whether it does. (Since some state and local laws also ban discrimination under more liberal standards, you also should check with your state or local human rights or fair employment practices offices; ask the labor department if your state has such laws.)

The second decision you have to make is whether you want to pursue the matter. Individual settlements with your employer can be made fairly quickly, if you can come to terms. If you cannot, you will have to go to court and file a lawsuit, which can drag on for years. The federal Equal Employment Opportunity Commission, which has jurisdiction over most antidiscrimination cases, has no power to enforce its findings without a court decision. Seven women reporters who worked for the Associated Press waited ten years before their class-action suit on behalf of women and blacks was finally settled in a consent decree. The decision cost AP $2 million and required the company to set up an extensive affirmative-action program. Close to $1,500,000 went for back-pay awards. However, by the time the case was settled, none of those named in the case still worked there.

Although it is illegal for your employer to harass you for filing a discrimination complaint, women who have gone through the process report that life at the office can become quite unpleasant. Employers have even been known to fire people despite the law—and fighting back requires taking them to court. However, as attorney Jane L. Dolkart points out: "A few individuals willing to file charges can end up helping many women who are afraid to risk their jobs or who do not understand that they are being discriminated against."

Sexual harassment. Obviously there are many forms of discrimination, all of them very difficult to deal with. But because sexual harassment is such a painful and delicate problem for so many working women, we'd like to spend some extra time on ways to handle it.

Although sexual harassment is not usually as extreme as rape, its victims have many of the same problems. For example, victims of sexual harassment tend to be blamed or to feel guilty, or both; the charge can be difficult to prove; and the whole experience can be acutely distressing.

If you are being harassed, one thing you can be sure of is that you are not alone. In a 1976 survey by *Redbook* magazine, almost nine-tenths of the 9,000 women who responded said that they had experienced some form of harassment on the job. Forty-five percent said that "they or a woman they knew had quit or been fired from a job because of sexual harassment." And a 1983 study at Harvard University found that 49 percent of nontenured women faculty members, 41 percent of women graduate students, 34 percent of undergraduate women, and 32 percent of tenured women faculty members had encountered at least one incident of sexual harassment.

What is sexual harassment? In 1980 the EEOC published guidelines for employers that include an excellent definition:

> Unwelcome sexual advances, requests for sexual favors, and other verbal or physical conduct of a sexual nature constitute sexual harassment when (1) submission to such conduct is made either explicitly or implicitly a term or condition of an individual's employment, (2) submission to or rejection of such conduct by an individual is used as the basis for employment decisions affecting such individual, or (3) such conduct has the purpose or effect of unreasonably interfering with an individual's work performance or creating an intimidating, hostile, or offensive working environment.

In other words, sexual harassment is conduct that is unwelcome to you, that involves your work, affects your ability to do your job, or affects your career (including whether you are hired for a job), or forces you to work in an offensive, unpleasant work environment. What's more, the EEOC holds your employer responsible for creating a work environment where such conduct is not tolerated. Yet a 1981 study of more than 1,800 male and female subscribers to the *Harvard Business Review*, conducted jointly by *HBR* and *Redbook*, found that few companies have formal policies that address sexual harassment.

Sexual harassment is often related to power—usually a more senior or powerful man harasses a less senior, less powerful woman. At Harvard, for example, 80 percent of women graduate students who reported harassment were harassed by men in the department in which they were enrolled; male faculty members usually did the harassing.

This is what you can do if you are being sexually harassed:

1. If possible, and if you know who is harassing you, confront the harasser and tell him that what he is doing is harassing to you. Tell him that you don't like it and he should stop right away. If he is a coworker, tell him that you will inform management about his behavior if he doesn't stop. Remember that harassment by a coworker can be just as illegal as harassment by a superior.

2. Put your complaint in writing and give it to him, keeping a copy for yourself.

3. Keep a detailed diary of each incident, writing down what happened and when. Precise documentation is extremely important. If the harassment takes the form of notes or pictures, save them, noting when and how you received each one. Keep the diary in a safe place—not in your desk, for example. Keep a trusted coworker informed of the incidents as well.

4. Talk to other women where you work to find out if they too have been harassed, or have noticed that you have been. Keep notes of these conversations, but be sure to check with the women before giving their names to anyone investigating your complaints. You also may want to discuss your problem with a women's group before proceeding further.

5. If your company or union has a grievance procedure for complaints of sexual harassment, and if confronting your harasser did not stop the incidents (or if you were unable to confront her or him), discuss your problem with management or a union representative. If no such formal setup exists, inform management in writing of the problem and ask them to take steps to end it, reminding them that sexual harassment violates Title VII of the Civil Rights Act of 1964. Keep copies of your letter and any response from management, and take notes at any meetings you have to discuss the problem.

6. If none of this puts an end to the harassment, you may decide to file charges with the EEOC (see Appendix A). If you are fired, denied a

promotion, or given a bad evaluation by your harasser, or because you have complained about the harassment, you'll need to make the decision as soon as possible. There is a strict time limit for filing charges under Title VII. (See Appendix A for how and when to file.)

Pregnancy discrimination. Another law that is particularly important to younger working women is the Pregnancy Discrimination Act (often called the Pregnancy Disability Act, or PDA) of 1978. This requires employers to treat women disabled by pregnancy and related conditions the same as employees with health problems that affect their ability to work. The PDA includes the following provisions:

1. An employer must hold open the job of a woman absent to bear a child on the same basis that jobs are held open for employees on sick or disability leaves. If the employer allows other disabled workers reduced work loads or less strenuous tasks, the same provision must be made for women disabled by pregnancy or the effects of childbirth. After maternity leave, a woman's seniority must be upheld or accrued on the same basis as for anyone else who had been on disability. Vacation and pay increases also must be awarded in a manner equal to that provided for those with other disabilities.

   However, if leave is extended beyond the time of medical disability, and unpaid leave or vacation time is used, the law does not protect the woman's job or salary. In this case the employee's rights upon returning to work are left to the discretion of the employer. Getting an employer's written promise to hold open a job for a longer period would, of course, provide job security.

2. The law also stipulates that health insurance must cover pregnancy-related expenses on the same basis as expenses for other medical conditions.

3. The law prohibits pregnancy discrimination in hiring, compensation, conditions of employment, and apprenticeship or other training or retraining programs.

4. The PDA applies to employers with fifteen or more employees, to employment agencies, and to labor organizations.

One shortcoming of the PDA is that it does not require employers to establish new programs where none currently exist. That is, if your company does not provide disability insurance to employees, it does not have to provide maternity disability benefits to employees for childbirth.

Defining your options. To win a discrimination case in court you have to prove that your charges are correct. To file a complaint with a government agency such as the EEOC or the Office of Federal Contract Compliance Programs, you don't have to supply any concrete proof at all. According to the American Civil Liberties Union, it is the agency's job to uncover discrimination in a company.

However—and this is a big however—agencies that deal with these cases are overworked and understaffed. Your complaint will have the best chance of being handled well if you provide as much detailed information as possible. Look at what kinds of jobs men and women hold in your company, at who gets promoted, at what kinds of education and training opportunities are available to men and women. Are pregnant women treated fairly, or are they forced to leave their jobs at a certain point regardless of whether or not they are able to work? Have you been denied opportunities because of your sex, race, age, or disability?

What the agency should do—using information your company may be required to provide—is prove that women as a group and/or you in particular are treated differently from others in whatever ways your complaint describes. It may also look at company documents and take the testimony of managers and other workers. Much of this research can be expensive, particularly when statistical evidence is collected, which is why it's best to let a government agency foot the bill if possible. If you are not pleased with the way the investigation has been conducted, though, it may pay to go to court on your own, if the law under which you are filing allows you to do so. (You can go to court on a Title VII or an Equal Pay Act case; you can't on an executive-order case. See Appendix A for details.) If you do go to court, your attorney should attempt to gather this same information from your employer in a pretrial process called "discovery."

Going to court or to a government agency is not the only recourse you have when you're seeking to fight discrimination at work. In fact, if you want to stay with your current employer, it could be the worst solution. "It's very hard to litigate and to continue with that employer," says Phyllis Segal, a Boston attorney and former legal director of the NOW Legal Defense and Education Fund. "You've put yourself in an adversarial situation by complaining to a third party. It's analogous to filing for divorce and continuing to live with your spouse—interpersonally it doesn't work."

Segal stresses the importance of assessing coolly what is going on, why it is going on, and what you want to have happen. "In some cases you want to continue with your employer but at a more favorable pay scale or without the harassment you have been experiencing," she explains. "Other times, the situation is so bad that you want to get out yourself but to make sure that no one else has to go through what you've gone through."

To help women who want to try a different approach to settling sex discrimination, some attorneys are experimenting with ways of helping clients plan strategies to negotiate with their employers instead of filing suit. This works best, Segal cautions, in cases where the violation of the law is clear (although some factual questions may exist) and the employer understands that if a negotiated settlement can't be worked out, the employee has solid grounds for a legal case. What the lawyer does is help a woman assess how good her case is, as well as what sort of relief she could negotiate. The American Arbitration Association has set up rules for arbitrating employment-discrimination suits, and some private negotiation/mediation firms also handle such cases. A number of corporations have their own in-house conflict-resolution programs, according to Segal. But to use these approaches, both parties have to agree to them.

Colquitt A. Meacham, another Boston attorney, handles such cases. In a report for the Ford Foundation she has developed a model that would provide incentives for employers to agree to have discrimination cases handled by an impartial third party rather than go the EEOC route. Meacham would like to see legislative reform that would require such procedures. "People think that the law is in place and they have some rights," she says. "But it's really hollow. The EEOC has no enforcement power and a large backlog. It takes five years and $10,000 to $15,000 to go through a case. Most plaintiffs don't have that kind of money and are out of work. They'll starve to death before anything happens." Without legal incentives to take a third-party approach, it's difficult to push many corporations into agreeing to negotiate, she explains, but she thinks mediation could be a good answer for both women and their employers: "It's very confidential, quick, cheap, and parties can fashion their own remedy rather than being limited by what the law says."

Attorney Donna Lenhoff of the Women's Legal Defense Fund disagrees. She fears that if the parties are left to "fashion their own remedies" in mediation, charging parties will end up bargaining away the relief to which they are entitled under law. Most experts on alternative dispute resolution agree that mediation is appropriate only when the two parties have equal bargaining power, and this is rarely, if ever, the case in employment discrimination situations, in which the charging parties generally continue to work for the employer with whom they must bargain. Most important, Lenhoff is concerned that reliance on mediation will remove the underlying purpose of the EEOC process: to insure that discriminatory practices are eliminated and corrected. In that process, as she puts it, "the EEOC staff person has a dual role—both to investigate impartially and to act as a champion of those whose rights have been violated."

Lenhoff agrees that there are major problems in the way discrimination cases are presently handled by the EEOC. "But the answer is not to throw out the baby with the bath water. To allow parties to come to their own agreement, in all cases, regardless of whether the law has been violated, would destroy the concept that violations of civil rights *must* be corrected."

At this point it has to be said that, whatever the merits of antidiscrimination laws, these laws can come and they can go. They can be voted away as easily as they were voted in, depending on the political makeup of the legislature. The one measure that would insure a permanent legal restriction against sexual discrimination would be the Equal Rights Amendment, which says that "equality of rights under the law shall not be denied or abridged by the United States or by any state on account of sex."

HEALTH AND SAFETY

Every worker has the right to a safe work environment. This is as much a legal right as the minimum wage or workers' compensation. People who work in a shipyard, people who work in a steel mill, people who work in a factory, and people who work in an office all are entitled to safety.

Office hazards are no small problem. Consider the potential dangers of sitting in a badly designed chair, under a flickering fluorescent light, next to a photocopier exuding chemical duplicator fumes, behind a chain smoker, in a building with bacteria in its ventilation system and asbestos lining in its walls: varicose veins, back pain, blurred vision, intoxication, headache, stress, respiratory ailments, contagious disease, and cancer.

The Occupational Safety and Health Administration and the Environmental Protection Agency tend to be more concerned about industrial worksites than offices. However, OSHA has set standards for safety and health in regard to the use of asbestos and to noise and fire prevention, and it has the power under the law to inspect any workplace at any time, especially if the inspection is requested by a person working there.

OSHA has no strict guidelines about video-display terminals, lighting, and photocopying chemicals. This isn't to say that these things aren't covered (there is a "general duty" clause which states that workers should be in an environment free from "recognized hazards"), but there is no specific set of requirements.

Some OSHA pointers:

If a health and safety problem is troubling you and notifying your employer has not resulted in remedial action, get in touch with the OSHA office in your area. If you are a member of a union, talk instead to your shop steward.

OSHA will conduct an inspection.

Your employer cannot legally retaliate or harass anyone who exercises her health and safety rights.

OSHA will set a deadline for the violation to be corrected.

The company may decide to contest the situation or fine.

The appeal process can take months.

You have the right to refuse hazardous work.

Pregnant women should be especially aware of work conditions that could harm the fetus or be hazardous to their own health. Some problematic situations are as follows:

A *quiet desk job* has its own problems. Sitting for long periods of time in the same position can exacerbate leg and ankle swelling in the late months of pregnancy. Sciatica (pain in the upper leg caused by pressure on the sciatic nerve), also common in the last trimester, is aggravated by prolonged sitting.

Jobs that require long periods of standing not only create more fatigue in late pregnancy but also contribute to varicose veins and sciatic pain.

If your company uses *chemicals or toxic substances*, stay away from them. Lead, mercury, cadmium, and ethylene oxide may harm the fetus. They may cause miscarriage, birth defects, and cancer in newborns and may play a role in causing genetic defects.

Pregnant women who work in *hospitals or other health care facilities* must avoid contact with anesthetic gases, biological contaminants, and X rays.

Concern has been expressed about potential danger to the fetus from prolonged, repeated use of *video-display terminals* (see further discussion of VDTs in Chapter 9, Psychological Issues).

YOUR BENEFITS

So much for your rights. All the really lush items, the things that make life in and out of work worth living, come from the other side of the package, the benefits side. Job benefits range from the vacation and insurance policies many of us expect to luxurious "perks" such as stock options, club memberships, or a company-chauffeured car. We'll start with some of the basics.

VACATIONS AND HOLIDAYS

No federal or state statutes require employers to provide vacation time. The practices most employers follow are the results of a kind of consensus achieved through decades of collective bargaining and individual employee negotiations. These negotiations have bestowed about ten days of paid vacation leave annually on the average worker in the United States. Compared to many European nations, where paid vacations are a legal right, we make a pathetic showing. In France, for example, workers are entitled to two and a half days' vacation for every month worked (after the first six). In Germany more than 90 percent of the workforce received four weeks' vacation in 1980—a pattern repeated in Britain, Italy, Scandinavia, Spain, and the Soviet Union.

In this country the following seven occasions are usually paid holidays: New Year's Day, Christmas, Thanksgiving, Martin Luther King's birthday, and Memorial, Independence, and Labor days. Some other occasions celebrated optionally include "President's Day" (Washington's and Lincoln's birthdays), Veterans' Day, and Columbus Day. Federal legislation has increased the number of three-day weekends by insuring that several of these holidays are celebrated on Mondays, a practice followed in Canada for at least three decades.

Oddly enough, more vacation time would not be welcomed by all Americans. A René Plesser Associates survey of 210 executives earning between $50,000 and $75,000 annually revealed that almost 50 percent had failed to take their allotted vacations the previous year. This may not be good news. Most psychologists believe that vacations are not only beneficial to the individual but actually improve on-duty performance. This is a notion generally accepted in many European countries, where subsidized holidays (vacation bonuses, company resorts, and other such benefits) are not unusual.

"Job burnout is definitely related to lack of vacation time in our society," says psychotherapist Stephen Shapiro. "Vacationing in this taut world is not a luxury; it is a necessity."

SABBATICALS

Until recently college teachers were among the few employees granted sabbaticals, paid breaks of months or even a year designed to allow them to refresh their minds with different work (usually a research project), and often in a new setting. Now the idea is catching on in some of the nation's more forward-looking companies.

Although the American Management Association reports that "The fully paid sabbatical is not a benefit that is widely granted," it is gaining ground. One of the more generous deals is offered by the high-tech Tandem Corporation of California, which allows a fully paid six-week sabbatical every four years. The result is a much lower personnel turnover than in competing companies. The Xerox Corporation's program is even more comprehensive, and more unusual. It is restricted to what Xerox calls "social service leave," a plan under which employees at any level of the company who have at least three years' service may apply to work with a nonprofit, nonpolitical organization for up to one year. During this time the employee is paid full salary and receives all benefits. Up to two hundred employees apply each year; a committee of employees approves about fifteen to twenty of the applications. Most employees return to their guaranteed jobs, either the one they left or a better one. A few decide they prefer their new responsibilities and leave Xerox to pursue their new careers full time.

SICK PAY

Sick leave is enormously important, not just to employees but to employers. People who are not allowed to rest when ill can become dangerously rundown and subject to more serious illnesses. They can also spread infection among the rest of the staff.

Here, too, practices vary. Some companies allow a certain number of sick days each year; others require a doctor's note if deductions from the pay check are not to be made. Some grant no paid sick days at all.

DISABILITY INSURANCE

Company plans for disability insurance—which may be dispensed as sick leave pay—are usually quite limited. There are two kinds of plans. Short-term disability (used for maternity leave, for example) lasts for a period of several weeks or months. Long-term disability generally goes into effect after you have been unable to work for a certain period. These benefits may be paid for the rest of your life, if you are severely disabled, and some of them replace a major portion of your last salary. Companies may offer one or both of these plans as part of a benefits package. It's a good idea to examine your company's plan carefully; you may decide you need an additional plan of your own. Check with your personnel department and, if necessary, get more information from an insurance agent.

MEDICAL AND DENTAL PLANS

No federal laws require a company to provide medical insurance for its employees (although some states have insurance laws outlining what must be included in such plans). Yet medical plans are widely available, at least in larger firms, if only because it would be hard for the employer to compete in the marketplace without one.

Typically, a medical plan is in three parts. The first covers a specific number of days in the hospital (120–180 days is fairly common). The second pays doctors for specifically identified procedures, as long as the fee represents "reasonable and customary charges." The third, a major medical plan, includes fee deductibles (if you pay the first $50 of a medical bill) and some cost sharing (the plan will cover only a certain percentage of each bill).

Generally one plan covers all employees, but some companies have an additional plan for executives over and above the basic agreement.

A survey by *Fortune* magazine of 130 of the largest U.S. companies showed that most companies (66 out of the 72 responding) provide regular physicals for their managers and professionals, with about 25 percent of the firms extending the free examination to all their employees. Dental plans have also become fairly common but are much less usual than the medical plans.

Some companies also provide complete medical coverage through a Health Maintenance Organization. HMOs offer total services for a flat fee. Users must accept a doctor from among the HMO's staff, but many HMOs provide more services—free routine physicals and consultation with staff specialists, for example—than a traditional insurance package does.

FLEXIBLE BENEFITS

A fast-growing new trend is the so-called flexible benefits plan, sometimes described as "cafeteria-style" because the employee is able to choose the benefits she wants from a menu of options.

It works like this: The employee can supplement a basic core plan of, say, health, life, and disability insurance with other choices. Typically, a flexible benefits scheme allots to each employee a specific number of credits based on the individual's age, salary, dependents, and/or length of service. On top of the core plan each employee may get, say, thirty credits to spread over a list of options such as eye care, legal counsel, car insurance, child care, and prescription drugs. Additional credits can often be purchased for a small fee.

A flexible benefits plan makes an attractive package because it recognizes that the age, personal situation, savings goals, and leisure needs of employees vary.

As far as the corporation is concerned, flexible benefits give a measure of control over spiraling benefit costs. Both individuals and corporations were very disturbed in May 1984, when the IRS threatened to ban one popular form of cafeteria benefit which allowed workers to pay medical and other expenses in pretax wages and take back in cash the unused portion. At press time, Congress was trying to create a compromise plan that the IRS would accept. Meanwhile, thousands of workers were waiting to hear whether they owed back taxes and penalties on benefit payments. If you have flexible benefits, be sure to check with your personnel office about your plan.

PENSIONS

The subject of corporate pension plans is so complex that it merits careful study by all who participate (for a discussion of pension law, see "Your Pension, earlier in this chapter). In 1974 few pensions, even when combined with Social Security, added up to as much as 70 percent of final salaries. And a recent survey of 989 pension plans revealed that 15,000 employees who had served thirty years retired on pensions equal to only one-fifth of their final earnings.

In *Executive Essentials*, Mitchell J. Posner urges those participating in pension plans to ask the following questions:

Is there a minimum employment period before one can take part in the plan?
How will the payout formula be affected by Social Security benefits?
In calculating my pension benefits does the company count bonuses as earnings? (IRS guidelines discourage but do not prohibit this.)
What periods of employment are "credited" in terms of pension? What about leaves of absence? What if there is a company merger?
Is the plan contributory or company paid? How much will it cost me?
What provisions exist for an early retirement? What if I become disabled before I retire?

Because women have a longer life expectancy than men, until recently many insurance and pension plans required female employees to make larger contributions than male employees for an equal amount of benefits. This requirement was declared illegal in a 1983 Supreme Court decision. As a result many pension plans may soon be revised.

THE REAL GOODIES

Executive perks. Beyond all these basic benefits are the coveted perks. Once available only to top corporate officers, they are beginning to filter down to middle management, and some are becoming available to nonmanagement employees through union negotiations. To get an idea of what's available—at least to those at the top—look at the chart of executive perks on page 169. A 1983 *U.S. News and World Report* study, done with Hay Associates, produced the smaller chart on page 170, outlining the perks offered to the top brass at industrial companies and banks. Such benefits are designed to provide the "golden handcuffs" that keep highly productive top executives from jumping ship to the competition. This may be why some companies have been known to offer a sign-up bonus (see page 170) to new executives to help make up for what they have lost by leaving their old employer.

How do you make sure you get your slice of the pie? The time to negotiate for perks is usually when you are getting a new job. A few pointers:

Don't sell yourself short. Get documentation on what is typical for your category. Know what you are worth and what you are entitled to.

Let the company offer things first. Though this takes some negotiating skill, it boils down to an old market haggling technique: don't let them know what you'll go for, let them tell you what they'll give you.

Be bold about asking for such things as relocation funds. (This will be the commonest area of intense negotiation at the mid-salary level.)

Don't oversell—or undersell—yourself.

Get everything in writing. Make sure that any special agreements you have discussed are noted in your final offer letter from the company.

EXECUTIVE PERKS

Salary	Health and Life Insurance, Pension	Employee Contract or Termination Benefits	Relocation Expenses
Less than $40,000	The usual: major medical, life insurance disability;* dental; pension vested in five to ten years under ERISA	Contract very rare, except for noncompetition clause; few termination benefits except two weeks' to three months' salary	Shipping household goods, house-hunting trip, temporary housing, swing loan, closing costs, realtor's fees, settlement fees, legal fees, points, discretionary money
$40,000–$79,999	All of above, plus larger pension	Contract uncommon; two weeks' to one year's salary, outplacement services, use of office, phone, and secretarial help	All of above; third-party purchase of home, interest differential, auto shipment, house-hunting trips with spouse, more discretionary money
$80,000 and above	All of above, plus medical expenses paid 100 percent through use of discretionary medical fund; unusual pension benefits and pension settlements; much more insurance of every kind	Contract common, involving lump-sum settlement and payment over a period of years, use of private secretary in outplacement	All of above; company may provide housing and shipment of special items (boats, etc.)

	Car, Clubs and Membership, Travel Privileges	Bonuses, Stock Options, Deferred Compensation	Other
Less than $40,000	Health clubs, professional-society dues, car only if in sales/marketing	Sign-up, performance, guaranteed early annual review, profit sharing	Spousal placement, tuition refund, longer vacation, special training
$40,000–$79,999	All of above, plus greater choice of car (expensive sports cars are popular) or car allowance, social clubs, luncheon clubs	All of above, plus stock options, deferred compensation	All of above; gross-up factor, special executive-training programs, travel rights for spouse to exotic locations (the sales meeting in Monte Carlo)
$80,000 and above	All of above, plus luxury car including gas, oil, maintenance, and driver; country club; use of company plane	All of above; substantial equity position in company	All of above; apartment near office, assistance for children's tuition, or schooling for children if assigned overseas, etc.

* If benefit is underlined, it's almost always granted. If not underlined, then benefit is negotiable.
Source: "Negotiating Extras," by Tom Wolpert, *Working Woman*, May 1983.

PERKS OF THE TOP BRASS

	Industrial Companies	Banks
	% of Firms Giving Executives	
Executive physical exams	88	89
Executive parking	73	79
Stock options	66	79
Assigned company car	62	75
Liability insurance	60	68
Country club membership	47	64
Luncheon club membership	45	57
Special vacation policy	41	50
Financial counseling	36	46
Deferred compensation	35	43
Assigned chauffeur	29	18
Executive dining room	22	14

Source: U.S. News & World Report and Hay Associates.

Understand that certain companies are more generous than others in dispensing extras, and the higher your rank, the greater your leverage. But also bear in mind that it's often the company perk, not the pay check, that adds some luxury and status to life.

Sign-up bonus. Though the bonus paid upon joining a new company was once restricted to the highest echelons, this benefit has begun to filter down to middle managers in finance, advertising, and production. Carl Menk of Boyden Associates reports that 15 to 20 percent of his firm's middle-management searches resulted in a signing bonus.

Sometimes the job seeker herself can make a good case for a sign-up bonus. The sums accumulated in her old pension and profit-sharing plans may be lost, for example, and one-time bonuses could make up for this.

"One thing is certain," says management consultant James R. Baehler. "No one ever received a bonus without asking for it . . . and, if nothing else, should the company refuse to pay anything, you gain insight into how valuable they feel you are or aren't, and how badly they want you or don't."

Expense accounts. Having an expense account means that an employee does not have to pay work-related expenses out of her own pocket. In fact, when expenses for entertaining or traveling are likely to be high, most executives are better off negotiating a generous expense account than a salary increase, because a business expense account must be listed as tax deductible by the company. Naturally, it is easier to convince the IRS that business-expense deductions are valid if they are on an expense account than if they are expenses—even legitimate ones—paid out of your own pocket. Business expenses are tax-exempt, although there are of course restrictions to minimize their abuse; they can usually be justified to the IRS's satisfaction if they are backed up by proper documentation.

Profit sharing. Defined contribution plans under which an employer promises to invest a share of company profits on your behalf each year may or may not turn out to be a bonanza. The company's deposits, based on the size of corporate earnings and supplemented by the employee's voluntary contributions, depend entirely on the company's variable income. Some years the profits simply are not large enough to be shared with employees. Even if, after monitoring the company's performance, you are satisfied with its profits, you may still not be better off financially because, even though the saved income is tax-deferred, deferred income is beneficial only when it is invested well; otherwise inflation can eat it up. Beware too of having most of your assets (your job and your savings) in one place.

Stock options. Much the same advice applies to the option you may be offered to invest in the company stock. If your assets are tied up in a single gamble, a reversal of the company's fortunes could cost you not only your job but your savings.

Often, though, the chance to contribute around 5 percent of your gross salary to buy the company stock is a good deal, if only because the company will partly match your own contributions to this nest egg. The preferable plan, of course, is the one into which the company puts the highest proportion of matching funds.

It may be necessary to wait three or four years after your first contributions until you are vested—that is, receive title to the stock paid for by the company's matching funds. In a solid company it may be well worth the wait. Just make sure you read the fine print carefully.

Deferred compensation. At the upper-income levels of business, one of the more common privileges extended to executives is the ability to defer a portion of salary until later, thus minimizing tax liability. Under the principle known as "constructive receipt," IRS liability begins when you actually get the money rather than when it was earned. Typically, a deferred payment is spread over several years or even withheld until retirement, when the executive's income and tax liability drop substantially. Obviously, when an employee leaves the company for a new job, her balance is paid to her.

Although very few companies extend this privilege to those below the senior ranks, there are signs that some version of it may be coming into general acceptance via the newly popular "salary reduction plans."

Deferred compensation is an important new area of benefits administration. Some idea of why can be gleaned by how fast the money multiplies. For example, a worker who started at $20,000 per year, received annual pay increases of 8 percent, and contributed 4 percent of her salary plus $2000 each year, would have a nest egg of $54,194 after ten years, assuming there had been no withdrawals and an investment return of 10 percent each year. The major risk of these plans is that you may lose some or all of your money if the company goes bankrupt. Again, read the fine print before you sign up.

Relocation. Sometimes a company will want your services badly enough to move you and your family clear across the country and foot the bill. This "benefit" is becoming more of a necessity for the newly hired or transferred employee. A scant seven or eight years ago the cost of moving a family of four a thousand miles was about $10,000. Today, reports Homequity Inc. (a large relocation service) the cost averages four times that, without even counting such additional relocation incentives companies offer as mortgage assistance or acting as last-resort buyer of the employee's previous home. Partly for this reason, the old policy of moving employees around to give them experience in the company's different plants or offices is no longer quite so commonplace. And even if the company decides that a move is cost effective, it may meet strong resistance from the employee, because many people in the twenty-five-to-forty-five age bracket are reluctant to uproot their families.

Nevertheless, moves are often considered essential—by the company, which needs a fresh approach in the new location, and by the employee, who interprets the transfer as a career advancement or fears a black mark in the personnel file if the transfer is turned down. Many Fortune 1000 companies still find and groom top managerial talent by transferring people around (IBM's nickname among company workers is "I've Been Moved"). These peripatetic staff members (moved every five to seven years in most companies) not only become more knowledgeable about their companies but also establish a network of corporate relationships.

Important as relocating can be for career development, some companies are having to come up with more enticements to keep their management on the move. Interest-free loans for down payments on houses, cost-of-living differential allowances, and reimbursement for added income tax liability are all possibilities. These are in addition to the more or less standard house-hunting and temporary living costs, and miscellaneous sums for other items. For two-career couples, another important benefit is company help for the spouse's job search, especially if company regulations prohibit hiring from the same family.

Children. A new kind of benefit is the policy of time off with pay for employees who adopt children. "Companies just hadn't thought of it before," says Christine Selz of Hewitt Associates, a Lincolnshire, Ill., management consultant firm. "But once it's brought to their attention there's a willingness to consider it because it makes for good employee relations and doesn't cost much. Not many people use it."

Emery World Wide Corporation, a freight company with headquarters in Wilton, Conn., allows thirty days' leave with full pay for adopting parents, and New York State allows up to seven months' leave without pay, the same as for biological parents.

In assessing the rights and benefits available in present or future jobs, remember that your rights as an employee are provided and limited by law, but your benefits are limited only by the funds and flexibility of your employer and your skills as a negotiator. James Baehler compares them to Christmas stockings. "A few items protrude, but underneath is a whole host of goodies that can only be suggested." His shopping list runs to fifty-three items in seven categories: Finessing the tax collector (for example, limousine and chauffeur); cash in your pocket (the freedom to do freelance work on your own time); relocation protection (settling-in allowance); peace of mind (paid-up life insurance); and financial leverage (low-interest loans).

It's all worth thinking about.

9
Psychological Issues

In addition to a briefcase full of important if unfinished work, women carry to and from the office a bundle of unfinished psychological business. They bring to their jobs many of the same psychological imperatives they carry throughout the rest of their lives. And the office situation itself may call to the surface problems rooted in hitherto unexamined ambivalences. Unfortunately, simply being aware of what can happen is not by itself enough to help a woman break through psychological barriers that may be hindering her progress.

Any woman who aspires to real power and who wants to savor her success must be willing to do her psychological homework. That means an investment of time, patience, courage, and rigorous honesty in some form of self-examination. "Know thyself" is the oldest injunction in the world, and it is especially important in the realm of psychology, where what you don't know is what hurts you.

THE POWER PROBLEM

Women are uncomfortable with the idea of power. In our culture, the word "power" has a grasping, exploitive connotation that makes it difficult for women to say that they want it. Jean Baker Miller, psychologist and author of *Towards A New Psychology of Women*, points out that "Power has generally meant the ability to advance oneself and, simultaneously, to control, limit and, if possible, destroy the power of others. Power . . . has had at least two components: power *for* oneself and power *over* others."

Yet there is another sort of power, one not of domination but of self-

174

determination and effectiveness. It means tapping the best potential in one-self and inspiring it in others. Rosabeth Moss Kanter calls it "productive power" as opposed to "oppressive power." To *use* such power, of course, a woman must have full access to the information and support networks within her organization. Many women's jobs are still structurally powerless. Each woman must determine if she has taken—or been maneuvered into—a low-profile position that keeps her from taking risks and being visible.

One of the first things to understand, therefore, is that clout can come from the way a job is structured, and women's jobs are often powerless by design. Nevertheless, women's psyches still play a large part in holding them back.

In 1968, Matina Horner, a distinguished research psychologist and the president of Radcliffe College, completed her now-famous study of sex differences and achievement orientation. It was a study that would become enormously influential, especially after it was popularized—and oversimplified—as the "fear of success syndrome." Horner found that working women were plagued by guilt, ambivalence, and other disturbing emotions. She postulated that these emotions arose out of women's conflict between their own "great expectations" that they gain power, and the expectations of society that they fulfill their traditional role.

Other surveys of the working woman's dilemma followed. For example, Alexandra Symonds, an M.D. at the Karen Horney Clinic in New York City, points out that many successful women have been denying "deeply buried dependency needs" for years. These women she says, are more vulnerable than their veneer of composure would lead one to believe. Having disavowed their own need for nurturance, they suffer from a kind of depression that goes hand in hand with psychological malnourishment. Despite their success, they are often confused about their identity. Despite their aura of unflappability, they suffer from inner conflicts and tensions which may be only vaguely understood, or which may derive from very "real" situations—the conflict between developing a career and starting a family, for example.

THE OFFICE FAMILY

Even women who have found a way to juggle career and family, work and love, often have to struggle to bridge the gap between their off-hours behavior and their corporate performance. Men, as we have mentioned, see business within the metaphorical framework of the military or team sports (this is where the traditional notions of power come from). Women tend to view business, or the office, as a kind of extended family.

This can be a terrible liability. Seeing your work world this way complicates an already complicated situation, and sibling rivalry is only one of the entanglements it can lead to. Part and parcel of viewing the office as a family is the "need to fit in," to be part of a friendly group. If you are a manager, you may find that keeping office friendships running smoothly takes precedence over good decision making. If you are in an entry-level position you may find that office friendships undermine your work. For instance, one young woman went to a new job filled with energy and enthusiasm and dozens of fresh ideas. The other people on her level spent much of their time at the coffee machine complaining about how awful everything was. The new woman found herself paying lip service to the malaise in order to "belong." Finally she realized that her new office family was undermining her morale, fostering her dependency and stymying her professional growth. She had to carefully extricate herself from the group and go her own way.

Why do we insist upon transforming the office into a family affair? Here's where a psychological phenomenon known as "transference" comes into play. Many psychological problems have their origins in childhood. The feelings you repress in childhood can surface in adulthood and distort your impressions of other people. For instance, someone who had an overprotective mother may, twenty years later, interpret as interfering her boss's sincere interest in her development. In turn this woman will begin to feel as if she is being treated like a child again, not trusted to take risks. She is simply transferring leftover ambivalent feelings about a parent onto a new authority figure.

The love-hate feelings that once characterized your childhood relationships with your parents can easily be projected onto your relationship with your boss, especially if you fuel the situation by trying to get attention and win approval. (You don't have to be Mary Tyler Moore to have your Lou Grant.) There are no "parents" in the business world; no strong protectors who know everything, no daddies or mommies who will praise us for our good deeds, or indulge our mistakes, or take care of us in return for our loyalty, or punish us when we have the temerity to branch out on our own. Our bosses are just people, and work for the same reasons we do.

Transference is a kind of straitjacket. To escape it you have to examine your feelings and do some digging into your family background, then ask yourself what it is about the situation that is making you feel, and behave, like a child? For example, if as a child you always felt left out of your family, it may be that your herd instinct, your urge to merge, is strong. Having recognized this, you may see that you have been putting a higher value on being liked by your colleagues than on genuine work concerns.

It can be extremely difficult for men or women at work to overcome these projections because business, like society itself, is still by and large paternalistic. It is up to each working woman to first recognize and second avoid the pitfalls of patronage and parentage, whichever the case may be. Only by taking responsibility for her responses and actions, and making a conscious effort not to transfer childhood hangups to the office situation can a woman make sure her work won't be undermined or her spirit broken.

THE IMPOSTOR SYNDROME

The office family is not the only phenomenon to watch out for at work. Another common psychological pitfall is something called the "impostor syndrome." Let's look at how it operates. A young woman we may call Laura Bell is an account manager for a large advertising agency in Chicago. Recently she landed two lucrative accounts for her company. But when Bell's coworkers invited her out to celebrate, she wasn't game. "The market surveys that Steve did had a lot more to do with bringing in those accounts than my work," she said. "As far as my own role in this is concerned, it was just a question of luck. I was the one who got first dibs at going after those accounts. I just can't take credit where credit isn't due."

In fact, the marketing forecasts had little to do with Bell's success. She had studied her two clients carefully, going over annual reports, trying to find out as much as she could about the kinds of advertising that had worked for them in the past and those that hadn't. Luck had nothing to do with it either. Wooing her clients over lunch, impressing them with her business savvy and her knowledge of their rivals' advertising plans, had gotten Bell her victory. But she was unable to acknowledge that landing the accounts had been a victory at all.

Psychologist Pauline Rose Clance and Suzanne Ament Imes, both at Georgia State University in Atlanta, would recognize Bell as a victim of the "impostor syndrome," a devastating problem for some men and for legions of professional women. In fact, the brighter the woman, the more apt she is to fall prey to it. Women like Laura Bell feel that they are fooling everyone, that the competence they exhibit is only an illusion, and that sooner or later they will be "found out." Other symptoms of the impostor syndrome are tendencies to brush off compliments and to set goals that are either too easy or too hard to reach.

Take the case of Maggie Cohen, who met with the manager of her division to take stock of her career and her options in the company, and spent the entire meeting underestimating herself and giving others in the department credit for her accomplishments. For Cohen, the inability to appraise her contributions to the company accurately and to acknowledge her own talents cost her a promotion, and left management with the impression that she would probably never be able to function above the level she had already reached.

In addition to self-deprecation and a visible anxiety in the face of praise, another frequent sign of the syndrome is procrastination. Putting things off until the last minute can be a woman's way of avoiding the fear that she is not equal to the task at hand. That is, if the project is a failure, she can attribute it to her lack of organization, and not to any inherent lack of ability. But if it is a success, her pleasure is contaminated by the fact that she was able to do it so easily. After all, any project easy enough to wrap up in a couple of days (instead of the month that had been allotted by management) is no big deal, so the sense of achievement from doing it well is bound to be soured.

Many women who suffer from the impostor syndrome are relentless perfectionists who fear being found out as imperfect. Others may indeed fear success. We are still plagued by ambivalent feelings about our own achievements and ambition, and denying these feelings is one way to avoid having to deal with them.

Breaking out of the impostor syndrome isn't easy, but Clance and Imes have some clear practical advice:

> Begin by accepting your achievements. Explain them in terms of your actions and abilities. Keep a journal of the positive feedback you get and analyze your reactions to it. Do you habitually dismiss compliments or deny their legitimacy? Do you accept them graciously but secretly doubt you have earned them?
>
> Talk about the impostor phenomenon with friends who may also have suffered from it. Together you may be able to assess how the habit of self-deprecation can ruin the quality of one's working life.
>
> Don't set impossibly high (or low) goals or hold yourself to unrealistic standards. If you spend too much time on a task, trying to do it perfectly, when you should be getting on to something else, your perfectionism is counterproductive.

THE SOCIAL WORKER SYNDROME

As if perfectionism were not enough of a problem, women also tend to bring a kind of "saintliness" to their relations with other people. *Working Woman* columnist Marilyn Machlowitz calls this self-effacing tendency the "social worker syndrome." It is an inclination to make other people's priorities more important than your own. Maybe you help a coworker with a project when you yourself are under a tight deadline, or you make allowances for work that is almost invariably (not occasionally) late. You accept phone calls at home and you're always, but always, ready to listen to other people's personal problems. If so, you are behaving like a social worker and this will cost you professionally as well as personally. If you miss a deadline because you were helping an assistant with a research problem, your excuse may not be acceptable higher up. You cannot count on others for the same graciousness that you extend.

Playing the office social worker is a hard habit to break. In certain instances you may not even want to break the habit, especially if you are in a position in which flexibility is an asset (personnel work is an obvious example). Still, there are going to be times when you must decide whether knowing you helped a coworker through a personal crisis at the expense of your deadline will be consolation enough when your raise or promotion is withheld.

LEARNING TO BE ASSERTIVE

Taken to the extreme, the social worker syndrome can mean that a woman becomes what is referred to by assertiveness-training people as a doormat. Women have a problem being selfish. Why? Carol Gilligan, a Harvard psychologist and author of *In a Different Voice: Psychological Theory and Women's Development*, believes that, because women are reared to be caretakers, they have an ingrained sensitivity to the needs of others. This sensitivity leads women to "attend to voices other than their own and to include in their judgment other points of view." While this may be laudable in certain circumstances, it can be debilitating in others. If a woman struggling to succeed is brought into direct competition with someone who engages her sympathy, she may hold back her opinions and concede too quickly. When push comes to shove, she may give up the fight for an interesting project or even a promotion. Interestingly enough, Gilligan defines "postconventional morality," or a true emotional maturity, as getting past this stage of always putting others before yourself. Women must learn to take a firm stand and give it everything they've got in order not to end up underfoot.

An integral part of assertiveness is a willingness to fight. Avoiding conflict often means being overcompromising; seeking it out is aggressive; confronting conflict, putting forward your side and defending your opinions while validating the other person's is assertive. Being assertive means that you ultimately benefit from the conflict.

One way of learning to be assertive is to practice explaining your feelings. Assertive people will say, "this is becoming very frustrating," aggressive people will provoke others to anger by exploding: "Just what do you think you are doing?" The thing that differentiates aggressiveness from assertiveness is that aggressiveness is often misdirected anger.

Another helpful assertiveness hint that can propel a woman forward, especially when it comes to asking for a raise or negotiating a promotion, is knowing that the word "no" has various interpretations. It can mean "not now, try again later," or "show me why I should say yes." Changing "no" to "yes" is a talent much needed in the corporate world. Having a substantial amount of convincing facts on hand and the right amount of persistence will often do the trick. If you are a manager, don't be surprised if some of your staff try to change your mind in much the same way. Fair is fair.

Sometimes, of course, you have to go beyond assertiveness. In many situations anger—a much-maligned emotion for women—may be a sensible reaction and may lead to a resolution of conflicts that otherwise would have continued to fester, causing problems for you and your company. Sometimes, for instance, controlled anger is the only way to draw out a sulky assistant or pacify two key coworkers who are at continual loggerheads. You can't manufacture anger, however; it has to be a genuine gut reaction.

THE WAY MEN SEE US

Although there are those who would like to think that many of the "traditional" images of women have fallen by the wayside, women still have a problem with how men perceive them. Although they may not admit it, many men do not like to see women outside of their wifely, motherly, sisterly, daughterly, secretarial role—submissive and, above all, supportive. For some men an assertive and successful woman is a threat, and so they need to label her as an unworthy opponent. Tom was one of those men. He knew he was on the slow track, and had credited the economy with keeping him from rising more rapidly up the corporate ladder. When Sue, whom he had trained himself, was promoted twice within a year, he began to wonder aloud exactly whom she was sleeping with. Tom's response is typical of a small, if vocal, minority of male workers who will resort to the old "wives or whores" way of categorizing a woman as a measure of self-defense. Men like Tom console their egos by making clothed but derogatory remarks about women: "her behavior was very flagrant," "she is intentionally provocative," "isn't that just like a woman?"

Rumors can fly freely behind the men's room door. Even for liberal males, reared in the 60s to believe in gender equality, deep-seated expectations of femininity can arise and distort their view of women. They may resort to the "sweetie syndrome," taking a very casual, if seemingly friendly, approach to their female coworkers by calling them "dear" or "hon" or, worse, "girl."

The important thing here is for women to realize that we are in a transition period (a period that will probably last most of our working lives), with women for the first time moving in substantial numbers into positions of power within organizations. Adjustments must be made on both sides—men must learn to trust women to do more than brew a nice cup of coffee and women must help make men comfortable with the fact that they are full, strong, and capable human beings. In this period of transition women need to be especially sensitive both to their own projections and expectations and to those of the people around them. We are all less free than we'd like to think and we all need to come to terms with each other.

Being sensitive does not, however, mean being indulgent or overtolerant. As Jean Baker Miller has pointed out in *Working Woman*, women need to assess what is admirable about the old roles, the old ways of interacting, and then use them *creatively* to enhance their power—go with the flow, but be a strong directional force.

COPING WITH STRESS

For a talented, ambitious, educated, confident, productive person *not* to work would be stressful. But that does not diminish the fact that devoting oneself to a full-time career creates special stresses that must be mastered if one is to work happily and well. And a working woman's stresses are compounded because of the many roles she juggles. Stress occurs when on the morning of a presentation to the board of directors the babysitter calls in sick; when a husband or lover issues the ultimatum, either put away the briefcase for one Sunday or else. . . ; or when the laundry piles up, the bills go unpaid, there is nothing in the refrigerator but sour milk, and the job is demanding twelve to sixteen hours a day. Even good news—a promotion, a better job—can add another source of stress to a woman's already overtaxed life.

Dr. Hans Selye, a leading authority on stress, defines it as the nonspecific response that the body makes to any demand—a broad definition that can mean simply the wear and tear of everyday living. Looked at that way, stress does not seem very alarming, but a stress overload can cause or exacerbate many conditions, such as headaches, heart trouble, high blood pressure, skin ailments, joint pain, menstrual problems, and digestive upsets such as irritable bowel syndrome and ulcers.

Until recently it was believed that the major issues of life, such as the death of a spouse or the loss of a job, were the most stressful. New research suggests the opposite: it is the daily hassles—getting stuck in traffic, waiting for a slow elevator—that get to us most. Furthermore, it's not so much a situation that causes stress, it's our response to it. That is encouraging news, because our reactions to these day-to-day occurrences are often within our control. If, for instance, you remind yourself that the bus's being late is beyond your control, and *use* that time to read, make a list, or talk with someone, you are gaining control of your response and the stress diminishes.

What happens to the body during a stressful situation? When you sense something threatening, your body readies itself to meet the challenge by releasing into the bloodstream a family of biochemicals called catecholamines. These chemicals help you get ready for fight or flight: your heart beats faster; your blood pressure goes up; you breathe faster; your muscles tense; your hands and feet may go cold and sweaty. Sometimes we interpret these signals as the energy to act—to flee an aggressor or turn on the pressure to finish a report. If we don't act—and we can't always run from the office or punch a difficult coworker—the body continues to release stress chemicals. You keep your mouth shut to keep your job, but the biochemicals stay in your bloodstream. If the stress continues, the body can usually adapt to it, but since we have limited resources for this adaptation, we become vulnerable to other stresses that may occur simultaneously. If you encounter too much stress over a long period of time, you can develop a stress disorder (when you're up against a deadline, say, you get the flu). Your target organ for stress—whatever weak spot you have—may be hit the hardest; if your stomach is your target organ, you may become easily nauseated or develop an ulcer.

To control the stress in your life you need to examine the particular cause or causes of your anxiety. Does your job make excessive demands on your time or subject you to brutal deadlines? Is the atmosphere at the office one of cutthroat competitiveness? Are you afraid of being fired—and is it a reasonable fear? Do you get along poorly with your boss, or come into regular contact with "difficult" people? Are you underemployed—in a job that makes little use of your aptitudes or talents? Does a recent promotion make you feel ill equipped to handle your new responsibilities? Or perhaps you are suffering from burnout, the feeling that your job no longer matters to you, or that it is taking more from you than it gives. Is your work area a disaster, with poor lighting or ventilation, noise, or a lack of privacy? Do personal stresses— marital problems, a sick child—add fuel to your anxiety at work?

These serious, stress-inducing situations can make you feel as if your life is out of control. But there are many steps you can take to regain a sense of mastery. The first thing is to remember that, in most cases, you are *not* locked into a job. If you find the atmosphere at work uncongenial, you can seek a similar post elsewhere; if your basic problem is burnout, you can look into translating your skills and experience into a different field. You can also remind yourself forcefully that few problems in life are unsolvable. If work conditions are intolerable, for example, you can join with others to negotiate for improvements. On occasion—when the problem is a pugnacious coworker or when you are going through a personal crisis—the answer may simply be to accept that the situation is unalterable, and go about your work as best you can. If a member of your family is in the hospital, say, take a moment to examine your job responsibilities, see how you can reorganize them in light of your immediate priorities, then concentrate on following your plan to cope with what you've got to do.

These changes in outlook can add a dose of fresh air to anxiety-producing situations. There are also many strategies you can use to survive or lessen the day-to-day stresses encountered at work. Not surprisingly, some of the suggestions apply to working well in general (see Chapter 4, Working Smart). They are even more important when you are under stress.

Don't aim for perfection. Set goals that are within your capabilities.

Set priorities. Divide tasks into A, B, and C categories. Delegate as much as possible.

Say no. No manager is responsible for everyone's every need; refuse to take on projects that take you away from your primary responsibilities. If you are a secretary and you feel that your boss is treating you like a personal servant, speak up.

Don't procrastinate. Tackle unpleasant jobs quickly so that you get them over with. In other words, take control of your work.

Analyze your day. Perhaps you're more productive in the mornings: do a high-priority task then. Make sure you are well prepared for stressful situations, such as meeting with your boss or making a speech.

Assess each situation. Should you fight or flee? Fight only for the things that warrant it.

Boost your self-esteem. When you suffer a setback, think about your past accomplishments. Don't castigate yourself for mistakes; everyone makes them.

Keep your sense of humor.

Take daily breaks. Pressured executives often believe that working nonstop will get the job done faster; instead, they leave themselves vulnerable to burnout.

Such survival strategies do not stop when you leave the workplace: the way you manage your personal life is also essential to your serenity. You should take good care of yourself by eating a balanced diet, getting enough sleep, and enjoying recreation. Vacations are a necessity; they help restore a sense of perspective about your life.

You may also want to look into certain techniques that can help defuse the tensions of daily life. Many women like to have regular massages, a good remedy for backaches, insomnia, fatigue, and stress. Meditation, in which you refocus your attention from the external to the internal, can also help quiet anxieties. Biofeedback, a way of learning how to control physiological responses with the help of a machine, has become a popular stress-reducing method in recent years. It is especially useful for people with migraine headaches, which are often triggered by stress.

If the stresses of life are wearing you out, you owe it to yourself to find some private time to wind down and relax. Even a bubble bath or a facial can work wonders. You should try, at all costs, to avoid chemical "solutions." Alcohol or tranquilizers may relieve stress temporarily, but they don't solve the problems that cause the stress and they are dangerous substances. People who suffer from extreme stress, and who feel that they can't get a grip on their problems, should consider seeking psychotherapy.

Exercise is an excellent stress antidote. Regularly pursued, exercise can improve endurance, sharpen the mind, and calm the nerves. A well-balanced workout should include exercises for flexibility, strength, and endurance— and it should be fun. The last thing you need is another stressful responsibility.

For the already overextended working woman, who may be managing a family as well as a career, finding the *time* to exercise may seem an insurmountable problem. Yet her multiple stresses make a regular program of exercise all the more important. Possible solutions may be an early morning run, an after-work aerobics class, or a swim at a health club during lunch hour. Engaging in such activities only twice a week, and adding tennis or biking on the weekend, could make the crucial difference in a working woman's energy level and her peace of mind. Exercise not only keeps the body fit, it is a natural tranquilizer.

You can also make exercise an integral part of your day. If you live and work in a city, you can walk to or from work, or walk to that business lunch across town instead of hailing a cab. Take mini-exercise breaks during the day. Stretching or doing shoulder rolls, and remembering to stand when you make phone calls, can help relax tense muscles and keep your blood moving.

Some corporations, such as Xerox, General Foods, and American Can, have invested in on-the-premises fitness facilities for their employees. The health benefits of such programs, many of which also emphasize proper nutrition, make them worthwhile. Top executives know this: a survey of Fortune 500 chief executive officers found that they exercise on a regular basis, watch their diets, have a low hypertension rate, and get a minimum of six hours of sleep each night.

Many corporations are responding to more than their employees' physical needs. More than 2,500 corporations, unions and nonprofit organizations provide employee-assistance programs. The purpose is twofold: to help the troubled worker and to save the corporation money in lost time and medical benefits, since employees' personal problems are often reflected in absenteeism, sick leave, and high turnover. Companies generally take one of two approaches in starting an EAP. They start in-house programs responsible to a department in the organization or contract with outside professionals for counseling services. Whatever the method of operation, EAPs (also known as employee health counseling, staff advisory services, human-service networks, troubled-employee programs, or employee counseling) concentrate on three main services. Counselors evaluate the problems and needs of the worker, perform short-term counseling, and, if it seems desirable, refer the person to a suitable outside agency or therapist.

Measures such as fitness centers and counseling services are part of the trend toward humanizing the workplace, a benefit for both employees and employers.

LIVING ON A PSYCHIC INCOME

We have seen that women still earn only 60 cents to every man's dollar. The economic consequences of lower pay are obvious, and as more and more women become the breadwinners for their families, bridging the gap is becoming more important than ever. Even at the top levels of America's most powerful corporations, the discrepancy between what men earn and what equally qualified, equally responsible women earn is a painful reminder of how far we still have to go.

This should be the stuff of revolution. Every unpaid dollar should add more kindling to the fire, pushing underpaid women closer to standing up en masse to corporate America and demanding an explanation. But there is a paradox here that, in one form or another, has intrigued many a psychologist, manager, and feminist. Almost all women admit that women in general are the victims of pay discrimination, but when it comes to sizing up one's own circumstances, acknowledgment is slow in coming. Why aren't more women angry?

The study by the Public Agenda Foundation (see page 21, Chapter 1,

Where We Are) documents this phenomenon. The differences in salary showed up in the survey, of course, but women in positions across the board, from clerical to professional, were as satisfied with their jobs as the men who work side by side with them. In addition, more women than men (56 percent to 48 percent) claimed to have an "inner need to do the very best I can, regardless of pay." Despite lower incomes, the women in the survey were more committed to the work ethic than their male counterparts.

Faye Crosby, an associate professor of psychology at Yale University, has studied this phenomenon. In a book published in 1982, *Relative Deprivation and Working Women*, Crosby reported the results of a survey of 405 men and women in Newton, Massachusetts. The women in Crosby's survey felt that, though women as a group were discriminated against, they personally were not. According to Crosby, this point of view may stem from an inability to assign guilt to individuals. Admitting that you are the victim of discrimination requires making your employer a villain and you an accessory to the crime. This in turn can lead to a painful severing of ties, shattered loyalties, and broken trust. Crosby warns women about letting "psychic income," the joy and self-esteem they derive from working, override their willingness to demand equal pay.

Whatever the roots of women's predicament at work, understanding it is the first step toward dealing with it in a constructive way. This is also true of another aspect of life that is often related to psychic income: workaholism.

The term "workaholic" has a negative connotation. The workaholic is typically seen as a person who cannot stop working, whether in the office, on vacation, or at home. She is the one who brings a beeper to the family Sunday dinner, a briefcase to the beach. The workaholic might be described as the woman who "doth sublimate too much"—meaning that her obsession with work grows out of her discomfort with another unfulfilled area of her life. Whether that is always true or not, the genuine workaholic *has* lost perspective about the meaning of her work and the need for rest. If you know someone strung out on work, yet totally dependent on it for her identity, chances are she doesn't recognize her own workaholism. Therapy may be in order, but first she must convince herself that therapy time is productive work time.

Marilyn Machlowitz, author of the book *Workaholics* and a self-proclaimed workaholic, contends that workaholism is not necessarily a character flaw. For Machlowitz, workaholics are simply people who must constantly be in motion, whether at work or at play. They are happy when they are busy. This describes a less tortured type of workaholism that may be quite healthy. Some people seem to have a strong desire for the stress related to hard work.

Theirs is a "healthy stress" which gives them the incentive and energy to keep on going.

Whether we work in a fashion approaching workaholism or not, we spend at least one-third of our lives at our jobs. Whether we are shooting for the top or just trying to make ends meet, we bring to a job all sorts of psychological needs. We must recognize what these needs are, and wear them, as the zen masters say, like a loose garment.

10
The Efficacious Office

Come the end of our working lives, most of us will have spent 2,500 hours a year—100,000 hours total—in our offices. This is easily as much time as the waking hours we spend at home, so it makes sense that the office environment plays an important role in our work lives. Despite this, office design has largely been given short shrift, the attitude of companies being "Sure it's nice to have an elegant reception area and executive suites to impress visitors, but such refinements are hardly relevant to the hardnosed world of corporate financial performance." As for the back-office areas, these have been mostly ignored, left to company purchasing agents and individual workers to organize and furnish.

Many offices reflect this neglect. The conventional arrangements of the insurance companies in the 1920s are still often the norm: managers secluded in outside offices while row upon row of lower-level employees sit in a central bullpen. Even fairly enlightened companies have failed to adapt their offices to the last two decades' dramatic changes in corporate hierarchies, technology, and work styles. It's one thing, for example, to have ten manual typewriters tapping away and quite another to have noisy photocopying machines and word processing printers side by side with a middle manager trying to devise a new sales strategy.

Poorly planned offices work against people. Bad layouts break up departments illogically, making communication awkward and time-consuming. People in badly designed cubicles have little privacy, many visual distractions, and too much noise. Computers are placed on tables too high for comfortable operation; chairs don't support users' backs; cheap materials wear out quickly;

and lack of storage and ill-thought-out mixtures of colors, styles, and furnishings make offices look cluttered and unattractive.

Workplaces needn't be like this, of course. The best are stylish and functional. Most important, they are effective "support systems" for the people working in them. Indeed, recent studies have shown that people who work in well-planned, pleasant environments are more productive, have better morale, and are also healthier. A 1983 study by the BOSTI, the Buffalo Organization for Social and Technological Innovation, for instance, showed that if companies invest in well-designed offices, they can expect their managerial, technical, and professional staff to increase their productivity by 5 percent. Translated into a dollar figure (based on an employee's annual salary), that comes to an average saving of $1,600 to $1,700 per person per year. And although the productivity increase for clerical staff is less—about 3 percent of their salary—annual savings still come to about $400 per person. Company executives worried about productivity, one of the most urgent issues on their agendas, are beginning to pay attention to such findings and reconsider their views on office design.

By knowing the fundamentals of good design, *everyone*—not just administrators—can make her surroundings more pleasant and thus more productive. By being aware of what makes for a well-planned office, you can:

Organize your own office or section for maximum efficiency.

Learn to compensate for flaws in your office's design.

Rearrange your office furniture or add some of your own equipment or furnishings to make better use of the space.

Lobby the company's purchasing agent for better storage.

Know what to push for when you do get a chance—as a manager or small-business owner—to influence office design. As an entrepreneur, especially, you may need to renovate an office space; you should at least be able to choose a well-designed office chair.

PLANNING

What goes into the planning of a successful work space? Ideally, the skills and tools of a professional interior designer. (To locate a qualified designer, see the list of professional associations and magazines in the Appendix B, Suggestions for Further Reading, page 328.) One of the first steps these professionals take, though, is to consult the people who will be using the space. That means talking not only to the department head but to every staff member, finding out the kind of work people do, who they do it with, what machines they work on, what storage they need, and so on. As the BOSTI study discovered, people like to be consulted about their office's design, and their performance on the job improves as a result.

Let's look at some of the other things that designers consider in planning an office. First, offices should be "P-places" (people places), not "O-places" (object places), according to the environmental psychologist Franklin Becker. Offices should *serve* people. They should not be just an arbitrary arrangement of objects but rather should support the activities of those who use them. This is especially important as more and more computer equipment is introduced into the workplace.

The "open plan" was one of the first attempts designers made to humanize the office environment. In the open office (which originated in Germany in the form of an "office landscape") walls were replaced by movable partitions, to encourage communication, and people were grouped according to function rather than rank.

For those in the bullpen, the move to partitioned work spaces was a step up. Many managers, though, felt that it meant a loss of status. Lack of privacy was a common complaint. Over the years, designers have become more conscious of these concerns and have fine-tuned open-office planning. At the same time, furniture companies have upgraded their products to make the office elegant, comfortable, *and* efficient.

The perfect office arrangement has yet to be found, but common sense and designers' experience dictate certain principles of layout, privacy, lighting, and so on.

LAYOUT

People should be grouped logically. According to office designer John Pile, the most active lanes of communication should be the shortest ones. In other words, those who work together most often should be nearest to one another. In this respect the flexibility of the open plan is advantageous: work space can be rearranged quite easily to accommodate temporary groupings such as task forces.

Everyone should have easy access to the telephone, the most common business tool, and people who frequently use other office machines (computers, copying machines) should be located reasonably close to them.

PRIVACY

People's need for privacy, both visual and acoustic, is much greater than had previously been thought. According to the BOSTI study, the visual privacy essential to good work performance can be provided by a work space that meets certain conditions: It must be enclosed on at least three sides by partitions that you can't see over when standing. Such privacy is lacking in many open offices. But the traditional closed office with a door is not necessarily the answer. "What really encourages interaction and employee communication," says Michael Brill, an architect who is the head of BOSTI, "is exactly the same thing that supports privacy: an open-office system with lots of enclosure and employee control over physical and visual access. . . . Too much visual access actually leads to decreased performance."

Walls are not the only way of insuring visual privacy. Screens, wardrobes, plants, and other accessories give some seclusion and break up long vistas. They also can give each worker a well-defined space, satisfying the proven psychological need for one's own turf.

Acoustic privacy is also important. People need to feel that they can talk without being overheard and at the same time not be disturbed by noise. It's all right if voices are somewhat audible, but you shouldn't be able to hear clearly what people are saying.

Acoustic ceilings, movable screens, and sound-absorbent surfaces can cut down on noises. The placement of work stations is equally important, says Suzanne Bates, director of interiors at Architectural Alliance, a design firm in Minneapolis. Two people should never be talking toward each other when they share a panel, and noisy machinery should be set up in a place where it won't disturb anyone.

Becker points out a number of simple tactics that are useful for increasing privacy:

Arrange your desk so that you don't directly face the door or opening of your work space (this will cut down on distractions from passersby).
Use a plant as a screen.
Place a solid cabinet or bookshelf a few feet inside your door (also to minimize distractions).
If company policy permits, use a personal stereo with headphones to control what you hear.
Mask disturbing sound with a white-noise machine "that can provide a form of privacy without offending anyone, as a closed door might."

LIGHTING

According to surveys of office workers, lighting is an extremely important aspect of the office environment. In fact, people's satisfaction with their offices is directly related to their ability to control the light. Poor lighting can lead to eyestrain and fatigue, which cuts down on productivity.

But what *is* proper office lighting? Dim light is obviously more suited to nightclubs than work spaces, but many offices, unfortunately, go overboard on the assumption that there never can be too much light. The result: vast banks of fluorescent lights flooding light across a work area, often producing glare that reflects off work surfaces and papers. The reflections and distortions caused by badly positioned and excessive light are a particular problem for the growing number of people who work at video-display terminals, whether a typist at a word processor or an executive at her personal computer.

More important than lots of overhead light is a comfortable general light in the room, supplemented by movable lamps that can be adjusted over your work. The amount of light needed varies not only with the type of work but with individual preference. Lamps should be easy to adjust; architect's lamps on swing arms are excellent for many uses. Other tips on lighting:

To reduce glare on your desk, move the desk between, rather than directly under, overhead lights. (If you are unsure where the glare is coming from, place a mirror on the work surface and look for light sources.) Try replacing fluorescents with lower-wattage bulbs and use a good lamp for close work and reading. Special diffusers are also available for fluorescent lights.

Reduce glare on VDTs by adding an antiglare filter. Many of the latest computers come equipped wth nonglare terminals, a fact that should influence purchasing decisions. Unfortunately, natural light often produces the worst glare on VDT screens. Position your terminal as far from the window as you can, and don't face a window either—the contrast in light is too great, and your eyes will tire more quickly.

Try to have a range of light levels in an office, and avoid working too long in any one light condition. Your eyes will tire less easily if they adjust to different light types and levels several times a day.

VENTILATION

There's not much an individual can do to change an office building's ventilation system, but you should be alert to signs of poor ventilation. The problem with sealed buildings is that any contaminants in the building will continue to circulate inside and affect the occupants' health. These pollutants can range from carbon monoxide (released by smoking) to chemicals (from office machinery such as photocopiers) to allergens (from various cleaning fluids, typewriter ribbons, and so on).

When office workers complain of chronic headaches, breathing problems, or sore eyes, for which no clear medical cause can be found, the office environment is sometimes the culprit. If you suspect you have a problem caused by something at the office, certain specific steps may help. Smoking can be restricted to one designated area, and office machines can be kept in enclosed rooms away from general work areas. If you develop an allergy to a specific substance, you may be able to work in a different area of the building where the substance is not used.

TEMPERATURE

Office temperature may not present a health risk but it does affect people's comfort on the job. In a 1980 Louis Harris survey, more than half the office workers polled said that their office temperature was not right. No one temperature will be just right for everybody, but Joel Makower, in his book *Office Hazards*, suggests some comfortable ranges: with light summer clothing, the temperature should be between 75 and 81 degrees F; with heavy winter clothing, between 67 and 74 degrees F; and with between-season clothing, from 72 to 78 degrees F.

STORAGE

The paperless office may be the wave of the future, but for the time being most of us have enough papers, documents, books, magazines, and files to choke any office. Before you begin considering how to store all this paper, think about what you can throw out. Ann Hoffman, head of records management at the Pillsbury Company in Minneapolis, did just that. When the dust settled, she had cleared out 42 tons of records and 348 barrels of miscellaneous items, ranging from a pair of shoes dating back to the 1920s to flower pots. What she kept she consolidated: 365 boxes of paper went into storage and another 305 were microfilmed. The upshot: 400 fewer file cabinets, 45 percent less file space needed.

After the cleanup, make an inventory of what needs to be stored—now and six months from now. Make a note of the amounts and sizes of materials and how accessible they need to be. Decide the length of time each item should be kept, and schedule "paper purges" at regular intervals.

File drawers and shelves are not the only storage answers today. Blueprints and large drawings or charts can be hung on special racks or laid flat in plain files like the ones architects use. Computer printouts and disks can be stored in specially designed hanging files, thus freeing desk space. Try organizing papers, pamphlets, and magazines into standard-size cardboard file boxes (available at stationery stores). These can then be stored neatly on a bookshelf. If your desk faces a wall, think about putting up a wall-mounted storage unit above your desk, within easy arm's reach but allowing you more desk surface. Swamped by books? You may be able to move some of them to a central area in your department.

FURNITURE

The best office furnishings look good *and* work well. They rank the human need for easy movement, physical comfort, and health as high as aesthetics. To produce such user-friendly furniture, manufacturers use ergonomics, the study of the physical relationship of human beings to machines. Ergonomics recognizes that people vary considerably in size and proportions and that furniture must accommodate these differences. Some tips for buying office furnishings:

> The people who will actually use the equipment should test it before purchase, looking for obvious "bad fits." Many women, for instance, will find that desks are too high and chairs are overscaled.
> Buy high-quality materials and products. They may cost more, but they will wear better, support the user more effectively, and ultimately be a sounder investment.
> Look for full lines of furniture from which you can choose a variety of chairs, desks, tables, and storage units. This will give you flexibility should your needs change or grow, while allowing you to maintain a coherent style in the office.

CHAIRS

Office chairs haven't yet been labeled with warnings that "sitting may be hazardous to your health," but a growing opinion suggests that they should be. Back problems, stiff muscles, stress, and fatigue can result from badly designed office seating. Here's what to look for in a good office chair:

> *Support.* The chair should support your back when you're sitting in a normal working position. The lower back, especially, needs firm support to help you sit up straight.
> *Proper seat dimensions.* The chair seat should not hit the backs of your knees. An overlong seat will cause you to slump in your chair, and that prevents the back rest from supporting your back. The front edge of the seat should be rounded, since sharp edges restrict circulation in the legs.
> *Adjustability.* The best way to sit for most work is with your upper and lower legs at right angles and your feet flat on the floor. To allow this, your chair's height should be adjustable to your dimensions. But sitting too long in any position can cause tired muscles, constriction of blood

vessels, and pressure on nerves. The more easily adjustable the chair, the more accommodating it can be to a variety of sitting positions during the day. (It can even be used comfortably by several different people working at one station at different times of the day.) Naturally, a chair that adjusts without your having to get up (by means of a handy lever, for instance) is the best choice. If a chair isn't easily adjustable, people just won't bother to change it, even if they are uncomfortable.

Stability. The chair should stand on a five- (not a four-) spoked base and should be mounted on casters for easy movement.

DESKS

The conventional notion of a desk—a 30-by-60-inch rectangle with drawers tucked underneath on both sides—is giving way to new ideas. For instance, a manager who rarely writes more than a few lines can choose to have a smaller writing surface but opt for a much larger conference table for the many meetings she conducts. Some newer furniture systems offer a kit of parts that let you customize an office to your particular needs. Parts may include typing tables, computer keyboard supports, even a small swing-away telephone stand. The key to planning a rational work space is to tailor the work surfaces as much as possible to your own work style. Some tips:

Size. Many desks are too high for women. Ideally, your arms should rest horizontal to the desk surface as your work; your wrists shouldn't be higher than your elbows. This means, of course, that typing or computer tables should be even lower than writing surfaces, to take into account the height of the keyboard itself. Again, as for chairs, look for adjustability.

Killing clutter. Desk tops intended to be work surfaces too often become unsightly storage places for piles of paper, office equipment, and knick-knacks. This clutter reduces your productivity (you waste a lot of time looking for papers), and it gives others the impression that you are too busy to see anyone or badly organized. Studies have shown, though, that extreme neatness doesn't give the best impression either. "Organized stacks" are the better solution. As Becker comments, "People know that you are active and involved but also see you as in control."

Tactics for gaining control of your desk top begin with analyzing the kind of work you do on your desk. Perhaps some equipment (the stapler or the telephone) can be moved to another surface. Or you may want a separate small table, kept free of everyday business, for meetings with visitors. Try moving your in/out trays off the desk to a nearby shelf. To organize the paper you work with regularly, use one of the many organizers available: wall-mounted or desk-top racks in which you can keep your most active files. These also help prevent the in tray from becoming just another storage box. Keep souvenirs, awards, and knickknacks to a minimum. Decide which are the most important personally and professionally, and stick to them.

THE COMPUTER

In the much heralded "new office," white collars will turn pinker as executives are able to produce reports or calculate complex statistics at their own desktop terminals rather than leaving these jobs to secretaries or assistants. At all levels of corporate America—managerial, secretarial, technical—more and more people will be using some sort of computer on their jobs, be it a personal computer, a word processor, or a terminal hooked to a larger system. Yet studies conducted in 1980 and 1981 by the National Institute of Occupational Safety and Health, an agency of the U.S. Department of Health and Human Services, raise some concern about working on video-display terminals. NIOSH found that VDT operators have more health complaints than nonoperators. For example, 91 percent report eyestrain, compared to 60 percent of nonusers. NIOSH further concluded that VDT users are more prone to stress problems. They are more anxious, depressed, and fatigued than nonusers. In fact, the study found "higher levels of job stress than have been observed on assembly lines."

Several precautions can help alleviate stress and prevent health problems. NIOSH recommends a work/rest regimen: one fifteen-minute break after two hours of continuous VDT work under moderate visual and work-load demands; one break every hour if visual and work-load demands are high. You should have an eye examination before starting work on a VDT. Because you will be shifting focus continually from keyboard to screen to document, you may want to consider getting eyeglasses specifically prescribed for the viewing distance from your eyes to the screen. Although radiation has been discussed as a possible danger for VDT users, tests of VDTs by the U.S. Bureau of Radiological Health illustrate that the likelihood of being exposed to harmful levels is very low indeed. As a precaution, use only machines for which the manufacturer has provided information about emission levels.

Good design of the terminal and the work station can do a lot to reduce potential stresses. Indeed, it is a must. Some pointers:

The screen should tilt and turn as the user wishes.
The keyboard should slope slightly and should have palm rests.
The keys should be large enough to see easily.

The keyboard should be detachable from the terminal so that you can use it in different positions.

The top edge of the screen should be no higher than the viewer's eye level.

The viewer should be able to adjust the brightness and contrast of the characters on the screen.

There should be special provisions for controlling glare, such as a screen hood or an antiglare filter.

Images on the screen should not flicker.

Letters should be squared, have upper and lower case, and have true descenders and ascenders (the g should drop below the line and the h should rise about it).

Proper lighting is essential, of course (see "Lighting," page 191). It should be indirect, bounced off upper walls and ceilings to reduce glare.

Computer furniture is as important as the machine itself, but despite the huge interest in computers, few furniture manufacturers have come up with creative, thoughtful responses to their rapid rise in the business world. The sheer speed of computerization is partly to blame, with new products introduced almost daily. It wasn't so long ago that computers *were* furniture— bulky, complicated objects confined to their own hermetic environment, with few terminals or operators—and the number of people directly affected by computer technology was relatively small. Silicon chips and the quick drop in prices have changed all that. Terminals and personal computers are everywhere.

Computers bring new efficiency to the office, but they also bring problems, often because they are purchased without adequate support furniture. Crowding of scarce desk-top space, noisy printers, incorrect keyboard heights, and unsightly (even dangerous) cable tangles are some of the most obvious drawbacks. In one New York office, for example, two word-processing operators are crammed into a hallway. One operator has intense, glaring light falling on her screen. The other sits in virtual darkness. Although the terminals are on adjustable stands, the stands are not adjusted and the machines are too high. There is inadequate space for papers and other desk work, people frequently pass by the work stations, and a printer clatters away under inadequate noise cover.

Management failed to carry through on the investment in the original equipment, and this technological sweatshop is the result. Two employees and $80,000 in computers are being misused for want of proper attention to the environment and to basic furniture.

The scene is being repeated all over the country. It is not technology that is the problem but the introduction of "half a technology." The total technology of office automation should include both the computer hardware and the support equipment that enables people to use the hardware in comfort and safety.

These are not trivial concerns. The problems associated with computerizing an office can reduce the effectiveness of new technologies. If using computers is cumbersome and uncomfortable, managers will be slow to accept them. Companies may find, contrary to expectation, that productivity and efficiency actually decline after computers are introduced. Proper design and installation of computer furniture (as well as good training, of course) make computers more usable.

Tables are now available that tilt for optimum screen angle and height. There are keyboard supports that swivel for proper typing angle and swing out of the way when the computer is not in use. There are even elegant cabinets for printers that greatly reduce noise.

IMAGE

The standard-issue office is usually an anonymous place, but it needn't be. By personalizing it you can make it your territory. Remember, though, that your office is a place of business. Don't throw just anything up on the walls or shelves. Each object will say something about you to visitors. Photographs of you with a senator signal status as much as a mahogany desk; dime-store jokes and a Miss Piggy poster give quite another impression. If you have a reputation for being rather forbidding, however, you may want to include a funny or light touch—a business cartoon, say—to help break the ice with visitors. A cautionary note about family pictures: When a man keeps photos of his family in his office, he appears stable and mature. When a woman does, people may interpret this to mean that her children—not her work—take first priority.

Becker's studies suggest that small changes in your office layout can also greatly affect your image. How you position your desk, for example, can influence the impressions others have of you and thus how effective you are. According to Becker, "You should be clear about what kind of impressions you want to create and then use the environment subtly to help strengthen them." He points out, for example, that an open desk placement, in which your desk does not separate you from visitors, will make visitors feel more comfortable and welcome than an arrangement where your desk stands guard between you and whoever comes into your office. The open arrangement is particularly appropriate if you are considered difficult to know or aloof.

Moving to a more cooperative position (with your visitor at the side of the desk, for example) will make you more effective. If, on the other hand, you are viewed as lacking authority, "the distinct barrier of a desk may help reinforce your authority and responsibility."

Just as surely as your manner or dress projects an image, your office—its artwork, color, textures, furniture arrangements—can all be designed to create the impression you want: up-to-the-minute, creative, warm, powerful. A good office supports productive and effective work, but beyond that, it can work *for* you.

11

Improving the Quality of Work Life

Millions of women are struggling with the conundrum of motherhood plus career. Other women refuse to accept the possibility that devotion to career requires the quality of life to suffer. Still others believe simply that there should be more ways to work than nine to five, five days a week, fifty weeks a year, for forty-five years. For all working women who ever ask themselves, "Is this all there is?" there's hope. After a century and a half of rigid timekeeping, the tyranny of the standard work schedule is at last being challenged.

Though the movement toward a new flexibility at work may have been slowed down because of the current job shortage, some 21 million people in the United States already function under official work schedules and systems that fit their lives, instead of the other way around.

Many of the new ways of working were initially developed on the factory floor. Unions and management got together to work out steps to increase productivity without increasing cost, or to cushion the effects of cutbacks and avoid layoffs. They also wanted to see if they could improve the quality of workers' lives, an issue that eventually assumed more importance than wages.

This sudden concern for making work pleasanter is mostly enlightened self-interest. At the same time women flooded into the workforce, and men *and* women acknowledged they had priorities in addition to work, the old ways of running factories and other large organizations—ways which both management and unions tried to maintain for a long time—turned out to be inefficient. Their rigid time-keeping kept productivity low and costs unnecessarily high. For American industries to compete effectively in world markets they had to make radical changes in the way they operated. A system of flexible work schedules was one such change. Not only does flexitime boost productivity and raise employee morale, it also cuts down on expenses such as absenteeism and energy consumption.

Involving employees in discussions and decisions about new work rosters has, not surprisingly, proved rewarding. Hundreds of employers have harnessed their workers' brainpower in variously titled Quality Circles, Employee Involvement Teams, and Labor Management Committees in which both sides get together to come up with ways to make things work better. "Work innovations, based on grassroots employee involvement in decision making, are not a gimmick or a passing fad but a 'new look' in management," says Jerome M. Rosow, president of the Work in America Institute. "The recession will certainly end but the structural changes that have taken place in the economy will remain. In this tough, competitive environment, employers will turn increasingly to participation, cooperation and joint problem solving as a means of survival."

One consequence of such changes will be fewer layoffs and more jobs to go around. More than five years ago a Louis Harris poll reported that between 30 and 40 million workers would be willing to trade up to 10 percent of their pay for a proportional reduction in work hours. This alone, if implemented on a voluntary basis, could create the equivalent of three or four million full-time jobs, a considerable step toward achieving full employment in this country.

These innovations serve the interests not only of working mothers who want to be with their families but of many other women as well. Recent studies show that today's employees, with more education than those of previous generations, seek greater self-fulfillment from work. They want to use all their skills, and they expect to participate in decisions affecting their jobs and their workplace. Happily, management has found that acceding to these demands improves productivity, and employers and employees together are finding new ways of working to achieve common goals.

Today the most common variations on working nine to five, five days a week are flexible work plans, work- or job-sharing, and working part-time.

FLEXITIME

Still something of an ambiguous buzzword, flexitime in practice has become the fastest-growing of all the innovations in the workplace. Simply put, it allows employees to choose starting and quitting times within limits set by management. Since its introduction barely a decade ago, flexitime has spread to some 10 million workers, many of them federal employees. Since Congress authorized an Alternate Work Schedules experiment in 1979, more than 40 percent of government agencies have taken part.

Flexitime takes various forms, from a simple eight-hour day based on a starting time chosen by the employee, through variable day schedules, all the way to the so-called maxiflex system, under which employees are permitted to vary their hours every single day. In the most popular version of maxiflex, people can choose to work a full, thirty-six-hour week in four nine-hour days instead of five seven-hour ones. The system adapts to both white- and blue-collar jobs, the main difference in the latter being that some technological tasks require the worker's unbroken attention for at least a few hours at a time. But even with production-line operations, employers have started to allow shift swapping, so a worker wanting to take off all or part of a shift may arrange for a colleague of comparable skill to substitute for her.

The key to a good flexitime system seems to be the employer's effort to design jobs so that employees have the maximum independence and responsibility. An atmosphere of trust and cooperation is another essential. Flexitime and time clocks don't go well together.

Hewlett-Packard, the Palo Alto, California, electronics firm that introduced flexitime at a single plant in 1972, now offers flexible hours to all its employees worldwide. Skill sharing is an important part of its system. Workers rotate jobs regularly and cross-training is continual. One of the company policies which aids in coverage and supervision is that at least two workers doing a job must be present at a location. Things are also arranged so the organization is decentralized. Units are small and autonomous and, even more important, employees are appraised by the work they produce, not the hours they work. Such additional criteria as quality, contribution to the workplace, teamwork, compatibility, judgment, initiative, and dependability are taken into account, and supervisors are also appraised on leadership, innovation, planning and organization, and employee development. The physical plant at corporate headquarters is an open system with no built-in status distinction. Managers and production workers sit side by side.

Flexitime, where it occurs on a community-wide basis, has yielded other benefits. It has eased the pressure of urban transportation, extending the rush-hour "window" by as much as two hours at the beginning and end of each workday. This not only makes commuting more pleasurable but improves energy efficiency, because more room on public buses decreases the number of people who have to drive to work. In Seattle, Washington, this conservational aspect of flexitime is being explored further. A federal grant from the Department of Transportation is allowing Seattle employers to offer workers a flexitime transit pass at a discount rate.

The introduction of new work schedules, and even the transition to a shorter week, has been received enthusiastically on all sides. The minor disadvantages, all on the employer's side—occasional problems with supervision, higher utility costs, overtime adjustments—have been offset by gains in productivity. Among the major industries, finance, insurance, real estate, public administration, and trade have found it easiest to adjust to shifting schedules, and the transition from five- to four-day weeks has been smoother than the earlier shift from six to five.

Many firms that have adopted a four-day week use multiple shifts of workers to extend the days and hours in which the firm does business. This is in marked contrast to the typical five-day week, which means that business grinds to a halt each weekend. "This might suggest," says the U.S. Dept. of Labor, "that adoption of a four-day week is a less radical step for employers than was the adoption of a five-day week."

Some of the changes, nevertheless, have had radical social consequences. In a handful of industries, notably textiles and rubber, the mandatory double or time-and-a-half pay schedules that prevailed on weekends have yielded to straight-time wages, with Saturdays and Sundays recompensed like any other day for those forty-hour workweeks.

Even more profound than the changes brought about by flexible schedules are the changes in the job classifications themselves.

WORK SHARING

Once each worker had only one specific part to play in the assembling of a product. Now duties are occasionally merged or overlapped, and workers are learning to interchange their skills. General Motors' Livonia, Michigan, plant is one of nine around the country that have introduced a "pay-for-knowledge" program, under which employees learn to do all the jobs in a particular section and are paid extra for each skill they acquire. This allows much more flexibility in working roles. And where productivity costs have become too high in relation to the goods produced, such work sharing has helped to counteract layoffs: skilled workers master seven separate jobs and stand willing to pitch in as needed.

The impact that layoffs have on the employee, the family, and the community at large is destructive and pervasive. When work sharing can prevent layoffs, there is minimal disruption of society in general, and everyone gains. Employers maintain productivity by retaining skilled employees; they avoid retraining costs and have more flexibility in their placement of people because more people can turn their hand to more tasks. Employees continue to enjoy earnings, benefits, and job security, and affirmative action gains are preserved. The community also gains in many ways, not the least of which is the preservation of tax revenues and the avoidance of welfare costs.

There have been other, less predictable side benefits of work-sharing plans. Finding they had more time for personal matters, employees began working with greater dedication. Supervisors and foremen found that reduced schedules and a drop in absenteeism gave them a chance to catch up on paperwork and administer training courses. All this, of course, reduces the employer's costs. Against this, some high-seniority employees may register lower earnings, and there are complications for those workers who do lose their jobs. Insurance laws in most states prohibit the collection of partial benefits for partial employment.

Recently legislators at both state and federal levels have tried to modify these laws, and in 1978 California became the first state to pass a law known as "short-time compensation." California's experimental Work Sharing Unemployment Insurance plan was extended in 1982. As of April 1982 it had covered more than 100,000 employees in about 3,000 different plans, with, on the average, claimants receiving payment for one day's unemployment per week.

One of its textbook successes was the Pinedale plant of the Vendo Company, a worldwide manufacturer of vending machines whose sales plummeted in 1979. Instead of laying off its workers, the company placed 253 of them (almost half its workforce) on a work-sharing plan under which they worked thirty-two hours a week for the remaining four months of the year. During this period employees received full fringe benefits (at a cost to the employer of about $100 per employee each month), and the combination of four days' wages, partial unemployment compensation, and already-scheduled wage increases provided take-home pay that was approximately the same as before.

Even without short-time compensation benefits, companies can sometimes achieve the same effects with a little ingenuity. In Indiana, Pennsylvania, management and union officials at a tire and rubber company devised a furlough plan under which one-third of the workers would be laid off each week on a rotating basis. During a four-month period each group of employees worked and was paid for two weeks out of three, collecting unemployment benefits for the third week, and retaining eligibility for all fringe benefits. Despite working nine weeks less in 1980 than in 1979, employees found their incomes at least the same because of previously negotiated cost-of-living adjustments, vacation benefits, and of course the unemployment compensation.

In the public sector in California some groups of employees have taken the initiative on work sharing. Through their service unions employees of Santa Clara County, for example, have won a variety of optional working plans. Under one of them each employee may, for six months at a time, request a reduction of work time and pay of either 2.5, 5, 10, or 20 percent. An individual may take the time reduction in the form of fewer hours per day, or days per week, or even in longer blocks of time during the month.

Given enough ingenuity, management and labor can develop schedules to meet the most diverse operating requirements and personal needs. When United Airlines announced during the 1980 recession that it had to lay off 200 flight attendants, their service organization, the Association of Flight Attendants, offered an alternative scheme. The attendants themselves formed work-sharing teams—usually consisting of one junior and one senior employee—and together they worked out the details of pay, benefits, and hours of work (in most cases alternating months or determining on a trip-by-trip basis who would fly). As a result, United was able to avert 125 of the proposed 200 layoffs.

These experiments in work scheduling reflect an enormous change in the attitude of organized labor, which at one time regarded productivity gains as merely a means to increase profits at the expense of workers. Many now see increased productivity as the source of wage gains and long-term security. Moreover, the exclusively adversarial role that unions once maintained has been tempered, and in some cases reversed, by a decline in public support, political clout, and diminished membership. Yet, ironically, the growing need to cooperate with former adversaries has strengthened the unions' position in many important ways.

Workers too have gained by their willingness to cooperate. No longer in the position of being merely "hired hands," they feel more like full and able members of the organization and are being treated as such. Robert Zager writes in the *Harvard Business Review* that "All over the country, in the private and the public sector, in organizations large and small, in union and non-union settings, employers are encouraging their employees to assume responsibilities formerly considered 'managerial.' "

JOB SHARING

One aspect of this new joint responsibility is the introduction of job sharing, in which two (or more) part-time employees share a position, working out their own arrangements to insure that the job gets done.

"It's a super arrangement," reports Bill Connolly, a recruitment and staffing manager at TRW Vidar, a California electronics firm, who supervises two women who share a $20,000 job as personnel representatives. "Having two job sharers means that I benefit from two points of view on every problem," he says.

In 1976 a woman employee was about to be fired from XYZ (a medium-sized manufacturing company) because of her absentee record. The woman suggested sharing her job with her sister-in-law and the firm approved the experiment. The idea worked so well that by the third year it had expanded to thirty teams and the following guidelines had been more or less stabilized:

Job sharers are responsible for finding their own partner.
Full-time employees only may cut back to job sharing: no new employees may come in as job sharers.
Job sharers are responsible for covering their own absences.
Each job sharer must work at least one day a week, and full days are required, no part-days.
Job sharers receive the same benefits as full-timers.
Only workers in the lower three job classifications may job share (about 40 percent of the employees at this plant).

In this company all sides seem to have benefited from the now well-established system. Absenteeism among the job sharers, many of them young women with children, has dropped to less than half of one percent compared with their former 7.6 percent absenteeism record as full-timers. For the company the cost of fringe benefits for the "extra" employees has been offset by the elimination of overtime pay and the temporary staffing that used to be needed to cover absences. The job sharers, needless to say, are happy at having more time for the other parts of their lives.

As this case history shows, job sharing is of particular interest to working mothers, some of whom are quoted in the book *New Work Schedules in Practice*, by Gretl Meier: "There's no way I could manage our family life if I couldn't sometimes ask my partner to cover" . . . "I'm better at work, better at home: I can look forward to both" . . . "I'm a better parent when I can come home refreshed and know that I've been doing a worthwhile job."

Job sharing also provides a way for employees in general to place their work and family responsibilities on a more equal footing. It can answer the needs of both male and female employees for fewer hours at work, not only to have more time with their children but to pursue hobbies, education, or community work.

New Ways to Work, a San Francisco-based clearinghouse on job sharing which operates as an advocacy group for nontraditional work patterns, reports that job sharing has contributed to a new appraisal of what part-time work can mean. Instead of being work that people do in their spare time, part-time work now often implies the mapping out of a career with a definite view to upward mobility. For the employer, of course, it provides continuity in job performance. If one member of a team does leave, the remaining person can pick up the slack until a new sharer is trained.

New Ways to Work offers some cautionary advice, too. To be successful, job sharing must:

Be voluntary
Have parity with full-time positions in regard to salaries, benefits, and job rights
Have the support of the supervisor
Have clearly understood expectations
Be well organized
Draw on strong communications skills
· Be conducted in a spirit of cooperation

It also identifies certain positions that are more likely to benefit from job sharing than others. Such positions would:

Require a broad range of skills
Alternate periods of intense activity with slack periods
Require creativity
Include monotonous duties
Be sufficiently high-pressure to warrant two people sharing the pressure
Require more than eight-hour-a-day coverage, for the same reason

So far the vast majority of workers who participate in job sharing agreements are women. This is partly because of their enormous influx into the labor force over the past three decades, and partly because society still retains a certain prejudice against men doing part-time work. The men who are job sharing tend to be in the younger (in their thirties) or older (over fifty) age brackets. Among the younger group are men in the vanguard of what may be called family work sharing. They share household and parenting tasks as well as income earning with their wives, and some of them share the same job. Some couples have rejected the idea of commuting marriages and turned to job sharing so they can find work in the same community. Others, many of them in college and university teaching or administration, simply want to combine professional and family responsibilities.

About job sharing in academia Robert Karsten, dean of Gustavus Adolphus College in St. Peter, Minnesota, declares: "We support it. We recruit for it. We see it as a way of getting the talents of two for the price of one." He could be referring to Assistant Professor Patricia Dean, who teaches one course in the Women's Studies Department, and her husband, Professor William Dean, who teaches two in the Religion Department. Together they share a full-time teaching contract with salaries pro-rated to reflect the differences in their teaching loads and credentials. (At the time *Working Woman* wrote about them in 1981 their joint annual income was $20,000.)

The Deans, who started their job sharing as far back as 1971 to allow time for child-care needs, say the arrangement allows them to focus on both sides of their lives, the domestic and the professional. As the children get older each parent is able to devote more time to research and special projects than would have been possible with a full teaching load, and they have constructed "a simple life style" that has withstood the ravages of inflation so that they are still content with part-time jobs. The college allows each of them full vacation time and complete life insurance coverage, together with a family medical plan. On retirement they will be eligible for standard benefits based on their combined annual salary.

There is a lingering misconception in some business circles that part-time employment works only at the lower levels, that it is not feasible for managers and professionals because such jobs require great skill and long years of training. Yet the basic rules seem to operate at all levels. "Training two people initially may take more supervisory time," says the National Council for Alternative Work Patterns, "but in the long run, the time involved will be reduced. Two people will absorb material faster and reinforce each other with new information." In fact, the most dramatic increase in part-timers employed by the federal government has been in the higher-grade levels, and a dozen states have initiated programs creating professional-level part-time positions.

The habits and responsibilities of upper-echelon employees remain the same whether they work full- or part-time: they're experienced and organized, they usually have excellent back-up staffs, and they take armloads of work home with them. Gretl Meier quotes a section chief at the Environmental Protection Agency about one of his part-time professionals: "My guess is that she does as much work when she is not here at the office. She leaves on Thursday evening and comes back with a wealth of new ideas on Monday."

Summarizing the pros and cons of part-time work, the Work in America Institute reports the advantages as

A better match for the employer between work load and employee hours, coupled with higher productivity on stressful jobs and easier recruiting
For the employee, more time for family and personal interests
For the community, more job opportunities and more flexible hours to suit those who neither want nor need full time jobs.

Offset against these positive factors are a few negative ones: fringe-benefit problems and occasional union opposition for the employer; lower pay and benefits and (sometimes) more difficult career paths for the employee.

Fortuitously, the most frequent users of voluntary part-time work are in the very economic sectors and occupations that are expected to grow fastest in the next decade, and it has become clear that many new entrants to the workforce—particularly single parents and/or women—would choose part-time work if it were available. Such jobs are also a boon to older workers. In a 1981 Harris poll, 79 percent of employees between fifty-five and sixty-four said they would prefer part-time work to retiring completely. Pensions eroded by inflation have added financial pressures to older people's lives. Many *need* to make additional money and various companies are trying to accommodate them. The Travelers Insurance Company, for example, allows qualified retirees to work up to 960 hours per year, almost half-time, without reduction of pensions. They often fill jobs that would have been staffed by workers from temporary service agencies, contributing a sense of loyalty and a knowledge of the company that translates into great productivity.

Other countries have had longer experience with such plans and proved them viable. In Sweden, workers in their sixties who are approaching retirement may ease the transition by choosing to share their jobs with other workers. More than 25 percent of eligible workers have done so.

WORKING BY THE YEAR

Sweden, whose trend-setting social welfare policies changed many assumptions, appears to be on the verge of yet another breakthrough in labor relations: the working-year contract. In a sense it is an inevitable reaction to the benevolent programs that have contributed to doubling the absenteeism of that country's workforce in recent years. Generous public health benefits have allowed workers so much time away from their jobs that on most days management is unable to plan ahead because it doesn't know how many people will show up.

Thus there is an ongoing discussion about offering workers greater freedom in selecting their hours on the job. For example, "Instead of forcing everybody into an eight-hour or six-hour day," Volvo's president Pehr

Gyllenhammer suggests, "we could allow individuals to decide before-hand the time they wish to devote to work every week. We assume that individuals have the independence and maturity to be able to decide for themselves their rhythm of life and ideal work input. They can enter into a form of agreement with their employer for a certain period of time. At the end of the period of agreement, they would be free to reassess their work input."

Other European countries have extended the debate. In France the presi-dent of the country's employers' organization, François Ceyrac, has com-plained that the present method of time allocation which divides the lives of workers into uniform slices is outdated, and actually undermines efficient pro-duction. Germany's Willi Haller, a pioneer promoter of flexitime, has advo-cated annual agreements between management and individual workers setting working hours for the coming year.

WORKING AT HOME

Probably the most significant shift in the way that business will be conducted in the future lies in the growth of what's come to be known as the "electronic cottage." This catchy term refers to people working at home on their word processors and computers.

Telecommuting has not only helped people make the transition from full-to part-time employment but extended job opportunities to single parents, the handicapped, and others who are tied to their homes.

Five million Americans are currently said to be in business at home, and futurists predict this figure will double by the end of the decade. Traditionally home workers were mostly self-employed entrepreneurs—writers, architects, lawyers, consultants—but the new breed includes those who were formerly tied to offices—managers, professionals, and clerical workers. Some of these will still be spending part of their time at the office (if only to keep in touch and prevent "cabin fever"), but mostly their work will be done in the com-fortable surroundings of their own home.

At first employers feared that employees might wind up doing the laun-dry, feeding babies, or sunbathing on company time, but such trepidation has proved groundless. In any event corporations developed techniques to check on their out-of-sight workers' output either by time logged on and off the computer or, more commonly, by allotting a specific block of work to be completed within a given time period.

There have been minor drawbacks such as these revelations from employ-ees at Denver's Mountain Bell Telephone Company.

One employee found that the lure of working at home was offset by the lure of the ever present refrigerator. Within three weeks she had put on twenty pounds from illicit snacks.

Another woman thought she could save on child care but found she couldn't work because of the noise. "Her kids treated her being at home as though it were a week full of Saturdays and Sundays."

A Mountain Bell programmer discovered that marital bliss was not enhanced by his working at home. There were fights because she liked to watch soap operas as she did the housework and he found it distracting.

Of more consequence have been the objections raised by unions and women's organizations who see in the electronic cottage system a vast potential for abuse. Karen Nussbaum, executive director of 9 to 5, the National Association of Working Women, regards computer homework as a disastrous return "to the cottage industries of the 1880s because of its potential to take advantage of workers who are unprotected by unions."

A 1938 federal law, the Fair Labor Standards Act, banned homework in the garment and jewelry industries, and in the opinion of the Service Employees International Union of the AFL-CIO the current type of home electronics has identical ramifications. "Unsafe working conditions and flagrant violations of minimum wage, overtime standards and child labor laws were prevalent [before]," states the SEIU's executive board, "and the potential for the same problems to arise in computer homework is tremendous." Home work smacks of piecework rates and contract labor, the unions maintain, and could lead to forced speedups.

There is some justification for these fears. An article in the *Nation* (April 2, 1983) reported that a woman in Elgin, South Carolina, spent fifty hours per week processing 2,000 Blue Cross claims at 16 cents per claim, ending up with a net weekly pay of a meager $100 after deductions for taxes and the obligatory rent paid back to Blue Cross for use of the computer terminal installed in her home.

Several companies have been studying this problem and considering whether, in view of the increased productivity of employees on the home work system (Mountain Bell reports it as high as 75 percent), it makes sense to increase the compensation paid.

Naturally, one reason why people working at home may become more productive is that they are happier with the job and able to manage their time better. Sherrie Masso, who files insurance claims through the computer terminal that Blue Cross of Washington, D.C., installed in her Virginia home, expected to have to quit work when she became pregnant but now is able to work as well as look after her baby.

"I'm making a little less than at other jobs," she says, "but there are other considerations. I have to take care of my daughter so I need flexible hours."

Many of the people who work at home prefer it for similar reasons; they have a sick relative, a disability, or other responsibilities. Many also enjoy the casual style, with no dressing up or business lunches or commuting. As a study conducted by a Dallas consulting service noted, home workers tend to be independent, self-motivated, and comfortable with being alone.

Representative Newt Gingrich of Georgia recently introduced a bill called the Family Opportunity Act, which would offer tax credits to families who purchase home computers for business and educational use. The bill is especially favored by conservative Republicans who believe that computer work at home has potential for keeping families together by allowing women to earn money while attending to their household responsibilities. Such a law might well be helpful, but support for it on that basis is not. It simply restates the idea that women are expected to do everything—load up the dishwasher, diaper the baby, *and* put in the required hours at the work station.

WORKING MOTHERS

For many years now working mothers have been the fastest-growing component of the job market. Since 1950, when only 30 percent of the working population was composed of women (it is now almost 48 percent), the number of working mothers has quadrupled and seems destined to increase even more.

But attitudes have not kept pace with facts. The 1982 Public Agenda Foundation survey analyzed in *Working Woman* found that although nearly nine out of ten working Americans agree that most working mothers need the money, more than half don't approve of mothers working, especially mothers of young children. If a woman wants to work instead of staying home and caring for children, a majority feel, she should not have them in the first place.

"Regardless of what people think about the social-political-sexual issues," comments Villanova University's John Immerwahr, who worked on the survey, "they can agree that many women need to work for financial reasons and therefore that there must be some arrangements for the care of their children. They also agree that employers must show some flexibility in helping these women and that there is a particular need to help poor women who currently may be on welfare."

The issue is a far-reaching one. Currently there are about 32 million

American children under eighteen—almost 8.5 million of them under six—whose mothers hold paying jobs. Surveys show that when asked who should be responsible for these children—parents, government, or employers—most respondents think parents should take the prime responsibility. Yet most respondents also think the government should help in some way, perhaps through tax breaks to employers that provide day care or some type of family allowance.

In the Public Agenda Foundation's survey, government-funded day-care centers and nursery schools actually ranked quite low on a list of possible child-care options. At the top of the list of preferences was day care on company premises. Such facilities are now available only at 230 hospitals and less than 100 other worksites. Compared to health care, child care is just beginning as a company benefit.

But it is working well for such companies as Wang Laboratories of Lowell, Massachusetts, which opened a day-care center in 1980, and the American Can Company, which added a child-care benefit option to its flexible benefits plan in 1983. It seems more and more likely that adding optional day care benefits will enable companies to remain competitive, attracting and holding top-quality people and perhaps reducing the costs of turnover and absenteeism. This is what appears to have happened with PCA International, Inc., a photoprocessing firm in Matthews, North Carolina, which claims that the stream of job applicants that followed the company's installation of a day-care center has reduced costs related to recruiting and turnover by $50,000 a year.

At the Corning Glass Works, in Corning, New York, personnel-development manager Marie McKee is quite emphatic. It's clear to her that the Corning Children's Center "has given us a competitive edge in recruiting and retaining excellent people. . . . It's equally important that the center is benefiting one of our secretaries and one of our plant workers who's a single father. Because of Corning's attitude toward child care many women have told me they're no longer afraid that having children will create guilt and career conflicts. That's very positive for them and us."

The Corning Children's Center, a warm, cheerful, active place that uses space in a church near company headquarters, is funded by the Corning Foundation, which has a long tradition of supporting community programs. The church charges a nominal rent, a hospital provides low-cost lunches, and volunteers from both Corning's board and the community have donated hours of administrative, legal, and accounting services. The center is nonprofit, charging parents only 86 cents an hour ($43 weekly for fifty hours of care), the $25,000 annual deficit being absorbed by the Corning Foundation.

Programs are based on the most up-to-date knowledge of young children's intellectual, social and emotional development, and the center, though small (twenty-four children initially, with plans to extend the program to infants and toddlers) is a model that similar corporations might beneficially study. "We provide an environment that is supportive to women and men," comments board chairman Amory Houghton, Jr. "We feel it is the right thing to do."

At Intermedics, Inc., in Freeport, Texas, parents whose children use the day-care center—the largest in any industrial plant in the country—pay a mere $15 weekly in an area where day-care costs average nearer to $40. The company covers three-quarters of the center's actual cost, maintaining that as it was established to increase productivity its contribution is a tax-deductible business expense. This claim seems to be accurate. Turnover decreased 60 percent in the center's first two years of operation and also diminished absenteeism by thousands of hours.

About two-thirds of the company's 1,300 employees are women with technical training who work in production; just over one-third are single parents. Each day almost 300 children attend the center, whose director, Alice Duncan, says: "Having a large dedicated staff makes it possible to offer youngsters lots of individual attention. There are specially designed areas for each age group, with equipment chosen to stimulate the children's curiosity and develop new skills." There are filmstrips and a playhouse for the three-year-olds, for example, preschool skills lessons for older children, and plenty of scooters, tricycles, tire swings, and tunnels.

At most centers the highest costs are for staffing. Teacher salaries burn up around three-quarters of the budget, which is usually shared in varying proportions by the parents using the center and the corporation. Operating costs for a high-quality center serving from twenty-five to seventy-five children are between $50,000 and $150,000 per year, approximately two or three thousand dollars per child. Parents' fees per child can be as low as $15 and as high as $68 a week, but $35 or $40 is the average.

Start-up costs—anywhere from $70,000 to more than double that figure—depend on whether the premises are donated by the company or rented separately, but in both cases costs can be a deductible business expense for the company if it can establish that the center increases productivity. Not every company, of course, wants the problems inherent in starting up day-care centers from scratch, although many are becoming aware of the advantages of having one. A solution for some has been to engage the services of one of the already existing chains, the largest of which is Living and Learning, a New England group which, after merging with Kinder Care, became the country's largest for-profit day-care-center chain, with 729 facilities.

Connecticut General Life Insurance Company, with headquarters near Hartford, Connecticut, contracts with L & L to provide day care just as it contracts with other firms to provide such employee services as retail shops, a sports center, and a cafeteria. In return for guaranteeing forty enrollments at the child-care center, the company received a 10 percent discount off L & L's usual rates which it was able to pass on to its employees. In spite of this, rates are comparatively high (although not compared with those of other local centers), ranging from $44.10 per week for preschoolers to $67.50 for infants, including lunch and snacks.

Both company and employees have benefited, reports Rita Triano, Connecticut General's director of employee services. "The center has helped attract new employees, smooth corporate transfers, and ease the return to work after maternity leaves. But the tangible benefits aren't our primary motivation. We see day care as an opportunity to exercise social responsibility in a meaningful way."

Even when a company doesn't see a central day-care center as being viable it can still offer help in that direction. For example, Honeywell, Inc., an advanced-technology company in Minneapolis, Minnesota, has more than fifty worksites in the Twin Cities area. Parents at virtually all of them were reporting that the stress of doing their jobs and looking after their children was lowering their productivity. It was difficult to find sitters who matched their working hours and when they were absent it was often because the sitter was ill rather than themselves. Sonia Sands, in the rare job of parents' resource coordinator, helped the company search for solutions. One was to provide funding and staff assistance toward setting up a computerized information and referral system. Now this Child Care Information Network offers parents help in finding suitable day care by providing data on hours, fees, enrollment, and distance from major bus routes, highways, and public schools.

"Corporations are mindful of the problems of two-career families and of the potential negative effects of these problems on recruitment, employee morale, and productivity, but corporate practices lag behind their more responsive attitudes" a Catalyst survey reports. Catalyst suggests that options corporations might explore include:

Credits for child care offered through a flexible benefit program
Financial contributions to expand and upgrade existing child-care facilities

Purchase of corporate "slots" in existing community child care

Working with employees to establish both corporate-run and not-for-profit child development centers both on-site and nearby

Paternity leave, virtually nonexistent among the survey's respondents, was likely to exist only at the larger companies, but almost all mothers employed when their babies were born took time off. The median time was twelve weeks, with 68 percent of the mothers back at work four months after giving birth.

Corporations are slowly becoming more responsive to the needs of working parents, but there is still much to be done.

THE AUTOMATED OFFICE

"Automate, emigrate or evaporate," warns James A. Baker, a vice president of the General Electric Company. Though he was talking about the factory, many have felt that office automation is to business what robotic technology is to the assembly line.

Every day seems to bring an announcement of new wonders—electronic work stations, camera computers that store images, voice-activated "keyboards"—and the immediate challenge is to integrate all the components so they provide seamless links among the thousands of information producers and consumers in the contemporary corporation.

Working Woman's Randy Goldfield lists some of the reasons why the computer revolution is necessary and inevitable:

To make the best of valuable information resources

To prevent workers from doing things more than once

To give decision makers as much information as possible, in an intelligible form, when they need it

To increase the amount of goods a company can produce

To coordinate better the corporation's management of people, machines, and money

To help people finish their jobs during the day so that they don't lose sleep worrying about undone tasks

According to Dataquest, Inc., a market-research firm, the information processing market will more than double, from its current $65 billion to $155 billion, by 1987. The investment is widely viewed as imperative to arrest the alarming decline in white-collar productivity in recent years. The international consulting firm of Booz, Allen & Hamilton reports that along with this decline, the costs of running an office have been increasing by 12 to 15 percent each year; thus more and more people have been generating less and less revenue.

Oddly enough, most business people seem not to be intimidated by the technological changes in store, apparently believing that they will make work more interesting and challenging. In the Public Agenda Foundation survey on work, only 27 percent of the respondents said they expected jobs to become more routine, boring and dehumanizing. Only 8 percent thought the changes would eliminate their jobs, although the percentage was slightly higher among the lower-income groups.

Most authorities agree that no matter how dazzling the latest technological marvel is, unlocking office automation's potential will depend on how well the people who operate the technology are managed. One survey, conducted by Index Systems, Inc., a Massachusetts consulting firm, found that fifteen out of the eighteen systems studied failed, not because the technology was unsatisfactory but because management failed to pay attention to employee resistance.

Some firms have taken this lesson to heart. They have set up ways for their employees to learn what they need to know to feel more comfortable about computers. One such course, at the Ciba-Geigy Company, has taught more than 300 staffers—in small groups at a time—where the information is stored and how they can use it. The eight-hour course (which includes about two and a half hours of video shown in short segments) emphasizes the use of information more than the dazzling technology. This orientation attempts to overcome what Bruce E. Bergen, Ciba-Geigy's director of information systems, describes as "cypherphobia" (fear of symbols).

Do people automatically resist automation? Absolutely not, says Alvin Toffler, whose provocative book *The Third Wave* is partly about the new work environment. Toffler believes that given the right conditions workers embrace automation, but that if it is rammed down their throats or threatens them with unemployment, demotion, or family dislocation, they have every right to resist it and would be stupid not to.

"We're very good at creating machine systems," he writes, "but terrible at thinking intelligently about human systems and human reactions. There is no machine which cannot be sabotaged or delayed or diverted from its purpose by employees who resist and who are frightened of it. Companies that want to introduce word processing, teleconferencing, multipurpose executive workstations, and other advanced technology into their office systems need to begin years in advance to assure their employees that there is a role for them, that they will be consulted, that they will be treated with dignity, that they will not suffer in consequence. Companies that think that is expensive are making a mistake. What's expensive is trying to make the transition the hard way."

Toffler points to the contrasting cases of the London *Times,* whose introduction of office automation prompted a year-long strike that nearly bankrupted the paper, and the *Times's* equivalent in Japan, the *Asahi Shimbun,* where years ahead of the transition the company explained it to the workers and guaranteed that no one would be discharged. Closer to home is the example of the World Bank, which, before automating its East African regional office in Washington, D.C., took pains to alleviate its employees' justifiable fears about the effects of working with VDTs.

A widely distributed survey conducted in 1979–80 by the National Institute for Occupational Safety and Health had found that VDT operators in strictly clerical jobs demonstrated higher levels of stress than any group of workers the Institute had ever studied, including air traffic controllers. Eyestrain, muscle aches, high levels of anxiety, depression, and fatigue were among the problems cited. To deal with these concerns, the World Bank held seminars on radiation, bringing in ophthalmologists and other experts to reassure the staff; instituted regular eye examinations; installed easily adjustable chairs in rooms with shaded lights and walls painted to reduce glare; and scheduled the work so that employees spent no more than four hours a day on the machines and could take breaks as needed.

"We tried to address the ergonomic questions," says office technology coordinator Janet Damron, who prepared for her task by reading everything she could find about office automation.

The negative side of the picture can be illustrated by any number of horror stories, among them the one described by Jill Casner-Lotto in *Working Woman* in November 1983. Before the back-office collections department of a large discount store was automated, collectors had total control over their work, with each responsible for certain customer accounts. Then the system "de-skilled" their jobs, pooling all accounts and distributing them randomly. The level of judgment and skill needed was substantially diminished, and within a year turnover among the office staff reached almost 100 percent.

"Office automation is like any other organizational change. It just happens to involve computers," says Marty Gruhn, a research director for the Sierra Group, a research and consulting firm in Tempe, Arizona. Gruhn, after fifteen years' experience introducing new office systems, declares that "there aren't enough people who know how to combine the use of automation and people effectively."

Experts on the quality of work life have long argued that humanizing work improves productivity but the reverse is also true: mechanizing work leads to decreased productivity. A review of the research literature reveals that when control over the pace of the work is taken away from the worker—as happens with the monitoring systems that often accompany automation—"errors tend to increase . . . anything from 40 percent to 400 percent depending on the situation (one is) dealing with." This conclusion is from a memo prepared by Cleveland's Working Women Education Fund. It goes on to say that even when the speed of the work is not changed, if the worker has no control over the speed, she *perceives* the pace as faster and experiences greater anxiety and stress. In self-paced work a person can compensate for errors, whereas in machine-paced work she cannot.

Office: Technology and People, published in 1982, takes the argument even further. Its authors, J. Gregory and K. Nussbaum, charge that the evolution of office automation does not represent a disinterested advance of technology but rather the advancement of particular interests. "Scientific invention is being defined to provide management with ways to reduce both the cost of employees' labor and, eventually, the size of the workforce. Office technology is being used to destroy the positive aspects of clerical work, while reinforcing the worst features. Corporate leaders encourage the development of labor-displacing technologies without regard for the social consequences. The current direction of technological development is irrational in any but management terms."

Nevertheless, the changes are almost certainly irreversible. A report by Siemans, the West German high-technology firm, estimates that 40 percent of the work done in today's office is suitable for automation by the end of the decade, which will result in a reduction of the labor force by 25 or 30 percent. For employers the attractions are obvious: the cost of computers is declining at a time when clerical workers are demanding more pay and other benefits—demands which computers never make—and even in conventional office setups computerization tends to restrict workers' freedom and hence cut down on "wasted time."

Gregory and Nussbaum point out that the new jobs will redefine the meaning of clerical work. Traditionally clerks, typists, and secretaries not only performed routine tasks but made decisions, ordered priorities, and brought to their work a personal style. Soon "most women office workers will find themselves in jobs which are closely supervised and increasingly 'specialized'—meaning that they do even smaller fractions of the larger task. Each job thus requires less training and offers less potential for advancement." There are exceptions: at the American Hospital Association headquarters in

Chicago, computerization of the filing and registration system has relieved secretaries of the more mundane tasks and allowed them to take on additional responsibilities. But most of the new breed of clericals work with computer terminals that are strictly programmed to perform only one task. "One woman expresses the frustrations of many office workers when she says: 'I feel like asking my boss, What do you think I am—an extension of the machine?' "

12

The Dress-for-Success Debate

Examining the question of what women wear to work brings up some large issues. For example, should a woman try to look like a man? Should what you see be what you get? Must the same person play different roles in different fields? Why and when should we conform and when stand out? Perhaps fortunately, there are no simple answers, but women's accumulated experience in the work world seems to point in certain directions.

THE IMAGE FACTOR

Image does count. In the best of all possible worlds people's appearance would matter not a jot—all that would count is sheer ability. As every woman knows from her very first interview, though, ability *isn't* the only issue in business. She may learn in school that beauty is only skin deep, but the fact remains that everyone is judged by appearance a good deal of the time. In a split second people form impressions, often permanent ones, based entirely on what they see. Even experienced recruitment executives admit that they often make snap decisions about candidates using only stereotypical information. People who are attractive, who look right, get jobs easier and get promoted faster.

A 1978 study done for Clairol, Inc., by Judith Waters, a professor of psychology at Fairleigh Dickinson University in New Jersey, put a number on what an attractive appearance is worth in the job market. Potential employers were shown photographs of women before and after their hair had been styled and colored and their makeup changed. No drastic changes were made, and the makeup was discreet. Clothing and facial expressions were the same in both pictures, which were attached to similar résumés. The personnel directors, none of whom saw both before and after photographs of the same woman, were asked to rate each job applicant and estimate how much she could expect to earn.

The study showed that mean salaries for the made-over women ranged from 8 to 20 percent higher than for their "before" versions. And the personnel directors' incidental comments were even more revealing: "Doesn't look like an organized person. Should pull herself together." "Not very neat. I wouldn't hire her, even though it seems she is qualified from what she has done." "Looks very business-oriented. Looks efficient." "She looks like she'd have to stay in a nonprofit type of organization. Doesn't seem to have corporate business image."

Exactly what our appearance tells viewers varies from time to time, of course, but the language can be learned—and spoken. Once you know what a certain image communicates, you can if you wish arrange your own looks, props, and backdrop to create a particular idea about yourself. Learning this "impression management" is particularly important for professional women, because self-presentation, especially in an alien world, is one of the few ways you have of maintaining control over what happens, what people think of you, and how they respond. It is the core idea behind dress-for-success, and its importance is illustrated by all the personal shoppers (at $100 a day), image consultants (at $6,000 a corporation), and how-to-dress authorities that are in business today.

Your image has two levels: first impressions, such as when you walk into an interview or a boardroom; and constant credibility, as you function day to day at work. Wearing the right executive suit does not make you an executive if you don't speak management's language and know your way around the fourteenth floor and can't get anyone to listen to you at a meeting. Image building goes far beyond what you wear. It is all the parts that go into your self-presentation: clothes, hair, and makeup; accessories and possessions; voice, carriage, attitude, and behavior; how you communicate; your skills with people; your degree of visibility at work. Other parts of this *Working Woman Report* look at how women speak, how they handle their problems with assertiveness, how they can politic and network to benefit their images, and more aspects of what could be called image development. In this chapter, however, we want to concentrate on dress and grooming, starting with the easiest image for women in business, its drawbacks, and how to move beyond it as you move beyond entry level.

Since women don't look like traditional business people—meaning men—they generally need to spend more time than men on packaging themselves. They need that extra edge. But working on an image does not mean you're erecting a false front. Rather your own image insures that you are read right in the context of your career. "*I* know I'm competent, I just want to be sure people in my company do too," says a young manager who is as organized about her wardrobe as she is about her spreadsheets.

THE DRESS-FOR-SUCCESS CODE

Once you acknowledge the importance of image, you come to best-selling author John T. Molloy, who in the mid-1970s applied market-research techniques to the question of using clothes as a tool for getting ahead in business. He conducted extensive interviews, recorded and tabulated people's reactions to various articles of men's—and later women's—dress. From these data he worked out the ideal business image, including style and color scheme of clothes; accessories; and even haircut. His look was not based on what was fashionable or even smart, but on what tested best in the studies round the country. Unsurprisingly, Molloy's winning style is an encoding of the standard upper-middle-class look that has always won approval in the male business world.

According to Molloy's research, this dress code—written or implied—exists in corporate America for the following reasons:

Subordinates work harder and longer for bosses who dress in upper-middle-class authority garments. Company loyalty is based on a sense of security, and employees' security depends on how they think of their company, which comes from how they see their boss.

In turn, properly dressed executives find it easier to deal with associates and subordinates.

People make moral judgments of other people based on dress. The same goes for a company. If the receptionist or secretary looks in some way cheap or incompetent, a person visiting the company will think the company is second rate.

Executives who wear upper-middle-class business clothes are morely likely to succeed than those who do not.

Dress-for-success has become something of a joke. It *is* unashamedly conformist and snobbish, and it *does* encourage the managerial herd instinct. Molloy's prescribed look—and he permits no deviation—is indeed bland, conservative, and sexless. Nevertheless, ten years after *The Woman's Dress*

For Success Book was published, Molloy's wardrobe (below) still seems to be guiding neophyte businesswomen.

THE DRESS-FOR-SUCCESS WARDROBE FOR WOMEN

Man-tailored, dark-colored, traditionally designed, skirted suit: jacket with a blazer cut and matching skirt. The jacket must be cut full enough to play down the contours of the bust, and it should not be pinched in at the waist. Skirt should fall just below the knee. Color: the gray of the average men's suit, or medium-range blue (also that of the average men's suit).

White blouse without frills, neckline equivalent to that of a man-tailored shirt, with only one button open. White blouse with stock-tie bow also acceptable. Blouse collar should go inside jacket.

Camel-colored wraparound winter coat.

Good-quality plain leather pumps in a dark color with a closed toe and heel. Heel should be one and a half inches high.

Skin-colored hosiery only.

Woman's fedora hat.

Scarf worn at neck.

Dark leather gloves.

Hair worn above shoulders, not too curly; most important, the same style must be worn consistently. Brunettes have more authority than blondes.

Perfume is not appropriate at the office.

Glasses should be worn when possible, and one or two pieces of good jewelry.

Carry a gold or silver pen, attaché case, no handbag.

The result is obvious at any corporate headquarters. With substantial numbers of women now working beside men in management, anyone can see that both sexes wear a business uniform. *Fortune* calls women's combination of dark suit, plain shirt, and bow tie "a grim little number" and worries about its eradicating all signs of femininity in the bright young MBAs entering the corporate world. It would appear, though, that despite—or perhaps because of—their uniform suits, boy managers are meeting girl managers without any difficulty. Like still attracts like.

Though it shouldn't be taken too seriously, updates and variations on the Molloy uniform do serve a useful purpose. When you are a new arrival in the corporate world, and are worried about fitting in, finding and following a dress code can be a huge relief. There are other things to worry about when you're new on the job; the easy, safe uniform can save you some worries about this part of your image and let you concentrate on building your career.

Wearing the uniform also signals that you are serious about business. In this conservative decade, men too have settled down to dark suits, white shirts, and tight ties. The 1950s man in the gray flannel suit is back. Sartorial expansiveness of any sort is out, and rules (usually unspoken) about what is appropriate for the office are firmly back in place.

The corporate dress code is particularly rigid at entry level, and men and women who flout it risk their careers. "Five years ago," says Molloy, "when I talked to companies about how they wanted recruits to dress, the message was 'We'd like the young man to wear a suit, but won't hold it against him if he doesn't.' Three years ago, the message was 'We demand that the men wear suits, and would like the women to, but won't hold it against the women if they don't.' Today I hear 'We have so few jobs and so many qualified applicants, we're looking for ways to eliminate candidates. Those who won't dress appropriately we'll eliminate.' "

Fortune says wearing the right thing has become a sort of heraldic symbol of a young manager's dedication to the corporation, especially in the case of the young woman manager. According to the magazine's experts, if a recently promoted woman executive uses the occasion to trade in her suit for dresses and bangles, management may infer that she doesn't want to rise any higher. According to *Fortune*, to prove they really want to be in the business world, women have to show that they will make a sacrifice, in this case of their individuality as women.

THE IMPORTANCE OF FASHION

One of the things Molloy got wrong was telling women not to pay any attention to fashion. Fashion is not only inescapable but dangerous to ignore. Some people, disturbed at the importance of dress, label the whole subject "fashion" and try to keep it at a convenient distance. "Fashion" smacks of mindless vanity and commercialism, and surely couldn't have a place in the lives of serious businesswomen. If clothes are only fashion, then clearly they are not important. Furthermore, we all know that fashion—or worse still, high fashion—is the last thing to wear to work, unless your work happens to be fashion.

But you can't ignore fashion. Everyone has to buy clothes, even those who try not to spend any mental energy on shopping. Fashion has a way of creeping up on you; you will suddenly feel like a fool in what you are wearing and have to go shopping. Fashion makes even business clothes change. Social commentator Ann Hollander says, "Writers of how-to-succeed-through-clothes books forget that even a well-cut, conservative suit can stay in the closet too long. In the darkness it may develop too shapely or too straight a cut, too wide or too narrow a lapel to produce the look of success; when it is exposed to the lights, it may unhappily suggest a tacky hick."

No woman will appear businesslike and in command if she looks out of fashion. "Updating is an important ingredient in looking right for business," says image expert Jacqueline Warsaw. "One of the biggest complaints personnel interviewers voice about women trying to reenter the work world is that their clothes are outdated. Even worse, they dress as though they haven't looked at themselves in years."

Reading about, looking at, and shopping for attractive, fashionable clothes keeps you in touch and able to build the office wardrobe that will work best for you—and it may also give you pleasure.

TOWARD A WORK STYLE

While it makes sense to play it safe and wear your own version of "the uniform" when you begin your career, you may later choose to develop a more individual style. There comes a point, usually five to ten years into the work world, when you can take advantage of your natural extra visibility there. You can decide whether, and how, you want to draw attention to yourself. Do you want to be noticed as up-and-coming? Build an image as a creative, competent, or conservative executive? You use your image to signal these messages to the outside world. As Kathy Fox, a career counselor at Harvard, puts it, "It is vital to a woman's success to express her individuality. When she makes that psychological jump into her own identity, rather than imitating her peers, her career enters a new, much more successful phase."

When a group of female Harvard Business School graduates of the last fifteen years were asked about the importance of image in their careers, 75 percent said they felt it had been very important to their success. The majority also said that they had worn the uniform early in their careers, but now they found themselves wanting to assert themselves more. "From the beginning I paid attention to how I was coming across," says an MBA from another college. "When I started my career I was all suits and ties, but now I am branching out. I know who I am, and I feel established enough at work to express my individuality. The interesting thing is that the style I am expressing is very different from the image I'd have chosen to show the world ten years ago!"

Once a woman decides to establish her own work style, to step beyond the safety of the uniform, she takes into consideration five things: her occupation, her industry, the level of her job, the region where she works and lives, and her own sense of what's right for her.

As women move up or become established, they can loosen up their dress codes, but only within the limitations of their circumstances. Different industries have different images, and even within an industry there are subtleties of rank and area. Take banking, for example. A woman bank vice president who deals with consumer loans and is on the bank floor may wear a suit to distinguish her from the tellers, but she may choose that suit in a bright color and wear it with a frilly blouse, so as not to distance herself too much from her customers. Her counterpart at the bank headquarters who negotiates large commercial loans must dress in a closer approximation of the banker's pinstripe, perhaps wearing a gray flannel suit and white blouse and a little expensive jewelry. And the female investment banker will show she belongs in the glamor side of banking by wearing expensive, conservative clothes by such design firms as Calvin Klein or Anne Klein.

Like the financial world, insurance, manufacturing, civil service, and the legal profession expect a conservative, substantial appearance. Service industries generally allow a more lively look—as in the hotel industry, for example, and in packaged goods—but in some cases a corporate culture overrides the industry norm. Dark suits and white shirts are *de rigueur* for executives of both sexes and all levels at IBM.

Heavy industry—the world of steel, construction, chemicals—probably has the most conservative image of all for women, but in this, as in all fields, standards are more relaxed in the Southwest. Southern California is more casual than Illinois, although even in Los Angeles few executive women go so far as to wear pants when image-building. The only fields where it's possible to get away with pants—and then only when they are well made and becoming—are the so-called creative jobs in advertising and media.

These industries allow considerable latitude, even flair, in dress, with television and advertising ahead of publishing. Dress is counted as part of the creative process for jobs in some of these fields. Art directors of either sex are looked at askance if they wear suits and ties, and there is a joke that camera people may not get their union cards if they're not wearing dungarees.

Women with "outside" jobs have to pay even more attention to their image than those who are always "inside." A saleswoman who must constantly meet clients can never get away with a day when her clothes and makeup are not fully pulled together from the start. But the woman who knows she won't be meeting anyone because she's busy in her office all day should be aware that inevitably the day she didn't bother is the day she has to go see the chairman of her company. Don't take the chance, ever.

Once you know your industry's conventions, you begin developing personal style. It can be a simple signature, like dressing only in one color family or wearing interesting jewelry. For example, one New Jersey banker wears only extremely conservative suits, but to go with them she has a wonderful collection of blouses, everything from ruffles and lace to silk and hand embroidery. The important point, though, is consistency. To develop your image you cannot appear as one person one day and another the next. The signals get confused, and change makes superiors nervous.

Remember, too, that as Molloy says, "People who look well-educated and successful receive preferential treatment in almost all their business and social encounters." The look he is talking about is conservative and high quality. It is probably the most successful business image for women, and the easiest to achieve. Also known as "dressing rich," it does not have to be expensive.

Women in business don't have to wear something different every day, any more than men do. A lean wardrobe keeps costs down and also makes it far easier to keep your image clean and consistent. In fact a work wardrobe should probably consist of only three basic looks—which can be varied, mixed or matched, and built on. Spend on quality, not quantity, and apply the cost-per-use theory: Divide what you'll pay for something by the number of times you'll use it. If you spend $300 on a beautiful briefcase and use it every work day for three years, it is costing you less than 30 cents a day. But if you spend $200 on an evening blouse and never go out in the evening, you've made a bad buy no matter how much of a bargain it was.

You build a serious, quality look; then you maintain it. The look has to have polish: well-kept hands and face, hair that's shaped and short (or worn up), stockings, good, shined shoes, nothing casual, and nothing that jingles or dangles. "A businesswoman does not have to look dowdy," says Mary Cunningham, "but she should avoid wearing anything that attracts more attention than what she says or the work she does."

Employers want to know that people who work for them mean business. Commitment and loyalty are valuable to them because of the dollars invested in developing each worker. Especially at managerial level, an employer has to feel an employee is serious about staying. Because of the stereotype that she is just waiting to meet a white knight who'll take her back to domestic city, it is especially important for a woman to communicate long-term commitment. Employers interpret provocative clothes as an indication that the wearer's mind is on other things than computer printouts, while the woman who dresses for the job she wants as well as the one she's got already has a foot on the ladder up.

What work style boils down to is common sense. It can be used to make points about ourselves in the work context, and as such can be used as just another professional tool or skill. It also involves our creativity and imagination, and it is very directly linked to how we feel about ourselves. There comes a point, after we've learned the rules and can follow all the cues on how to look, when all of us need to remember that we dress for ourselves, for our own pleasure and comfort, as well as for success.

A WORKING WOMAN'S CLOSET

A woman's style can get lost in her closet if she is too busy to pay attention to it. Left to its own devices, a closet ruins garments, separates them forever from their natural mates. A properly organized closet yields up outfit after outfit, each projecting the owner's image to perfection. Here, then, are some tips on closet organization prepared by Susan Dresner, author of *Managing Your Business Image,* for a Dupont/*Working Woman* seminar:

> *Rotate.* Rotate your wardrobe seasonally—every fall, winter, spring, and summer. Remove from your closet the clothes you're not wearing this season and store them. Pack with clean sheets, never in dry-cleaner's plastic bags, because plastic, which does not breathe, retains moisture and can fade and discolor garments. Inspect clothes for stains and clean them before storing. Breathing space between garments in closets and drawers prevents wrinkles. Fabrics containing polyester are more wrinkle-resistant and easier to maintain.
>
> *Edit.* If it doesn't work with your other clothes, if you have not worn it in three years, if it's too tight, if it was a mistake from the beginning . . . *get rid of it!*
>
> *Organize.* Get a closet organizer or an additional rod for hanging blouses and jackets. Invest in shoe racks or bags to keep shoes organized, clean, and easy to find. Hang your separates together by category, jackets with jackets (yes, break up suits), skirts with skirts, pants and blouses together. This will allow you to mix and match with greater freedom.
>
> *Subdivide.* Subdivide your separates along functional lines: clothes for business, casual wear, evening, and travel. If you have more than one closet, use one for business and the other for nonbusiness clothes.

WHAT WORKING WOMEN SHOULD KNOW ABOUT SKIN CARE

Always wear a moisturizer to protect your skin from the drying effects of indoor heat and air-conditioning.

Keep a mister full of water or a small humidifier in the office to help keep moisture in the air.

Fluorescent lighting makes the skin look sallow. Use a shade of foundation that is close to the skin's natural color and add blushers with pinkish tones to counter the lighting.

Use discreet matte eye shadow in the office. Save iridescent and frosted shadows for evening wear.

Use a gray, blue, or brown eye liner (liquid or pencil) and smudge the line to soften it. Black around the eyes tends to make you look hard and too made-up.

People who wear glasses need more defined eye makeup. Add an extra coat of mascara or use a shadow that harmonizes with your frames.

Avoid resting your head on your hand or pulling at your face during the day. Constant tugging on the skin stretches it and can lead to premature wrinkling. Touching also spreads dirt and germs to the face.

Keep duplicates of makeup essentials (cleanser, moisturizer, foundation, eye shadow) handy in a desk drawer for touch-ups.

CHANGING IN THE OFFICE

Maintaining a social life is a challenge for working women today, because few of them have the time to go home after a hard day at the office and primp for a night on the town. Looking glamorous after hours is based on careful planning.

Buy dresses with soft or slim lines rather than bouffant gowns for evening. They are easier to carry and store in the office.

Keep black sandals, an evening bag, makeup, hairbrush, and extra stockings in the office.

Change to a dressy blouse or camisole to make a tailored suit appropriate for almost any occasion.

Buy a two-sided stand-up mirror (regular and magnifying) for applying makeup.

Keep hair ornaments, dressy earrings, and a travel-size bottle of perfume in a desk drawer.

> Before getting ready for an evening out, close your office door and do some stretching exercises, or dim the lights and close your eyes. The point is to relax and come down from the day's hectic pace.
>
> For black-tie business events, common sense should govern your decision.
>
> Keep your evening fashion within the conceptual framework of the company. No need to display cleavage if it's a high-neck company.

BRIEFCASES AND ATTACHÉS

A briefcase, or attaché, is a portable desk as well as an image-making accessory. According to Jim Fisk and Robert Barron in their *Official MBA Handbook*, business cases are the "number-one power accessory." They are also an accessory that should last from three to five years, so shop carefully. If your case is not well chosen, it can be extremely unflattering.

Remember, though, you may not *have* to have one. Not all men carry briefcases; it's not *de rigueur* in all business settings.

There is a lot of talk in luggage circles about which case projects the most power, but convention has it that the attaché case—a solid frame with metal fasteners—is the most professional. Elizabeth Anthony, head of advertising at T. Anthony, a leading luggage company in New York, says that attaché cases account for about 70 percent of all business sales in their store, even though attachés generally cost more than briefcases. On the other hand, we have yet to see a woman who looks really elegant carrying an attaché case.

Good briefcases and attachés start at $100. If you are investing in a case, look for solid brass fixtures and top-grain cowhide. Take your size into account: small hands require small handles and short women should choose small cases. If your case is for papers and extras like makeup and a hairbrush, go for a briefcase or portfolio, which will hold more because of its extra inside and outside pockets. And of course consider the predominant colors of your business clothes: unless you intend to buy a whole wardrobe of cases, stick to black or brown.

As for the handbag or shoulder bag quandary—to carry it separately or put it inside your case—*Working Woman* recommends the latter.

13
On the Road

It was 1967, and housewives across the country were angling to join their husbands on business trips. "Take me along," they pleaded as they packed his case; "take me along," they wrote on the bottom of coffee cups raised to their husband's line of vision at the breakfast table. The man's reply was (on-cue jingle): "I love you little cutie, but the office is my duty."

This was the scenario of United Airlines' most successful commercial.

United's ad campaign in 1978 featured a woman stockbroker. Indeed, the times they are a-changing.

One out of every six business travelers in the United States today is a woman. The number of women on the road for business reasons is increasing at a rate three times faster than that of men, and by the end of the century it is likely that the number of men and women travelers will be equal. The business traveler is the bedrock customer of the hotel and airline sectors of the travel industry, and both have at last woken up to the fact that working women are among their best prospects.

Some airlines have conducted seminars for inexperienced female travelers, and hotels now stock skirt hangers and shower caps. More important, both industries are making efforts to improve the way women are treated. Ramada Inn, for instance, instructs its staff not to assume that a woman traveling with a male business partner is his secretary or wife or mother. In spite of such consciousness raising, however, females still do not get equal treatment when traveling alone. Blatant discrimination is less likely to mar your trip, but the annoyances remain.

A woman is often served last and seated worst; she may be ignored or assumed to be in the company of a man when at a check-in desk; women are considered fair game for unattached men; and, when she is the host at a business meal, a woman may find that the waiter automatically hands the check to her male guest. Women have valiantly been cultivating assertiveness to counteract such boorish behavior, but the dilemma remains. Travel is still more stressful for businesswomen than for businessmen.

READY TO GO

People who don't travel on business often have the misconception that an out-of-town assignment is like a vacation on company time and money. The neophyte soon finds out that working away from home is still working. Far from being the glamorous extra that her nontraveling peers envy, it can be an exhausting responsibility.

On top of work pressures—business trips are expensive and are expected to be cost effective—comes the stress of coping in a strange situation. Problems of language and custom as well as geography may have to be surmounted before you get to the business of doing business. In fact, the first step to setting up a business trip is to establish if it's really necessary. Must you go? Can you do the same job from your office by electronic means? Conference calls, electronic conferences, electronic mail, all might allow you to accomplish your goal without hopping on the next flight.

If a trip is inevitable, there *are* ways to make it work. The primary ingredients for successful business traveling are good advance planning which anticipates the worst (especially in the case of international travel) and an independent attitude. When traveling, a woman has to do things for and by herself. It is a mistake to depend on business contacts to take care of either professional or personal requirements. Strangers can't be relied on to make your arrangements or take you out to dinner on your own time, for example.

In the future you will be able to plan, book, and pay for trips using videotex services on interactive computer systems, but for now, ordinary efficiency must suffice. Here are some pointers:

Begin planning as early as possible. The success of a business trip is directly related to the degree of advance preparation.

Don't try to do everything yourself. Your travel agent, not you, should be searching out the most sensible route, the most efficient ticketing, the best car-rental service, and so forth. She should have on record your preferred plane seating and any special meal requirement.

Remember that the cheapest way to go is not always the best. Using your time and energy efficiently may often mean paying more in order to get to your destination when you need to be there. You cannot afford to use cut-rate transportation or fly stand-by if it means you might miss an important meeting or tie up other people. Similarly, it makes sense to travel ahead of time, pay for hotel rooms, and get a good night's sleep before conducting important business.

Make itineraries in triplicate. Take one copy with you, leave one at home with your family, and leave another at your office. This way you are reachable at all times. The itinerary—on a single piece of paper, if possible—should contain flight numbers and other travel arrangements, arrival dates and times, destinations, who's meeting you, where you're staying, and all contact phone numbers. (This is not only efficient but also a good security precaution. If you don't check in when you said you would, people have a head start on finding you.)

Carry written confirmation of all reservations. You or your secretary should telephone a day ahead of arrival to reconfirm arrangements, even when you have written confirmation.

Carry credit cards even if you intend to pay in cash. Hotels often demand them for identification and as a credit check.

If a plane is filled before you arrive to board it, the airline must make restitution and find you another flight. If your hotel room has been given to someone else, there is no such requirement. Avoid this inconvenience by paying for hotel accommodations ahead of time. Or use your American Express number and your hotel room will be held until you arrive, even if you're hours late. (You will, of course, be charged for the room no matter what happens.)

As you become a more experienced traveler, you may wish to do your own planning. An office travel library should include at least these tools: *The Travel Planner*; the *Guide to Airport Facilities in America*; the *Hotel and Motel Red Book*; the *Hotel & Travel Index*. If you travel a lot, also get the *North American OAG Pocket Flight Guide* ($30 per year for twelve monthly issues, from OAG Publications, 2000 Clearwater Drive, Oak Brook, Illinois 60521). This is a smaller version of the huge *Official Airline Guide*. It offers nationwide flight information and is updated every month. *The Europe and Middle East OAG Pocket Guide* is also available. You might consider joining an airline club; it doesn't cost much (about $30 a year), and it allows you to get away from waiting rooms and into VIP lounges where you can get seat assignments and take advantage of private meeting rooms, bar service, newspapers, television, and phones.

Plan for your arrival before you depart. Know how to get around a new city, for example. If your expense budget is limited, it would be careless to hop into a taxi at the airport in Pittsburgh instead of finding the limousine service to the downtown area. Most airports now have good bus links to their city centers, but in smaller cities you should be prepared to rent a car if necessary because it's often the only way to get around.

PACKING

Try to travel with only a garment bag, a briefcase (your traveling office with your purse inside), and one big tote or soft-sided suitcase that can slip under the seat of a plan. (These three can be carried on to the plane on most major airlines.) Don't lug along the contents of your bathroom cabinet; in the United States you can buy virtually anything you may forget. Remember, though, that because state laws vary, you may not be able to get certain drugstore items over the counter when you are away from home, and that refilling prescriptions will be expensive (in long-distance phone calls) if not impossible.

Take, and wear, the same clothes you wear to the office. Business dressing is basically the same everywhere.

Packing and dressing are infinitely easier if all the clothes you take are in the same color family. Shades of brown, black, navy, or wine are best. For warm climates use lighter classic colors; off-white, beige, pale gray. Prints, especially big ones, are not versatile and look unprofessional. If your home base is 30 degrees hotter or colder than your destination, remember to dress in layers that can be added or shed at will. Blazers, jackets, and raincoats make good layers.

If you do check luggage on a plane trip, pack spare toiletries plus an extra garment in your carry-on bag in case your case gets lost in transit, and make sure that you have baggage insurance. You may be covered through other general policies such as your homeowner's policy, or through your credit card if you have charged the trip. If your property is worth a lot, airlines can sell you fairly cheap additional coverage that will offer small reimbursements for lost luggage. However, they are responsible only if the luggage is lost while in their care. If you want broader travel insurance, to cover any possible mishap, buy what you need from your travel agent or an insurance broker; but if your trip is made at the last minute, get some protection at the airport insurance counter. As soon as you are covered make a list of all the things in your luggage and remember to have receipts for large items—you will need them if you have to collect.

Here are some pointers on packing:

Shoes should go opposite the handle of your suitcase (along the hinges of the case, if it's hard-sided), so they won't shift and crush everything else when the case is carried. Save space by tucking small, soft things inside shoes.

Fold sportswear so that one garment is cushioned in the folds of another, to prevent wrinkling.

Gloves, scarves, and stockings can go in pockets or odd corners; belts can be tucked along the rim of the case.

If you travel frequently, have a permanently packed toiletries kit.

Place your most delicate dress (folded into thirds lengthwise, toward the back of the garment) in the middle of the suitcase, with other dresses and blouses on top, also folded into thirds.

To pack a suit, button the jacket and bring sleeves around to the back. Fold the skirt into thirds.

Pack a small cache of office supplies—scissors, tape, stationery, pens and pencils, paper clips, notebooks, expense account forms. Carry a small, zippered pouch for receipts.

EXPENSE ACCOUNTS

On the whole, women use their expense accounts too conservatively. The "good little girl" pattern appears, and they want to show top management how little they spend of the company's money. This is a shortsighted approach to doing business and likely to be appreciated only by the shortsighted employers. The point of a trip is to be effective, and you should spend whatever you need to insure that you are.

Find out the norm for acceptable expenses among your peers on the job, but remember that your expense-account charges may not be identical to those of your male counterparts. For example, it may be essential to get your hair done on the road. Don't hesitate to charge to your expense account these little things that make your travel easier: hairdressing, dry-cleaning, airline-club membership, and so on.

When traveling on business, request receipts wherever possible so you will have full documentation. This is especially important when you think a charge will seem high to the person who has to approve your accounts. Carry blank receipts; if someone you ask for a receipt says it's not possible, you can fill one out yourself and have the person sign it. It's extremely important to keep track of all expenses as they are incurred. Record them in a small notebook at the time or at least at the end of each day. If you leave this task until the end of the trip, you risk forgetting things, and your business travel will end up being very expensive to you.

YOUR COMFORT

You should live as well on the road as you do at home, perhaps even better to compensate for the extra demands on you. At least you deserve a room that is safe, clean, comfortable, reasonably priced, and conveniently located. You also need efficient, prompt service. The easiest way to meet these requirements is to stay in chain hotels with a national reputation until you can use your own network of contacts and experience to find alternatives.

One way to insure security, good service, and maximum comfort is to use a hotel's executive or business floor. Some women feel the first-class treatment and business facilities they get are worth the extra cost of 10–20 percent to them or their companies. They like the floor's clublike facilities, where they can socialize comfortably without feeling like pickup candidates at a hotel bar, and they appreciate the little luxuries such as fresh flowers and a phone in the bathroom.

Women traveling on business and needing to see clients privately have a special problem. The presence of a large bed in your hotel room can set the wrong tone, yet rental costs for meeting rooms can be prohibitive. Solutions include asking for a room with a foldaway bed, a "parlor suite," or a room that divides off the bed area. Hotels are increasing the number of such accommodations, in part because of women's requests.

Another facility women are asking for, and getting, is a means of staying fit while traveling. Many more hotels now have jogging courses or health clubs and pools on the premises. Others supply addresses of nearby clubs or maps of places to run in the neighborhood.

TIPPING

Tipping is often awkward. It is not easy for any woman to overcome the general attitude that many tip earners have toward women. Cab drivers, waiters, and waitresses say women are finicky when it comes to the tab; that they seem to add up every check, almost hoping to find an error; and that the tip is often small compared to the trouble and fuss. Businesswomen are helping to chip away at these negative attitudes by tipping generously, especially when they plan to return to the restaurant or hotel again.

Some general guidelines will make tipping in the United States easier: Most people know that waiters and cab drivers get 15 percent of the bill. One easy way to figure the restaurant tip in states where the sales tax is about 8 percent is to double the tax and make that the tip. The usual tip for airline and hotel luggage attendants is 50 cents per bag or a minimum of $1, and the hotel doorman should get a dollar for calling a cab. For the chambermaid who cleans your room give 50 cents to $1 per day. Exactly what you give a maître d' depends on the restaurant and the service, but it usually ranges from $1 to $10. Wine stewards get 10 percent of the wine bill.

With all this in mind, it is wise to carry around several dollar bills and a good supply of change, so you won't get caught short and reinforce the myth that women are poor tippers.

SECURITY

Safety is the number-one concern for both men and women business travelers, and it is a fact of life that women must take special precautions. Fortunately, hotels are beginning to focus on women's security needs. Well-lit lobbies and hallways, dead-bolt locks on room doors, and responsible check-in and key-handling procedures are a few of the improvements they are offering.

Here are some security pointers:

Do not let people around you see or hear your name or room number at the front desk. The easiest method is to hand over your business card as you check in. This relieves you of the necessity of announcing yourself, establishes your authority as a business traveler, and puts your business address rather than your home address on record.

Ask for a room fairly near the elevators. It may be less quiet, but the approach will be well lighted and safe.

Have a bellhop escort you to your room. Make sure he joins you in a quick inspection of the room, including the closets and the bathroom, to be sure there's no one there.

Never take a room in the motel section of a hotel. These rooms are the most isolated and the easiest to break into.

Don't travel with expensive jewelry or items you can't wear all the time. Lock your suitcases whenever you leave the room.

Don't display your room key in public. Do not leave it on restaurant tables or in other places where it might be noted or stolen.

To deter robberies, leave a radio or television on when you leave the room.

Don't display large amounts of cash when making purchases.

If you hear strange noises when you open the door to enter your room, do not go in. Close the door, lock it, and report what you've heard to the front desk immediately.

If you come in late and the corridors are deserted, don't hesitate to have someone from the hotel escort you to your room.

Double-lock the door and bolt the chain, and check balconies and windows, before going to bed.

Before you stay at a hotel, call ahead and ask about its sprinkler and smoke-detector systems, its height (lower floors are generally safer in case of fire), and its safety record.

All traveling executives should carry a survival kit that includes an ionization smoke detector (check to make sure it works properly before leaving on your trip) and a flashlight. Keep the flashlight and your room key next to your bed, along with a hotel fire/safety survival checklist that contains phone numbers for the front desk, the fire and police departments, and the number and location of emergency exits.

Never use elevators in a fire emergency. Elevator shafts are a flue for smoke. Use emergency stairs.

If a fire breaks out in the hallway or in another part of the building and you cannot exit through your room door, call the front desk, the fire department, and the police. Turn on the bathroom exhaust fan and soak some towels in cold water, placing them along the bottom of the door to seal out the smoke. If the window in your room opens, hang a sheet out the window to signal the fire department that you are trapped. Meanwhile, place a damp towel over your face and lie on the floor near the window.

EATING ON THE ROAD

Many women who travel talk about the discomfort and the hassles of eating alone. Dining alone terrifies some people, and when they have to do it they feel they must supply themselves with paperback books, postcards to write, or a notebook to scribble in so as not to feel self-conscious. Many women would rather go hungry than eat alone, and sometimes their fears are not unfounded. Barbara de Portago, who lectures on traveling, says, "A woman alone in many hotel dining rooms is treated by the maître d's and waiters as someone who has failed, failed to get a man. Some of them initially act as though you are invisible and when you finally get a table, often in a terrible location, they try to ignore you."

One way to avoid this kind of treatment is to phone and make a reservation. If it's important to you to be well seated, make a special request. If it's important to be given excellent service, avoid the rush hour.

When you're entertaining other people in a restaurant, especially if you're not in a big city, you may have a different kind of problem. The people who run the restaurant and the clients you are entertaining, or both, may have some ancient ideas about who gets the check. The standard evasion tactics for this problem are to call ahead and make special arrangements, to prepay the check, or, better still, to pay with a credit card. Have your card out and ready when you say firmly to the waiter, "May I have the check, please." If your client protests, hold on to the check and remind him that your company is paying for the meal, not you yourself.

You'll find that as you gain experience, handling such matters with authority becomes second nature.

TAX DEDUCTIONS

While most large and medium-size companies reimburse business travel and convention expenses, women who are self-employed or work for small companies may have to cover their own expenses. All such work-related expenses are tax deductible. According to tax legislation that took effect on January 1, 1981, the number of meetings you can deduct a year is not restricted as long as your expenses are "reasonable." Remember that you may have to justify your expenses and that, as when filing for company reimbursements, you will need good documentation. In the event of an audit, you must be able to substantiate expenditures of over $25 and you must present a less formal accounting of everything else. Record all your expenses in an account book—meals, lodging, business entertainment, fees for a facility used, and other items. Records must be credible. You should record such expenditures in your book at or near the time they are incurred.

If your spouse accompanies you on a business trip, the part of the expense attributable to travel, meals, and lodgings for him is not deductible unless you can prove that his presence served a bona fide business purpose. Incidental services he might perform, such as typing notes or helping you entertain customers, do not warrant a deduction.

If you travel abroad for a meeting or a convention, you must also establish that the meeting is directly related to your business, and show that it is "as reasonable" for the meeting to be held outside North America as within it. Cruises are not eligible.

The IRS publishes three booklets of interest to business travelers: *Your Federal Income Tax* (#17), *Tax Guide for Small Business* (#334), and *Travel, Entertainment and Gift Expenses* (#463).

All are available free from your local IRS office.

CONVENTIONS

There's a time for work and a time for play, and both are usually provided at an annual convention or meeting. As part of doing business organizations ranging from Fortune 500 companies to local community associations gather each year to introduce new products, train members, build morale, network, reward employees, and socialize. In 1981 more than 9.5 million Americans attended conventions and 5.6 million got together for national sales meetings. The price tag for all these gatherings, according to *Meetings and Conventions* magazine: $24 billion.

Whether it's a full-fledged convention (defined by some hotel/motel industry authorities as at least 250 rooms booked) or a meeting (any gathering using less than 250 rooms), get-togethers are a standard business tool. People from different locations and backgrounds who have a common interest—the corporation they all work for, the profession they are in, the hobby they pursue—routinely gather to share information.

Most groups make a big event of their gatherings, often staging them in first-class hotels in major cities or at faraway resorts with multimedia exhibits (video or slide shows, live musicians or sound tracks). Thus a meeting of this kind is an invaluable experience for networking, meeting the big honchos, and learning about your organization.

And what happens when people trade in their business suits for bathing suits? The temptation to eat or drink or party too much can be strong at out-of-town gatherings, and a number of careers have probably been ruined because of overindulgence. It's important that you remain alert and courteous. You can't get lax; nobody wants an embarrassing situation, you least of all.

Here is the schedule for a typical convention:

Day One. Day-long registration. A chance to get acclimated, or to recover from jet lag if you've come that far. Registration is always hectic in the morning. Waiting until late afternoon is better—you may breeze right through. At the registration area you will pick up a schedule of events (if organizers haven't sent them in advance) listing seminars, special sessions, cocktail parties; an information package about the hotel (beauty salon, exercise facilities, secretarial services) and the goings-on about town (theater, museums, points of interest); and possibly a "convention survival kit": antacids, aspirins, sewing kit. Every conventioneer receives a name tag. It is a work tool and the best way to learn names.

The support systems of a convention are usually stationed at the registration area. A travel agent will probably be on hand to help with return arrangements or extend your stay. There is usually a notice board, blackboard, or desk for leaving messages. Some conventions start their meetings on day one, and most at least have some exhibits in place. These areas are open every day throughout the convention, after the general sessions.

The first day is a good time to have your own minimeetings, perhaps lunch or afternoon sessions with people you work with across the country but haven't met. Set these up in advance: it's important to have a plan when attending a convention.

Day Two. Time for the big show. Everyone gathers to hear the opening remarks of the head or heads of the organization. The opening address, invariably positive, is a time for the powers that be to reiterate and redefine the company image, and to weld a diverse group together.

In the evening there will no doubt be a welcome party. Even if parties are not your style, attend. It is your chance to chat with the president or other key executives.

Day Three. Today information overload may set in; your personal schedule should include some free time, and by now you'll need it. You may find yourself with an open evening. You could arrange a dinner meeting with colleagues you met at other conventions or keep clear in case you're invited to a bash in the president's suite. Whatever you do, think of the convention as a twenty-four-hour job. Forget about laundry and manicures until you get home.

Final Day. Today there are the wrap-up, rev-up speeches. Everyone should go home feeling enthusiastic about the company or the association, reaffirmed about its goals, and ready to work with renewed vigor.

In all probability, the first part of your body to give out at a convention will be your stomach. It is hard not to overindulge at the breakfast meetings, coffee breaks, heavy lunches, cocktail parties, dinners, and late night get-togethers, all of them taking place under unusual stress.

When you get your convention schedule, decide which meals are important to you: the general banquet, the breakfast with colleagues from around the country, a district manager's luncheon? Omit the meals that aren't a necessary part of the convention or useful for meeting people. Convention-goers warn that this is not the time to sample exotic food. Their advice is to eat sparingly, resisting the temptation to eat everything just because it is included in the package cost.

Evening meals at conventions are often formal. You may need a long gown or at least a cocktail dress, plus accessories. Although there's usually no need to pack sports clothes unless the convention is at a resort, do bring a bathing suit; your hotel may have a pool.

Before you go to the convention, talk it up. Send a memo to key people in your company telling them you plan to attend. Attach a photocopy of the program.

If you're attending a convention to job hunt or hone your professional skills, take ten copies of your updated résumé and a supply of business cards. Put together samples of your work; you may be able to arrange a critique or use them in a workshop. Take a map of the area you're visiting in case you're interviewed by a company headquartered off the beaten track.

Play the name game. Note names of speakers and their biographies in the preregistration material. Get a list of people who'll be there and take it with you. Pick out those you'd like to meet. Who are the top people in your field? What do they predict for the future in your occupation? Who might be useful to your future? The important speakers, organizers, and other notables are likely to arrive early for pre-meeting sessions. Set up a breakfast, lunch, or dinner meeting with them. Be ready to pick up the tab.

FOREIGN TRAVEL

Traveling overseas isn't that much different from traveling in America for business, just more complicated. Here are some general tips about travel abroad, followed by information about some foreign centers of business, with information about customs and traditions as well as hard-core facts. Women do business regularly in the parts of the world we describe, and there are no unusual taboos.

Apart from the usual passport and visa and immunization checks, arrange for the special services and equipment you may need. Always find out about hours of business and local or national holidays and customs that will affect your functioning in the foreign country. Know about attitudes toward women in business, and work within them.

Your problems overseas may stem less from the fact that you are a woman than from the fact that people may not instantly recognize *who* you are and *what* company you work for. One of the most important rules concerning foreign business travel is that you have (or seem to have) the status to conduct business and the complete backing of your company. This is especially important in Japan, where there are many American-owned subsidiaries, and where people coming from the United States are often lower in rank than Japanese executives presiding over subunits of the American companies.

You will encounter a similar problem doing foreign business if you represent a company that is not very well known. Women who work for multinational corporations are at a distinct advantage when conducting business overseas.

For these reasons it is especially important to travel with a number of different business cards printed in Japanese, Arabic, or whatever languages are used in the countries on your itinerary and to present yourself as a consummately competent professional.

Everyone has communications problems when working overseas. Telephones are particularly challenging: ringing and beeping have different meanings in different places; certain phones take coins, others tokens; many hotels, especially in France, Germany, and Switzerland, have as much as a 300 percent markup on calls you make from your room, and practically all switchboards waste precious minutes. Tips: Call collect or from a phone center (often in a major post office), get a room with a direct phone line, use hotels that have Teleplan.

Business people often forget to use the services of their own government when preparing for a trip overseas. For example, the U.S. Commercial Service of the Department of Commerce, which has offices in major cities, can supply you with research facilities and expert help. It can also tell you the best market for your products and services (through its Agent Distribution Service), give you tips on contacts, business advice, and general information. If you need background on a foreign corporation, the Commerce Department will prepare a report for you, with facts about sales, credit ratings, capitalization, etc. This service costs $40 and takes time, so request it well in advance.

A note on foreign languages: If you want to take a crash course in a particular language, there are several methods available for business people. Before investing in any form of instruction, consider how fluent you need to be. You should take into account your business needs, the customs of the country you're going to, and the time you have for studying. The Berlitz and Inlingua schools, the biggest and best-known chains, offer intensive conversational learning programs for short or long periods. Many community colleges offer language instruction as well.

Most guidebooks are written for tourists and will help only with part of your travel. The best handbook for business people abroad is the *Multinational Executive Travel Companion* ($35; available from Guides to Multinational Business, Harvard Square, Box 92, Cambridge, Massachusetts 02138).

FRANKFURT

Business in Germany is formal. On an average work day you can expect to find a person in the office between 9:00 A.M. and 1:00 P.M. and again between

3:00 P.M. and 5:00 P.M. But there is a growing trend to close offices early on Fridays, so make your end-of-the-week business calls Friday morning.

Americans consider West Germany one of the most difficult countries to do business in. It is a particular problem for women, who often feel unnerved by staunch Germanic negotiating styles. Assertiveness is never more important than when doing business in Germany.

GENEVA

Geneva, though a small city (population about 175,000), is a thriving international crossroads. Combining modernity and old-world charm, Geneva is known as one of the cleanest and safest cities in Europe. Many find it a pleasure to do business there.

HONG KONG

Hong Kong is devoted almost entirely to business: It is a base for international trading, multinational business, and manufacturing. Because of this Hong Kong is geared to the business person's needs. Most first-class hotels can provide negotiating rooms, secretaries, communication facilities, and other services. You can hire a translator easily, usually from Riggs Associated Services. These services are not cheap but they are efficient. For the woman traveler, Hong Kong is a safe city to move around in, as tourist areas are in most of the Orient. It is considered perfectly acceptable for a woman to have a drink or a meal alone at any of the hotels. Dress professionally, as you would at home.

Most business travelers stay in Central Hong Kong, on Hong Kong Island. This is the city's business and financial center, and it has three first-class hotels: the Mandarin, the Furama Inter-Continental, and the Hilton International. The last two cater almost exclusively to business people. Business hours are 9:00 A.M. to 5:00 P.M.

MADRID

Though the siesta still lives in Spain, the mañana philosophy is less evident in the capital city. Business hours in Madrid are from 9:00 A.M. to 1:00 P.M. and 4:30 to 8 P.M., and appointments during these hours are kept. Because of this daily business schedule, women travelers are sometimes reluctant to dine out alone at the traditional hour of 9:00 P.M. Don't be, or you'll miss a good deal of Madrid's flavor.

MILAN

Milan is sometimes called Italy's second city, but it is of primary importance in fashion, finance, publishing, and the arts. Milan's leadership in the fashion world is displayed on the elegant Via Monte Napoleone, Via della Spiga, and Corso Buenos Aires. The combination of industrial activity and an artistic past create an energetic atmosphere. The fast pace is constant because of the many industrial exhibitions and conventions, including the annual International Trade Fair in April. The work day usually begins at 8:30 A.M. and ends at 6:30 P.M., with a two-hour lunch break.

MOSCOW

A business trip to Moscow can be less comfortable than a trip to other major foreign cities, and it requires more preparation. All foreigners entering the Soviet Union, whether for business or tourism, deal with the Soviet National Tourist Board (Intourist). You must pick your hotel from a list provided by Intourist, and you probably won't get your first choice. You learn where you are staying only after you arrive. After you go through customs, an Intourist guide will take you directly to your hotel. There you submit your visa and passport, which the hotel's management holds till your departure. There is a concierge on every floor, and in most hotels you pick up your key from her and leave it with her whenever you go out; in the newer hotels you pick up the key from the desk. All foreign trade corporations (responsible for importing specific goods and services), Soviet ministries, and other governmental organizations are located in Moscow. Most businesses are open from 9:00 A.M. to 6:00 P.M., sometimes as late as 8:00. Public transportation is excellent, but most foreign visitors are driven around by Intourist guides.

For most of your stay in Moscow your hotel will be the center of your world, for eating, sleeping and doing business. Service bureaus run by Intourist in every hotel offer telexes, car rentals, translation services, and interpreters. Interpreters should not be necessary, because you get a business visa to the Soviet Union only when the appropriate connections with the Soviet government have been made, including English-speaking contacts.

PARIS

Though Paris is synonymous with romance, business dealings there can be cutthroat. Most Parisians speak at least a little English, but some will feign ignorance and just let you struggle and stutter. Polish up your schoolgirl French for getting around. For business dealings, don't take chances. Ahead of time request that someone who speaks English be present. Business hours are 9:00 A.M. to 5:00 or 6:00 P.M.

High surcharges are usual on hotel telephone calls; use *jetons* (tokens) for some public phones, for others use regular coins. *Jetons* can be purchased in any *"tabac"* shop or café that sells cigarettes. There you can also buy postage stamps and Métro tickets and *carnets* (ticket books).

TEL AVIV

If you're doing business in Tel Aviv, get ready for the hectic pace of a Western European business center—with a Middle Eastern flavor. Hebrew and Arabic are the official languages in Israel, but most people also speak English. Business hours are usually 8:00 A.M. to 1:00 P.M. and 4:00 to 7:00 P.M. Be well informed about religious customs when scheduling weekend appointments—Friday is the Moslem Sabbath, Saturday the Jewish, and Sunday the Christian. Business dress is informal, probably because of the Mediterranean climate. Bus and taxi transportation is excellent within the city. Remember that a phone token (*asimon*), which you get at a post office or a kiosk, is necessary to use the public phones, and that the Israeli ring sounds like an American busy signal.

JET LAG

Plane travel is an art unto itself. One of the first things you learn is to rest and relax as much as possible. This will help you with the problem of jet lag.

When you fly across time zones, you have to reset not only your watch but also your body timers. This is the root of jet lag: the bodily clocks set to function on the schedule of your place of departure have not yet found their new setting for the place of arrival. If you fly through more than three time zones, you can expect jet lag. Symptoms may include an exhaustion that makes it almost impossible to concentrate, remember, do anything, or pay attention to where you are. You may also suffer constipation or diarrhea, loss of appetite, headaches, bad vision, insomnia. The effects of jet lag can last up to three weeks, depending on your loss of physical strength and on environmental factors. Jet lag, on top of culture shock, can make a business trip a complete disaster.

If you have serious problems with jet lag, you may need to follow an anti-jet lag program which involves altering your sleeping and eating patterns an hour a day in the week before a trip. If you are going to lose time—that is, fly east—sleep and eat later. To combat less extreme travel fatigue:

Set your watch to the time of destination as soon as your trip starts, and behave as though you are on the new schedule for eating and sleeping. Eat lightly and avoid salty foods.

Relax and exercise your body during the flight.

Take a sleep shade, wear loose clothing, and bring slipper socks. Wear loose shoes: your feet may swell a couple of sizes and you'll want to take your shoes off and get them back on. Try to make use of empty seats to stretch out and rest. Get a pillow or blanket.

The atmosphere in a plane's cabin is literally as dry as the Sahara Desert, with humidity as low as 5 or even 2 percent. Drink a lot of fluids but avoid alcohol, which increases dehydration. Eliminate or cut down on smoking. The carbon monoxide in cigarette smoke reduces the blood's ability to carry oxygen and can cause headaches or slight dizziness while in flight.

If you wear contact lenses, consider removing them while in flight so that your eyes will not become tired and irritated because of the extremely dry atmosphere in the cabin.

You may also want to use extra moisturizer on your face.

In between your rest periods, get up and move around the plane as much as possible to keep your circulation active. Scandinavian Airlines' *In the Chair Exercise Book* (published by Bantam Books) has a wonderful collection of exercises you can do mostly sitting in your airplane seat. Moving all your limbs around and exercising your muscles as much as possible can make an amazing difference in how you feel at the end of a long flight.

Get all of this under your belt and you're ready to go. *Bon route!*

14

Women and Men and Work

Once there was a woman who had a huge, important freelance editing assignment. With everything else she had to do, she just couldn't get the freelance job done. The deadline was approaching and it was driving her crazy. Her husband had been in that kind of pressured work situation before, so he knew exactly what to do. He put fifty dollars' worth of good food in the refrigerator and left town for a long weekend. He gave her the stretch of time she needed to get the work done and lifted a great burden off her shoulders.

The life of a dual-career couple: when it works it's the best of all possible worlds. They are a team working together toward personal and joint goals, each cheering the other on, both sharing a firm foundation of love and support. When it doesn't work, two careers in one family can make life very complicated.

. It has been a generation since the typical family was one in which the father worked and the mother stayed at home to look after the kids. Even by 1968, according to the Bureau of Labor Statistics, dual-salary families equaled the number of "traditional earner" families. By 1981 we had almost come full circle—more than two-thirds (68 percent) of married couples were receiving two pay checks, whereas the number of "traditional" households had shrunk to a mere 16 percent. Today working mothers and working couples are the norm.

Some of the reasons are economic. We all need to support ourselves, and given the precarious state of the economy, two pay checks are better than one. But the financial incentives are only a part of the picture. The dual-career family thrives because more and more people believe that the old "patriarchal" family was a constraint to women and men alike. Women today no longer value the idea of being supported by a man; they want to contribute to the family finances and honor their own ambitions. And a woman's ability to earn income relieves her husband of the burden of ceaselessly providing, year in, year out. He is now freer to consider the options that some women have had for years—to change careers, to relocate, to say no to certain jobs, and even to take time off to engage in a pursuit that offers more personal rewards.

For these reasons and more, dual-career couples are the wave of the future. Estimates now put the number at 30,000,000 (a figure that includes both married couples and cohabitants). The baby boom generation has grown up, bringing with them increased expectations. Today work and achievement figure higher on the scale of components contributing to a woman's sense of well-being than do marriage and children, according to a 1980 study.

However exciting, these changing outlooks have placed a certain stress on the dynamics of relationships. Even the choice of a mate has taken on new meaning, especially for men of an executive stripe. At one time an ambitious young man sought as a bride the kind of well-brought-up, attractive young women of whom the boss (and the boss's wife) would approve, somebody who would do a good job of running his home, raising his kids, and entertaining his clients. Today this junior executive's idea of a good mate is often a woman with great prospects of her own—exactly the kind of person his mother would have called a "good catch" when talking to his sister. And the situation is much the same in reverse. Women executives are seeking men at least as successful as themselves, if not more so—an ambition that, statistically speaking, becomes less possible to fulfill with every passing year. In some relationships status may become an overriding issue, even more important than romance.

In a *Working Woman* article entitled "Does He Love You for Your Money?" Sheila Eby suggests that the marriage game has turned into a money game. She reports on a slew of romances that ultimately failed to turn serious: the young broker who told his lover, a novelist, that she'd better turn her writing skills into a job as an advertising copy writer because he could afford to get serious only about a woman who had a "real career"; the junior banker who told his would-be fiancée to forget about quitting work to have a child because he expected her to help pay for the house and car that he had in mind. "Men looking for mates today," one disgruntled woman complained, "check out a woman's résumé the way they used to look over her mother."

This describes one wrinkle in the fabric of our changing society, and there are others. Although people may now apply different criteria to establishing relationships, men and women continue to meet and fall in love. Boy meets girl, but he is less likely to do so at college, family gatherings, church events, or even singles bars. Increasingly it is the employer that acts as the new matchmaker, and as a result complications abound.

LOVE, MARRIAGE, AND THE OFFICE

Now that women perform high-level jobs, working *with* men rather than *for* them, the office has become a natural environment for romance to grow. It is, after all, a place where people are together eight hours a day, five days a week, seeing one another at their best, dressed for success, wielding power, asserting themselves, taking risks and performing well. "Success is sexy," reckons William J. Goode, a Stanford University sociologist who predicts that "women managers will in the future be perceived as much sexier and more womanly than now."

Yet mixing business and pleasure can have serious personal and professional repercussions. "A love relationship constitutes a threat to business," according to Eliza Collins, a senior editor at the *Harvard Business Review*. It is a harsh view, and one that Collins says she arrived at with great reluctance. She also says the conclusion was inescapable; that at present such relationships can erode an organization's stability and undermine the effectiveness of the individuals involved. She makes another point. In these matters it is almost always the woman who becomes the scapegoat; she is the one who eventually loses her job. Since women are generally lower on the corporate totem pole than men are, they are more likely to be considered unessential to the company, or cheaper to replace.

Collins says companies should consider affairs of the heart between their executives dangerous to everyone involved. Her advice to management is pointed and uncompromising:

Treat the relationship as a conflict of interest.
Advise the couple to get outside help.
Persuade the couple that either the person least essential to the company has to go or both have to go.
Help the ousted executive find a new and perhaps better job.

The expression "love conquers all" never had the corporation in mind. If you fall in love with a fellow executive, be prepared for management's reaction.

Not all companies take a hardline position on office romance, however.

Some have bent old nepotism rules to permit married couples and, in some cases, cohabitants to work at the same place. The Bank of America, for example, allows married couples to work together at all levels of the organization except in the same branch—and that exception is for security reasons rather than fear of favoritism or a drop in productivity. Nevertheless, in such situations individuals must conduct themselves professionally. They must exercise good judgment about the shop talk they can share and the information that must remain confidential. Corporations have a right to expect their employees to act at all times in the best interest of the company.

Other, more private occupational hazards can make life difficult for couples working together. Occasionally the two people are so worried about favoritism that they overcompensate by being harsher on each other than on their coworkers. It is also possible that little touches of self-importance ("She's too busy to call *me* back?") can sabotage a relationship, causing resentment or jealousy. Keeping your job, relationship, and sanity all depend on communicating clearly and openly with your partner and establishing ground rules in advance.

Such measures are especially vital when couples go into business together. In a recent *Working Woman* story, "24-Hour Partnerships," Andrea Fooner told of the troubles Marcel and Rachel Akselrod encountered when their comfortable but traditional marriage became a business partnership. Rachel had started a gourmet food import and distribution business at home that grew so fast she called on her husband's financial and managerial expertise and invited him to become a coowner. Suddenly there were bitter arguments. Marcel had expected to exercise his authority, but Rachel, who had started the business, was used to being in charge. The conflict made working together a misery, and ate away at their personal lives too. "It's hard to be lovey-dovey at night when you've been fighting at work," Rachel ruefully concluded.

Business counselor Roger Goodeve, whose Windham, Vermont, General Business Services advises many such couples, agrees that togetherness can be "an unexpected strain" for couples who haven't thought through its implications. Says Goodeve, "You need a marketing plan, a financial plan, and an operating plan. The couple also must be very clear about which areas of responsibility belong to the wife and which to the husband. Each spouse needs to be boss in a different area. Otherwise there will be an inefficient duplication of effort and many irritations."

The dual-career couple, whether they work together or separately, has to withstand stresses and juggle priorities that the traditional couples of yesteryear could not have envisioned. Happily, they also enjoy many more advantages:

Dual-career couples have a deeper understanding of each other's lives. They not only share responsibilities, they share the special pleasures—and tensions—that both jobs and homemaking bring.

Dual-career couples can afford a better life style, acquiring material possessions that would otherwise be denied them.

Dual-career couples are usually better parents. Their children have the benefit of a more self-assured mother and a less remote father.

Dual-career couples enjoy a special sense of security. If one partner loses a job, the other still contributes to the "breadwinning."

The shift in gender roles and family life is not being accomplished without difficulty. Some of the problems were pinpointed in a 1981 Catalyst survey, *Corporations and Two-Career Families: Directions for the Future.* Responses from 374 top companies and 815 two-career couples identified four major problems that are troubling to both men and women.

Allocation of time
Financial issues
Poor communication
Conflicts over housework

Many more wives than husbands mentioned role conflicts, though fewer than might be expected expressed worries that their husbands would resent their success. Competition was not a serious concern for most couples.

The report highlighted another important trend. It seems that most couples, while satisfied with their careers and demanding a high performance of themselves at work, rate family as even more important than career. This orientation is one explanation for the changing attitudes of both couples and companies toward relocation.

WILL YOU FOLLOW?

When two careers are heading in different geographical directions, conflicts inevitably arise. These days the conflicts take on a new dimension. At one time it was, invariably, the woman who followed the man to his job; now it may well be the other way around.

Working Woman carried matching stories—eighteen months apart—by members of a Detroit couple who moved to Dallas after the wife was offered a better job (with a 25 percent salary increase) as assistant features editor of the *Dallas Morning News.* In the first piece, "My Wife the Breadwinner" (published in March 1982), Dennis Holder told of his unsuccessful attempts to find an equivalent job in Dallas. He decided to move anyway, and take up a new, precarious life as a freelance writer and full-time househusband. He found, he wrote, that although the decision worked out well for the couple themselves, it was not well understood by many of their acquaintances, who "have rigidly fixed ideas about the proper roles for a man and a woman."

In the later piece his wife, Elizabeth Franklin, wrote about the time she came home after an exhausting work day and found her husband "fluffed out on the sofa reading a novel instead of writing or doing the housework." The role reversal seemed funny but also unsettling. There were money problems, too. "It had been easy to love as a man and woman of independent means," she wrote. "It was less easy and gave new depth and breadth to caring to have to plot pennies together." In the end, however, this couple agreed that their decision had been a wise one.

Some couples often doubt the wisdom of their decision, perhaps especially the so-called commuting couples who have opted to live apart when one partner is asked to relocate. Sociologists Harriet Engel Gross and Naomi Gerstel coauthored a 1983 study of 50 professional commuting couples, many of whom confessed to feeling that they were "missing something." Some individuals reported irritating encounters at the office, where peers assumed that their living arrangements meant they were "up for grabs." Others lamented marital strains, such as constant discussions about whether the time they spent together was worth the money it cost to commute. Almost all the couples in the Gross-Gerstel study felt their careers were important enough to put up with commuting. They tended, however, to define their condition as temporary—an attempt, Gross explains, to "normalize" the situation so as to accept it.

According to Patricia Light, chief psychologist at Harvard Business School's counseling service, commuting should be regarded only as a short-range option. "The problem of loneliness is enormous," she says, adding: "I'm not too optimistic about people who do it over the long haul; I think a marriage or a relationship requires a minimum level of contact and communication. Things like phoning and spending weekends together help keep things going but after a while they're not enough."

WHO DOES THE DISHES?

When both partners in a marriage are working there never seems to be enough time for anything. When a child or children are involved too, the marriage takes on some of the aspects of a nonstop merry-go-round. Foremost among the areas of conflict about time are those to do with housework and child care. Despite all the current talk about sharing, men still contribute only about 22 percent of the time and effort needed for domestic tasks (up from 14 percent a few years ago, according to the Urban Institute). At the same time, however, working women are estimated to spend some twenty-six hours a week doing household chores. That may be less than half the time spent by the "unemployed" housewife, but it is a harrowing burden for the woman who works full time.

The central problem is that men, although they may be willing to do housework, still see their role as *helping* rather than taking responsibility. As Caroline Bird writes in *The Two Paycheck Marriage*, "That means that she does the worrying about dinner, even when he does the shopping as well as the cooking. She, not he, does the worrying about the dwindling supply of clean socks even if he does 'her' laundry."

The theoretical solution for dual-career couples would be to employ household help, but more than one family has found that this cost, in addition to the other costs necessitated by both partners going out to work (transportation, clothes, lunches out, babysitting) cancels the gains from the second pay check. On the other hand, paid help can be worth the investment if the wife is building a career.

The real-life solution to the domestic debate is much simpler and more obvious: *Let the housework slide.* Women who work are beginning to deprogram themselves. They don't care about waxy buildup, they buy take-out food, they vacuum once a month only. And life does go on.

Even if a career woman sheds the homemaker image, she has to make difficult choices about how to allocate her precious private time. Opportunities to visit friends or read a novel or just goof off are scant. "What I would like more than anything—more than a raise or a bonus—would be the privilege of going to exercise class at three in the afternoon," says one woman who rises at six o'clock to go work out. What most successful women with families crave in their time off from the office is not excitement or glamorous vacations but more sleep.

MONEY AND POWER

As if the balancing of multiple roles were not enough, women in dual-career marriages must wrestle with another, often unresolved conflict: money.

Separate checking accounts and a joint savings account, separate savings accounts and a joint checking account, separate everything, joint everything: the way a couple decides to handle money reveals a lot about their relationship, and about themselves. Fights over money are often really fights over things such as power, sharing, trust, and security. Combined pay checks can be a source of solidarity or conflict.

A woman's salary contributes about 40 percent to the average dual-career income. And where there is a disparity between what individuals are contributing to the family coffers, there is usually an equally disparate balance of power.

According to Caroline Bird, the woman's income in a two-career marriage is often trivialized by making it the "family budget." She pays for the "little things"—groceries and so on—and he pays for the "big things"—the mortgage, the car. Such an arrangement can make the wife resentful. Studies have shown that the closer the woman's pay check is to the man's, the more willing he is to share responsibilities, and that couples who pool their funds to pay the bills seem to have a smoother time. But the ideal arrangement, according to some marriage counselors, is to share some money, putting it into joint checking and savings accounts, and to separate the rest. That way each partner has personal funds. Handling money this way symbolizes that the power in the relationship is shared, yet it also affirms the importance of autonomy within the marriage. The happiest marriages, says Bird, are those in which the husband and the wife are equal—in other words, the ones where power is *not* an issue.

Don and Becky Powell, a Dallas, Texas, couple interviewed by *Working Woman* in January 1982, agreed that sharing their money meant working together. "If one person is making a lot of money and not sharing it," said Becky, "the other mate feels like a child. I think a lot of people feel trapped when the other isn't sharing."

Stress and strain over money problems can best be solved by frequent discussions about common goals. But no matter how a couple chooses to manage their money, they should try to maintain a sense of mutual respect. There is no "perfect" arrangement. "What is important," says New York clinical psychologist Michele Berdy, "is that people be as comfortable as they can with what money means and that they be as flexible as possible in dealing with the other person."

Does the decision not to have children eliminate one of the biggest conflicts from a dual-career couple's life? Probably yes. Childlessness doesn't seem to affect the happiness of a marriage, provided both partners have fulfilling careers. But having children changes things irrevocably.

The next chapter explores the inevitable transformation that occurs in a working couple's life when two becomes three, or four, or more.

15

Motherhood and Career

"Motherhood isn't like anything else I've ever done," says Elizabeth Stone, professor of media studies, author, and mother. In the September 1982 *Working Woman* Stone described the inherent conflicts between careers and motherhood: "Those who talk about working and mothering as if they were parallel activities—just two of the several 'hats' that working women wear— miss a crucial point. Whatever mothering and working have in common, in a very important way they involve opposite rather than compatible impulses. If mothering is at its best selfless, working insists we be selfish. If mothering requires us to be other-centered, and asks that we give up a certain kind of control, working demands that we take control, that we be, in the best sense, self-centered, self-asserting, self-promoting."

Nearly a hundred years ago Sigmund Freud described love and work— *"Liebe und Arbeit"*—as the two most important components of life. Achieving a balance between them and deriving fulfillment and satisfaction from them were both the goals and the characteristics of healthy adults. Freud, of course, did not intend this prescription primarily for women. For most of them, anatomy was destiny, and their fulfillment was to be found exclusively in the roles of wife and mother.

Today psychologists and others who study the human race are willing to include women in the company of healthy adults. An array of research studies, the writings of our best thinkers, and the day-to-day experience of countless women confirm that a combination of work and love is necessary to everyone for a satisfying, challenging life.

Consider the research of Faye Crosby, a professor at Yale. In a large-scale study of working women, nonworking women, and working men, she found that working women who are married and have children seem to enjoy their work more than those who are not wives and mothers. Crosby concluded that family life both enhances career satisfaction and puts job problems into perspective. "The people who love their jobs the most are the parents," she reports. "Multiple roles are very protective psychologically. If something goes wrong in one role, I can shut it out when I switch roles."

In a study of 300 women between the ages of thirty-five and fifty-five, Grace Baruch, Rosalind Barnett, and Caryl Rivers found that work has a profound effect on a woman's sense of self-worth, her feelings of being in charge of her life, and her chances of avoiding anxiety and depression. In *Lifeprints: New Patterns of Love and Work for Today's Women*, these authors conclude: "A woman's well-being is enhanced when she takes on multiple roles. At least by middle adulthood, the women who were involved in a combination of roles—marriage, motherhood and employment—were the highest in well-being despite warnings about stress and strain."

One thing we often forget in our current debate about working mothers is that the idea of a mother devoting her whole life to the care of her children is relatively new. In other cultures, and in preindustrial American society, women always combined work and motherhood. Most people lived off the land or practiced their crafts and trades in the same place they lived. Wives worked alongside their husbands, in the fields or the workshop, contributing to the support of the family. Children were cared for by the whole family, especially by those too young or old to work. It was only after the Industrial Revolution that the role of middle-class women began to be limited to that of homemaker and mother.

American society in the 1980s is not an agrarian economy, nor is it an aggregate of tradesmen or home-based businesses. And it does not, for the most part, include the kinds of family support systems that regularly provide free child care. This leaves women who want to combine paid work with motherhood prey to conflicting demands and often to guilt, anxiety, stress, and fatigue.

Martin V. Cohen, a clinical psychologist at New York Hospital–Cornell Medical Center, describes three sources of stress for women who combine careers with motherhood: "The first is guilt," he says. "Most women have grown up in non-dual-career families and have unrealistic ideas of what a mother should be. Inevitably, they have a sense of guilt over not doing enough—of not being as good a wife and mother as *their* mother was. Second, the woman has additional anxiety over her career. New to the marketplace, she may not yet be comfortable about career advancement or office politics. Third, there is the additional stress of the husband's unresolved fantasies of what a wife and mother should be like. If the wife is working and taking care of the kids, she may not be as sexually available as he would like, and this creates a strain."

Nancy Roizen, a thirty-six-year-old California pediatrician and mother of Jeffrey and Jennifer, describes with anxiety her inability to "give 100 percent to either her career or her family." For many women, this is the most stressful aspect of working motherhood.

"I felt a split loyalty," says Barbara Keck, a Harvard MBA and a former manager at a Connecticut manufacturing concern. "There is plenty of time to do the career, but children are small for a very short time." Keck left the company to found a thriving consulting firm that employs other highly trained working mothers.

Chicago editor Linda Matthews comments, "Though I am deeply absorbed in my work while I'm doing it, in the evenings, at lunchtime, at odd moments of the day, I am conscious of missing my daughter. And I can't help feeling that if I miss Sarah, she must miss me, too. More often I am convinced that some such struggle is inevitable, that there can be no easy transition from work to working motherhood."

And there isn't. But the good news is that most children of working mothers not only survive, they thrive. Frances Fuchs Schachter, a clinical child psychologist, compared 32 children of employed mothers with 38 toddlers from similar backgrounds whose mothers did not work. She found no discernible differences between the two groups in language development or emotional adjustment. What she did discover was that the group with employed mothers was more peer-oriented and self-sufficient, while the group with nonemployed mothers appeared more adult-oriented and dependent. Other studies have found that the adolescent offspring of working mothers feel better about themselves, are better adjusted socially, and get along better with their families and their friends at school.

When judging the effect of a mother's employment on her child, researchers say, the crucial issue is the mother's attitude. A mother who stays at home when she wants to be out working or when her family sorely needs money will transmit her depression and frustration to her child. All the same, the life of a working mother requires considerable stamina, and the challenge begins even before her first child is born.

MANAGING YOUR PREGNANCY

You are pregnant. The news is announced by your gynecologist, confirmed by a pregnancy detection test, or divined by you as you cope with swollen, uncomfortable breasts, midafternoon sleepiness, or sudden bouts of queasiness as you sit in a meeting. You are alternately thrilled and frightened—fascinated with the changes in your body and the idea that a new life is growing inside you, and simultaneously resentful of the fetus's demands that sap your energy and strength. All of this is a normal reaction to a major life crisis.

According to Tobias Brocher, M.D., pregnancy can arouse serious conflicts and ambivalence, especially if the woman is working. "The first pregnancy is a crisis," says Brocher, who is the director of the Center for Applied Behavioral Sciences at the Menninger Foundation, "because a woman realizes that she is entering a new stage of life. She is becoming a mother, which means not just a pregnancy but a commitment of fifteen years or more. Most women need some time to come to terms with this change."

Coming to terms with this change—adjusting to the reality of impending motherhood—is a crucial phase for a newly pregnant woman. Meg Wheatley and Marcie Schorr Hirsch, authors of *Managing Your Maternity Leave*, strongly advise that a woman defer announcing her pregnancy to her boss and coworkers until "after she has made her own initial adjustment and dealt with her conflicts and ambivalent feelings about being pregnant." Social worker Elizabeth McKamy adds that a woman who is adjusted to the idea of her pregnancy is "better able to weather co-workers' reactions and respond to the worries and anxieties they arouse." The news *should* be shared before the pregnancy is glaringly evident. Wheatley and Hirsch point out that it is vitally important to respect office protocol and inform key individuals (immediate supervisor, division manager, and the like) before announcing it to friends over lunch or at the water cooler.

Pregnancy evokes a variety of rational and not so rational reactions. Your boss's initial reaction may be to the imminent loss of the "old you." You may have been his or her confidante, social support, link to line staff or other departments, his or her trustworthy, dependable "anchor" during times of stress. He or she is wondering, "How will I fill the void in my support system during her absence?" If your boss is a woman who has decided against childbearing in the interest of her career, she may feel a resurgence of ambivalence about her decision or a fleeting sadness at the lost opportunity. If she is single, she may be somewhat jealous of your marital status and blossoming motherhood. If she is a married woman who stayed home to raise her children, she may resent your determination to combine two demanding careers.

A pregnant woman is obviously not responsible for these myriad responses, but if she intends to keep her job she has to deal with them. Her first tool is her awareness of a boss's potential reactions and biases. Armed with this awareness, as well as sensitivity to her boss's managerial style, the pregnant woman must negotiate one of the most important business deals of her career—her maternity leave. Like any other business deal, you need thoughtful preparation. Wheatley and Hirsch break the process into four steps:

1. Assess your job and determine which functions or responsibilities are most valuable to your employer. Calculate your replaceability index. The more difficult you are to replace, the more bargaining power you bring to the negotiations.
2. Anticipate the problems that may result from your leave, problems for your boss, coworkers, or subordinates. Develop and present a well-thought-out plan for countering organizational or personnel difficulties.
3. Identify and set priorities for the issues you will need to settle when you present your plan. Typical negotiation points include length and timing of leave, paid vs. unpaid leave, return to same or different job, choice of part-time employment after the leave is exhausted, flexible scheduling, or the option of working at home. Which points are subject to compromise? Which are nonnegotiable?
4. Have a series of renegotiations—a second round of discussions about the kind of leave you have, the handling of your work load, and so on—close to the time of your departure.

These are not the only issues you will need to consider in negotiating maternity leave. Other factors come into play.

Pace of change. Is your organization or department changing? Redefining its priorities? Refocusing its goals or purposes? Consolidating functions or personnel/staff responsibilities? Will your role and responsibilities remain static during the months you are away, or will you be returning to a different job with new responsibilities?

Seasonal demands. Does your "due date" coincide with your organization's busiest time? While your absence may be acutely felt, decisions will have to be made and procedures changed without your input. Wheatley and Hirsch advise planning job coverage carefully and remaining in contact with allies who will represent your interests. Some women have even managed to time their pregnancies to coincide with slack periods, a feat that obviously takes luck as well as planning.

Unwritten rules. Have other women in your department or organization successfully negotiated maternity leave, or are you the first? Has someone's career suffered badly because of her leave? If you can find out the unwritten part of your company's maternity leave policy, you can probably predict your success.

You cannot, in your fourth or fifth month of pregnancy, anticipate how you will feel at the end of the eighth month or six weeks after delivery. Some women work through their ninth month, but leaving at the end of the eighth month often makes good sense. It allows time to prepare yourself psychologically for the baby's birth and homecoming, and to make the transition from working full time to being at home for a while. By this time, too, commuting to and from work, sitting at a desk for extended periods, and concentrating during late afternoon meetings may become herculean tasks. Some women make it a matter of personal pride to resist succumbing to the demands of their bodies and deny or dismiss the fatigue and discomfort they are feeling. This can be a mistake; it's crucial to listen to your body and respond to its needs, to insure your own and your baby's health.

Most organizations offer a six-week paid maternity leave, which you take before or after the birth, as you need it. Many experts, however, consider a three-month leave ideal. At six weeks, the uterus has just begun to return to its normal size, breastfeeding has finally become synchronized, the baby may have begun to sleep through the night, and postpartum fatigue may be finally waning. In addition to considering these matters, you have to look at your own needs and goals. Women who are deeply involved in their work may find it important to return very soon after the birth. Others may find it more desirable to take a longer leave or devise a scaled-down work schedule that leaves more time for child rearing. Either way, having a child means a major change, one that even the best-prepared new parents can find harrowing. What's in store?

THE TRANSITION TO MOTHERHOOD

The first chapter of *Mother Care* begins, "After the birth of your baby, life will never be the same." In interviews with the authors, Lyn DelliQuadri and Kati Breckenridge, women describe the impact of a newborn on their previously well-ordered lives. They remember feeling as if their own identity had been submerged or absorbed by the baby, that they had "suddenly lost their pasts and their futures." They talk about exhaustion and an insatiable need for unbroken sleep. They talk about losing control of their lives.

Are these women suffering from severe postpartum depression? Are they women who are easily flustered, disorganized, overwhelmed? Not according to DelliQuadri and Breckenridge. These women are experiencing the "temporary scrambling" of their lives and identities as they make the transition to motherhood. Easing this transition, the authors advise, takes "acknowledging your need for time and activities apart from the baby."

Many mothers, particularly women who deferred childbearing until their thirties or had difficulty conceiving a child, often feel guilty about admitting they need time to themselves. They think they should want to devote every minute to nurturing, cuddling, and caring for the baby. Parenthood is full of such "shouldisms," warn the authors of *The Private Life of Parents*. Roberta Plutzik and Maria Laghi point out that many women hold themselves up to an idealized, madonnalike image of the perfect mother, the mother who is never angry, never tired, never depressed or distracted. What a new mother must remember, the authors maintain, is that perfect parenthood is an illusion. "Look after yourself," Plutzik and Laghi advise. "Well-being for parents means striking a balance between responsibility to one's child and responsibility to oneself and partner."

Being a perfect mother is not the only impossible goal. Perfection in the business world is equally impossible, as working mothers soon learn. Dianna Silcox, coauthor of *Woman Time*, head of her own consulting business, and full-time working mother, says, "My job is no longer my top priority, but neither is my child. I've had to downshift my expectations of myself. Having a baby means giving up the idea that you can excel in every area of your life." It also means learning to set limits on what you can do, and sharing responsibility as much as possible.

Happily, fathers are increasingly willing to share child-care responsibilities. The growing numbers of women working full time, the shift in child-development theories to stress involving both parents, and the emergence of the "we" philosophy, with its increased emphasis on sharing and giving to others, all promote a much larger role for the father in the life of his child. In the past ten years fathers have begun attending natural childbirth classes, witnessing their child's birth, and routinely caring for their children. Some fathers have even chosen to reduce their professional responsibilities and limit their schedules to spend more time with their children.

Fathers attest to the personal rewards and expanded vision that more responsibility for their children has given them. "It was difficult, exasperating and a lot of joy," says New York sculptor Ansell Bray, describing in *Working Woman* his years raising his five-year-old daughter. "I have a relationship with Samantha I wouldn't have had otherwise, and it certainly changed the way I see women."

Fathers who choose to assume full-time responsibility for their children while their wives work may suffer unexpected penalties when they decide to reenter the job market. Don Demers, a thirty-four-year-old industrial engineer, quit his job to care for his two daughters while his wife finished medical school. After a two-year hiatus, Demers began job hunting. He could not find a job.

"The hurdles men face when returning to the job market are about three times greater than those faced by women," says the president of a Los Angeles–based employment firm. "There isn't a male I know of in an executive position who would accept raising kids as a legitimate excuse for not working for three years."

No firm statistics are available yet, but an increasing number of large corporations are recognizing and responding to men's desire to share actively in the care of their children. AT&T, for example, offers an unpaid, six-month care-for-newborn-children leave to both men and women. IBM offers a year's personal leave to women and men, and CBS has a specific six-month paternity leave. The Ford Foundation offers fathers and mothers an eight-week paid leave of absence, followed by an eighteen-week unpaid leave after the birth of a child.

Such remarkable changes in corporate policy have not, however, altered corporate prejudices against the nurturing man. "The family man is actually penalized in the business community," writes Letty Cottin Pogrebin. "If he cares too much about his children, his career 'commitment' is suspect. He is likely to be overlooked for promotions and he may even lose his job. Fathers who voluntarily devote *all* their time to children, even temporarily, are seen as social deviates. Before men can comfortably devote more time to their children, the values of the workplace must change. But that is the task of the whole society, not of the individual father."

YOU'RE NOT ALONE

Working mothers are an anomaly no longer. There are more than 32 million mothers in the labor force today, and more than 18 million of them have children under the age of six. Almost 60 percent of all mothers with children under eighteen, and 50 percent of those with children under six, are working full time. The fastest-growing group entering the labor force is the mothers of children under three.

Unfortunately, neither American society nor American attitudes have caught up with this reality. According to the 1982 survey by the Public Agenda Foundation mentioned earlier, 54 percent of working men and 46 percent of working women think working mothers weaken the family, and 63 percent of working men and 52 percent of working women believe that a woman who wants to work outside the home should not have children. Paradoxically, though, 60 percent of the men and 70 percent of the women think that "a woman's need for self-fulfillment through work is just as important as her children's need for the best child care."

These conflicting attitudes and beliefs (work is important for mothers, bad for children and families) serve to complicate the political and practical issues that not only working parents but employers and legislators must confront and resolve. The question is not whether mothers with young children should work. It is how a nation set up on the assumption that most children have stay-at-home mothers can readjust to the reality that most kids don't. It is up to all of us—parents and nonparents—to speak up in favor of policies and practices that help two-pay-check families cope and their children flourish.

But even if society were more responsive to working parents than it is today, motherhood would still have a detrimental effect on a woman's career development. Even though fathers are participating more actively in child rearing, more often than not the role of "psychological parent" falls to women. It is mother who arranges for child care, stays home when a child is sick or the babysitter doesn't show up, keeps track of the pediatrician's visits and all the other minutiae that only grow greater as soccer practice and ballet lessons come into the picture.

Some women adjust to these demands by cutting back, working part-time or standard full time instead of their previous sixty-hour weeks. Others, lucky enough to work for forward-looking corporations, take advantage of flexitime to stagger their hours. In many hard-pressed families, parents work different shifts so they can care for their children without much outside help. Still other women leave the traditional job market and start their own businesses, a task that cannot be called relaxing but may give a woman greater flexibility. The really clever ones plan ahead and set up these new routines before the baby arrives.

And what about the rest? They grit their teeth, open their pocketbooks, and pay for full-day or more-than-full-day care for their children. This is generally much easier on the child than it is on the parents.

WHO CARES FOR THE KIDS?

As soon as a woman decides to return to work, she and her husband must confront the complex problem of choosing a caretaker or caretakers for their child. The decision will be influenced by their work schedules, their ability to pay for care, the willingness of the husband to share child-care responsibilities, how many children are in the family, and their ages and temperaments.

There are five types of child care: child-care centers; preschool programs (usually part-day nursery schools); "family" day care given in a home other than the child's; play groups (informal arrangements made by several families who split the costs); and traditional babysitters who care for the child in the home.

Parents' feelings about the child-care options available to them vary. In the Public Agenda study, half of all working parents and two-thirds of the mothers interviewed pointed to day care on company premises as an "excellent solution" to the problem of child care. Other acceptable options were a private nursery school or day-care center; in-home care from a licensed child-care worker or neighborhood babysitter; or leaving the child with a relative. Least popular was group care in a neighbor's home, and government-funded day-care centers and nursery schools also ranked quite low.

Despite parents' preferences, a recent Census Bureau study indicates that the reality of child-care arrangements is somewhat different. In 1977, 29 percent of the children of women who worked full time remained at home and were cared for by the father, by relatives or by other caretakers. Forty-seven percent were cared for in someone else's home.

CHILD CARE AT HOME: CHOOSING A BABYSITTER

Every working mother has heard the horror stories: the psychotic sitter who desperately craves a child of her own and kidnaps the one she is caring for; the preoccupied sitter, glued to the television or telephone, who ignores the baby's crying; the mindless sitter who meets the child's physical needs but does not talk to him; the insensitive sitter who lavishes attention and love on a male child while ignoring his sister. Then there's the other fear—the sitter who is so competent, experienced, wise, loving, gentle, unflappable, and inventive that she "steals" the children's love and allegiance. In the face of these horrors—fortunately more imaginary than real for most families—working mothers' feelings of guilt, ambivalence, anxiety, and intimidation abound.

Attorney Jane Stevens, mother of twin daughters, describes her first experience with a babysitter: "The fact of her broad experience with children presented a slight problem: There was some ambiguity about authority. She was older and more experienced; I was the employer and mother. For the first month or so, there was competition between us about the decision-making power. I felt twinges of jealousy and possessiveness. Those feelings of jealousy were the first hints of a low-key, subtle competition for the babies' affection that continued for a long time."

Linda Matthews talks about the guilt: "I felt betrayed and like a betrayer in leaving Sarah to babysitters five days a week. Why had I become a mother if I could spare so little time for my baby?"

A working mother must cope with such emotions, and they may never be fully resolved. They peak and diminish as old, trusted sitters leave and new ones must be hired and adjusted to; as the child goes through potentially stressful developmental stages like teething, toilet training, starting school; during holidays or summer vacations. Accepting the existence, and the persistence, of these feelings is probably the first step in coping with them; they are, after all one of the realities of being a working mother. Equally important is realizing that no one can replace you in your child's eyes. You will be the permanent figure in your child's life; the sitter, however loving and involved, is likely to be temporary.

The final evidence is your children. If they are thriving, happy, involved with school, activities, and peers, if they are not afraid of or intimidated by the sitter, and can separate from you in the morning with a degree of equanimity, then your concerns should be alleviated.

If, however, you think something is wrong with your babysitting situation, you should trust your instincts and take immediate action. Come home unexpectedly in the middle of the day, or arrange for a relative or friend to visit unannounced. Watch your children's behavior at night for clues to their daytime activities. Are they so exhausted that you know there were no quiet playtimes or rest periods? Or are they so rambunctious that you suspect they were forced to sit quietly all day? What do they say about their experiences with the sitter? Listen carefully to your children.

Firing a sitter will disrupt a working mother's (and one would hope a working father's) schedule at home and at the office, but often there is no alternative. The best thing to do is end the situation quickly. The fair way is to give the sitter one or two week's wages in lieu of notice. Firing someone is not a pleasant experience, but having an inadequate sitter continue to watch your children is not a good idea.

FINDING A DAY-CARE CENTER

Sometimes child care at home is not a realistic alternative because of financial or other considerations. Whatever the reason, the idea of a child-care center evokes its own horrors in parents. You may be haunted by images of your helpless infant or barely verbal two-year-old surrounded by wailing babies, older, aggressive children, and overworked, overextended caretakers who are too busy to single out a scared or lonely child for affection and attention.

These things can happen, of course, but many researchers have much happier news to report. A University of Chicago study found that children in day-care centers may develop intellectual, verbal, and social skills earlier than their peers who remain at home. Although other researchers are not totally convinced about the positive effects of day care on child development, Dr. Lois Hoffman asserts that the "research done has thus far not demonstrated adverse effects of quality day care for infants and young children."

But what constitutes "quality day care"? Estelle Kramer, early-education specialist and supervisor of a Los Angeles day-care program, characterizes a good program this way: "An accommodating administrator, a good adult/child ratio (three infants to one adult or ten older children to one caretaker), a responsive curriculum, nurturing caretakers, flexibility in routine and an awareness that at the end of the day, parents returning from work are as tired as the youngsters."

The day-care relationship is a triad made up of the working parent(s), the child, and the day-care staff. Good communication between and among all those involved is essential. Parents need to provide medical information about the child, participate in conferences, advise the staff of any changes or occurrences in the family that may affect the youngster's behavior or temperament, and maintain an active interest in center activities.

The staff, in return, should provide ongoing, honest communication about the child's activities and adjustment to the center. You may want to make a point of talking to the staff regularly. Sometimes caretakers hesitate to tell parents that a youngster cries frequently or is withdrawn and apathetic, for instance.

Parents can also take certain steps to help a child adjust to day care. Taking children for a short visit to the center before they actually start can avoid much of the fear of the unfamiliar, and arranging to visit the center yourself during the first few days can ease the transition. Children should also be encouraged to talk about their experiences and helped to define their feelings. Is your child sad when you say goodbye in the morning, or scared of the other children? On the practical side, remember to dress the child in comfortable clothes that can get dirty and are easy to unbutton.

A difficult adjustment does not necessarily indicate a poor center or an insensitive staff. It also does not mean that the child is not suited to or will not ultimately benefit from day care. It may mean that center staff and the youngster's parents need to discuss strategies for coping with this behavior both at home and at the center.

THE STRUGGLE TO IMPROVE CHILD CARE

The availability of good-quality day care for the children of working parents is no longer the idiosyncratic concern of a small minority of women. According to Sheila B. Kamerman, D.S.W., professor of social policy and planning at Columbia University School of Social Work and author of *Parenting in an*

Unresponsive Society: Managing Work and Family Life, "the contemporary reality is that most American mothers are not at home with their children."

Another fallacy, Kamerman continues, concerns day-care consumers. Day care is not solely for, nor used exclusively by, poor people. "Changes in the labor force have made child care an essential service for the majority of American children," says Kamerman. "The issue no longer is whether we need such services, but rather how to assure access to good ones."

Kamerman and other child-care experts worry about the quality of care available to the children of working parents. In her eloquent new book, *The Day-Care Dilemma,* Marian Blum educational director of the Wellesley College Child Study Center, gives a vivid picture of the kinds of stresses that plague even good child-care facilities: lack of privacy for children and teachers, constantly changing (and overworked, underpaid) caregivers through the day, insufficient individual attention available for children, sometimes less than sanitary conditions.

It's crucial that working parents put themselves at the forefront of local, state, and national efforts to do something about these problems. As Kamerman points out, federal standards for child-care facilities could help. But parents, teachers, employers, and the society at large must give serious consideration to the needs of children for "a healthy, secure, consistent, loving, disciplined, warm, caring, nurtured, unpressured infancy and childhood," Blum writes. "Society must rethink its priorities," she says. "If children are as important as offshore oil; if they are as interesting as computers; if they are as vital to the survival of these United States as nuclear missiles . . . then *someone will have to raise them.* And, someone—including parents and the larger society—will have to pay for that care."

If we don't find solutions to the problem of child-care our children will be the victims. And through them, the nation will suffer the consequences of our failure.

THE CHILD-CARE TAX CREDIT

ELIGIBILITY

If you pay someone to care for your child or other dependent while you work, those expenses may entitle you to a tax credit for part of the money you spend. The credit amounts to 20 percent of your household or personal-care outlays.

Who is a dependent? A dependent is defined as: (1) a dependent child under the age of fifteen for whom you can claim an exemption on your tax return; (2) other dependents who are physically or mentally "incapable of self care" and for whom you pay over half of the cost of support; (3) a spouse who is physically or mentally incapable of self care.

You must earn income from a job or self-employment and must maintain a home for the dependent you claim.

EXPENSES

Expenses include in-home or outside-the-home costs that permit you to take, keep, or actively search for a job. Such expenses include payments for a housekeeper, nurse, or caretaker; payments to a nursery school, day-care center, day camp, or babysitter. Payment for transportation to the center or school is not considered a deductible expense. Allowable care expenses also include payments to a relative, provided you do not claim that relative as a dependent.

OTHER PROVISIONS

Divorced or single parents are eligible for the credit if: (1) each partner files a separate return; (2) your spouse did not live with you during the last six months of the year; (3) the child or dependent has lived in your home for six months of the year; (4) you paid half the cost to keep up your home for the year.

PAPERWORK

Compute your tax credit on Form 2441 and enter the amount on Form 1040. Attach Form 2441 to form 1040.

SCHOOL-AGE CHILDREN

Though the pressures of child care ease up when children reach school age, the strain on working parents is by no means over. They are confronted with structuring after-school hours and summer vacations, attending school plays and PTA meetings, coping with the sudden onset of tonsilitis or the need for two dozen home-baked cookies.

And parents also have very real fears for children in this age group, including kidnapers and burglars and emergencies, such as fires or serious injuries, that a young child would be unable to cope with. "Latchkey kids," children not supervised by an adult after school, are at particular risk.

In *The Handbook for Latchkey Children and Their Parents*, Lynette and Thomas Long advise parents to encourage youngsters to talk about their fears of being alone in the house. Children often cope with such fears, the authors state, by conducting elaborate security checks of their house each afternoon, turning on all the lights, or, if frightened, hiding in the bathroom or closet. The authors also found that many of the 5.2 million American children who are left alone at some time during the day panic when their parents don't appear as expected. "It's important for parents as well as children to keep each other informed of their whereabouts or if they'll be late."

What other measures can parents take to make youngsters at home alone feel safe—and be safe? The Longs advise:

Fire. Children should know that in the event of a fire, they should leave the house or apartment immediately and call the fire department. To prepare children for such an event, parents should plan and practice home fire drills, devising an escape route from each room in the house. Secondary escape routes should also be planned. Children who live in apartments should be taught safety tips appropriate for apartment residents.

Injuries. Children must be taught to recognize an emergency that requires them to call the number for the police, fire department, or rescue squad. A list of emergency telephone numbers should be posted, at the youngster's eye level, in a prominent place near the telephone. All children who stay alone should be aware of the treatment for burns, insect bites, broken bones, and cuts and scrapes.

Break-ins. Children should know what to do if they are at home when a break-in is attempted, and what to do if they approach the house and something looks amiss.

Assault. Children must be alerted to the dangers strangers pose. Children must be taught never to talk to strangers, get in a car with strangers, or accept gifts from strangers. Children should walk home from school with friends on main, well-lit streets. If a stranger approaches your child, he or she should be taught to run away and find safety where there are other people.

Appliances. Parents should indicate which appliances children are permitted to use and which are forbidden, and should teach children how to use those that are allowed.

Sally Wendkos Olds also advises that children not tell strange phone callers or visitors that they are at home alone, and that they should never allow anyone they don't know to enter the house. In addition to encouraging children to express their fears about being at home alone, or to talk about their loneliness during the afternoon hours, working mothers and fathers also can use the telephone as an important link to their youngsters at home. A brief call lets the parent know that a youngster is home from school safely or that a special event at school—an exam, a spelling bee, an assembly program—went smoothly. Children should have their parents' work numbers but should understand what constitutes a legitimate call.

Because a parent's work-related concerns are foreign to a youngster, telephone calls to and from home should be cheerful, and concerned primarily with the youngster's needs or experiences. Kids like to hear their parents say, "You're just the person I wanted to talk to." Having children visit parents' offices can help. It makes the parents' jobs seem real and allows kids to visualize them at work and know they aren't really so far away.

Working parents encourage, and indeed expect, their school-age children to be independent, self-reliant, and resourceful. Happily, children benefit from such expectations. "The school-age children of working parents benefit from two conditions of family life," says Olds. "They tend to live in more structured homes, with clear-cut rules. Also, their parents usually encourage them to be independent."

Independence and responsibility usually go together. Helping youngsters accept responsibility for household chores, schoolwork, and often the care of younger siblings is another task of working parents. Basic rules should be posted on the refrigerator, advises Robin Pappas. This is particularly important when the oldest child is put in charge of younger children. A list of rules reminds younger family members that their older sibling is enforcing parental requirements. "The eldest child needs the strong support of parents in enforcing house rules," Pappas says. "It is very frightening when younger children do not obey. Without backup from parents, the eldest may become a tyrant or lose self-confidence in his or her relationships with others."

Pappas also encourages working parents to spend time alone with each of their children whenever possible, and to allow their children to spend time away from each other, pursuing their own interests or hobbies.

The most stressful time for many working parents is the first hour after getting home. Children often cannot understand that their parents need to "wind down" after a day at the office and bombard them with their problems, news, and needs as soon as the tired parent enters the door. "There is an immediacy about children's needs," Pappas says. "They can't wait to pour out the explosive news they have been holding in for the past several hours of waiting."

Olds has devised a list of strategies for easing the transition between work and home. These include: Lie down on the couch or bed for fifteen minutes or half an hour, issuing an open invitation to all family members to share their news as you rest. Change from work clothes into comfortable shoes and a caftan as soon as you get home. Have informal appetizers—cheese, carrot sticks, yogurt dip—right away so you can relax and serve dinner a little later. Take a fifteen-minute herbal bath or bracing shower.

Despite your best planning, some events in life will demolish the most sophisticated organization. No one can be prepared for every emergency.

Illness. What happens when a school-age youngster with working parents gets sick or injured in the middle of the day?

The youngster's school should, of course, have the daytime numbers of both parents, and be aware that both parents are available in the event of an emergency, or that one parent may be more accessible than the other. "Schools have to break out of sex-stereotyped roles," Olds warns, and recognize that often a father's work schedule is more flexible than a mother's. Schools should also have the telephone numbers of responsible, accessible friends or relatives to notify in an emergency. A trustworthy neighbor, relative, or babysitter (if one is employed) should be given a notarized statement authorizing him or her to approve medical treatment in your absence.

When a sick child has to spend several days at home, the working mother's guilt, ambivalence and anxiety resurface. Many women reserve their sick or personal leave for such occasions. Others share the responsibility with their husband, neighbors, or accommodating relatives. There are no easy solutions.

Jane Greengold Stevens describes the difficulties involved in handling her twin daughters' allergies and asthma. "In lives like ours, so full and so tightly scheduled, there is little margin for crises. Every childhood illness and crisis puts a strain on our resources of time and energy, reminds us how precarious is the balance that allows us to parent and to work and to make art."

School holidays, Christmas, and summer vacation. Most parents schedule their vacations to correspond with their children's time off from school. Yet schoolchildren have far more free time than working parents, who sometimes solve the problem by enrolling their children in overnight or day camps. Adolescents, however, may resist or resent the suggestion of summer camp. Alternatives for them include volunteering in a hospital or child-care agency, enrolling in art, dance, or drama classes, or taking enrichment or skills courses in summer school. Parents who feel compelled to structure every minute of their youngsters' vacation may find Dr. Stella Chess's advice reassuring. "Vacation isn't vacation," she says, "if every minute is scheduled, no matter how pleasant the program. Thirteen-year-olds should have a chance to practice independence."

Chess also urges working parents to pressure school boards to expand or change programs and schedules to be more responsive to their needs. The National Committee for Citizens in Education, a private nonprofit organization and advocacy group, surveyed working parents and found a need for before- and after-school care for children and for increased sensitivity to working parents' difficulties in arranging conferences, and special school activities.

School plays and sudden calls for baked goods, custom-made costumes,

274 · THE WORKING WOMAN REPORT

and other assorted guilt-inducing events. Be prepared for these events to occur regularly, and for the guilt and anxiety you will feel when you miss your daughter's performance in *The Nutcracker Suite* or her tenth touchdown. And don't try to do everything. Parents have to learn to forgive themselves.

As Jane Whitbread puts it: "Don't expect a perfect child, a perfect household, or a perfect husband." Or, we might add, a perfect job, a perfect boss, or a perfect self. In the final analysis, being a working mother means making compromises, having reasonable expectations, being flexible and organized, accommodating and structured. It means balancing two jobs and two areas of responsibility. It also means deriving satisfaction, pleasure, and fulfillment from both.

In her 1981 book *The Second Stage*, Betty Friedan argues that there has been "a blind spot in feminism that is both personal and political in its implications and consequences." She is referring to the letters she receives from young women asking how they can possibly combine a career and a marriage and motherhood without making terrible compromises. "How can I make it in a man's world indifferent to the needs of children?" "Will taking time off to raise a family do irreparable harm to my career?" Neither Friedan nor other feminists have answers for these types of questions, but women are going ahead anyway, trying the best they can to have it all.

16
Catch-35

A contemporary professional woman approaching middle age is a pioneer. Such women—in midlife and midcareer have never before existed in meaningful numbers. There have been a few forerunning women who built lives outside the traditional daughter-wife-mother mold: we call them role models and examine their lives for clues to how to behave and what to expect. But just because they are so rare, their lives have been different. There really are no guidelines for arranging the adult lives of today's adult women, and no easy answers for questions never before asked.

Professional women today have business degrees and career paths that they can expect will actually lead them somewhere. It makes sense to them to see how far they can go before worrying about such traditional things as husbands and children. There is plenty of time to deal with that. Career now, marriage and motherhood later.

And so, time passes, you struggle, move ahead, get your career established. Your name is on the office door, you have a home with furniture you've paid for, you can afford good suits and nice vacations. Then, suddenly, "later" is here and the issues you've put off for some future date can no longer be ignored. The future is now—and "now" often becomes the crisis we call Catch-35. The Catch-35 phenomenon is characterized by depression, anger, anxiety, and extreme behavior. You may be thinking about quitting your job, going back to school, or starting another career "before it's too late." At home, the big debate may be whether or not to be a mother.

For women in their mid-thirties, the choices that loom large can be either personal or career related, and are often both at once. Because choices concerning one aspect of your life can affect other aspects, this is a very crucial time. The New York psychologist Mortimer Feinberg thinks that an urge to change your life at midpoint should be dealt with cautiously, since thoughts of a career change at that time are often reactions to a midlife personal crisis. "A crisis in oneself or in one's relationships can be a very important trigger [to job dissatisfaction]," he says. "You should never make decisions at the time of a divorce, at the time of a crisis, or when you're very tired." Home life is a vital element to consider when a career change looks enticing.

THE BIOLOGICAL CLOCK AND LATE PARENTHOOD

Suddenly, at thirty-five, women who have been concentrating on their career wake up to the fact that their childbearing years are almost over. As their time begins to run out, single women may develop a new interest in marriage. Some revise their criteria of what represents an acceptable mate and look at men who are younger or from a different background. Others talk of becoming mothers through artificial insemination or single-parent adoption. For almost all women, being childless in the late thirties means pain and soul-searching.

A woman measures the number of years she has left to bear children and watches as each passing year shrinks the pool of available partners. The biological clock ticks louder and louder, and she is forced to look ahead at a childless future. Often it's only when she has to face the prospect of never having children that she discovers how much she now wants them. The pain and wanting are real, but it is important to get them into proportion to make them manageable.

Whether you are married or not, having a baby does not necessarily make a flawed life better. And motherhood infinitely complicates the life of a woman who works, as we saw in Chapter 15. Ellen Peck, an advocate of the positive points of childlessness, believes women who are committed to careers or professions should think especially deeply before pursuing motherhood. She has a useful set of questions that, if answered thoughtfully and honestly, will help you gain some perspective:

Do I care about my job? If you are devoted to your job, would you be willing to give less time and attention to it? Would you be willing to give it up altogether for a while? Are you willing to abandon the "fast track" of career advancement and salary increases? Can your occupation be adapted to at-home work or part-time hours? Is your desire for a child strong enough to make you consider a change of occupation?

Do I care about maintaining or improving my present standard of affluence? "Motherhood is not only a job that fails to pay," Peck contends. "It costs." She describes children as competing in two ways with a higher standard of living: First, they consume; and second, they prevent one spouse (most frequently the wife) from working as fully as before. Would your income drop if you had a child? How much? How would your personal spending patterns have to change?

Do I have illusions about parenthood? Children do not remain the darling babies with beatific smiles so lovingly portrayed on Mother's Day cards. The realities of children include hard work, long hours, sleepless nights. Children can be disorderly, disobedient, obnoxiously defiant, and have learning problems and asthma, or need braces. They certainly mean a loss of privacy and personal freedom.

Do I have illusions about combining parenthood with my job? Do "Supermom" stories seem realistic to you? The notion of kids at the office is an illusion, Peck says. "The practical demands of the typical business day are simply bound to be in conflict with the equally insistent requirements of small children for attention, supervision, physical contact and general care."

Do I genuinely like and enjoy children of all ages? Can you picture yourself in the role of a mother beyond your child's infancy? Are you equally comfortable with and happy about mothering a boy or a girl?

It may be that the women's movement and women's magazines have unintentionally done women a disservice over the past few years. Coming of age in the seventies, women who were torn between, on the one hand, their parents' pressures to settle down and start a family immediately and, on the other, the new freedom and opportunity offered through feminism, sought advice and counsel from the women's media. "You needn't be locked in," said articles and talk-show guests. "It's not an either/or situation" . . . "Ignore your mother, do other things, women can have children up to forty at least." Women read it, heard it, and decided not to be pressured into tying themselves down until they were ready. They got fitted with the latest in contraception and went on to pursue their careers.

Ten or fifteen years later those same women are back at the gynecologist, primed and ready to have a baby. But they may be in for a big shock. When the media said "women can have children up to forty" the emphasis was wrong, the sentence incomplete. It might more accurately have read, "Women *can* have children up to forty . . . but often, many can't." Those glowing articles about "elderly primogravidus" had not addressed the fact that as women, and men, get older, the odds increase that whatever can go wrong will. From the mid-twenties onwards, complications are more and more likely, and it becomes harder and harder to get pregnant. Many women who assumed they could come back after a decade and take up the baby-making business where they left off now find that they've left it too long and that getting pregnant is difficult or impossible, and that even if they conceive, as they get older they are more likely to have to face the heartbreak of miscarriage or birth defects.

"Twenty-four is when a woman's fertility is at its peak," says Dr. Wayne Decker, surgeon in chief of the Fertility Research Foundation in New York. "As a woman gets older she will have more trouble getting pregnant, staying pregnant, delivering the pregnancy, and the babies will have more trouble after they are delivered."

As many as a third of all women now have their first baby in their thirties, and the marked increase in the number of women visiting fertility clinics like Decker's reflects both the women who have lately heard their biological clocks ticking louder and those younger ones who realize that if they want to have children, or even to keep their options open for the future, they must plan ahead.

The best way to keep a biological clock from turning into a time bomb is to find out if you (and your partner, if you have one) are fertile several years before you think you might want to have children. Treatment for infertility is at best an inexact science, consisting largely of eliminating possible causes one at a time, and each step can take months or years. You should know that infertility can be caused by endometriosis, a condition in which patches of the tissue lining the uterine cavity implant outside the uterus that is called the "career woman's disease," because it is found disproportionately in working women and gets more serious with age. You should also be aware that with age comes increased likelihood of troublemakers like fibroids, pelvic inflammatory disease, and blocked tubes. Medical techniques are now able to surmount such obstacles to pregnancy more often, but even then only with time and advance notice.

Artificial insemination and single-parent adoption are possibilities for women without mates who are determined to be mothers, but neither is easily available. Choosing either option is also an extremely serious decision.

For these reasons and others, not all women can, should, or will have children. Some women, fifteen years into their careers, realize that now they may not find mates because of the shortage of males available for their age group. Coming to terms with such facts represents a huge life step for working women. It is not a step that is taken quickly, lightly, or easily. Typically it seems to take up to two years to make the transition, and the phases can be compared to those associated with a death: denial and isolation, anger, bargaining, depression, acceptance. Here is one woman's story: "For several years, five actually, I tried to get pregnant. At first I wasn't too worried, each month I'd expect it would happen the next time. Then I began the rounds of doctors and I started to be aware I might not be fertile. My husband didn't seem to worry, but I got very depressed and hated every pregnant woman I saw. But I kept on hoping, test after test. Finally I knew it was hopeless. Over the next few months we pursued some new experimental therapy, and I used that time to let my subconscious get used to the idea. When we finally had to accept the situation I had learned to live with it, though the pain stays. But at least I know where I am and can get on with the rest of my life now."

THE KEY TO HAPPINESS

The other side of life, over which women have a bit more control than whether they will find a partner and whether they want to or can have children, is work. Work too is an area many women take a hard look at as they approach their late thirties.

Their first step may be reassessing what work means to them. The German existentialist Martin Heidegger is supposed to have said, "You are your projects." If that is an acceptable way to live for men, can it also work for women? The Wall Street psychiatrist Jay B. Rohrlich says that for most people identity is largely a function of successful, productive achievement. "Nothing else with which we associate ourselves," he says, "can give us the sense of objective identity that work can." Compare this statement to the famous revelation when 75 percent of the respondents to a questionnaire by the columnist Ann Landers said that if they had it to do over again they would *not* have children.

Researchers used to report that what makes a woman feel good about herself is marriage and children. Many women accept these findings as givens. It turns out that not only are they not givens, but following these old patterns can be downright harmful. New reports such as the work done by Grace Baruch, Rosalind Barnett and Caryl Rivers (see page 258, Chapter 15, Motherhood and Career) emphasize that work and achievement are also central issues when it comes to happiness. The study, which compared working and nonworking women, tried to get at what contributes to a woman's sense of well-being. There are, the authors say, two distinct components of well-being, "mastery" and "pleasure"; and both should be equally present in a woman's life. "Mastery" is defined as feeling important and worthwhile. "Pleasure" means finding life enjoyable. Often the two have different sources.

Your sense of mastery is closely related to the "doing" side of your life. It involves your self-esteem and sense of control over your life, and reduces your level of anxiety and depression. Pleasure comes from the personal, emotional side of life and most typically is supplied by love relationships, including motherhood. The study shows that working women are significantly higher in mastery than nonworking women. Thus it follows that work is a large part of what makes you feel good about yourself.

To be absorbed in work, we now know, is rewarding and fulfilling. Some women who have grown accustomed to the reality that they will not have families increase their investment in careers. They accept challenging new responsibilities, take the courses needed to qualify for another step up, or perhaps agree to a relocation that will further their careers, even though it will probably not help find eligible bachelors. This is the point too, when women stop being mentored and themselves begin to find satisfaction in mentoring and teaching. Many then find time for formal and informal teaching and helping of people more junior than they are. All this involvement in work can be enormously fulfilling, and it becomes unhealthy only when it is the only thing in a woman's life, or when it won't allow anything else in.

Other women find contentment by adjusting the balance and focus of their work lives. For most self-supporting single women, dropping out is not a viable option, but starting on a new career may be, if they have the energy, or wish, to go back to school or start all over again from the bottom. And this is the time in life when many women get serious about starting their own businesses. They decide to take the skills and contacts they have acquired thus far in their careers and put them to use for themselves instead of an employer. Women start businesses based on silicon chips and make millions, and they also open inns in Vermont where they don't make much money but they have a lot of fun. (See Chapter 17, Being Your Own Boss.)

Sometimes women blame their lack of love or social life on their careers, but they shouldn't be tempted to throw off a career too lightly. That's what happened to Carolyn Lewis, the pseudonym of a woman who was the first female partner in a well-known national consulting firm. "Chief executive officers do not lead balanced lives," she told Jane Adams for *Working Woman*, just before taking a six-month leave of absence from her job. "I want a balanced life more than I want the president's office. I want to make room in my life for love to find me." Adams reports that by the end of her leave love had not found Carolyn Lewis, but she had chosen to burn her professional bridges rather than return to work. Today Lewis lives collectively with friends whom she describes as "other success dropouts." She admits that she is not much happier than she was a year ago. Adams thinks that, by taking out of her life the source of many of her psychic rewards, Lewis has in fact impoverished herself.

Lewis's drastic action may not have brought much happiness, but other women take less extreme steps at midlife to improve the elements of life other than work.

Not all childless working women in their late thirties are in crisis. Some are happy, their lives comfortably filled with their work and their pleasures. They begin reaping the rewards their careers have earned them by traveling, or buying a house, or just expanding their horizons. They find time they didn't seem to have before for their families and to build warm, rewarding friendships and close relationships with a variety of other people, including other people's children.

Single or married women can adopt children, or find part-time formal or informal fostering arrangements, or formal, national ones like the Big Sister Program. Some women marry into ready-made families. But most pause, assess, agonize, adjust, and get on with building full lives. These lives may not be turning out the way the women expected when they started, but they are having a good time, and are in good company as they go. The future, for a growing group of talented women who have achieved a great deal in the first half of their lives, is what they make it.

17
Being Your Own Boss

In the annals of American business, the greatest heroes have been those singular individuals who, with pluck and ingenuity, created and built empires from practically nothing. The tough, striving entrepreneur is a larger-than-life figure in this nation's consciousness; the dream of "being your own boss" is a durable one.

Today the entrepreneurial spirit is stronger than ever, with people all across the United States starting businesses in record numbers. These small enterprises are creating most of the country's new jobs and are the major source of our industrial innovation.

What is new about *this* entrepreneurial wave, though, is that women are leading the way. In fact, the number of self-employed women increased by 56 percent from 1970 to 1979—more than five times the rate for men, according to the U.S. Bureau of Labor Statistics. At least three million women now run their own businesses. And according to the Department of Commerce, these businesses bring in gross receipts of more than $40 billion.

Almost half of these women's businesses are in the service sector and another 30 percent are in retail trade, both areas where capital requirements—and, unfortunately, return on investment—are low. But given the increasingly important role that the services play in our economy (creating some 60 percent of all new jobs), women may be in the right place at the right time. And even in the service and retail sectors, women are not just running beauty shops and keeping the books in Mom and Pop enterprises; they are financial planners and business consultants too.

Women business owners are also making inroads into other sectors of the

282

economy. They own computer companies, banks, manufacturing plants, public relations firms, even construction companies and auto repair shops. From 1972 to 1982, the number of women-owned construction businesses and manufacturing outfits almost quadrupled. In finance, insurance, and real estate, the number nearly tripled.

More and more women are making it very big indeed. The latest Department of Commerce figures record more than 5,000 women-owned businesses grossing over $1 million. Consider:

Debbi Fields, twenty-eight, who in seven years has built a $30-million chocolate-chip cookie empire from scratch.

Sandra Kurtzig, thirty-seven, who took her software company, ASK Computer Systems, Inc., public in 1981. As of 1983, she was a "paper millionaire" with holdings valued at an estimated $53 million.

Tricia Fox, thirty-six, whose Fox Day Schools, Inc., took in $1.2 million last year and is franchising in thirty-eight states.

Muriel Siebert, fifty-two, the first woman to buy a seat on the New York Stock Exchange, whose discount-brokerage firm grossed more than $3 million last year.

Lane Nemeth, thirty-six, whose direct-sales toy company, Discovery Toys, earned $22 million in 1983, just six years after being launched in a garage for $50,000.

Why are so many women taking the plunge and going into business? For many of the same reasons that have spurred men to do so. Entrepreneurship is still the one best way to create wealth, rather than merely earn an income. Independence, too, is a strong motivation to strike out on one's own.

Certain social and technological forces are improving the general climate for entrepreneurs, according to David Gumpert, associate editor of the *Harvard Business Review* and a contributing editor to *Working Woman*. First, he says, it has become more socially acceptable to be an entrepreneur, especially in comparison to the late 1960s and early 1970s, when antibusiness sentiments were strong. (Interestingly, more than a few of the "alternative" ventures started during those years—*Rolling Stone* magazine and Celestial Seasonings herb teas, for instance—have become thriving businesses.) Second, this acceptance of entrepreneurship has brought with it more managerial and educational resources to support the budding entrepreneur—seminars, magazines, books, courses. Third, those starting a small business have access to a much wider variety of financing sources than twenty years ago: commercial finance companies, leasing companies, venture capital firms, "informal" investors, life insurance companies, and state and federal agencies, in addition to banks, the traditional source. A fourth impetus, according to Gumpert, is technology. Small, inexpensive computers now give small businesses access to data banks so that they can do the kind of market research that was previously available only to large companies. Businesses can also handle accounting, payroll, even sophisticated financial planning, much more easily and cheaply by computer.

Women have special reasons for becoming entrepreneurs. One is frustration. After years of experience in corporations, a woman may find that she hits a glass ceiling, that despite long service and considerable managerial talent, she is not getting near a top position. She's ambitious, has the self-confidence and business acumen to make it, and is tired of waiting indefinitely for someone to give her the chance to do so. So she bails out of corporate life and opens her own business.

Take Dianne Sullivan, co-owner of Miraflores Designs, Inc., a New York company that manufactures and packages toiletries for hotel chains. Sullivan quit her job as an aerospace contract negotiator at NASA's Jet Propulsion Laboratory because, she says, "I wanted to work harder, push harder, accept more responsibility. . . . I'm not very good at being an employee." Her company reached $3 million in sales last year.

The career/motherhood conundrum is another reason women decide to become their own bosses. Even though some corporations are becoming responsive to the needs of working mothers (see Chapter 11, Improving the Quality of Work Life), they are still in the minority. Most women still face difficult problems when they try to combine motherhood and a career. Although entrepreneurship may seem like a more-than-full-time job in itself, it can provide professional satisfaction—and income—while still allowing a flexibility that is often impossible in a large corporation. Barbara Keck, the consultant, has even built her business around the needs of other working mothers, matching part-time business consultants with corporations. The consultants are mothers who want part-time professional work that leaves time for them to raise their children.

NEW PIONEERS

Although many of the classical images of the entrepreneurial hero are male, recent evidence shows that women bring special strengths to business ownership. Studies conducted by Harold Welsch and Earl C. Young of DePaul University in Chicago and by Robert Hisrich of Boston College and Candida Brush, a Boston consultant, show that women entrepreneurs differ from men in several ways.

Women tend to do more research and digging before starting their businesses or making business decisions. They are also more likely to attend seminars and courses, particularly in such areas as business accounting, retailing, and taxes. This bodes well for women, considering the high number of failures of new businesses in general, many owing to a lack of planning. Successful entrepreneurs are good risk takers, not wild gamblers.

Women are more attuned to the conditions around them. For instance, an American Management Associations study found that women are much more realistic about the kinds of sacrifices necessary in the first few years of business, whereas men seem to be more concerned with power and status. The men surveyed were more likely to close down a business if it didn't make profits as early as they had expected.

Women entrepreneurs do face special obstacles, however, both in themselves and in the outside world. According to studies, women entrepreneurs consider themselves weak in the area of financial management. It isn't that women are innately unable to work with money, but that many of them have never been trained to do so. This lack of financial savvy can hold a business back or even drive it into the ground. The Office of Women's Business Ownership at the Small Business Administration reports that many women still undercharge for their service or product. Dun & Bradstreet has found that lack of money—undercapitalization—is a major pitfall for small businesses. To get a business started and keep it growing, you need money. And you need to feel comfortable with number crunching to keep track of how your business is doing—how much money is coming in, how much is going out, what the cash-flow position is at any particular point.

Complicating the financial issue is the fact that women still experience credit discrimination from lenders (but see "Equal Credit Opportunity," page 287). According to Hisrich, this helps explain why women feel they have to rely on their personal assets and savings to start businesses rather than borrow heavily as men do. Women entrepreneurs have to work extra hard at establishing themselves as credible business people.

Women business owners also tend to feel pulled in too many directions, especially between family and career. The strain of trying to fulfill multiple roles is one that few men entrepreneurs experience.

Women encounter other barriers. Although an increasing number come to entrepreneurship with business degrees and years of corporate experience, many still lack the business record that potential investors or lenders are looking for. The idea that a woman's place is not in business lingers. Even seasoned businesswomen, confident of their authority, report that male clients, customers, suppliers, and advisers don't take them seriously.

Women entrepreneurs tend not to be unduly discouraged by such obstacles, however. In fact, meeting obstacles head on may make them stronger business people. According to business consultant Charlotte Taylor, "The ability to cope with frustrations and anger and to turn the forces of prejudice to their advantage appears to be a key ingredient to women's business success." Women entrepreneurs are in many ways the new pioneers. The greater their number and the more spectacular their successes, the easier it will be for all women business owners.

It must be remembered, too, that women and men business owners face similar challenges and problems. Being in business is tough. When interest rates soar or credit tightens, small businesses are the first to feel the pinch. Half of all businesses fail in their first five years, according to the Small Business Administration. Businesses that are thriving one day may encounter unpredicted setbacks the next. The story of Vector Graphic, the Thousand Oaks, California, computer company cofounded by Lore Harp, is a case in point.

In 1976, Lore Harp and her friend Carole Ely, "bored with tennis," decided to market a computer memory board designed by Harp's husband, Robert. By 1981 they had parlayed the initial $12,000 investment into a $30 million-plus corporation producing microcomputers for the small-business market. Then they took the company public. Venture capitalists and financial analysts praised Harp for her excellent management skills, financial acuity, and flair for marketing.

But then the game changed, and suddenly Vector was scrambling. IBM introduced its version of the microcomputer and within a year had grabbed 17 percent of the market. Other computer firms began to fight over the remaining market share, which had shrunk because of an economic recession. Vector had anticipated the IBM challenge, but it had not reacted quickly enough. The company had failed to upgrade its technology to match the IBM machine, and hadn't recognized how radically the market would change with such an impressive new contender. In 1983, Vector's profits plunged.

Although Vector may not have been the only company to misjudge the new business environment, other factors combined to make its position precarious. The company was straining because of its rapid growth during the previous years. Personal problems intruded, with the divorce of the Harps and the departure of Carole Ely.

In an attempt to provide more professional management for the company, Harp hired a seasoned corporate executive as president. She felt confident enough to take time off to remarry, but things continued to slide at

Vector, and Harp decided to take charge again. She fired the president after only a year, laid off a quarter of Vector's employees, and tried to reestablish the close ties with the company's dealer network that had been one of Vector's strong points. (The dealers responded by sending flowers to celebrate her return to the helm.)

Harp's emergency measures included establishing short-term task forces to deal with inventory control, receivables, quality control, and working capital, areas that had slipped during her hiatus. She went so far as to ban memos to insure fast action on serious problems. Harp insists that she will bring the company back into the black, and many analysts are optimistic. Aggressive marketing and advertising, a more effective management team, and a new range of products directed specifically to her old customers—small businesses—may help revive a company that almost allowed spectacular success to become spectacular failure.

Business failure is not rare, unfortunately, but every owner or prospective owner can reduce the odds of failing by paying close attention to certain key aspects of small-business management such as planning and financing. (For sources of more detailed information, see Appendix B, Suggestions for Further Reading, p. 331.)

EQUAL CREDIT OPPORTUNITY

Here is an outline of your rights under the Equal Credit Opportunity Act of 1974, as amended:

Who can complain? People or organizations (acting on their own behalf, or that of others) who feel discriminated against in obtaining credit.

Who can be accused? Those who regularly extend credit—for example, banks, finance companies, department stores, credit-card issuers, and government agencies, such as the Small Business Administration.

Provisions. Bans discrimination against applicants for credit on the basis of sex, marital status, race, color, religion, national origin, age, receipt of public assistance, or good-faith exercise of federal consumer-protection rights. Covers all aspects of a credit transaction and all types of credit, including credit for business, consumer goods, home financing, and education. The definition of discrimination is treating one applicant less favorably than another.

Enforcement agency. Various federal agencies are authorized to enforce the act. Banking agencies handle banking complaints, for example. The Federal Trade Commission has enforcement power in areas not specifically assigned elsewhere in the act, including retail credit and small-loan companies.

Do you need a lawyer? You do not need a lawyer to complain to a federal agency. If you decide to sue in federal court, you should have a lawyer.

Anonymity. May be available, although anonymity may make investigation more difficult. Check with the agency involved.

Time limitations. You must bring suit within two years.

Procedure. This depends on the agency to which your complaint is directed. If you are unsure to whom you should complain, write to the Division of Consumer Affairs, Board of Governors, Federal Reserve System, Washington, DC 20051, or to Equal Credit Opportunity, Federal Trade Commission, Washington, DC 20580.

No special complaint form is required, merely a letter or telephone call to the appropriate federal agency. There are no uniform procedures. Response time varies according to the agency and agencies may not investigate all complaints.

You may file a lawsuit in federal court with or without using the agency-complaint procedure.

Relief/Penalties. Enforcing agencies may use any powers the law gives them to deal with credit complaints, including cease-and-desist orders and fines. If you file an individual suit in court, you can sue for several kinds of money damages, such as the actual financial loss incurred or punitive damages not exceeding $10,000. In a class action suit, punitive damages may not exceed the lesser of $500,000 or 1 percent of the creditor's net worth. Injunctive relief, attorneys' fees, and court costs are also available.

STARTING UP

You have an idea that you think will make you rich but how do you know it will pay off? Do you have what it takes to be an entrepreneur? Books on small business often begin with impressive checklists of "entrepreneurial" qualities and personality traits: high energy level, ability to commit oneself to long-term projects, self-confidence, ambitious, goal-oriented, well organized, independent, a self-starter, a risk taker, a persistent problem solver. To be sure, entrepreneurship does demand many of these characteristics, but there's much more to starting a business.

Are you certain about your personal and financial goals—what you want to get out of the business? Do you know if there's a market for the product or service you have in mind? Many successful businesses grow out of a personal interest or hobby, and if you're going to be working sixteen hours a day, you've got to like what you're doing. Previous experience in the business you're going into will considerably increase your chances of success. If you want to start an employment agency, for instance, it helps to have worked in one for a while. As Beatrice Fitzpatrick, head of the American Woman's Economic Development Corporation, has said, "Learn on someone else's time and money."

Another point to consider: Do you have the financial resources and the contacts to get your business off the ground and keep it going? You should be able to last at least two years without taking any profit out of the business. Make a list of your start-up costs as well as projected regular expenses. Start-up costs might include such items as fixtures and equipment, starting inventory, office supplies, renovation of office space, installation of equipment, deposits for utilities, legal and professional fees, licenses and permits, advertising, operating cash, and your own "draw" or salary (if any) during the start-up time. Such items as salaries, rent, utilities, insurance, taxes, and bad debts, would come under expenses.

THE BUSINESS PLAN

Once you've decided to go into business, planning is crucial. Unfortunately, it is one of the most neglected entrepreneurial skills. Both for budding entrepreneurs and for those with established businesses, the central planning tool is the business plan—or, as one small business expert calls it, "the blueprint for building a business." Preparing this comprehensive document forces the entrepreneur to think through every detail of a business operation objectively and unemotionally.

The finished plan serves several purposes and is well worth the many hours it will take to research and prepare. It is the basis of any financing proposal you make to a bank or potential investor. It serves as a guide for making decisions as the business grows and changes. It helps orient staff to your goals for the company. Even more important, writing a business plan will give you a clear picture of whether your business idea is worth pursuing; if it is, you have just turned a "good idea" into a sound business concept.

To prepare a plan, you'll have to decide on such issues as your target market, the price you'll charge for your product or service, who your competition is, where your business will be located. You'll have to devise a marketing strategy, establish a staffing plan, and choose a legal structure (sole proprietorship, partnership, corporation, S-corporation). And you'll have to make detailed financial projections for at least three years.

A business plan should be tailored to your particular business and circumstances; there is no one correct form. Here is an outline of the usual contents of a business plan:

SUGGESTED OUTLINE OF A BUSINESS PLAN*

Cover Sheet: Name of business, names of principals, address and
  phone number of business
Statement of Purpose
Table of Contents
  I. The Business
    A. Description of Business
    B. Market
    C. Competition
    D. Location of Business
    E. Management
    F. Personnel
    G. Application and Expected Effect of Loan (if needed)
    H. Summary
  II. Financial Data
    A. Sources and Applications of Funding
    B. Capital Equipment List
    C. Balance Sheet
    D. Breakeven Analysis
    E. Income Projections (Profit and Loss Statements)
      1. Three-year summary
      2. Detail by month for first year
      3. Detail by quarter for second and third years
      4. Notes of explanation
    F. Pro-Forma Cash Flow
      1. Detail by month for first year
      2. Detail by quarter for second and third years
      3. Notes of explanation
    G. Deviation Analysis
    H. Historical Financial Reports for Existing Business
      1. Balance sheets for past three years
      2. Income statements for past three years
      3. Tax returns
  III. Supporting Documents: Personal résumé, personal financial require-
    ments and statements, cost of living budget, credit reports, letter of
    reference, job descriptions, letter of intent, copies of leases, contracts,
    legal documents, and anything else of relevance to the plan.

* This outline is from the *Business Planning Guide* (Copyright 1981), Upstart
Publishing Company, Dover, New Hampshire.

FINANCING

If you're starting a business, chances are you'll have to rely to a great extent on your own savings, loans from family or friends, and perhaps a bank loan. According to *Working Woman*'s 1982 survey of small-business owners, 80 percent of the respondents used their own money to start their businesses. If you're prominent in your field, or in a high-growth area like computer technology, you may be able to attract funding from outside investors such as venture capitalists. As your business gets off the ground, a number of financing options will open up.

Bootstrap financing. Many entrepreneurs are unaware of one of the easiest ways to generate funds for a business: internal or "bootstrap" financing. Basically, this involves speeding up the cash coming into a business and slowing down that going out, to keep cash at work in your company as long as possible. Some ways to do this are to bill promptly, collect outstanding accounts aggressively, and offer a cash discount policy to encourage early payment of bills.

There are other ways to find hidden cash. You should assess your inventory regularly to make sure that goods are not languishing in warehouses any longer than necessary. (Remember, the ideal situation is to buy goods, sell them, and collect the receivables before your payment for the goods is due.) You can examine profit-and-loss statements for places to trim costs. Or you can turn fixed assets (old equipment you no longer use, for instance) into cash.

Debt financing. Borrowing money is another source of funding. If you're starting up, a *personal loan* may be the only kind you can get. If you have a longer track record, you may qualify for a *commercial loan,* a type of loan which usually has to be repaid in three to six months. Through *accounts-receivable financing,* you're able to exchange unpaid invoices (receivables) for cash in the form of a loan valued at 75 to 85 percent of the invoices. In *inventory financing,* a bank advances money against inventory. For established businesses, banks may extend a *line of credit.* Under this arrangement, you are free to borrow repeatedly, on a revolving basis, as long as you don't exceed a maximum limit.

Life insurance companies, consumer finance companies, savings and loan associations, and credit unions also offer loans at various rates and terms. In all cases the lending institutions will want evidence of your company's profitability, your management expertise, and your credit history. The business plan is essential for getting such funding.

Factoring is another form of debt financing. A factoring company buys your company's accounts receivable from you and then collects the amount due. Although factoring is expensive (you typically pay a high interest rate plus a fee on each invoice collected), it can allow a growing company to reach higher sales and profits.

Certain government agencies also provide funding for small businesses. The Small Business Administration grants few direct loans any more but does guarantee loans obtained through private institutions. Go to your local SBA office for more information on its loan programs.

Equity financing. Another way to raise capital is to give up a share of the company in return for an investment in it. *Risk or venture capital* is one example. A venture capital firm might invest money in your business over a five-year term for a percentage of the profits. After the five years, you can decide to refinance and regain full control of the company. Experienced business owners advise that you always maintain a majority interest in your company, however. In the past few years a new source of equity capital has come to light: so-called informal investors, who are usually experienced business owners who want to invest in other businesses. When your business's financial needs can no longer be satisfied by venture capital, a *public stock offering*, in which you offer shares of your company to the public, is an attractive option. Again, you give up some control, but you gain leverage so that you can expand.

Getting funds is only one part of the finance picture. Once you have them, you'll need to pay attention to financial controls and accounting. Break-even analysis, cash-flow projections, pro-forma statements—these are terms that make most people's eyes glaze over. But entrepreneurs ignore accounting at great peril. Too many businesses still work out of a shoe box filled with receipts—and their financial picture often reflects it.

Keeping good financial records is the only measure you have of how your business is doing and what it will be able to do in the future. You'll need records of business transactions to make up financial statements that can tell you at any given moment what your exact cash-flow status is, whether you are carrying enough inventory, how sales are going, whether you're making a profit. In addition, the government requires businesses to keep certain records pertaining to income taxes, payroll, sales taxes, and so on.

The first step is to establish an exact and up-to-date bookkeeping system. It is best to get a professional bookkeeper or accountant to do this, since the information must be properly organized and recorded to be any use to you. In various ledgers or journals you'll record all your business transactions—cash receipts, cash disbursements, sales, purchases, payroll, capital equipment, inventory, and expenses. This information is the raw material for an analysis or accounting of your business. Following are some of the most common accounting tools and what they can tell you about your business:

Balance sheet. This gives a company's assets, liabilities and net worth at a particular time.

Profit-and-loss statement. Also called an income statement, this provides a picture of the company's financial activities over a period of time. It includes the amount of income earned, how it was spent, and the profit or loss that was left over.

Cash-flow statement. This shows the flow of cash into and out of a business over a period of time—an aid to predicting your financial needs.

Breakeven analysis. This tells you how much you have to sell in order to break even (no profit, no loss), given certain fixed costs and prices for your product.

PEOPLE

Smart entrepreneurs know that there's no such thing as going it alone. They rely on "human capital" as much as they do on venture capital. When potential investors consider financing proposals, one of the factors they look for is a strong management team. As you formulate your business plan, ask yourself: Do I lack certain of the skills necessary to make my business a success? Can others—whether a partner or employees—fill the gap?

Certain key advisers are also very important to business owners: your banker, your accountant, your lawyer. By getting to know your banker, you'll probably get better service from the bank. And a banker who is familiar with your business will, of course, be able to give you better financial advice. Don't just open an account in a bank; make an appointment with a bank officer and get to know her or him.

An accountant provides several important services to your business. He or she can set up and maintain an accounting system. An accountant can also prepare regular financial statements, as well as your income tax returns and various social security, withholding, and personal property tax documents that you need to file, especially if you have employees. If your business is fairly small, a bookkeeper may be able to provide many of these services. Or you may want to have an accountant or a CPA (certified public accountant) set up the books and then have a staff member keep them up (or do it yourself). Make sure that you understand any system an accountant puts in place and that it is simple enough to use.

As a business owner you will probably need a lawyer when you form your business, especially if it's a corporation or a partnership. But don't lose contact with your lawyer after the initial documents are signed. You should consult her or him for other business transactions—for example, when you sign a contract, buy equipment, purchase or sell a business, buy property, or if you need to know about equal opportunity laws or work with a union.

Beyond having a sound management team and reliable advisers, entrepreneurs need a network of contacts and business relationships from which to gain new business, hear industry news, buy needed services and products, or get advice. If you can establish good relationships with suppliers, for instance, you may be able to extend your bill payment time when you hit a cash-flow crunch. It's especially important to keep expanding your contacts so that you can keep developing new business.

Scores of associations, agencies, and educational institutions are available to help entrepreneurs with their problems. The Small Business Administration is especially helpful; it offers various management assistance programs as well as seminars and workshops. Under the SBA's auspices the National SCORE Association, a group of retired business executives, provides free advice to business owners. Through the Small Business Institute program entrepreneurs can benefit from the counseling services of graduate students under the supervision of faculty members. The Small Business Development Centers program offers private consultations, seminars, and workshops run by university faculty members and professional consultants. In addition, the SBA publishes free pamphlets on such subjects as profit planning and meeting tax obligations, as well as workbooks on preparing a business plan. Call your local SBA office for information about any of these services.

There are also a number of associations specifically for women business owners. Here are some of the best:

- The American Woman's Economic Development Corporation was established in 1977 to help women business owners develop their business skills. It offers individual counseling, conducted in person or on the phone (a 1-to-1½-hour session costs $25); an eighteen-month training program for women who have been in business at least six months ($350); and a program for women planning to start a business ($175). In addition, AWED publishes a quarterly magazine, offers specific courses on starting, building, and managing a business, and has a hotline (800-442-2933 in New York; 800-222-2933 in other states) to deal with "quick" questions. For ten minutes, and the answer to one question, the service costs $5. (It operates Monday to Friday, 10:00 A.M. to 5 P.M.) Address: 60 East 42nd St., New York, N.Y. 10165; 212-692-9100.

- The National Association of Black Women Entrepreneurs was formed "to train black women to develop themselves and their businesses and to do business with one another." To this end NABWE publishes a monthly newsletter, conducts workshops, and holds an annual national conference. NABWE also enters the political arena by testifying before Senate committees on women and minorities in business. Address: P.O. Box 1375, Detroit, Mich. 48231; 313-963-8766.
- The National Association of Women Business Owners is a national organization with twenty chapters. It conducts seminars and monthly programs related to the business interests of chapter members. Other programs look at "wider issues" such as economic trends or the role of business in the cultural community. The organization emphasizes the accessibility and visibility of its members, some of whom have been in business for twenty-five years. NAWBO publishes directories of women-owned businesses and a monthly newsletter. Address: 500 North Michigan Ave., Suite 1400, Chicago, Ill. 60611; 312-661-1700.

HANDLING GROWTH

You've worked hard at your business and you're a success—every entrepreneur's dream. Yet hard as it is to anticipate, success can be a problem. If, for instance, you suddenly get three times the number of orders you were expecting, you may not have the financial resources to increase production. And even if you do, you may not be able to fulfill the orders in time, risking the loss of disappointed or irate customers. When growth comes too rapidly, it can put you out of business.

The best way to meet the challenges of expanding your business is good planning. Use your business plan as an operating document. Review it every month, or every couple of months, and adjust it when necessary. Building in a cushion for unpredictable swings in business will help you weather the good and the bad times.

One of the hardest moves for many entrepreneurs is to give up some control, either by bringing in professional managers or by giving up a share of the company in return for a capital investment necessary for growth. Even hiring the first employees can be difficult. But as Charlotte Taylor points out, "Entrepreneurial brilliance can create a company but only employee brilliance can build it." Entrepreneurs need to have the confidence to hire people who are even better than they are at a particular job, and they also need to learn the difficult lesson of delegation. Too many entrepreneurs insist on staying involved in every single aspect of a business, long after the company has grown beyond this stage. As a result a business may falter. At the very least it will fail to grow.

Being an entrepreneur means taking risks, including the one of letting go of parts of the business. Entrepreneurs are not blind optimists in the risks they take, but they do take them. And for the increasing number of women who are taking the entrepreneurial route, the rewards—independence, money, excitement—seem to be more than worth the risks.

18

Where Most Women Work: The 80 Percent

I've been on the linotype since 1945. I started out in South Carolina. We had two kinds of high schools there, the ones that prepared you for college and the ones that gave you on-the-job training. I knew I'd never go to college, so I went to the other one. I was being trained as a secretary to a small job printer. The boss came to me after I'd been there a short time and said, "You're going to have to learn how to operate the linotype." All the men were going to the war. I went home and cried all night. I wanted to be a secretary.

I'm happy it happened that way. I came to love it. I'm much better off being a linotype operator. Of course, after the war they didn't want women, wanted rid of us. We had to fight to stay on then. We also had to fight to get into the union.

—Lerline M. Santos

The work life of "the rest"—the 80 percent of the female workforce not in white-collar jobs—has always been something of a fight. The road to the vice presidency isn't paved with roses, but it isn't the constant struggle of being a blue- or pink-collar worker.

In November 1978 the Consolidated Coal Company of Pittsburgh agreed to pay $370,000 in damages to women it had refused to hire as miners. The company agreed to employ these women in the mines, and to hire one inexperienced woman miner for each experienced man until women composed over 30 percent of the workforce. Does Consolidated's forced change of heart, allowing women to work underground, constitute an upward move for women?

It does.

Mining is dark, dirty, and dangerous work, but it pays substantially more than the average woman in a mining town can earn at a traditional female job. As we saw in Chapter 2, What Women Earn, women's work almost invariably pays less than men's. And mining certainly isn't the only field in which women's progress has been blocked. When you eliminate discrimination at any level, you take a big step toward eliminating sex-based discrepancies in salary and breaking down the barriers that keep women from career advancement.

This applies to women assemblers in the electronics industry, who may never have the opportunity to advance to foreman or move to the better-paying job of forklift operator. It applies to women sales clerks in the clothing sections of department stores, who have been restricted from switching to comparable but more lucrative jobs selling furniture. It applies to secretaries whose career fortunes are linked to their bosses' and who are never even considered for advancement to managerial positions. In short, it applies to the vast majority of the women sales, service, factory, and office workers who together make up 80 percent of the women who work.

The story of these 80 percenters—their entry into the labor force in great numbers, their dramatic and hard-won advancement into jobs previously considered the exclusive domain of men, the continuing concentration of the vast majority in low-paying, low-status jobs—closely parallels that of professional, technical, and managerial women. There are other similarities too. Working women in both sectors need to explode the myth of "women's work," to develop clearer attitudes toward career preparation and advancement, and to support organizations that uphold their interests. These solutions are the subjects of this chapter.

First a note on terminology: "Blue-collar" has long been used and "pink collar" is increasingly used in reference to some categories of 80 percenters. A blue-collar worker is a factory worker, a construction worker, an auto mechanic, or the like. A pink-collar worker is one who works in a female-dominated occupation, such as a secretary. The terms are not mutually exclusive. A sewing-machine operator, for example, could be blue or pink. We use the two terms sparingly here, and in such a way that this sort of overlapping should not make a difference.

THE MYTH OF WOMEN'S WORK

Though the physical demands of some jobs, such as stevedore, may be beyond the capacities of many women, this is not sufficient grounds for excluding *all* women from those jobs. Nor can we accept blithe statements about women being concentrated in certain jobs because they are "appropriate" for women; such presumptions dissolve under close scrutiny. Yet, justified or not, among the 80 percent as among the 20 percent, the majority of working women are more or less confined to a limited number of occupations, and in them they "enjoy" a virtual monopoly. The following table illustrates how alarmingly little has changed in this respect over the last two and a half decades:

WOMEN AS A PERCENTAGE OF EMPLOYED WORKERS,
FEMALE - PREDOMINANT OCCUPATIONS, *1960–1982*

Occupation	% 1960	% 1970	% 1974	% 1976	% 1982
Secretaries	97.1	97.6	99.2	99.0	
Retail sales workers	63.3	64.6	69.4	70.7	
Waiters and waitresses	86.6	88.8	91.8	90.7	
Cashiers	76.9	83.5	87.7	87.7	
Private household workers	96.4	96.6	97.8	97.3	
Typists	95.1	94.2	96.2	96.7	
Nursing aides, orderlies, and attendants	88.2	84.6	86.9	86.8	

Source: *Work in America: The Decade Ahead*, ed. by Clark Kerr and Jerome M. Rosow. (Van Nostrand Reinhold, 1979).

Women have not always been congested in these particular jobs. Before the turn of the century we find a rather different picture of women's employment. No better example exists than that of clerical work, the number one women's occupation today but nothing of the sort in 1870. At that time there were relatively few office workers; they enjoyed considerable status and, not surprisingly, they were almost all men. The prestige of these "gentlemanly" clerks derived from their separation from manual workers and their special relationship to management.

But the situation changed. Business thrived. There were more records to be kept, more letters to be sent. The introduction of office machinery "deskilled" jobs to a certain extent. And as an increasing number of people were hired to perform these tasks, the special status of office work was lost. Salaries declined.

Predictably, many of these new clerks were women. By 1880 they constituted a fifth of the clerical force, and by 1920 half. People began to say that because of their "natural passivity" women were ideally suited for jobs involving an endless series of repetitive clerical tasks. Women were also said to have greater manual dexterity than men, a belief that abetted the introduction of the typewriter into the office.

Office work today is 99 percent female at the clerical level. Women there face problems such as lack of respect and sexual harassment. But one of the biggest drawbacks reported is the low chance for advancement, which results in stalemated salaries.

No one invoked that imaginary manual superiority when it came to factory work. In the early days of industrialization, when the economy was still largely agrarian, able-bodied men were needed to work in the fields. Women took most of the first factory jobs that became available, and those were primarily in the textile industry. But as agriculture became mechanized, farm jobs dwindled and immigration further enlarged the pool of "surplus labor." Men routed women from the factories. The mill town of Lowell, Massachusetts, for example, was almost entirely populated by single, female mill workers in the 1830s. These women worked thirteen hours a day, six days a week, for an average weekly pay of $2 plus board. By the second half of the century, Lowell's textile mills were worked by men. Ironically, the laws finally enacted to protect women from the dangers of industrial work, though fundamental safety measures, also helped drive them out of many fields that eventually provided high-paying blue-collar jobs for men. Sally Steeland, deputy director of the National Commission on Working Women, an advocacy organization for the 80 percent, notes that job segregation by sex has, to an extent, been mandated by law. In Pennsylvania, for instance, a century-old law prohibited women from working in the state's coal mines until 1974. (Hence the significance of the Consolidated Coal agreement.)

"Women's work," then, is to some degree different now from what it was yesteryear. We might also observe that even today the sex classification of jobs is subject to regional and geographical variations that show just how whimsical it is. In the Midwest, for example, cornhuskers are traditionally women, while trimmers are almost always men; in the Far West the situation is reversed. In 1971, 25 percent of insurance sales personnel in Boston were women, but that was true for less than 5 percent in New York City.

There are even variations from industry to industry. In 1960, though 44 percent of all factory assemblers were women, they were concentrated in certain fields. Only 16 percent of auto assembly workers were female, while women made up the majority of assemblers in electrical concerns. Within an industry there may be variations from firm to firm. One business establishment will hire only women as elevator operators but another favors men; some restaurants will employ either waiters or waitresses but not both.

THE TRAINING TRAP

Arbitrary or not, job sex-typing victimizes women, and the problem is exacerbated by women's failure to make career preparations that will help them avoid dead-end jobs. Such preparations should begin in high school. Too often they do not.

School guidance counselors frequently route female students in ways that perpetuate the pink-collar ghetto. Sally Hillsman Baker, a project director in the Research Department of the Vera Institute of Justice in New York City, says, "One former junior high school guidance counselor told me that the vocational-interest test used for years in her school was constructed so that any interest in marriage or motherhood automatically lowered a girl's scores in all other areas of vocational interest." As a result, girls in this school who were not pressing to go on to college were encouraged to take a noncollege-preparatory general curriculum supplemented by minimal skill-preparation courses such as typing. According to Baker, this practice is not uncommon.

Girls following a vocational education curriculum are rarely encouraged to enroll in programs that would prepare them for high-paying skilled jobs. Though in 1979 female students made up over three-fourths of the students studying home economics and preparing for office-related occupations, they accounted for less than one-fifth of the students in agriculture and in technical programs (electrical, mechanical, and automotive technology) and under 15 percent of those in trade and industrial programs (such as carpentry, plumbing, and drafting).

Once out of school, women's access to career education is further curtailed. In a survey conducted by the National Commission on Working Women in 1979, half of the respondents reported that they had no chance to train for a better job. Sex discrimination by employers limits female workers' access to training programs. Clerical workers who want to take courses outside their companies to improve their chances for promotions may be denied the tuition reimbursement that is routinely granted to men. In one large bank, for instance, a woman was denied reimbursement for a course in economics on the grounds that it wasn't "job-related"; six months later a man in a similar position received a full refund for a course in English literature.

Women themselves are sometimes self-defeating. Jenny Farley, in her book *Affirmative Action and the Woman Worker*, reports that the few women office workers selected by their firms for management training have a tendency, when given the choice, to select inappropriate courses. They are "far too likely to elect group dynamics or self-awareness courses when they should be studying accounting or budgeting."

Women with families often concur in family decisions against training to enhance their market potential. Family resources are usually allocated to the husband or the children; very often a mother works to help pay their college bills. The few families that do invest in the wife and mother's training usually settle on the briefest programs available, the ones that prepare women for the least rewarding jobs.

It is also true that women are not well informed about alternative job opportunities. According to statistics cited in congressional hearings on vocational education in 1975, less than one percent of all registrants in apprenticeships are women. The reason for this is that women lack the information they need to enter apprenticeships. Women are not encouraged to prepare for traditionally male jobs, and by the time they enter the labor market with serious intentions to do so, they may be too old to apply. The usual age limit for apprenticeships is twenty-four to twenty-seven.

NEW HORIZONS

Clearly, as Mary Lindenstein Walshok shows in her book *Blue-Collar Women,* the 80 percenters need a push. "More than half the women interviewed," she writes, "indicated no prior interest in nontraditional work, and they described their movement into nontraditional fields as directly related to the appearance of better opportunities. A number of the women we interviewed said they had no prior knowledge of the jobs they currently hold until someone came along and gave them an opportunity."

One woman in Walshok's book was making $3.25 an hour as a keypunch operator at a West Coast naval facility when a recruiter came through her office looking for women to apprentice to blue-collar trades. Here was an opportunity to enroll in a four-year community-college training program at company expense and on company time. The result: an eventual job as foreman making $9.06 an hour, nearly three times as much as she had earned in her preapprenticeship days. Another woman, wanting to break out of years in the typing pool, went to a career opportunities and counseling center for women in the city where she lived. The center got her into a training program for machinists. Generally employers have found women for nontraditional jobs through such outside agencies. Except for service industries and public utilities, which do recruit from within, most industries have few women in their ranks to draw on to meet equal opportunity criteria. Many of the women Walshok interviewed got their jobs through the help of women's groups and government agencies.

Despite the legendary ineffectiveness of antidiscrimination legislation such as the Equal Pay Act, government—at state and local levels as well as the federal level—has helped women make a dent in some of the more highly paid blue-collar jobs. In 1977, in response to pressure from the women's movement, the U.S. Labor Department issued a series of regulations requiring companies with federal contracts of $10,000 or more to meet specific goals for hiring women in construction craft jobs. Such efforts have hardly ended labor market segregation, but they have led to what the Labor Department's 1975 *Handbook on Women Workers* calls "perhaps the most dramatic shift that occurred between 1960 and 1970 . . . the large influx of women into the skilled trades." In 1970 almost half a million women were working in skilled occupations (including craft and kindred workers), which was three times as many as in 1960. This was eight times the rate of increase for men in the skilled trades. Women machinists nearly doubled, increasing from 6,700 to 11,800. Plumbers rose from 1,000 to 4,000, auto mechanics and carpenters more than tripled. Though women still account for only a tiny percentage of workers in these employment categories, their rate of increase certainly indicates that the trend is going to continue.

GETTING ORGANIZED

Over the years women workers have organized to improve their lot. Around the turn of the century office workers united in a variety of organizations, as teachers did also, and such women's labor organizations as the Women's Protective Association and the Women's Trade Union League arose. By the mid-1930s, however, though unionizing was in full swing across the country, these groups had died out. It wasn't until the 1970s, as labor historian Barbara Wertheimer has noted, that a new consciousness arose, and with it a drive to increase women's involvement in unions. One sign of this change was the establishment in 1974 of the Coalition of Labor Union Women. Another indicator was the increase in women's union membership, which, according to the Bureau of Labor Statistics, more than doubled between 1970 and 1977. By 1980 30 percent of workers belonging to labor organizations were women (this includes employee associations, such as the National Education Association, as well as unions).

Women are also beginning to take leadership roles in the formerly male-dominated unions. One such trailblazing union leader is Alice Puerala, who in 1976 became the first woman president of a local in the history of the United Steel Workers Association. And, in October 1977, though women accounted for only 858 of the 277,000 members of the United Mine Workers, a woman, Mary Maynard, was elected president of Local 1971 in Rum Creek,

West Virginia. She was succeeded the following year by another woman, Pauline Shine, and that same year Linda Triplett became president of Local 4172 in northern West Virginia. Together, as delegates to the United Mine Workers national convention, they were able to get the international to adopt a motion for paid maternity leave. Recognition from labor-union leaders finally came in 1980 with the appointment of Joyce Miller, head of the Coalition of Labor Union Women, to the AFL-CIO Executive Council, the first woman to be so honored.

Outside the blue-collar sphere—where union membership has earned women an average of $647 per year more than nonunionized blue-collar women make—unionizing has not taken a strong hold. Union representation among white-collar workers has risen by 50 percent in the past twenty years, but most of these workers are teachers and hospital personnel. Clerical workers have historically been difficult to organize, partly because of their close relationship to management. For this reason and others—for instance, the old claim that women are only temporary workers—existing unions have not tried to woo clerical workers until recently.

The vacuum was filled by the various women's groups that sprang up around the country. In 1973, for instance, several hundred women in Boston founded 9 to 5, drawing up an "Office Workers' Bill of Rights" that demands equal pay and promotion opportunities, detailed job descriptions, overtime pay, maternity benefits, and the right to refuse to do personal errands for an employer (see text below). In Chicago's Loop area a group known as Women Employed in Chicago was formed; in New York City, 1973 saw the establishment of Women Office Workers; and women on the West Coast started Union WAGE and other organizations. Except for Women Employed in Chicago, Women's Alliance for Pay Equity in Philadelphia, and Women Organized for Employment, active in Chicago and Washington, most of these groups, have now either folded or been subsumed into 9 to 5, which has grown spectacularly into a national organization. By 1983, 9 to 5, the National Association of Women Office Workers had eighteen chapters in major cities around the country and representatives in many towns not large enough to support chapters.

With growth came change. "You learn as you grow," says Janice Blood, director of information for 9 to 5. One change the organization has made is to allow voluntary, as well as staffed, chapters. Under this arrangement, in which office workers can volunteer time rather than work full days for a chapter, Blood expects the number of chapters to jump to fifty by 1985. Interest is strong; Blood reports sixty to a hundred requests for information per week.

One reason interest is so high is, quite simply, that 9 to 5 gets results. In 1980 the group won a quarter of a million dollars in back pay for female—and male—workers in an age-discrimination suit against the Provident Institute for Savings in Boston. To take another example from Boston, in the late 70s the group was responsible for getting equal pay in several job categories and promotions for a dozen women at the New England Merchants National Bank. But the group's most resounding victory up to now is probably its success in getting the Department of Labor, under the Ford and Carter administrations, to extend affirmative-action enforcement to office jobs and to initiate investigations into the practices of banks and insurance firms, where so many clerical workers are concentrated. Progress slowed under the Reagan Administration, but 9 to 5 regards any action as an important philosophical or political victory. Anything that 9 to 5 does keeps the issue of office work alive in the public mind.

The group expects to remain active on the national policy level, but part of the thrust of the office workers' movement, ultimately, is unionization. A union is the necessary prelude to contract negotiation and collective bargaining to achieve such benefits as medical care, which are provided by governments in other countries but only by businesses in the United States. For this reason, some see clerical workers' groups as halfway houses on the route to unionization. Already 9 to 5 has established Local 925 of the Service Employees' International Union in Boston, and in 1981 it spawned the creation of a totally new union, District 925. Unionization may not be the answer for all clerical workers, partly because some offices may not warrant or be able to support a union. But a group such as 9 to 5 may do much on a national level to increase employers' awareness of—and response to—office workers' concerns.

THE 9 TO 5 BILL OF RIGHTS

The right to respect as women and as workers.

The right to fair and adequate compensation, based on performance and length of service; regular salary reviews; and cost-of-living increases.

The right to written, accurate job descriptions specifying all job duties, and the right to choose whether to do the personal work of employers.

The right to fair and equal access to promotion opportunities, including a job posting program announcing all openings and training programs that give each employee an opportunity for job growth.

The right to a say over office policies, and the right to participate in organizing to improve our status.

The right to an effective, systematic grievance procedure.

The right to fair treatment in every aspect of employment without regard to sex, age, race, or sexual preference.

WILL AUTOMATION HELP?

The much-heralded increase in office automation may serve as an impetus for the unionization of office workers. Without the right to have direct input into how office work is designed—a right it may take unionization to win—office workers may face worse job conditions under automation than they have now. The National Institute for Occupational Safety and Health reports that employees who work all day at video-display terminals suffer the highest stress levels it has ever recorded. One reason is that in many cases automation destroys the very aspects of a job that clerical workers once enjoyed: variety, contact with coworkers, and a measure of control over work style. Working on terminals, women find that they end up with only one task to perform, one that they must repeat over and over again—not at their own pace, but at the pace set by the machine. In some companies keyboard operators are even instructed to enter material exactly as it is presented to them, errors and all. And impotence in the face of errors is undoubtedly stress-inducing.

Workers in automated offices also have had little control over the design of their work stations—keyboard height, lighting, and so forth. As a result there have been numerous reports of physical discomfort associated with VDT work—backaches, blurred vision, even temporary paralysis of the face and hands. But a study conducted by NIOSH has found that most of these symptoms are greatly alleviated if workers are able to adjust the equipment. This right, too, is something unions may try to win. Already some unions, such as the Newspaper Guild, have won concessions from employers on the health score. At Time, Incorporated, in 1983, the Newspaper Guild won company commitment to periodic checks for radiation emissions, one of the major concerns of VDT users. (See Chapter 9, Psychological Issues, for more on the health effects of VDTs, and Chapter 10, The Efficacious Office, for how VDTs should be set up.)

However, if it is handled properly—if workers are consulted about planning and organizing their work, and if they are protected from the machines' possible adverse health effects—automation may extricate women from the female ghetto. Office automation could be an opportunity to redesign clerical jobs to make them more rewarding and less, not more, alienating. If workers' jobs could be defined, not according to tasks but according to departments, for example, workers could perform a task using a VDT but also have responsibility for an entire function related to that task. Such wide responsibility is also likely to give a worker a better understanding of the operations of a given department and make her more eligible for promotion.

GOVERNMENT, A SPECIAL CASE?

On the subject of promotions, some people maintain that federal, state, and local governments—huge employers of women—with their announced policies of equal opportunity and their competitive examinations, provide clear pathways from office worker to managerial position. In some ways this is true. In some ways it is not.

The competitive government exams are fairly administered; women who take them pass in the same proportion as men. Not nearly as many women as men get to *take* those exams, however. A 1980 survey of New York State job exams showed that only about 12 percent of the examinees were women, and there is reason to believe that comparable situations exist in other states. Why? Because in civil service, as elsewhere in the working world, there are women's jobs and there are men's jobs, and some of the women's jobs are not on career ladders that lead to exams. Large numbers of women civil servants simply aren't eligible to compete for promotions.

Female clerical workers have to learn to avoid civil service cul-de-sacs. First, before taking a job they should find out where, if anywhere, that job can lead. Women who suspect they are stuck in a job that will never put them in line to compete must speak up and ask about transferring to a position that offers better access to executive promotions. Second, women should remember that, with administrative approval, a supervisor can *redefine* a subordinate's position without going through the examination protocol. Even if a job is classified as clerical, when the functions and responsibilities a worker has justify the change, the job title can actually be redefined to put the employee in the running for increased upward mobility.

Just how far women can go in government is still open to question, however. Only 2 percent of the 28,000 higher level federal employees are women. On the highest levels, where positions are filled by appointment rather than on the basis of examination scores, the number of women depends on the political philosophy of the president. The Carter Administration appointed the largest number of women to high public office in the history of the United States. These women appointees in turn appointed and promoted women, many already in the career service. Under President Reagan, things have taken a turn for the worse. Daisy B. Fields, author of *A Woman's Guide to Moving Up in Business and Government*, reports that as of March 1983 women occupied only 45 of the 400 positions requiring Senate approval.

Job discrimination, then, exists in government as elsewhere. For every woman who escapes the pink-collar ghetto, many more remain, and those who do not escape must have higher wage levels. Current laws requiring equal pay deal only with identical jobs, not different ones, and few women, as we have seen, have jobs identical to men's.

That's why, as we said in "The Next Step: Pay Equity" (see Chapter 2, What Women Earn), the newest battleground for working women is pay equity: equal pay for jobs with equal responsibilities, skills, and difficulty. This requires evaluating different jobs within a company or organization according to their components (skills, training, responsibilities) and then assessing whether jobs of equal value held by men and women are paid equally. To no one's surprise, most of the studies done so far show that men's jobs are valued more highly. But a legal battle is shaping to change that.

Will unions, automation, and pay equity help the bulk of women in the 80 percent? That remains to be seen. But so far, they represent our best hope and our best chance of reaching equality at last.

The Legal Safety Net: An In-Depth Guide
to the Major Antidiscrimination Laws

What are the major laws against discrimination and whom do they cover? Discrimination issues are discussed in Chapter 8, Benefits and Rights of Work. This appendix is designed to help you distinguish among the different laws, and to figure out which of them, if any, apply to you or your company. (The Equal Credit Law is discussed in Chapter 17, Being Your Own Boss.)

Each section lists the workers and workplaces covered, the agency in charge, the basic provisions of the law, whether someone can file anonymously, what the time constraints are (if you miss a deadline, you can lose the best of cases), what the procedure is and how the cases are handled, and—most important of all—what "relief" (back pay, reinstatement in a job, etc.) a victorious discrimination victim can gain and what penalties an employer found guilty of discrimination can suffer.

We'll begin with the broadest law against discrimination, Title VII of the Civil Rights Act of 1964. This act created the Equal Employment Opportunity Commission, the federal agency that enforces not only Title VII but most of the other major federal antidiscrimination laws as well.

One other point: many states and localities have their own antidiscrimination laws. Check with your local EEOC office, or with your state's human rights commission (if it has one), before you file a discrimination charge.

TITLE VII OF THE CIVIL RIGHTS ACT OF 1964, AS AMENDED BY THE EQUAL EMPLOYMENT OPPORTUNITY ACT OF 1972 AND THE PREGNANCY DISCRIMINATION ACT OF 1978

Workers covered. Current, discharged, or former employees, applicants for employment, union members or applicants for union membership, apprentices or other job trainees or applicants.

Workplaces covered. Private companies with fifteen or more employees; federal, state, and local governments; labor unions with fifteen or more members; employment agencies.

Employers not covered. Smaller companies, religious groups, educational institutions.

Enforcement agency. U.S. Equal Employment Opportunity Commission.

Basic provisions. Prohibits discrimination in employment—hiring, firing, compensation, terms, conditions, or privileges—because of an "individual's race, color, religion, sex or national origin." Forbids employment agencies from discrimination in referrals for hiring and unions from discrimination in classifying members. Also prohibits discrimination in apprenticeship or training programs. Under the 1978 pregnancy discrimination amendment, this protection extends to women "affected by pregnancy, childbirth, or related medical conditions," who are required to be treated the same "for all employment-related purposes . . . as other persons not so affected but similar in their ability or inability to work." One of the most important effects of this amendment (also called the Pregnancy Disability Act) is that it requires that pregnant women be offered the same insurance and leave policies as other workers who become disabled. Among other things, this law forbids employers to force pregnant women to take a mandatory maternity leave whether they want to or not.

When to take action. Practices can be declared discriminatory if they fall into one of three classifications:

1. Overt discrimination—failing to hire women or some other protected class (people of a certain race, religion, color, or national origin) because the work allegedly is too dangerous, too heavy, etc., or because women, for some reason, "shouldn't" do a job. Practices that have been banned under this definition include discriminating against women on the basis of state protective laws (banning women bartenders, for example), sex-segregated help-wanted ads, discriminating against hiring or promoting mothers of preschool children (while hiring and promoting fathers of such children). The employer's only defense is that women are excluded because of a "bona fide occupation qualification" (BFOQ). Courts have found that very few jobs have a BFOQ requiring members of one sex only. The classic examples of jobs that do: wet nurse, sperm donor.

2. Practices that are neutral but have a discriminatory impact—for example, weight and height requirements that screen out more women (or Hispanics) than (white) men. You don't have to show that the employer intended to discriminate, but to defend him/herself against your charge the employer must show that the disputed practice is a business necessity. Under this provision companies may have to change their methods of recruiting and hiring women to insure a sufficient representation of women. Promotion policies that end up with women in jobs with fewer opportunities for promotion than men—or training policies that do not offer employee-training programs to allow lower-level employees to qualify for higher-level jobs—can also be classified as discriminatory if they affect a protected class, such as women.

Employers are granted an exception for seniority systems, even though these often fall most heavily on previously disadvantaged groups. When workers are laid off on a last-hired-first-fired basis, women and minorities recruited relatively recently under affirmative-action plans tend to suffer more heavily.

3. Employment practices that seem neutral but in fact treat men and women differently—for example, many more men than women are promoted to upper-management jobs although they are supposedly judged according to the same standards. Employers also cannot hire similarly qualified men and women but assign them to different kinds of jobs, giving heavy work only to men and light work only to women, say. These cases are the hardest to prove, because you must show that the employer *intended* to discriminate. Most Title VII cases fall into this category. Employers defend themselves here by trying to show that the salary promotion difference, or other difference in the treatment of men and women, is due to other factors—lower qualifications, more absenteeism, and so on.

Among the unequal practices that can occur despite outwardly equal employment policies are different pay for the same or very similar work, differential treatment of pregnant women, different pension benefits (declared illegal by the Supreme Court in

Los Angeles Water & Power Department v. *Manhart*, in 1978), and—in an emerging concept discussed in Chapter 2—pay inequities, in which jobs held primarily by women are paid less than jobs requiring comparable skill, effort, and responsibility held primarily by men.

Need for a lawyer. Title VII cases must be filed initially with the local office of the EEOC, unless you live in a state or city with a fair employment practices law. If you do, you must file first with the local FEP agency. There are FEP laws in Alaska, Arizona, California, Colorado, Connecticut, Delaware, District of Columbia, Florida, Georgia, Hawaii, Idaho, Illinois, Indiana, Iowa, Kansas, Kentucky, Maine, Maryland, Massachusetts, Michigan, Minnesota, Missouri, Montana, Nebraska, Nevada, New Hampshire, New Jersey, New Mexico, New York, North Carolina, North Dakota, Ohio, Oklahoma, Oregon, Pennsylvania, Rhode Island, South Carolina, South Dakota, Tennessee, Utah, Vermont, Washington, West Virginia, Wisconsin, Wyoming, and in Puerto Rico and the U.S. Virgin Islands. You may have a lawyer with you at any stage of the proceedings, but you do not need one as long as the EEOC or a state FEP agency is handling your case. If no settlement can be reached, the EEOC or local agency *may* sue on your behalf. Most often, though, you are then given a right-to-sue letter and will need a lawyer to take your case to the federal courts.

Anonymity. In general, within ten days after someone files a charge with the EEOC, the employer against which it is filed gets a notice that includes the name of the person making the complaint. To avoid this situation, you can have a women's or civil-rights organization file on your behalf. Eventually the employer will probably need to know your name for a settlement to be negotiated, unless you are part of a class-action complaint (on behalf of "all management women at the ABC Company," for example).

Time constraints. These time questions are nitpicking details, but they're the kinds of details that can cause you to lose your case. You must file charges with the EEOC within 180 days of the date on which you were discriminated against, unless your state or city has an FEP office. If it does, you must file first with that office. Most local laws allow 240 days from the date of the discriminatory incident for filing, but some require filing in a lesser time. You must then file your charge with the EEOC also. You can do that any time after you have filed with the local FEP agency—except that you *must* file with the EEOC within 30 days after the FEP agency has finished processing your case, or within 300 days of the discriminatory incident, whichever is *sooner*. This sounds complicated, but it's simpler than it sounds because you can usually file charges with both offices at once through the EEOC. Check with the EEOC first. To be safest, try to file your charges with both agencies within the shortest applicable deadline: 180 days after the discriminatory incident happened is the shortest time in any of the laws so far.

The other crucial time comes after the EEOC—unable to settle your case and unwilling to pursue it—releases it back to you with a right-to-sue letter. (You have the right to sue whether or not the EEOC finds "cause" to believe discrimination has occurred.) Once you get that letter, you have exactly 90 days to file a lawsuit, so it's crucial to have a lawyer ready to go on your case.

Procedures and timing for employees of the federal government (and often of state and local governments) who file Title VII complaints are different. Check with your agency's Equal Employment Opportunity counselor. One crucial time point for federal workers: you must file an original "informal" discrimination complaint with your agency (not the EEOC) within 30 days of the discriminatory events.

Procedure. Except for government cases, all Title VII cases begin with the EEOC or local FEP office. You cannot file a court case without going through this step, which is designed to give you a chance to avoid a lawsuit altogether. (However, if you accept an individual settlement and don't take the case to court, the settlement will affect only you and not all women in your situation—a consideration you may want to keep in mind to discuss with an attorney or a women's rights group.)

In many areas the local EEOC and FEP offices have set up work-sharing arrangements through which each office specializes in different kinds of cases to avoid duplicating the other's efforts or making you wait the 60 days for the case to move from the FEP to the EEOC. According to *The Rights of Women*, an American Civil Liberties Union handbook (revised edition, 1983), the EEOC does not routinely review state agency decisions, but you have a right to such a review if you request it. What we will summarize here is the EEOC procedure; the FEP agencies generally follow this type of procedure, at least at the early states of their case processing.

As the chart on page 313 demonstrates, an EEOC filing sets up a process that usually allows two opportunities for you and your employer to come to terms. When you file, your case will be assigned to an equal opportunity specialist, who will decide what data are necessary for a fact-finding conference and will contact your employer within ten days.

The conference is usually scheduled for about three weeks after your employer receives the notice. Both parties may present witnesses and have a lawyer present at the conference, but the lawyer will not be able to speak for them or to cross-examine the witnesses. At the conference, the specialist will present your complaint, listen to each side, and try to resolve the dispute. If a settlement is reached, it will be typed and signed by both you and your employer. The fact-finding conference is not a formal hearing, and it is not recorded by the EEOC.

If you cannot come to terms, your case will be sent on to the continued investigation and conciliation unit, where a specialist (usually a second one) will gather more information and analyze the case. When this is done, the EEOC will determine whether "reasonable cause exists to believe there is discrimination." If it finds cause, the agency will again try to settle, or "conciliate," the case. If it cannot do so, it will either issue you a right-to-sue letter or file the case for you in federal court. According to the ACLU, the latter situation is rare. If, on the other hand, the EEOC finds no cause, it will not try to settle the case. It will simply issue the right-to-sue letter, allowing you to proceed on your own.

In some cases the EEOC will bypass the fact-finding step and go directly to the investigation stage. This tends to happen when your complaint is similar to those of a number of other charging parties and the EEOC wants to handle them together and file charges in court as a class action suit on behalf of a group.

These cases are selected as part of what is called the early litigation identification program. The EEOC has a list of problems and employers selected for ELI treatment. Unlike the usual case, which takes 60 to 90 days to settle, ELI cases are being groomed for court; they can take at least six months to research and many more if they end up in the court system. You will be allowed to choose whether to participate or have your case handled individually, according to the ACLU.

If, by the way, your company harasses or fires you as a result of learning that you

Flow Chart: EEOC Procedures*

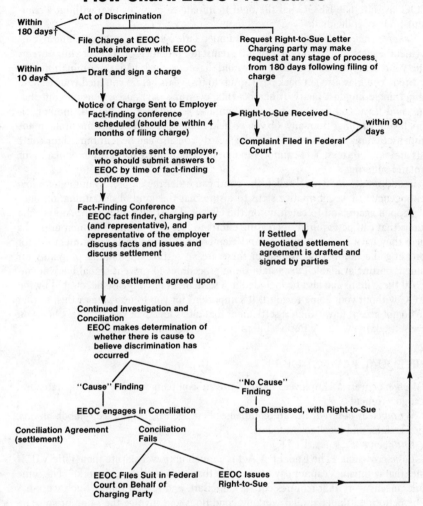

Within 180 days† — Act of Discrimination

File Charge at EEOC
Intake interview with EEOC counselor

Within 10 days — Draft and sign a charge

Request Right-to-Sue Letter
Charging party may make request at any stage of process, from 180 days following filing of charge

Notice of Charge Sent to Employer
Fact-finding conference scheduled (should be within 4 months of filing charge)

Interrogatories sent to employer, who should submit answers to EEOC by time of fact-finding conference

Right-to-Sue Received

Complaint Filed in Federal Court — within 90 days

Fact-Finding Conference
EEOC fact finder, charging party (and representative), and representative of the employer discuss facts and issues and discuss settlement

If Settled
Negotiated settlement agreement is drafted and signed by parties

No settlement agreed upon

Continued investigation and Conciliation
EEOC makes determination of whether there is cause to believe discrimination has occurred

"Cause" Finding

"No Cause" Finding

EEOC engages in Conciliation

Case Dismissed, with Right-to-Sue

Conciliation Agreement (settlement)

Conciliation Fails

EEOC Files Suit in Federal Court on Behalf of Charging Party

EEOC Issues Right-to-Sue

* This chart applies to the procedures that are used by the federal Equal Employment Opportunity Commission (EEOC) for charges under Title VII of the Civil Rights Act of 1964. Local agencies, such as the District of Columbia Office of Human Rights, follow similar procedures.
† In jurisdiction where there are state or local laws prohibiting employment discrimination such as the District of Columbia, this period will be longer.
Source: Copyright © 1981 Women's Legal Defense Fund/Women's Rights Clinic of the Antioch Law School.

have filed an EEOC charge, you can file a second charge (or amend your first charge) and, following the same procedures, ultimately sue the company for damages. The EEOC is allowed to bring an immediate lawsuit in your name for "temporary and preliminary relief" in such cases. If the agency refuses to do so, you can sue the company yourself, and if you win, the company will be forced to pay damages or reinstate you in your job.

If you work for an employer whom the EEOC has chosen to target for "systemic" discrimination affecting a large group of women, you may also find yourself part of an EEOC lawsuit. The EEOC has the right to initiate cases on its own without a complaint from an individual.

Relief/Penalties. If you win a lawsuit under Title VII, your employer/union/employment agency may be ordered to hire, reinstate, promote, or transfer you, or reinstate your seniority at the level it would have reached had discrimination not occurred. You may also get back pay (for up to two years before you filed your EEOC charge), including lost salary, fringe benefits, overtime pay, raises, pension contributions, and leave and vacation pay. You can also get interest on the lost monies, although your earnings from any job you've held in the interim plus any unemployment compensation may be deducted from the award. You also can be reimbursed for court costs and lawyer's fees. You cannot, though, receive punitive damages or damages for pain and suffering.

In addition to individual relief, the court can order the employer/union/employment agency to take affirmative steps to insure that this kind of discrimination does not happen again, and to catch up on the effects of past discrimination. Among the actions that can be required: increasing efforts to hire and promote women into jobs where they have been excluded or underrepresented (using goals and timetables for increasing the number of women in these areas); setting up training programs for women; posting available jobs; establishing procedures to prevent sexual harassment.

All these items can also be included in a settlement of your case negotiated by the EEOC without your going to court. It's important for you to be aware of this, so that you do not accept unwittingly a settlement that offers less than you are due. Once you have settled, it's virtually impossible to bring further charges later on.

THE EQUAL PAY ACT OF 1963

Workers covered. Employees of most private companies and of federal, state, and local governments.

Workplaces covered. Private companies "engaged in commerce," labor unions, federal, state, and local governments.

Enforcement agency. EEOC.

Basic provisions. The Equal Pay Act is a much narrower statute than Title VII. It states that companies cannot pay women less than men for the same work. "The same work" means work that requires equal skill, effort, and responsibility. Such work has to be performed under similar working conditions and involve the same or substantially similar tasks. What's more, the men and women must work for the same establishment in the same location.

Once you have established "equal work" under these standards, the employer may be able to defend against your claim by showing that the unequal pay was based on (1) a seniority system; (2) a merit system; (3) a piecework payment policy; or (4) "any factor other than sex."

Causes of action. The Equal Pay Act deals only with sex discrimination in pay. Complaints involving pay inequities according to religion, or involving other kinds of sex discrimination, must be brought under Title VII. To win a case you must establish that it meets the "same work" criteria listed above. Among the jobs that have been found to be equal are janitors and maids in colleges, nurses' aides and orderlies in hospitals, and sales clerks in different departments in stores. Women bank tellers, inspectors, and laboratory technicians have also won cases.

It is often a good idea to bring charges under both the Equal Pay Act and Title VII, so that if you can't prove the "equal" jobs criteria you still may win.

Need for a lawyer. Under Title VII, the Equal Pay Act gives you a choice of filing your complaint with the EEOC or bringing a lawsuit on your own. You do not need a lawyer if you work through the EEOC.

Anonymity. One big advantage of filing under the Equal Pay Act is that the EEOC does not have to—and usually won't—reveal your name, although if you have an unusual job, your employer may figure out who you are. If your charge is also filed under Title VII, though, staying anonymous is more difficult (see page 311). If you skip the EEOC and file suit on your own, you will obviously have to reveal your name.

Time constraints. You have two years from the time the discrimination takes place to file an Equal Pay lawsuit in court—three years if you can prove the discrimination was "willful." As will be detailed below, if you file a complaint with the EEOC and the agency finds pay discrimination, it will start a lawsuit on behalf of you and other women in your situation at your workplace. But this law, unlike Title VII, does not permit you to meet the deadline by filing a charge with the EEOC: you have to get to court within the specified time period. This is crucial if you were discriminated against in the past and your employer no longer discriminates against women. If the pay inequities are continuing, the time clause will not affect your ability to sue.

Procedure. If you go directly to court, your attorney will explain the procedure to you. But it may be better to work through the EEOC, because the agency will do the investigation for you free. If it finds pay discrimination and decides to file a lawsuit about it—this happens very rarely, though—you won't have to pay for the lawyer either. In addition, the courts provide more kinds of benefits for EEOC cases than for those filed by individuals (see "Reliefs/Penalties," below). And the EEOC can file a class action lawsuit on behalf of all women in your situation, while you can file a case only on behalf of yourself and of women who specifically authorize you to use their names.

When you complain to the EEOC, investigators from the agency's Equal Pay Division will go to your company. If they find a violation, they will attempt to collect the back wages due to underpaid women and have the company sign a formal agreement to equalize the wages of men and women. (The company must do this by raising the women's wages—it's illegal to comply with the act by lowering men's wages.) If the EEOC cannot come to terms with the violator, the agency may file a lawsuit in federal court.

Relief/Penalties. If you win a lawsuit you bring to court on your own, you may get back all lost wages for two years from the date you filed your case, plus an equal amount as damages. Thus in contrast to Title VII cases, Equal Pay Act victors get double back wages. If you can prove your employer discriminated "willfully," you can recover three years of lost wages, doubled.

But if the EEOC brings your case, in addition to double back pay the judge may require your company to raise your salary—and that of other women in your firm—to equal that of men with jobs like yours.

TITLE IX OF THE EDUCATION AMENDMENTS OF 1972

Workers covered. Teachers and staff in institutions that receive federal funds for education.

Workplaces covered. All institutions that receive federal funds for education, including not only schools and universities but also some libraries, museums, and similar institutions. Recently, this law has been the subject of a major controversy. For years, receiving any federal funds (including money for student loans) was considered to make all parts of an institution liable under Title IX. But a February 1984 Supreme Court ruling (*Grove City College* v. *Bell*) narrowed this interpretation considerably. Currently, only those departments in an institution that actually get federal money—not the whole institution—are covered by Title IX. This is likely to be interpreted to mean that if a biology department gets federal grant money, it cannot discriminate against its women students, faculty, or staff. But if the athletic department in the same college does not receive federal funds, it is free—for example—to provide better facilities and more staff for male athletes than for female athletes. As this book went to press, Congress was considering proposals to mandate that the previous broad interpretation be reestablished.

Enforcement agency. Complaints should go to the office of civil rights in the federal agency that provided the funds to your employer. This is usually the U.S. Department of Education but could be another agency—the Department of Health and Human Services for a medical school, for example.

Basic provisions. This law provides a broad range of protection against sex discrimination for students, teachers, and staff members. It also requires that employers document their compliance with the law and authorizes investigations to monitor this. However, because the Supreme Court did not definitely uphold the right of women to sue for sex discrimination in employment under Title IX until 1982, the law is still unclear about which practices are banned specifically. Some that are very likely covered include granting tenure to men but not women professors in a university and paying male and female staff members inequitably. Since employees protected by Title IX are also protected by Title VII of the Civil Rights Act and the Equal Pay Act, they should review their options carefully. Attorney Jane Dolkart believes that the relief for women employees under Title VII is likely to be broader. You can pursue cases under all statutes at the same time, if you wish to. Title IX has more lenient time requirements for lawsuits (though not for complaints); you may wish to file under it if you have missed the Title VII or Equal Pay Act deadlines. Title IX also has one rarely invoked but powerful penalty for violation that is not available under Title VII: cutoff of federal funds.

Need for a lawyer. You do not need to file a charge with the U.S. Department of Education or other funding agency in order to go to court. If you file agency charges, you will not need a lawyer. If you choose to go to court, obviously you will.

Anonymity. None. If you complain, your name will be listed on the charge.

Time constraints. You have 180 days after the discrimination has occurred to file your complaint with the U.S. Department of Education or other agency. If you file a private lawsuit in court, the only time requirement is your state's statute of limitations, which may range from 90 days to three years.

Procedure. When the U.S. Department of Education or other agency receives your complaint (the Department of Education will forward your charge to the proper agency if it belongs elsewhere), the department has 15 days to tell you whether you have included all the needed information. If you have not, you have 120 days to supply the missing pieces, or the investigation will be ended.

When the complaint is complete, the department must inform you and your employer when and how the investigation will be conducted. After interviews with you, school officials, and other witnesses, a letter of findings will be issued. If the agency finds discrimination, it will first attempt to persuade the school to comply with the law. If this does not work, it has 30 days to bring administrative action against the school or other employer for a cutoff of federal funds to the institution.

How vigorously federal agencies enforce these powers depends on who is in charge. It took a 1977 lawsuit against the backlog of sex-discrimination cases under Title IX in the Department of Health, Education and Welfare (predecessor of the Department of Education and the Department of Health and Human Services) to produce the timetable outlined in this paragraph. Between 1972 and 1976, the agency had managed to resolve only one-fifth of the complaints, according to the ACLU.

Penalties/Relief. The penalty of cutting off federal funds to the employer can be enforced by the U.S. Department of Education or other federal agency, but it is unclear whether a judge can order this penalty if you bring an individual lawsuit in federal court. What other relief you can win in court is also unclear, because the right of individual women to sue is so newly won.

EXECUTIVE ORDER 11246, AS AMENDED BY EXECUTIVE ORDER 11375 AND IMPLEMENTING REGULATIONS AND REVISED ORDER NO. 4 (THE AFFIRMATIVE ACTION REQUIREMENT)

Workers covered. Employees and applicants for employment of covered federal contractors.

Workplaces covered. All companies and agencies that have federal contracts of $10,000 a year or more (those with 50 employees and $50,000 or more in contracts are also held to Revised Order No. 4), plus their subcontractors and those receiving federally assisted construction contracts. Unions are not covered.

Enforcement agency. The Office of Federal Contract Compliance Programs of the U.S. Department of Labor.

Basic provisions. The Equal Employment Opportunity clause of this law, which each federal contractor is required to sign, reads: "The contractor will not discriminate against any employee or applicant for employment because of race, color, religion, sex, or national origin. The contractor will take affirmative action to insure that applicants are employed, and that employees are treated during employment without regard to this race, color, religion, sex, or national origin. Such action shall include, but not be limited to the following: Employment, upgrading, demotion, or transfer, recruitment or recruitment advertising, layoff or termination; rates of pay or other forms of compensation; and selection for training, including apprenticeship."

This order, originally signed by President Lyndon Johnson in 1965 to cover race discrimination (sex discrimination was added two years later), is the source of the term affirmative action. The difference between this order and the laws discussed elsewhere in this appendix is that federal contractors are ordered to take active steps to make sure that women and other protected groups are not discriminated against or risk debarment of their federal contract. (Under Title VII, the requirement that employers end discrimination and correct the effects of past discrimination is enforced only if a court or the EEOC finds that discrimination has occurred.) The original executive order merely required federal contractors to promise in writing to uphold these terms, but in 1971 President Richard Nixon signed Revised Order No. 4, which put teeth into the rule, at least where major contractors are concerned.

Now all contractors with contracts totaling $50,000 and 50 or more employees must prepare and institute written affirmative-action plans. (Note that the Reagan administration is trying to relax this requirement.) The plan must include an analysis of all parts of the company and specific numerical goals and timetables for increasing the number of women and other protected groups in jobs where they are underutilized. The goals should be "significant, measurable, and attainable" by "every good faith effort." The methods by which the company plans to attain and evaluate its progress on these goals—and the specific personnel responsible for meeting them—must be detailed in the plan, which must be kept by the company to be submitted to the OFCCP should it request a copy, and updated annually.

And there's the rub. Unlike Title VII and most other antidiscrimination acts, individuals cannot sue in court under these orders. You can file a complaint with the OFCCP, which generally refers individual complaints to the EEOC to be processed under Title VII while investigating itself those filed on behalf of a class of employees.

The company, by the way, will not be punished if it does not meet its goals and timetables, as long as it can prove that it has made a good-faith effort to do so.

Need for a lawyer. None.

Anonymity. Not available, unless an organization files the complaint on your behalf.

Time constraints. The complaint must be filed within 180 days of the discrimination.

Procedure. If your complaint involves a class of employees (for example, all women applicants for mining jobs at the XYZ Coal Company), the OFCCP will investigate it, studying the relevant affirmative-action plans and the contractor's employment practices. If the agency finds that discrimination has occurred, it will attempt to get the contractor to comply voluntarily. If that does not work, the OFCCP can either have the case tried in a hearing before an administrative-law judge or refer it to the Justice Department for suit against the company for breach of contract. When the OFCCP follows the first route, as it usually does, the administrative findings are then referred to the Secretary of Labor, who can accept, modify, or reject them. (This is what has happened to the $12 million judgment that Women Employed of Chicago won against the Harris Bank in 1980. At the time this book went to press, Secretary of Labor Raymond Donovan had sent the award back to the administrative law judge for more evidence.)

The other, and more common, route by which the OFCCP investigates federal contractors for job discrimination is by the regular compliance reviews that it is authorized to carry out—even without receiving a complaint—under the terms of the executive orders. How vigorously it pursues contract compliance is up to the agency; some presidential administrations have pursued this line of action more rigorously than others, going after systematic discrimination in certain industries. Under an administration unsympathetic to strong affirmative action, the requirement of agency enforcement can be more a hindrance than a help.

Do these penalties help? A recent study, which the Department of Labor has been highly reluctant to release, reports that women and minorities working for companies doing business with the federal government—and thus subject to these executive-order affirmative-action requirements—have made significantly greater gains than similar employees in companies not covered by these regulations. Between 1974 and 1980, the rate of minority employment grew 20 percent in companies covered by the affirmative-action rules but only 12 percent in the other companies. Figures for women were even more striking—15.2 percent compared to only 2.2 percent, according to a report in the *New York Times*. In other words, affirmative action works.

Relief/Penalties. The OFCCP can hold back payment by the government of sums owed under contract until it gets compliance, including an affirmative-action plan approved by the agency. It can require companies to provide back pay for the people affected by discrimination (as in the Harris Bank case), or order other kinds of relief such as promotions. It can also bar the company from eligibility for future federal contracts—a penalty so powerful that it has been imposed fewer than thirty times in the first seventeen years the order was in effect.

THE AGE DISCRIMINATION IN EMPLOYMENT ACT OF 1967

Workers covered. Employees between the ages of forty and seventy in most private industries and in federal, state, and local governments. There is no upper age limit for federal employees.

Workplaces covered. Employers of 20 or more people engaged in interstate commerce, an industry that affects interstate commerce, employment agencies, unions with more than 25 members.

Enforcement agency. EEOC.

Basic provisions. Prohibits discrimination in hiring, firing, and other terms and conditions of employment, in referrals for employment, and in membership in a labor union. Among the practices the act forbids are firing older workers (who have often worked up to higher wages or salaries) in favor of younger workers and refusing to count experience as a substitute for educational qualifications. Older workers also cannot be forced to accept reduced wages in lieu of being fired in favor of younger (cheaper) workers.

One major exception provides a loophole for age requirements in apprenticeship programs. These programs can still refuse to admit candidates above a certain age (although there is some dispute whether such limits are legal). This can be a special problem for women who decide to change jobs and enter one of the nontraditional fields now otherwise open to them but requiring an apprenticeship program.

Causes of action. As in Title VII, one defense for employers is that a certain age is a "bona fide occupational qualification" for the job. This is defined narrowly but has been upheld in cases in which people have tried to contest mandatory retirement ages for employees of fire and police departments and for airline pilots. It is legal for employers to provide special benefits for older employees (longer vacations or increased severance pay, for example). But employers in some cases may provide reduced fringe benefits for older employees where the cost of providing benefits for them is greater than it is for younger workers and might discourage hiring older workers. Unlike Title VII, the Age Discrimination Act does not provide for class-action suits. You—and any other employees who want to join your case—must be named in your lawsuit from the beginning.

Need for a lawyer. Your charge must first be filed with the EEOC, and you will not need a lawyer for that stage of the proceedings. You will need one if you take the case to court by filing your own lawsuit.

Anonymity. As in Title VII cases, it is difficult to file charges anonymously.

Time constraints. You must file your EEOC charge either within 180 days of the alleged age discrimination or—if your state has a law prohibiting age discrimination—within 300 days of the discrimination or within 30 days of getting a notice that the state proceeding against your employer is over. States with age-discrimination laws are: Alaska, California, Connecticut, Delaware, District of Columbia, Florida, Georgia, Hawaii, Idaho, Illinois, Iowa, Kentucky, Maryland, Massachusetts, Michigan, Minnesota, Montana, Nebraska, Nevada, New Hampshire, New Jersey, New Mexico, New York, Oregon, Pennsylvania, South Carolina, Utah, West Virginia, and Wisconsin. Also covered: Guam, Puerto Rico, U.S. Virgin Islands. Note that ages covered by state laws may differ from those specified in the federal act.

Sixty days after you have filed a charge with the EEOC, you can go to court on your own. Unlike Title VII cases, suits under the age-discrimination law do not require you to have a right-to-sue letter to go to court.

There is one other important time element: you must file your civil court case within two years after the age discrimination occurred. If you can prove in court that the act was "willful," the time limit is three years.

Procedure. The EEOC generally processes age-discrimination charges in the same way it handles Title VII cases (see pages 312–14). However, the law does not require the agency to investigate your charges or issue formal findings the way it must in Title VII cases. Usually it will go through a fact-finding process and attempt to settle your case.

Penalties/Relief. The employer can be required to hire, reinstate, or promote you and to pay you any unpaid compensation (wages, fringe and other benefits). If you can prove the act was "willful," you are entitled to double damages. Other kinds of damages may be available.

THE REHABILITATION ACT OF 1973, AS AMENDED

Workers covered. Employees and job applicants to employers covered by the statute. Such employees and applicants must be handicapped, which is defined as having "a physical or mental impairment which substantially limits one or more of such person's major life activities."

Workplaces covered. The federal government (Section 501), companies and agencies with federal contracts (Section 503), recipients of federal grants (Section 504).

Enforcement agency. EEOC for federal government cases under Section 501;

OFCCP for federal contractor cases under Section 503; the Office of Civil Rights in the agency that made the federal grant for cases under Section 504.

Basic provisions. The Rehabilitation Act is an immensely complicated statute, with different avenues for complaints depending on what kind of employer is accused of discrimination.

In general, covered employers are forbidden to discriminate against otherwise qualified individuals with handicaps who can perform the essential functions of the job with "reasonable accommodation." Reasonable accommodation can mean providing access to the workplace, adjusting furniture to accommodate those in wheelchairs, providing assistance for employees who are deaf or blind, and so on. The requirements and protections for federal employees under Section 501 are similar to those provided by Title VII (see pages 309–14); under Section 503, they are similar to those required by Executive Order 11246 (pages 317–19). Section 504 cases are probably handled like Title IX cases, but because the law is still unclear, it would be best to check with an attorney or an organization for the handicapped.

Among the practices that may be illegal are discrimination in hiring, promotions, accommodations on the job, pay, and other benefits. It is probably not illegal to refuse to pay insurance benefits for a preexisting disability (if this restriction also applies to nonhandicapped employees with other medical problems, such as high blood pressure). But it is illegal for your employer to require you to sign a waiver stating that you will not claim benefits if you are injured on the job—for example, if a woman on crutches slips at work.

Need for a lawyer. Under Section 501, you will not need a lawyer unless you decide eventually to file a lawsuit on your own. Under Section 503, you have no right to file a private lawsuit and can only complain to the OFCCP—no lawyer needed. Section 504 is still unclear. However, the requirements are so complex that it is worth checking with an attorney or an organization for the handicapped, says Kim Swain, staff attorney of the Disability Rights Education and Defense Fund, a California advocacy group. Her organization will not handle out-of-state cases but will give advice on filing complaints. You can reach it at 2032 San Pablo Avenue, Berkeley, CA 94702 (415-644-2555).

Anonymity. Possible with the EEOC under Section 501; not offered under Section 503 or 504.

Time constraints. Federal employees filing under Section 501 must inform the Equal Employment Opportunity counselor in their agency within 30 days of the act of discrimination in order to be covered. Other time limits of 501 are similar to those for Title VII cases. For complaints under Section 503, the time limit is the same as under Executive Order 11246—180 days.

Procedure. Section 501 follows the Title VII procedures set down for federal employees. Section 503 follows the OFCCP procedures. Section 504 follows Title IX procedures, except that it is unclear whether a handicapped person can sue privately in court for a violation.

Penalties/Relief. What is available to the handicapped person depends on which section the discriminatory employer fits into. Check with an attorney or advocacy organization. Back pay, retroactive seniority, reinstatement, and affirmative action may well be available if employment discrimination on the basis of a handicap is found.

Appendix B
Suggestions for Further Reading

FINDING A JOB

GENERAL

Abarbanel, Karen, and Siegel, Connie McClung. *Women's Work Book.* New York: Praeger Publishers, 1975.
Contains a wealth of general information on choosing a field, writing a résumé, interviewing, etc. Includes a directory of occupational organizations, career counseling services, women's centers, educational opportunities, and books, magazines, and newsletters.

Bolles, Richard Nelson. *What Color Is Your Parachute?* Berkeley: Ten Speed Press, 1981.
This class job hunter's and career changer's guide is a great motivator. Contains exercises to help the job seeker identify skills and interests, and a comprehensive listing of books and services.

Catalyst staff. *When Can You Start? The Complete Job-Search Guide for Women of All Ages.* New York: Macmillan, 1982.
Comprehensive and straightforward, this book offers good tips on networking and job interviewing.

Kanter, Rosabeth Moss. *The Change Masters: Innovation for Productivity in the American Corporation.* New York: Simon and Schuster, 1983.
A professor and management expert analyzes successful innovations in America's major corporations and argues that participative management is the way to tap skills of our managers and increase U.S. competitiveness.

Kanter, Rosabeth Moss. *Men and Women of the Corporation.* New York: Basic Books, 1977.
The classic book on corporate structure and how it affects the way men an women work.

Reich, Robert B. *The Next American Frontier.* New York: Times Books, 1983.
A mixture of social comment and business analysis, this book recommends a new course for American business, which should integrate high-tech realities with human needs.

Wright, Dick. *Hardball Job Hunting Tactics.* New York: Facts on File, 1983.
The solid, no-nonsense job-hunting tactics described in this book are based on a single law: the person who best understands what the employer is looking for is the one who lands the job.

REENTERING THE JOB MARKET

Berman, Eleanor. *Re-entering: Successful Back-to-Work Strategies for Women Seeking a Fresh Start.* New York: Crown Publishers, 1980.

322

This guide, the classic work for the reentry woman, makes use of the methods employed in a highly successful workshop for returning homemakers at Hunter College in New York. It includes first-person accounts illustrating such topics as self-evaluation, résumé writing, and going back to school. The appendices list state-by-state resources for job counseling, education, financial planning, and career information.

Fader, Shirley Sloan. *From Kitchen to Career: How Any Woman Can Skip Low-Level Jobs and Start in the Middle or at the Top.* New York: Stein and Day, 1977. Offers practical advice on how to use your everyday living and volunteer experiences to get a middle-to-upper-level job. Contains an interesting section on how helping a husband in his business has supplied many women with skills that would qualify them for non-entry-level jobs.

Mouat, Lucia. *Back to Business: A Woman's Guide to Reentering the Job Market.* New York: New American Library, 1979. A practical, encouraging book full of helpful guidelines for landing the job you want.

Shield, Laurie. *Displaced Homemakers: Organizing for a New Life.* New York: McGraw-Hill, 1981. A narrative describing the Displaced Homemakers movement from its beginnings in the early 1970s to the passage of a Displaced Homemakers Bill and the founding of the Alliance for Displaced Homemakers and the Displaced Homemakers Network. The author also shares some of the techniques used at various Displaced Homemakers Centers to help women regain a sense of self and set short- and long-range goals.

MID-LIFE CAREER CHANGES

Brodey, Jean Lisette. *Mid-Life Careers.* Philadelphia: Westminster Press, 1983. Written in an informal, anecdotal style, this book imparts much information on gaining work experience and getting a foot in the door. The author explores options such as network interviews, internships/apprenticeships, education, and volunteer positions.

Miller, Anne. *Finding Career Alternatives for Teachers.* New York: Apple Publishing Company, 1979. Useful for anyone who would like a career change from teaching, this book includes self-evaluation exercises designed to help you identify your strongest skills and direct you to an appropriate new career.

STRATEGIES FOR SUCCESS

MASTERING OFFICE POLITICS

Fader, Shirley Sloan. *Successfully Ever After.* New York: McGraw-Hill Paperbacks, 1982. Offers good, solid advice for the young woman in her first job. Topics range from how to work effectively with your boss to the dos and don'ts of succeeding after a promotion.

Harragan, Betty Lehan. *Games Mother Never Taught You.* New York: Warner Books, 1978.

A classic book for the working woman on the structures, maneuverings, and underlying assumptions—foreign to most women—that are encountered in the business world. Compelling and necessary reading.

Kaplan, Glenn. *The Big Time*. New York: Congdon and Weed, 1982.
Each career has its own rules. What gets you promoted in an ad agency may get you fired at a bank. Written with the participation of three hundred of America's most successful men and women, this book tells you exactly how the game is played.

Mazzei, George. *The New Office Etiquette*. New York: Poseidon Press, 1983.
This guide offers sound advice for getting through the bewildering maze of office etiquette.

The Editors of Working Woman. *The Working Woman Success Book*. New York: Ace Books, 1981.
A compilation of articles from *Working Woman* magazine.

THE ART OF SELF-PRESENTATION

Flacks, Niki, and Rasberry, Robert. *Power Talk: Theater Techniques That Have Helped Thousands of Executives Give Successful Presentations*. New York: Free Press, 1982.
An actress and a business-school professor offer a wealth of tried and tested theatrical techniques and exercises for professional people. For those who want to have a powerful delivery and overcome habitual nervousness.

Kenny, Michael, for Eastman Kodak Company. *Presenting Yourself*. New York: John Wiley, 1982.
This book teaches the art of successful business presentations. It offers step-by step advice to help anyone prepare and deliver a polished, professional, and convincing presentation. Covers such topics as sales pitches, exhibits, and audiovisual shows.

Stone, Janet, and Bachner, Jane. *Speaking Up: A Book for Every Woman Who Wants to Speak Effectively*. New York: McGraw-Hill, 1977.
Contains a wealth of helpful hints on giving presentations, nerves, introductions, and projecting authority. Distinctly feminist in nature and tone, this is one of the more interesting books on speaking.

Thompson, Jacqueline, ed. *Image Impact: The Aspiring Woman's Personal Packaging Program*. Reading, Pa.: A & W Publishers, 1982.
Eighteen nationally acclaimed image consultants help women match "outer" speech, dress, body language, and business manner to "inner" talents and aspirations. Offers advice on public speaking, assertiveness, and personal marketing strategies for job offers and promotions.

NETWORKING AND MENTORS

Collins, Nancy W. *Professional Women and Their Mentors: A Practical Guide to Mentoring for the Woman Who Wants to Get Ahead*. Englewood Cliffs, N.J.: Prentice-Hall, 1983.
One of the few books on mentors, and the only book on women's mentors. As such it is useful, though a little overreverent about the institution of mentoring. Based, in part, on the author's personal experiences.

Missirian, Agnes K. *The Corporate Connection: Why Executive Women Need Mentors to Reach the Top.* Englewood Cliffs, N.J.: Spectrum/Prentice-Hall, 1982.
A concise, well-organized, and clearly written account of a study of one hundred leading corporate women and their experience of having—or not having—a mentor.
Welch, Mary Scott. *Networking.* New York: Warner Books, 1981.
A classic on the subject, this book offers useful information on many women's experiences of networking and its various styles.

GETTING A RAISE

Chastain, Sherry. *Winning the Salary Game: Salary Negotiations for Women.* New York: John Wiley, 1980.
A very good game plan for getting what you feel you are worth—or more.
Kennedy, Marilyn Moats. *Salary Strategies.* New York: Rawson Wade, 1982.
How your salary is determined and how to raise it. This is an excellent book for anyone who wants to understand the salary sysem and make it work for her.

TIME MANAGEMENT

Januz, Lauren and Jones, Susan. *Time Management for Executives.* New York: Charles Scribner's Sons, 1982.
An excellent guide to time management at work.
Lakein, Alan. *How to Get Control of Your Time and Your Life.* New York: Peter H. Wyden, 1982.
A highly useful basic text written by one of time management's gurus.
Winston, Stephanie. *The Organized Executive.* New York: Norton, 1983.
Time management and organization tips for becoming an effective, as well as an efficient, executive.

MANAGEMENT

Brownstone, David M., and Franck, Irene M. *The Manager's Advisor.* New York: John Wiley, 1983.
A practical, personal handbook for the new manager, including succinct information on all the basic topics, among them handling subordinates, managing workload, and hiring and firing.
Collins, Eliza G. C., ed. *Executive Success: Making It in Management.* New York: John Wiley & Sons, Inc., 1983.
Thirty-two of the most influential and widely discussed articles from the *Harvard Business Review* were collected for this definitive management text in which top business minds offer creative ideas and concrete advice on attaining leadership.
Deal, Terrence E., and Kennedy, Allan A. *Corporate Cultures: Rites and Rituals of Corporate Life.* Reading, Mass.: Addison-Wesley, 1981.
According to the authors (of the Harvard Business School and the management consultant McKinsey & Co., respectively) the health of a company is not guaranteed by an army of MBA's but by the company's corporate culture—its inner values, rites, and rituals—which make or break the success of the group.
Drucker, Peter F. *The Effective Executive.* New York: Harper and Row, 1966.

Management guru Drucker discusses the essential characteristics of the effective executive—how he or she manages time, makes decisions, handles meetings, etc. His short case studies are revealing and applicable to everyday management responsibilities.

The Editors of Fortune. *Working Smarter.* New York: Viking Press, 1982.
Clear writing makes this book instantly appealing. The premise is that the key to pulling U.S. business back into the front of the world business scene lies in a better management, sensitive to the needs of the workers themselves. The answer is not to work harder but better, say the authors.

Grove, Andrew S. *High Output Management.* New York: Random House, 1983.
A clear, well-planned, documented handbook written with common sense and insight by a chemical engineer and Ph.D.

Hennig, Margaret, and Jardim, Anne. *The Managerial Woman.* New York: Anchor Press/Doubleday, 1981.
A classic study of the differences between men and women in management. Essential reading.

Kotter, John P. *The General Managers.* New York: Free Press, 1982.
Based on extensive observations of the day-to-day work of managers in some of the largest U.S. corporations. It raises a number of questions for anyone aspiring to join the ranks.

Larwood, Laurie, and Wood, Marion M. *Women in Management.* Lexington, Mass.: Lexington Books, 1977.
Written by two women with business experience and academic backgrounds, this book discusses what women need to enter and remain in management positions. It profiles both successful women who have staying power and women who have been burned by the "system" and are pursuing discrimination suits.

Ouchi, William G. *Theory Z: How American Business Can Meet the Japanese Challenge.* New York: Avon Books, 1982.
Ouchi outlines why and how Japanese business practices can and should be applied to Western corporations. Theory Z is a style of management which draws upon Japanese traditions.

Posner, Mitchell J. *Executive Essentials.* New York: Avon Books, 1982.
A comprehensive book dealing with many subjects: time and information management, key personal skills, health, career paths, compensation, office politics, and travel. Useful, clearly written, and highly recommended.

Sargent, Alice. *The Androgynous Manager.* New York: AMACOM (A division of American Management Associations), 1981.
The best managers have both male and female characteristics: this book presents its
. increasing viewpoint convincingly.

WOMEN AND THE LAW

Burnett, Barbara A., ed. *EveryWoman's Legal Guide: Protecting Your Rights at Home, in the Workplace, in the Marketplace.* New York: Doubleday, 1983.
One of the most comprehensive books on women's legal rights, covering everything from automobile ownership to starting your own business to rape. An excellent resource.

Ratner, Ronnie Steinberg, ed. *Equal Employment Policy for Women.* Philadelphia: Temple University Press, 1980.
A compendium of institutional discrimination, with strategies for achieving equality in the workplace.
Ross, Susan Deller and Barcher, Anne. *The Rights of Women.* New York: Bantam Books, 1983.
An American Civil Liberties Union handbook covering women's rights in an accessible fashion.

COMPUTERS

Blank, Hannah. *Mastering Micros.* Princeton, N.J.: Petrocelli, 1983.
A good, well-written book on everything you need to know about using and buying computer software and hardware.
The Directory of Information Word Processing Equipment and Services: A Guide to Office Automation. International Information/Word Processing Association, 1982.
A comprehensive hardware directory divided into two sections, equipment, and services. Companies are listed with addresses and descriptions of products; names and addresses of professional consultants are given.
Flores, Ivan. *Word Processing Handbook.* New York: Van Nostrand Reinhold, 1982.
A detailed textbook on word processing written on three levels: a descriptive analysis of word processing, a discussion of its theory and application, and operation techniques.
Marschall, Daniel, and Gregory, Judith, eds. *Office Automation: Jekyll or Hyde?* Boston: Working Woman Education Fund, 1983.
A compilation of the major speeches from the first international conference on office work and new technology, which took place in Boston, Massachusetts. It is a comprehensive look at the major questions concerning office automation. Leaders in the field provide the latest information in key areas such as job loss, radiation dangers, retraining, the quality of work, health and safety, collective bargaining, and the impact of office automation on women.
McWilliams, Peter A. *The Word Processing Book: A Short Course in Computer Literacy.* Los Angeles: Prelude Press, 1983.
An informal overview of the word processing industry, including the history and development of microcomputers and word processors and their applications in businesses of various sizes.
Mullins, Carolyn J., and West, Thomas W. *The Office Automation Primer: Harnessing Information Technologies for Greater Productivity.* Englewood Cliffs, N.J.: Prentice-Hall, 1982.
A basic guide to the planning, installation, and evaluation stages of office automation. Illustrates how automation increases productivity in word and data processing, photocomposition, electronic mail, telecommunications, scheduling, and message switching. Includes checklists and other tools for analyzing your needs, tips on winning cooperation from your staff, and methods for evaluating data on different products. In general, this book describes how office automation changes office activities.

THE OFFICE ENVIRONMENT

Becker, Franklin. *The Successful Office*. Reading, Mass.: Addison-Wesley, 1982.
A useful, well-written book covering all areas of office planning and design. Becker is an expert in the field.

Klein, Judy Graf. *The Office Book: Ideas and Designs for Contemporary Work Spaces*. New York: Facts on File, 1982.
A large, colorful book with great graphics and photographs.

Pile, John. *Open Office Planning: A Handbook for Interior Designers and Architects*. Whitney Library/Watson-Guptill Pubns., Inc., 1978.
A more technical book for those interested in planning. Very interesting nonetheless.

THE WORKING WOMAN'S IMAGE

Cho, Emily, and Grover, Linda. *Looking Terrific*. New York: Ballantine Books, 1978.
Cho, a well-known personal-shopping consultant, assumes you not only want to appear businesslike but also want to project a personal flair. Hers is one of the best wardrobe guides available.

Feldon, Leah. *Dressing Rich: A Guide to Classic Chic for Women with More Taste than Money*. New York: G. P. Putnam's Sons, 1982.
A guide for women who want to dress with elegance and taste without spending a fortune.

Fiedorek, Mary B., and Jewell, Diana Lewis. *Executive Style: Looking It, Living It*. Piscataway, N.J.: New Century Publishers, 1983.
Tells the success-bound woman how to create a professional image and develop a personal wardrobe acquisitions strategy based on a studied insight into what works and why.

Molloy, John T. *The Woman's Dress for Success Book*. New York: Warner Books, 1978.
A classic. Molloy conducted large studies and concluded that dressing in the business "uniform" of the executive suite would help women achieve credibility at work. Molloy's views are hotly debated; nevertheless, this is worthwhile reading. The book also offers excellent advice on comparison shopping for a fast-track look at lower prices.

Schrader, Constance. *Nine to Five*. Englewood Cliffs: Prentice-Hall, 1981.
The beauty book for the working woman.

HEALTH AND THE WORKING WOMAN

Boutelle, Jane, and Baker, Samm Sinclair. *Jane Boutelle's Lifetime Fitness for Women*. New York: Simon and Schuster, 1978.
Boutelle's exercise program is designed for those who are not able to do strenuous exercise. It involves a series of easy calisthenics that involve little muscle strain and includes a section for those with physical impediments.

Brody, Jane. *Jane Brody's Nutrition Book*. New York: Norton, 1981.
A basic guide to good nutrition by the Personal Health columnist of the *New York Times*, covering a wide range of topics such as vitamins, cholesterol, food additives,

weight control, and the special nutritional requirements of pregnant women, babies, children, the elderly, the athletic. Includes tables and charts on calories and nutrients.

Hayden, Sandy, Hall, Daphne, and Stueck, Pat. *Women in Motion: The Basic Stuff to Keep You Going to Total Fitness.* Boston: Beacon Press, 1983.
A different kind of women's fitness book that discusses such diverse areas as your movement history, how to begin moving, health clubs, and the wilderness challenge. Good reading.

Liebman, Shelley. *Do It At Your Desk: An Office Worker's Guide to Fitness and Health.* Washington: Tilden Press, 1982.
Outlines simple exercise routines such as knee bends and push-ups that can be incorporated into a busy work day. They are designed to reduce stress as well as increase your fitness level. Includes tips on how to sit and stand for long periods without causing lower back pain, the correct breathing techniques for exercise, and how to choose the proper chair.

Rowen, Lillian, with Winkler, Barbara. *The Working Woman's Body Book.* New York: Rawson Associates, 1978.
A diet and moderate exercise program geared to help you increase energy and stamina, relieve tension, and improve your figure. Includes exercises you can do on a plane, while waiting in line, even in the shower.

Verney, Peter. *The Weekend Athlete's Fitness Guide.* New York: Van Nostrand Reinhold, 1982.
Shows the weekend athlete how to avoid aches and strains while improving her performance.

Winter, Richard E. *Executive Fitness.* New York: McGraw-Hill, 1982.
For anyone who has a sedentary job. Includes sections on running, aerobics, stretching, weight training, and weight reduction. There is a chapter on how to exercise at the office.

BUSINESS TRAVEL

Ehret, Charles F., and Scanlon, Lynne W. *Overcoming Jet Lag.* New York: Berkley Publishing Corp., 1983.
A wealth of hints on how to stave off the dreaded jet lag, including some from Henry Kissinger and other well-known world travelers.

Murphy, Patricia, and Taylor-Gordon, Elaine. *The Business Woman's Guide to 30 American Cities.* New York: Congdon and Weed, 1982.
Recommendations from a network of seasoned travelers on where they prefer to stay, eat (alone or with clients), shop, visit. Also lists vital services (car rental, messenger, photocopying, taxis, etc.) and emergency numbers.

Naylor, Penelope. *The Woman's Guide to Business Travel.* New York: Hearst Books, 1981.
A thorough, detailed guide to all major aspects of travel, including planning, packing, planes and hotels, trips abroad, doing business on the road, and having a good time. Includes useful checklists.

Walker, Jane, and Ambrose, Mark, eds. *Business Traveler's Handbook: A Guide to Europe.* New York: Facts on File, 1981.

Just one in the Facts on File series of guidebooks, *Europe* offers general information on countries, geography, climate, currency, electricity, telephones, hotels, restaurants, and useful addresses. Other books cover Latin America, the Middle East, Africa, Asia-Australia-Pacific, the United States, and Canada.

LOVE AND WORK IN A CHANGING SOCIETY

Barnett, Rosalind, Baruch, Grace, and Rivers, Caryl. *Lifeprints: New Patterns of Love and Work for Today's Woman.* New York: McGraw-Hill, 1983.
This extensive study examines what makes women feel good about themselves and their lives these days. An interesting, readable account of the contemporary woman and her changing needs.

Bird, Caroline. *The Two-Paycheck Marriage.* New York: Pocket Books, 1980.
A highly readable, informative book about today's dual-career couples.

Blumstein, Philip, and Schwartz, Pepper. *American Couples: Money, Work, Sex.* New York: William Morrow, 1983.
An insightful survey of American couples of all stripes, delving into all aspects of a couple's relationship and revealing what has and hasn't changed over the years.

Catalyst staff. *Corporations and Two-Career Families: Directions for the Future.* New York: Catalyst, 1981.
Profiles of two-career couples who have found satisfying ways of combining work and parenthood.

Hot, Louis B., and Dalke, J. David. *The Sexes at Work: Improving Work Relationships Between Men and Women.* Englewood Cliffs, N.J.: Prentice-Hall, 1983.
How men and women can learn to treat each other better and with more respect.

Machlowitz, Marilyn. *Workaholics.* New York: Mentor/New American Library, 1981.
Thoroughly explores the phenomenon of the obsessive worker and contends that workaholism need not to be a bad trait.

Michaels, Joanne. *Living Contradictions.* New York: Simon and Schuster, 1982.
Michaels, through extensive interviewing, traces the effects of the turbulent sixties on the women of the baby-boom generation, most of whom are now in their late twenties and early thirties. An in-depth look at their life styles, goals, and special problems.

Rohrlich, Jay B. *Work and Love: The Crucial Balance.* New York: Summit Books, 1980.
Written by a distinguished Wall Street psychiatrist, this is a fascinating and intelligent discussion of the opposing requirements of work and love.

WORKING MOTHERS

Filstrup, Jane Merrill. *Monday Through Friday: Daycare Alternatives.* New York: Teachers College Press, 1982.
Nine families offer ideas on day care, covering topics from the househusband to the nanny to cooperative nurseries.

Lichendorf, Susan S., and Gillis, Phyliss L. *The New Pregnancy.* New York: Random House, 1979.

The active woman's guide to work, legal rights, health, and other topics relating to modern pregnancy.

Morrone, Wenda Wardell. *Pregnant While You Work.* New York: Macmillan, 1984.
A first-rate book on how families can make it all work.

Olds, Sally Wendkos. *The Working Parent's Survival Guide.* New York: Bantam Books, 1983.
A handy listing of everything a working parent needs to know if she or he is trying to balance home, marriage, children, job, and self.

Wheatley, Meg, and Schorr, Marcie Hirsch. *Managing Your Maternity Leave.* Boston: Houghton Mifflin, 1983.
A good resource book. Remember, the Pregnancy Disability Act does not guarantee paid maternity leave for all women.

Whelan, Elizabeth M. *A Baby? . . . Maybe.* New York: Bobbs-Merrill, 1975.
A useful guide to help you make the big decision.

SMALL BUSINESS

Brandell, Raymond J., in collaboration with Brandell, Raymond E. *The Dynamics of Making a Fortune in Mail Order.* New York: Frederick Fell, 1980.
An in-depth, step-by-step plan for making a successful start in the mail-order business. Included: choosing the right products, writing sales copy, getting free advertising, sample ads and letters, day-to-day operations, production requirements, and a list of publications that perform well for mail-order advertisers.

Brandt, Stephen C. *Strategic Planning in Emerging Companies.* Reading, Mass.: Addison-Wesley, 1981.
For those whose companies are experiencing fast growth, this book demystifies the notion of strategic planning and sets up a framework for long-term strategy.

Cohen, Jules A. *How to Computerize Your Small Business.* Englewood Cliffs, N.J.: Prentice-Hall, 1983.
Useful introductory text.

Diener, Royce. *How to Finance Your Growing Business.* Englewood Cliffs, N.J.: Prentice-Hall, 1981.
A succinct but thorough explanation of how to make modern domestic finance work for you.

Finn, Richard P. *Your Fortune in Franchising.* Chicago: Contemporary Books, 1980.
A good introductory text for prospective franchise owners. It describes how to investigate opportunities and explains rights, location, training, promotion, financial management, and opportunities for minority and female owners.

Gumpert, David E. and Timmons, Jeffrey A. *The Insider's Guide to Small Business Resources.* New York: Doubleday, 1982.
Lists and describes small-business resources in areas such as education, international trade, government procurement, and financing. An excellent source book.

Lowry, Albert J. *How to Become Financially Successful by Owning Your Own Business.* New York: Simon and Schuster, 1981.
Useful advice on cash flow, legalities, tax considerations, etc.

Phillips, Michael, and Rasberry, Salli. *Honest Business: Superior Strategy for Success.* New York: Random House, 1981.
A guide to establishing and managing a successful small business in an open and honest manner. The authors advise focusing energies on serving customers and responding to their needs. They also suggest the use of "open books," available to any customer or employee who wishes to examine them. Refutes the idea that to be a success in business one has to be an aggressive cutthroat.

Revel, Chase. *184 Businesses Anyone Can Start and Make a Lot of Money.* New York: Bantam Books.
Ideas and advice for self-made success. Explains the high and average profits, as well as the minimum and average investments, you can expect to make when you start your business.

Rubin, Richard L., and Goldberg, Philip. *The Small Business Guide to Borrowing Money.* New York: McGraw-Hill, 1980.
Discusses all major forms of financing along with the advantages and disadvantages of each, and offers guidance for approaching financing sources.

Seltz, David. *Franchising: Proven Techniques for Rapid Company Expansion and Market Dominance.* New York: McGraw-Hill, 1980.
A step-by-step guide to expansion from a consultant.

Shilling, Dana. *Be Your Own Boss.* New York: Penguin Books, 1983.
The owner of a company that makes "plain-English" business forms puts clear speaking to work in this practical, how-to book, which explains the nuts and bolts of opening a new business.

Taylor, Charlotte. *Women and the Business Game: Strategies for Successful Ownership.* New York Cornerstone Library, Venture Concepts Press, 1980.
One of the most thoughtful and clearly written books for and about women business owners.

Whittlesey, Marietta. *Freelance Forever.* New York: Avon Books, 1982.
How freelancers in creative fields such as art, writing, editing, and acting can learn to manage their lives with good business acumen. Includes legal and tax advice; tips on money management; helpful hints from freelancers themselves on practical and psychological issues; lists of professional associations, artists' colonies, and the like. Must reading for the motivated freelancer.

PERSONAL MONEY MANAGEMENT

Block, Julian. *Tax Saving: A Year-Round Guide.* Radnor, Pa.: Chilton Book Company, 1981.
Written by a former IRS agent and organized by topic, this is a comprehensive guide to saving money on your taxes.

Cook, John A., and Wool, Robert. *All You Need to Know About Banks.* New York: Random House, 1983.
How to get what you want from a bank; advice on choosing a bank, establishing a relationship with an individual banker, getting a loan, and winning special treatment.

Grace, William J., Jr. *The ABC's of IRA's.* New York: Dell, 1984.
A useful guide to making this "must" investment.

Kahn, Arnold D. *Family Security Through Estate Planning*. New York: McGraw-Hill, 1983.
Helps readers identify their estate planning objectives and determine how to reach them. Outlines basic estate plans and shows how changing personal circumstances alter individual goals and tactics.

J. K. Lasser Institute. *J. K. Lasser's Your Income Tax*. New York: Simon and Schuster. Updated yearly.
A popular all-round guide to tax preparation.

Rolo, Charles J. *Gaining on the Market: Your Complete Guide to Investment Strategy*. Boston: Little Brown, 1982.
The best introduction available to the world of investing—clear enough for the novice but sophisticated in its discussion and analysis.

Quinn, Jane Bryant. *Everyone's Money Book*. New York: Delacorte Press, 1979.
Contains a wealth of information from a well-known financial columnist.

Siverd, Bonnie. *Count Your Change: A Woman's Guide to Sudden Financial Change*. New York: Arbor House, 1983.
Goes beyond the traditional "how to invest" books and shows readers how to cope with changing financial circumstances, both good and bad.

VanCaspel, Venita. *The Power of Money Dynamics*. Reston, Va.: Reston, 1983.
This is the best overview of personal financial planning we've encountered, a breezy yet penetrating book to help you develop and implement your financial goals.

SALES

Culligan, Matthew J. *Getting Back to the Basics of Selling*. New York: Crown Publishers, 1981.
Culligan identifies the personal traits and skills of a good sales person and covers techniques on how to develop and use listening and speaking skills as well as how to cope with stress, nervousness, and rejection.

Hyatt, Carole. *The Woman's Selling Game: How to Sell Yourself—and Anything Else*. New York: Warner Books, 1979.
The classic book on women and sales, covering such essentials as setting goals, sales techniques, and maintaining success.

Kievman, Beverly. *The Complete Success Workbook for Today's Saleswoman*. Englewood Cliffs, N.J.: Prentice-Hall, 1982.
Kievman gives practical advice on what sales managers look for when hiring saleswomen; how to use power, intimidation, and humor in your sales presentation; and how to analyze and manage your time.

Lewis, William, and Cornelius, Hal. *Career Guide for Sales and Marketing*. New York: Monarch Press, 1983.
A practical, informative overview of the sales profession—how to evaluate sales training programs, find a job, and advance in your chosen sales field.

Micali, Paul J. *The Lacy Techniques of Salesmanship*. New York: E. P. Dutton, 1982.
A classic book, newly revised, with excellent information on developing a winning sales personality, creative selling, and sales strategies.

Vipperman, Carol, and Mueller, Barbara. *Solutions to Sales Problems: A Guide for Professional Saleswomen.* Englewood Cliffs, N.J.: Prentice-Hall, 1983.
Examines the pros and cons of sales as a career and the advantages and disadvantages of being a woman in sales. Good coverage of such topics as preparing your sales presentation, overcoming obstacles during the sales call, and time and territory management.

GENERAL

Baehler, James R. *Book of Perks.* New York: St. Martin's Press, 1983.
If you don't know what to ask for, you won't get anything. This book tells you everything that is available, and more.
Bartos, Rena. *The Moving Target: What Every Marketer Should Know About Working Women.* New York: Macmillan, 1982.
A look at women as a market with purchasing power. This book demonstrates that women's needs and values go beyond those assumed by marketers and advertisers. A persuasive book.
Cox, Allan. *The Cox Report on the American Corporation.* New York: Delacorte, 1982.
One of the most comprehensive surveys of American corporations, this book answers five main questions: What do corporations value? How do they function? How do they succeed and fail? What are executives like? How do they succeed?
Easton, Susan. *Equal to the Task: How Working Women Are Managing in Corporate America.* New York: Seaview Books, 1982.
Monitors how women are really doing in the corporate world.
Farley, Lin. *Sexual Shakedown.* New York: Warner Books, 1978.
Described by the *New York Times* as the "definitive" study of sexual harassment on the job.
Fisk, Jim, and Barron, Robert. *The Official MBA Handbook, or, How to Succeed in Business Without a Harvard MBA.* New York: Wallaby/Simon & Schuster, Inc., 1982.
Executives looking for a break from the all-important budget report or marketing strategy can get some relief from this book. Nicely sacrilegious.
Friedan, Betty. *The Second Stage.* New York: Summit Books, 1981.
A very important book. Takes up where *The Feminine Mystique* finished. As she puts it: "new questions for the eighties for the young men and women now living in terms of the movement for equality."
Gilligan, Carol. *In a Different Voice: Psychological Theory and Women's Development.* Cambridge, Mass.: Harvard University Press, 1982.
An excellent book covering various areas where different ways of thinking (male and female) come into play.
Howe, Louise Kapp. *Pink Collar Workers: Inside the World of Women's Work.* New York: G. P. Putnam's Sons, 1977.
An impressive survey of the needs, feelings, and status of the women of the pink-collar ghetto—beauticians, sales clerks, waitresses, clerical workers, and homemakers.

Jordan, Jane. *Women Merchants in Colonial New York.* Early working women. Most interesting.

Kandel, Thelma. *What Women Earn.* New York: Simon and Schuster, 1981.
A useful book to have at your fingertips, but it is not very extensive.

Kanter, Rosabeth Moss. *Men and Women of the Corporation.* New York: Basic Books, 1979.
Illuminating description of life in the large corporate bureaucracies, told from the inside. Kanter's thesis is that people's attitudes and behaviors are shaped by their work experiences (especially as they relate to power vs. powerlessness) and therefore as long as organizations remain the same, replacing men and women will not make much of a difference.

Kerr, Clark, and Rosow, Jerome M. *Working in America: The Decade Ahead.* New York: Van Nostrand Reinhold, 1979.
One book in the Work in America series. Very insightful, with essays from people such as Daniel Yankelovich and Eli Ginzberg.

Medsger, Betty. *Women at Work: A Photographic Documentary.* New York: Sheed and Ward, 1975.
A photographic and oral history of contemporary working women of all kinds.

Naisbitt, John. *Megatrends: Ten New Directions for Transforming Our Lives.* New York: Warner Books, 1982.
Naisbitt's best seller takes a look at the powerful forces that are shaping today's postindustrial, informational society. Compelling reading.

Peters, Thomas J., and Waterman, Robert H. *In Search of Excellence: Lessons from America's Best-Run Companies.* New York: Harper and Row, 1982.
A long-time best seller, this book is based on a McKinsey and Company study and reveals the conditions and qualities that make America's best-run companies the best.

Roman, Kenneth, and Raphaelson, Joel. *Writing that Works.* New York: Harper and Row, 1981.
One of the best guides to good and clear writing.

Trahey, Jane. *Jane Trahey on Women and Power.* New York: Avon, 1978.
An insightful look at the problem of acquiring power by a woman who did.

Wertheimer, Barbara. *We Were There: The Story of Working Women in America.* New York: Pantheon, 1977.
The definitive history of women in American labor unions.

Women's Legal Defense Fund. *It Pays to Be a Man.*
An information packet on pay equity from the Women's Legal Defense Fund. Available at: 200 P Street, NW, Suite 400, Washington, D.C. 20036.

Appendix C
Organizations and Other Resources

GENERAL

Catalyst
14 East 60th Street, New York, N.Y. 10022
   Founded in 1962 and funded by a wide-ranging group of business contributors, Catalyst is a national nonprofit association whose aims include furthering the upward mobility of women by helping to change the attitudes and practices of the corporate community, stimulating an awareness among young people of the full range of career options, reassessing the division of responsibilities within families. Informational brochures available on request.

National Abortion Rights Action League
825 15th St. N.W., Washington, D.C. 20005
   Political and public awareness action for pro-choice.

National Association for Professional Saleswomen
2088 Morely Way, Sacramento, Calif. 95825
   Conducts seminars and research projects on professional saleswomen, puts out a monthly publication (*Successful Saleswoman*), and holds a national convention.

National Commission on Working Women
2000 P St. N.W., Suite 508, Washington, D.C. 20036
   For women in low-pay, low-status jobs.

The National Council on the Future of Women in the Workplace
c/o The National Federation of Business and Professional Women's Clubs, Inc.
2012 Massachusetts Ave. N.W., Washington, D.C. 20036
   Founded in 1983 to investigate the effects of the technological revolution on working women. An advocacy group which develops model programs for responding to the changing workplace.

The National Federation of Business and Professional Women
2012 Massachusetts Ave. N.W., Washington, D.C. 20036; 202-293-1200
   Formerly the Business and Professional Woman's Foundation, this is the oldest and largest organization of American working women, founded in 1919. It disseminates information on economic, social, and political issues, in particular through *National Businesswoman*, published six times a year for the organization's 150,000 members.

National Organization for Women
425 13th St. N.W., Suite 1948, Washington, D.C. 20004
   One of the major national women's groups, primary promoter of the ERA, and action group for various women's rights (child care, divorce, disabled women, lesbian

336

rights, violence against women, minority women, reproductive rights, etc.). NOW maintains regional and local offices.

9 to 5, the National Association of Working Women
1224 Huron Road, Cleveland, Ohio 44115
Political action group for office worker's rights.

Ms. Foundation for Women
370 Lexington Ave., New York, N.Y. 10017
Established by Ms. magazine to help community-based women's groups.

Women's Bureau
Office of the Secretary, Department of Labor, Washington, D.C. 20210; 202-523-6653.
Established by Act of Congress in June 1920, the Women's Bureau of the Department of Labor monitors the status of women who work and uses its findings to make policy recommendations and analyze proposed federal legislation. The Bureau works with federal, state, and local governments to promote job training for women and enforce laws against sexual discrimination.

Women's Campaign Fund
1721 I St., Suite 515, Washington, D.C. 20006
To support the election of qualified women to public office.

The Women's Equity Action League
805 15th St. N.W., Washington, D.C. 20005; 202-638-1961.
WEAL, founded in 1968, is a national nonprofit research advocacy group specializing in economic issues. WEAL's 4,000 members receive regular monthly newsletters and the organization sponsors a national information center which monitors such subjects as women in the military, social security, insurance, pensions, and budgetary decisions of specific interest to women.

Women's Legal Defense Fund
2000 P St., Washington, D.C. 20036
Legal representation for women's rights. The WLDF conducts seminars and puts out a number of different publications concerning various women's legal issues (domestic relations, employment discrimination, pregnancy rights etc.).

Working Woman's Institute
593 Park Ave., New York, N.Y. 10021
Provides research and technical assistance for corporations and universities mainly in the area of sexual harassment.

OTHERS

American Association of University Women
2401 Virginia N.W., Washington, D.C.; 202-785-7700

American Medical Women's Association
465 Grand St., New York, N.Y. 10002

American Society of Professional and Executive Women (Business)
1511 Walnut St., Philadelphia, Pa. 19102; 215-563-4415

American Women's Society of Certified Public Accountants
500 North Michigan Ave., Suite 1400, Chicago, Ill. 60611; 312-661-1700

Council of Women in Business (A committee of the National Business League)
4324 Georgia Ave., N.W., Washington, D.C. 20011; 202-829-5900

Displaced Homemakers Network
c/o Older Women's League, 1325 G St. N.W., Washington, D.C. 20005

Executive Women International
2188 Highland Drive, Suite 203, Salt Lake City, Utah 84106; 801-486-3121

National Alliance of Homebased Businesswomen
P.O. Box 95, Norwood, N.J. 07648

National Association of Female Executives
160 East 56th Street, New York, NY 10022; 212-371-8086

National Association of Women Lawyers
1155 East 60th St., Chicago, Ill. 60637

The National Women's Education Fund
1410 Q St. N.W., Washington, D.C. 20009

National Women's Political Caucus
1411 K St. N.W., Suite 1110, Washington, D.C. 20005

Women in Advertising and Marketing (WAM)
c/o Ann Gilbert, Banker's Security, 1701 Pennsylvania Ave., Washington, D.C. 20005; 202-298-6225

Women in Communications
P.O. Box 9561, Austin, Texas 78766

Women Entrepreneurs
3061 Fillmore St., San Francisco, Calif. 94123; 415-929-0129

DAY-CARE AND EARLY CHILDHOOD EDUCATION PROGRAMS

For information on how to select a day-care program:

The Child Care Resource Center
187 Hampshire St.
Cambridge, Mass. 02139
The National Association for the Education of Young Children
1834 Connecticut Ave. N.W.
Washington, D.C. 20009

For further information:

The Children's Defense Fund
1520 New Hampshire Ave. N.W.
Washington, D.C. 20036

Day Care and Child Development Council of America
1012 14th St. N.W.
Washington, D.C 20005

School-Age Child Care Project
Wellesley College
828 Washington St.
Wellesley, Mass. 02181

For assistance in organizing and funding your own child-care program:

Bank Street College of Education
Consultation for Community Development and Self-Reliance
610 West 112th St.
New York, N.Y. 10025

Write to the National Association for Child Development and Education for a list of private day-care centers in your area. Enclose a self-addressed, stamped envelope.

National Association for Child Development and Education
500 12th St. S.W.
Washington, D.C. 20024

SAFETY IN THE WORKPLACE

The following sources provide helpful guidance:

"Guidelines on Pregnancy and Work"
American College of Obstetricians and Gynecologists
1 East Wacker Drive
Chicago, Ill. 60601

National Institute for Occupational Safety and Health
Parkham Building
5600 Fishers Lane
Rockville, Md. 20857

Occupational Safety and Health Administration
U.S. Department of Labor
200 Constitution Avenue N.W.
Washington, D.C. 20210

OFFICE DESIGN

To find a qualified professional, check with the following industry associations:

American Society of Interior Designers (ASID)
1430 Broadway, 22nd floor
New York, N.Y. 10013

Institute of Business Designers (IBD)
1155 Merchandise Mart
Chicago, Ill. 60654

Check interior-design magazines for designers whose work seems to suit your taste. Titles include *Interiors* and *Corporate Design*, both published in New York City.

PAY EQUITY

For general information contact:

The National Committee on Pay Equity
1201 16th St. N.W., room 422
Washington, D.C. 20036

The Comparable Worth Information Project
488 41st St., No. 5
Oakland, Calif. 94609

Index